PEARSON *LITERATURE*

CALIFORNIA

All-in-One
Workbook

Grade Seven

PEARSON

Upper Saddle River, New Jersey
Boston, Massachusetts
Chandler, Arizona
Glenview, Illinois

BQ Tunes Credits
Keith London, Defined Mind, Inc., Executive Producer
Mike Pandolfo, Wonderful, Producer
All songs mixed and mastered by Mike Pandolfo, Wonderful
Vlad Gutkovich, Wonderful, Assistant Engineer
Recorded November 2007 – February 2008 in SoHo, New York City, at Wonderful, 594 Broadway

ISBN-13: 978-0-13-367581-8
ISBN-10:   0-13-367581-5

11 12   VO39   14 13 12

TABLE OF CONTENTS

About the *California All-in-One Workbook* xiv
Correlations xv
About the California Content Standards xx
Building Your Vocabulary xxi

UNIT 1   Fiction and Nonfiction

BQ Tunes: **"Truth"** 1
Big Question Vocabulary 1 4
Big Question Vocabulary 2 5
Big Question Vocabulary 3 6
Applying the Big Question..7

"Three-Century Woman" by Richard Peck
"The Fall of the Hindenburg" by Michael Morrison

Listening and Viewing...8
Learning About Fiction and Nonfiction 9
Model Selection: Fiction..10
Model Selection: Nonfiction..11

"Papa's Parrot" by Cynthia Rylant

Writing About the Big Question 12
Reading: Use Context Clues to Unlock the Meaning 13
Literary Analysis: Narrative Writing 14
Vocabulary Builder 15

"mk" by Jean Fritz

Writing About the Big Question 16
Reading: Use Context Clues to Unlock the Meaning 17
Literary Analysis: Narrative Writing 18
Vocabulary Builder 19

"Papa's Parrot" and **"mk"**

Integrated Language Skills: Grammar..20
Integrated Language Skills: Support for Writing...21

from **An American Childhood** by Annie Dillard

Writing About the Big Question 22
Reading: Reread and Read Ahead to Confirm the Meaning..................................23
Literary Analysis: Point of View...24
Vocabulary Builder 25

"The Luckiest Time of All" by Lucille Clifton

Writing About the Big Question 26
Reading: Reread and Read Ahead to Confirm the Meaning..................................27
Literary Analysis: Point of View...28
Vocabulary Builder 29

from An American Childhood and "The Luckiest Time of All"

Integrated Language Skills: Grammar...30

Integrated Language Skills: Support for Writing.......................................31

from Barrio Boy by Ernesto Galarza
"A Day's Wait" by Ernest Hemingway

Writing About the Big Question 32

Literary Analysis: Comparing Fiction and Nonfiction...................................33

Vocabulary Builder 34

Support for Writing to Compare Literary Works 35

"All Summer in a Day" by Ray Bradbury

Writing About the Big Question 36

Reading: Recognizing Details That Indicate the Author's Purpose.......................37

Literary Analysis: Setting 38

Vocabulary Builder 39

"Suzy and Leah" by Jane Yolen

Writing About the Big Question 40

Reading: Recognizing Details That Indicate the Author's Purpose 41

Literary Analysis: Setting 42

Vocabulary Builder 43

"All Summer in a Day" and "Suzy and Leah"

Integrated Language Skills: Grammar...44

Integrated Language Skills: Support for Writing..45

"My First Free Summer" by Julia Alvarez

Writing About the Big Question 46

Reading: Use Background Information to Determine the Author's Purpose........47

Literary Analysis: Historical Context 48

Vocabulary Builder 49

from Angela's Ashes by Frank McCourt

Writing About the Big Question 50

Reading: Use Background Information to Determine the Author's Purpose........51

Literary Analysis: Historical Context 52

Vocabulary Builder 53

"My First Free Summer" and from Angela's Ashes

Integrated Language Skills: Grammar 54

Integrated Language Skills: Support for Writing 55

"Stolen Day" by Sherwood Anderson
"The Night the Bed Fell" by James Thurber

Writing About the Big Question 56

Literary Analysis: Comparing Characters 57

Vocabulary Builder 58

Support for Writing to Compare Literary Works...59

UNIT 2   Short Stories

BQ Tunes: **"Conflict Resolution"** 60

Big Question Vocabulary 1 63

Big Question Vocabulary 2 64

Big Question Vocabulary 3 65

Applying the Big Question..66

"The Treasure of Lemon Brown" by Walter Dean Myers

Listening and Viewing..67

Learning About Short Stories..68

Model Selection: Short Stories 69

"The Bear Boy" by Joseph Bruchac

Writing About the Big Question 70

Reading: Predicting 71

Literary Analysis: Plot 72

Vocabulary Builder 73

"Rikki-tikki-tavi" by Rudyard Kipling

Writing About the Big Question 74

Reading: Predicting 75

Literary Analysis: Plot 76

Vocabulary Builder 77

"The Bear Boy" and **"Rikki-tikki-tavi"**

Integrated Language Skills: Grammar 78

Integrated Language Skills: Support for Writing 79

from **Letters from Rifka** by Karen Hesse

Writing About the Big Question 80

Reading: Read Ahead to Verify Predictions and Reread to Look for Details 81

Literary Analysis: Character 82

Vocabulary Builder 83

"Two Kinds" by Amy Tan

Writing About the Big Question 84

Reading: Read Ahead to Verify Predictions and Reread to Look for Details 85

Literary Analysis: Character 86

Vocabulary Builder 87

from **Letters from Rifka** and **"Two Kinds"**

Integrated Language Skills: Grammar 88

Integrated Language Skills: Support for Writing 89

"Seventh Grade" by Gary Soto
"Melting Pot" by Anna Quindlen

Writing About the Big Question 90

Literary Analysis: Comparing Idioms 91

Vocabulary Builder 92

Support for Writing to Compare Literary Works 93

"The Third Wish" by Joan Aiken

Writing About the Big Question 94

Reading: Make Inferences by Recognizing Details 95

Literary Analysis: Conflict.. 96

Vocabulary Builder 97

"Amigo Brothers" by Piri Thomas

Writing About the Big Question 98

Reading: Make Inferences by Recognizing Details 99

Literary Analysis: Conflict.. 100

Vocabulary Builder 101

"The Third Wish" and **"Amigo Brothers"**

Integrated Language Skills: Grammar... 102

Integrated Language Skills: Support for Writing 103

"Zoo" by Edward D. Hoch

Writing About the Big Question 104

Reading: Make Inferences by Reading Between the Lines and Asking
Questions... 105

Literary Analysis: Theme.. 106

Vocabulary Builder 107

"Ribbons" by Laurence Yep

Writing About the Big Question.. 108

Reading: Make Inferences by Reading Between the Lines and Asking
Questions... 109

Literary Analysis: Theme.. 110

Vocabulary Builder 111

"Zoo" and **"Ribbons"**

Integrated Language Skills: Grammar... 112

Integrated Language Skills: Support for Writing 113

"After Twenty Years" by O. Henry
"He—y, Come on O—ut!" by Shinichi Hoshi

Writing About the Big Question.. 114

Literary Analysis: Irony 115

Vocabulary Builder 116

Support for Writing 117

UNIT 3   Types of Nonfiction

BQ Tunes: **"The Expert"** 118

Big Question Vocabulary 1 121

Big Question Vocabulary 2 122

Big Question Vocabulary 3 123

Applying the Big Question.. 124

"What Makes a Rembrandt a Rembrandt?" by Richard Mühlberger

Listening and Viewing 125

Learning About Types of Nonfiction: Expository, Reflective, and Persuasive 126

Model Selection: Types of Nonfiction: Expository, Reflective, and Persuasive...127

"Life Without Gravity" by Robert Zimmerman

Writing About the Big Question 128

Reading: Recognize Main Ideas and Key Points 129

Literary Analysis: Expository Essay 130

Vocabulary Builder 131

"Conversational Ballgames" by Nancy Masterson Sakamoto

Writing About the Big Question 132

Reading: Recognize Main Ideas and Key Points.. 133

Literary Analysis: Expository Essay 134

Vocabulary Builder 135

"Life Without Gravity" and **"Conversational Ballgames"**

Integrated Language Skills: Grammar... 136

Integrated Language Skills: Support for Writing.. 137

"I Am a Native of North America" by Chief Dan George

Writing About the Big Question 138

Reading: Understand the Main Idea.. 139

Literary Analysis: Reflective Essay 140

Vocabulary Builder 141

"Volar: To Fly" by Judith Ortiz Cofer

Writing About the Big Question 142

Reading: Understand the Main Idea.. 143

Literary Analysis: Reflective Essay 144

Vocabulary Builder 145

"I Am a Native of North America" and **"Volar: To Fly"**

Integrated Language Skills: Grammar... 146

Integrated Language Skills: Support for Writing.. 147

"The Legacy of 'Snowflake' Bentley" by Barbara Eaglesham
"No Gumption" by Russell Baker

Writing About the Big Question 148

Literary Analysis: Comparing Biography and Autobiography 149

Vocabulary Builder 150

Support for Writing to Compare Literary Works.. 151

"The Eternal Frontier" by Louis L'Amour

Writing About the Big Question 152

Reading: Classifying Fact and Opinion... 153

Literary Analysis: Persuasive Essay... 154

Vocabulary Builder 155

"All Together Now" by Barbara Jordan

Writing About the Big Question 156

Reading: Classifying Fact and Opinion 157

Literary Analysis: Persuasive Essay 158

Vocabulary Builder 159

"The Eternal Frontier" and **"All Together Now"**

Integrated Language Skills: Grammar 160

Integrated Language Skills: Support for Writing 161

"The Real Story of a Cowboy's Life" by Geoffrey C. Ward

Writing About the Big Question 162

Reading: Use Resources to Check Facts 163

Literary Analysis: Word Choice and Diction 164

Vocabulary Builder 165

"Rattlesnake Hunt" by Marjorie Kinnan Rawlings

Writing About the Big Question 166

Reading: Use Resources to Check Facts 167

Literary Analysis: Word Choice and Diction 168

Vocabulary Builder 169

"The Real Story of a Cowboy's Life" and **"Rattlesnake Hunt"**

Integrated Language Skills: Grammar 170

Integrated Language Skills: Support for Writing 171

"Alligator" by Bailey White
"The Cremation of Sam McGee" by Robert Service

Writing About the Big Question 172

Literary Analysis: Comparing Humorous Essays 173

Vocabulary Builder 174

Support for Writing to Compare Literary Works 175

UNIT 4   Poetry

BQ Tunes: **"Listen & Learn"** 176

Big Question Vocabulary 1 179

Big Question Vocabulary 2 180

Big Question Vocabulary 3 181

Applying the Big Question 182

The Poetry of Pat Mora

Listening and Viewing 183

Learning About Poetry 184

Model Selection: Poetry 185

Poetry Collection: Naomi Shihab Nye, William Jay Smith, Buson

Writing About the Big Question 186

Reading: Asking Questions to Draw a Conclusion 187

Literary Analysis: Forms of Poetry 188

Vocabulary Builder 189

Poetry Collection: Nikki Giovanni, Mary Ellen Solt, Bashō

Writing About the Big Question 190

Reading: Asking Questions to Draw a Conclusion 191

Literary Analysis: Forms of Poetry 192

Vocabulary Builder 193

Poetry Collections: Naomi Shihab Nye, William Jay Smith, Buson;
Nikki Giovanni, Mary Ellen Solt, Bashō

Integrated Language Skills: Grammar...194

Integrated Language Skills: Support for Writing...195

Poetry Collection: Naomi Long Madgett, Wendy Rose, Edna St. Vincent Millay

Writing About the Big Question 196

Reading: Connecting the Details to Draw a Conclusion.............................197

Literary Analysis: Figurative Language..198

Vocabulary Builder 199

Poetry Collection: Langston Hughes, Henry Wadsworth Longfellow,
Carl Sandburg

Writing About the Big Question 200

Reading: Connecting the Details to Draw a Conclusion.............................201

Literary Analysis: Figurative Language..202

Vocabulary Builder 203

Poetry Collections: Naomi Long Madgett, Wendy Rose, Edna St. Vincent
Millay; Langston Hughes, Henry Wadsworth Longfellow, Carl Sandburg

Integrated Language Skills: Grammar...204

Integrated Language Skills: Support for Writing...205

Poetry by Alfred Noyes and Gregory Djanikian

Writing About the Big Question 206

Literary Analysis: Comparing Narrative Poems..207

Vocabulary Builder 208

Support for Writing to Compare Literary Works 209

Poetry Collection: Shel Silverstein, Eve Merriam, James Berry

Writing About the Big Question 210

Reading: Reading Aloud According to Punctuation in Order to Paraphrase..... 211

Literary Analysis: Sound Devices 212

Vocabulary Builder 213

Poetry Collection: William Shakespeare, Eve Merriam, Louise Bogan

Writing About the Big Question 214

Reading: Reading Aloud According to Punctuation in Order to Paraphrase......215

Literary Analysis: Sound Devices 216

Vocabulary Builder 217

Poetry Collections: Shel Silverstein, Eve Merriam, James Berry; William Shakespeare, Eve Merriam, Louise Bogan

Integrated Language Skills: Grammar 218
Integrated Language Skills: Support for Writing 219

Poetry Collection: Edgar Allan Poe, Raymond Richard Patterson, Emily Dickinson

Writing About the Big Question 220
Reading: Reread in Order to Paraphrase 221
Literary Analysis: Rhythm, Meter, and Rhyme 222
Vocabulary Builder 223

Poetry Collection: Gwendolyn Brooks, Lewis Carroll, Robert Frost

Writing About the Big Question 224
Reading: Reread in Order to Paraphrase 225
Literary Analysis: Rhythm, Meter, and Rhyme 226
Vocabulary Builder 227

Poetry Collections: Edgar Allan Poe, Raymond Richard Patterson, Emily Dickinson; Gwendolyn Brooks, Lewis Carroll, Robert Frost

Integrated Language Skills: Grammar 228
Integrated Language Skills: Support for Writing 229

Poetry by Walt Whitman and E. E. Cummings

Writing About the Big Question 230
Literary Analysis: Comparing Imagery 231
Vocabulary Builder 232
Support for Writing to Compare Literary Works 233

UNIT 5   Drama

BQ Tunes: **"True Identity"** 234
Big Question Vocabulary 1 236
Big Question Vocabulary 2 237
Big Question Vocabulary 3 238
Applying the Big Question 239

***from* Dragonwings** by Laurence Yep

Listening and Viewing 240
Learning About Drama 241
Model Selection: Drama 242

A Christmas Carol: Scrooge and Marley, *Act I*, by Israel Horovitz

Writing About the Big Question 243
Reading: Preview a Text to Set a Purpose for Reading 244
Literary Analysis: Dialogue 245
Vocabulary Builder 246
Integrated Language Skills: Grammar 247
Integrated Language Skills: Support for Writing 248

A Christmas Carol: Scrooge and Marley, *Act II,* by Israel Horovitz

Writing About the Big Question 249

Reading: Adjust Your Reading Rate to Suit Your Purpose 250

Literary Analysis: Stage Directions 251

Vocabulary Builder 252

Integrated Language Skills: Grammar...253

Integrated Language Skills: Support for Writing....................................254

***from* A Christmas Carol: Scrooge and Marley, *Act I, Scenes 2 & 5,* by Israel Horovitz**

Writing About the Big Question 255

Literary Analysis: Comparing Characters 256

Vocabulary Builder 257

Support for Writing to Compare Literary Works.....................................258

"The Monsters Are Due on Maple Street" by Rod Serling

Writing About the Big Question 259

Reading: Distinguish Between Details to Write a Summary....................260

Literary Analysis: A Character's Motives 261

Vocabulary Builder 262

Integrated Language Skills: Grammar...263

Integrated Language Skills: Support for Writing....................................264

***from* Grandpa and the Statue by Arthur Miller**
"My Head Is Full of Starshine" by Peg Kehret

Writing About the Big Question 265

Literary Analysis: Comparing Dramatic Speeches 266

Vocabulary Builder 267

Support for Writing to Compare Literary Works.....................................268

UNIT 6   Themes in Folk Literature

BQ Tunes: **"Solidarity"**..269

Big Question Vocabulary 1 271

Big Question Vocabulary 2 272

Big Question Vocabulary 3 273

Applying the Big Question...274

"Grasshopper Logic," "The Other Frog Prince," and "duckbilled platypus vs. beefsnakstik® by Jon Scieszka and Lane Smith

Listening and Viewing..275

Learning About Themes in Oral Tradition...276

Model Selection: Themes in Oral Tradition 277

"Icarus and Daedalus" by Josephine Preston Peabody

Writing About the Big Question 278

Reading: Ask Questions to Analyze Cause-and-Effect Relationships 279

Literary Analysis: Myth 280

Vocabulary Builder 281

"Demeter and Persephone" by Anne Terry White

Writing About the Big Question 282
Reading: Ask Questions to Analyze Cause-and-Effect Relationships 283
Literary Analysis: Myth 284
Vocabulary Builder 285

"Icarus and Daedalus" and **"Demeter and Persephone"**

Integrated Language Skills: Grammar...286
Integrated Language Skills: Support for Writing.......................................287

"Tenochtitlan: Inside the Aztec Capital" by Jacqueline Dineen

Writing About the Big Question 288
Reading: Reread to Look for Connections 289
Literary Analysis: Legends and Facts 290
Vocabulary Builder 291

"Popocatepetl and Ixtlaccihuatl" by Julia Piggott Wood

Writing About the Big Question 292
Reading: Reread to Look for Connections 293
Literary Analysis: Legends and Facts 294
Vocabulary Builder 295

"Tenochtitlan: Inside the Aztec Capital" and **"Popocatepetl and Ixtlaccihuatl"**

Integrated Language Skills: Grammar...296
Integrated Language Skills: Support for Writing.......................................297

"To the Top of the World" by Samantha Larson
"The Voyage" *from* Tales from the *Odyssey* by Mary Pope Osborne

Writing About the Big Question 298
Literary Analysis: Comparing Treatments of Epic Conventions 299
Vocabulary Builder 300
Support for Writing to Compare Literary Works...301

"Sun and Moon in a Box" by Richard Erdoes and Alfonso Ortiz

Writing About the Big Question 302
Reading: Use Prior Knowledge to Compare and Contrast 303
Literary Analysis: Cultural Context...304
Vocabulary Builder 305

"How the Snake Got Poison" by Zora Neale Hurston

Writing About the Big Question 306
Reading: Use Prior Knowledge to Compare and Contrast..................................307
Literary Analysis: Cultural Context...308
Vocabulary Builder 309

"Sun and Moon in a Box" and **"How the Snake Got Poison"**

Integrated Language Skills: Grammar...310
Integrated Language Skills: Support for Writing.......................................311

"The People Could Fly" by Virginia Hamilton

Writing About the Big Question 312

Reading: Using a Venn Diagram to Compare and Contrast 313

Literary Analysis: Folk Tale..314

Vocabulary Builder 315

"All Stories Are Anansi's" by Harold Courlander

Writing About the Big Question 316

Reading: Using a Venn Diagram to Compare and Contrast 317

Literary Analysis: Folk Tale..318

Vocabulary Builder 319

"The People Could Fly" and "All Stories Are Anansi's"

Integrated Language Skills: Grammar..320

Integrated Language Skills: Support for Writing...321

"The Fox Outwits the Crow" by William Cleary
"The Fox and the Crow" by Aesop

Writing About the Big Question 322

Literary Analysis: Comparing Tone 323

Vocabulary Builder 324

Support for Writing to Compare Reactions to Tone 325

Reading Fluency Practice and Assessment

Reading Fluency Practice and Assessment 326

Daily Standards Reviews

Reading 1.0–3.0..CA 14

Writing 1.0–2.0...CA 44

Written and Oral English Language Conventions 1.0 ....CA 68

Listening and Speaking 1.0–2.0 ....CA 82

Writing Support for Essays

Written and Oral English Language Conventions 1.0..CA 106

Writing 1.0..CA 120

About the *California All-in-One Workbook*

The *California All-in-One Workbook* is designed to provide you with practice and preparation for standardized tests of California English-Language Arts content standards. The skills learned can be applied to your daily schoolwork and life, as well as to testing situations.

The *California All-in-One Workbook* includes the following types of pages.

- Each unit begins with a focus on the Big Question—lyrics to the BQ Tune, which features the Big Question Vocabulary for the unit, three worksheets that introduce and practice Big Question Vocabulary, and an Applying the Big Question chart, replicated from the Student Edition.
- Penguin Selection Worksheets—A Listening and Viewing worksheet, About the Genre worksheet, and a Model Selection worksheet support each Penguin author selection.
- Selection Pairings Worksheets—Worksheets supporting the paired selections include Writing About the Big Question, Reading, Literary Analysis, Build Vocabulary, Integrated Language Skills: Grammar, and Integrated Language Skills: Writing.
- Comparing Literary Works—Worksheets supporting Comparing Literary Works include Writing About the Big Question, Literary Analysis, and Build Vocabulary.
- Daily Standards Review—There is one Daily Standards Review for each standard. Each standard is stated, defined, and explained with examples. The test practice items are provided.
- Writing Support for Essays—There is one Writing Support activity for each tested Writing standard. Examples of tested prompts are featured with annotations and tips.

In addition, all items in Part 2 (Daily Standards Review and Writing Support for Essays) are correlated to California English-Language Arts content standards. This will help you single out and refine specific skills you need to improve upon.

Correlations to Daily Standards Reviews and Writing Support for Essays

Grade 7

California English-Language Arts Content Standards	All-in-One Workbook: Daily Standards Reviews	All-in-One Workbook: Writing Support for Essays
READING		
1.0 Word Analysis, Fluency, and Systematic Vocabulary Development		
1.1 Identify idioms, analogies, metaphors, and similes in prose and poetry.	pages CA 14–15	
1.2 Use knowledge of Greek, Latin, and Anglo-Saxon roots and affixes to understand content-area vocabulary.	pages CA 16–17	
1.3 Clarify word meanings through the use of definition, example, restatement, or contrast.	pages CA 18–19	
2.0 Reading Comprehension (Focus on Informational Materials)		
2.1 Understand and analyze the differences in structure and purpose between various categories of informational materials (e.g., textbooks, newspapers, instructional manuals, signs).	pages CA 20–21	
2.2 Locate information by using a variety of consumer, workplace, and public documents.	pages CA 22–23	
2.3 Analyze text that uses the cause-and-effect organizational pattern.	pages CA 24–25	
2.4 Identify and trace the development of an author's argument, point of view, or perspective in text.	pages CA 26–27	
2.5 Understand and explain the use of a simple mechanical device by following technical directions.	pages CA 28–29	
2.6 Assess the adequacy, accuracy, and appropriateness of the author's evidence to support claims and assertions, noting instances of bias and stereotyping.	pages CA 30–31	
3.0 Literary Response and Analysis		
3.1 Articulate the expressed purposes and characteristics of different forms of prose (e.g., short story, novel, novella, essay).	pages CA 32–33	
3.2 Identify events that advance the plot and determine how each event explains past or present action(s) or foreshadows future action(s).	pages CA 34–35	

California English-Language Arts Content Standards	All-in-One Workbook: Daily Standards Reviews	All-in-One Workbook: Writing Support for Essays
3.3 Analyze characterization as delineated through a character's thoughts, words, speech patterns, and actions; the narrator's description; and the thoughts, words, and actions of other characters.	pages CA 36–37	
3.4 Identify and analyze recurring themes across works (e.g., the value of bravery, loyalty, and friendship; the effects of loneliness).	pages CA 38–39	
3.5 Contrast points of view (e.g., first and third person, limited and omniscient, subjective and objective) in narrative text and explain how they affect the overall theme of the work.	pages CA 40–41	
3.6 Analyze a range of responses to a literary work and determine the extent to which the literary elements in the work shaped those responses.	pages CA 42–43	

WRITING

1.0 Writing Strategies

1.1 Create an organizational structure that balances all aspects of the composition and uses effective transitions between sentences to unify important ideas.	pages CA 44–45	pages CA 120–121
1.2 Support all statements and claims with anecdotes, descriptions, facts and statistics, and specific examples.	pages CA 46–47	pages CA 122–123
1.3 Use strategies of note taking, outlining, and summarizing to impose structure on composition drafts.	pages CA 48–49	pages CA 124–125
1.4 Identify topics; ask and evaluate questions; and develop ideas leading to inquiry, investigation, and research.	pages CA 50–51	pages CA 126–127
1.5 Give credit for both quoted and paraphrased information in a bibliography by using a consistent and sanctioned format and methodology for citations.	pages CA 52–53	pages CA 128–129
1.6 Create documents by using word-processing skills and publishing programs; develop simple databases and spreadsheets to manage information and prepare reports.	pages CA 54–55	pages CA 130–131
1.7 Revise writing to improve organization and word choice after checking the logic of the ideas and the precision of the vocabulary.	pages CA 56–57	pages CA 132–133

California English-Language Arts Content Standards	All-in-One Workbook: Daily Standards Reviews	All-in-One Workbook: Writing Support for Essays
2.0 Writing Applications (Genres and Their Characteristics)		
2.1 Write fictional or autobiographical narratives: a. Develop a standard plot line (having a beginning, conflict, rising action, climax, and denouement) and point of view. b. Develop complex major and minor characters and a definite setting. c. Use a range of appropriate strategies (e.g., dialogue; suspense; naming of specific narrative action, including movement, gestures, and expressions).	pages CA 58–59	
2.2 Write responses to literature: a. Develop interpretations exhibiting careful reading, understanding, and insight. b. Organize interpretations around several clear ideas, premises, or images from the literary work. c. Justify interpretations through sustained use of examples and textual evidence.	pages CA 60–61	
2.3 Write research reports: a. Pose relevant and tightly drawn questions about the topic. b. Convey clear and accurate perspectives on the subject. c. Include evidence compiled through the formal research process (e.g., use of a card catalog, *Reader's Guide to Periodical Literature*, a computer catalog, magazines, newspapers, dictionaries). d. Document reference sources by means of footnotes and a bibliography.	pages CA 62–63	
2.4 Write persuasive compositions: a. State a clear position or perspective in support of a proposition or proposal. b. Describe the points in support of the proposition, employing well-articulated evidence. c. Anticipate and address reader concerns and counterarguments.	pages CA 64–65	
2.5 Write summaries of reading materials: a. Include the main ideas and most significant details.	pages CA 66–67	

California English-Language Arts Content Standards	All-in-One Workbook: Daily Standards Reviews	All-in-One Workbook: Writing Support for Essays
b. Use the student's own words, except for quotations. c. Reflect underlying meaning, not just the superficial details.		
WRITTEN AND ORAL ENGLISH LANGUAGE CONVENTIONS		
1.0 Written and Oral English Language Conventions		
1.1 Place modifiers properly and use the active voice.	pages CA 68–69	pages CA 106–107
1.2 Identify and use infinitives and participles and make clear references between pronouns and antecedents.	pages CA 70–71	pages CA 108–109
1.3 Identify all parts of speech and types and structure of sentences.	pages CA 72–73	pages CA 110–111
1.4 Demonstrate the mechanics of writing (e.g., quotation marks, commas at end of dependent clauses) and appropriate English usage (e.g., pronoun reference).	pages CA 74–75	pages CA 112–113
1.5 Identify hyphens, dashes, brackets, and semicolons and use them correctly.	pages CA 76–77	pages CA 114–115
1.6 Use correct capitalization.	pages CA 78–79	pages CA 116–117
1.7 Spell derivatives correctly by applying the spellings of bases and affixes.	pages CA 80–81	pages CA 118–119
LISTENING AND SPEAKING		
1.0 Listening and Speaking Strategies		
1.1 Ask probing questions to elicit information, including evidence to support the speaker's claims and conclusions.	pages CA 82–83	
1.2 Determine the speaker's attitude toward the subject.	pages CA 84–85	
1.3 Respond to persuasive messages with questions, challenges, or affirmations.	pages CA 86–87	
1.4 Organize information to achieve particular purposes and to appeal to the background and interests of the audience.	pages CA 88–89	
1.5 Arrange supporting details, reasons, descriptions, and examples effectively and persuasively in relation to the audience.	pages CA 90–91	
1.6 Use speaking techniques, including voice modulation, inflection, tempo, enunciation, and eye contact, for effective presentations.	pages CA 92–93	

California English-Language Arts Content Standards	All-in-One Workbook: Daily Standards Reviews	All-in-One Workbook: Writing Support for Essays
1.7 Provide constructive feedback to speakers concerning the coherence and logic of a speech's content and delivery and its overall impact upon the listener.	pages CA 94–95	
1.8 Analyze the effect on the viewer of images, text, and sound in electronic journalism; identify the techniques used to achieve the effects in each instance studied.	pages CA 96–97	
2.0 Speaking Applications (Genres and Their Characteristics)		
2.1 Deliver narrative presentations: a. Establish a context, standard plot line (having a beginning, conflict, rising action, climax, and denouement), and point of view. b. Describe complex major and minor characters and a definite setting. c. Use a range of appropriate strategies, including dialogue, suspense, and naming of specific narrative action (e.g., movement, gestures, expressions).	pages CA 98–99	
2.2 Deliver oral summaries of articles and books: a. Include the main ideas of the event or article and the most significant details. b. Use the student's own words, except for material quoted from sources. c. Convey a comprehensive understanding of sources, not just superficial details.	pages CA 100–101	
2.3 Deliver research presentations: a. Pose relevant and concise questions about the topic. b. Convey clear and accurate perspectives on the subject. c. Include evidence generated through the formal research process (e.g., use of a card catalog, *Reader's Guide to Periodical Literature*, a computer catalog, magazines, newspapers, dictionaries). d. Cite reference sources appropriately.	pages CA 102–103	
2.4 Deliver persuasive presentations: a. State a clear position or perspective in support of an argument or proposal. b. Describe the points in support of the argument and employ well-articulated evidence.	pages CA 104–105	

About the California Content Standards

The purpose of the California English-Language Arts content standards is to help you achieve by defining the language arts knowledge, concepts, and skills that you should acquire at each grade level.

The skills that fall under Language Arts are reading, writing, listening, and speaking. These skills are interrelated and should not be taught independently of one another. Reading, writing, listening, and speaking skills need to be woven together into a strong core curriculum that aims to not only teach these standards but also apply the language arts skills to other curricular areas.

Mastery of the English-Language Arts content standards will help you go on to higher education and enter the workplace as a capable communicator.

Building Your Vocabulary

Academic Vocabulary

Academic vocabulary is the language you encounter in textbooks and on standardized tests. Understanding these words and using them in your classroom discussions and writing will help you communicate your ideas clearly and effectively. The words listed in this chart appear throughout your literature book.

Word	Definition	Related Words	Word in Context
analyze (AN uh lyz) *v.*	break down into parts and examine carefully	analytical	Out assignment is to analyze the story's ending.
appreciate (uh PREE shee ayt) *v.*	be thankful for	appreciative appreciating	Once I read Frost's poem, I learned to appreciate his use of symbols.
assumption (uh SUHMP shuhn) *n.*	belief or acceptance that something is true	assume assuming	The assumption in the essay is well supported by facts.
attitude (AT uh tood) *n.*	mental state involving beliefs, feelings, and values	attitudes	The writer's attitude toward his subject was respectful and full of admiration.
awareness (uh WAIR nehs) *n.*	knowledge gained from one's own perceptions or from information	aware	It is important to develop an awareness of the writer's message.
bias (BY uhs) *n.*	tendency to see things from a slanted or prejudiced viewpoint	biased	You must consider if an advertisement contains bias or tries to mislead the reader.
culture (KUHL chuhr) *n.*	collected customs of a group or community	cultural	Folk tales reveal the values of a culture and teach a lesson.
challenge (CHAL uhnj) *v.*	dare; a calling into question	challenging challenged	Ted invited me to challenge him to a debate.
characteristic (kar ihk tuh RIHS tihk) *n.*	trait; feature	character characteristically	One characteristic of a legend is a human who is larger than life.
common (KOM uhn) *adj.*	ordinary; expected	commonality	It is common for an essay to contain humor.
communicate (kuh MYOO nuh kayt) *v.*	share thoughts or feelings, usually in words	communication communicating	It is important to be able communicate thoughts and feelings in writing.
communication (kuh myoo nuh KAY shuhn) *n.*	activity of sharing information or speaking	communicate	There seemed to be a lack of communication between the mother and daughter.
community (kuh MYOO nuh tee) *n.*	group of people who share an interest or who live near each other	communities	Local newspapers serve the community where the paper is published.

Ordinary Language:
I was able to **explain the meaning of** the story's plot quickly.

vs

Academic Language:
I was able to **define** the story's plot quickly.

Building Your Vocabulary

Word	Definition	Related Words	Word in Context
conclude (kuhn KLOOD) *v.*	bring to a close; end	concluding conclusion	The writer was able to conclude the essay with a positive memory.
contribute (kuhn TRIHB yut) *v.*	add to; enrich	contribution	Editorials contribute to a public discussion about an issue.
convince (kuhn VIHNS) *v.*	persuade; cause to accept a point of view	convincing	It is important to convince readers of the character's dream.
debate (dih BAYT) *v.*	argue in an attempt to convince	debated debating	The two students tried to debate whether or not the new website was helpful.
define (dih FYN) *v.*	determine the nature of or give the meaning of	defined definition	I was able to define the story's plot quickly.
discover (dihs KUHV uhr) *v.*	to find or explore	discovering discovery	The writer tries to discover the reasons for the character's behavior.
diversity (duh VUR suh tee) *n.*	variety, as of groups or cultures	diverse	Reading works from different writers provides diversity.
environment (ehn VY ruhn muhnt) *n.*	surroundings; the natural world	environs environmentally	The essay described the beautiful environment where the writer lived.
evaluate (ih VAL yoo ayt) *v.*	judge; determine the significance of	evaluated evaluation	The character was unable to evaluate loyal friends from disloyal ones.
examine (ehg ZAM uhn) *v.*	study in depth; look at closely	examining examination	In order to examine the evidence, it was necessary to research the subject.
explain (ehk SPLAYN) *v.*	make plain or clear	explaining explanation	I will explain three key factors in the story's success.
explore (ehk SPLAWR) *v.*	investigate; look into	explored exploration	I wrote a research report to explore my ideas.
facts (fakts) *n.*	accepted truths or reality	factual	I supported my statement with facts and details.
focus (FOH kuhs) *n.*	central point or topic of investigation	focused focusing	The focus of the essay was to provide information about water safety.
generate (JEN uhr ayt) *v.*	create	generated generating	Before researching, I tried to generate several topics that I would explore.
identify (y DEHN tuh fy) *v.*	recognize as being	identification	How do you identify the meaning of this poem?
ignore (ihg NAWR) *v.*	refuse to notice; disregard	ignored ignoring	If we ignore the message, we miss the purpose of the writing.

Ordinary Language: In order to **think about** what had been said, I took some quiet time.

vs

Academic Language: In order to **reflect** on what had been said, I took some quiet time.

Word	Definition	Related Words	Word in Context
image (IHM ihj) *n.*	picture; representation	images imaging	The image in the book helped me to visualize the story.
individual (ihn duh VIHJ oo uhl) *n.*	single person or thing	individuals	The story is told from the perspective of one individual.
inform (ihn FORM) *v.*	tell; give information about	information	The purpose of the research paper was to inform the reader about whales.
inquire (ihn KWYR) *v.*	ask in order to learn about	inquiring inquired	We were assigned to inquire about weather patterns and present our findings.
insight (ihn syt) *n.*	ability to see the truth; an understanding	insightful	My teacher shared her insight with us about the characters.
investigate (ihn VEHS tuh gayt) *v.*	examine thoroughly	investigated investigation	As a team, we were able to investigate each aspect of the problem.
media (MEE dee uh) *n.*	collected sources of information, including newspapers, television, and the Internet		The media is an everyday source of information and entertainment for the public.
opposition (op uh ZIHSH uhn) *n.*	state of being against	oppose opposing	The villain in the story presented the opposition to the hero's happiness.
outcome (owt kuhm) *n.*	way something turns out		We found the outcome of the problem to be a favorable solution.
perceive (puhr SEEV) *v.*	adopt a point of view; see	perceived perception	I was able to perceive Jenny's character through her actions and words.
perception (puhr SEHP shuhn) *n.*	the act of becoming aware of through one or more of the senses	perceive perceptive	My perception of the character changed over the course of the story.
perspective (puhr SPEHK tihv) *n.*	point of view		I did not agree with the perspective of the writer.
produce (pruh DOOS) *v.*	make; create	produced producing	In order to produce a new show, the writing team must provide a script.
reaction (ree AK shuhn) *n.*	response to an influence, action, or statement	react	I had a strong reaction to the claims made in the commercial.

Ordinary Language:
Each writer has a ***one-of-a-kind*** way of telling a story.

vs

Academic Language:
Each writer has a ***unique*** way of telling a story.

Building Your Vocabulary

Word	Definition	Related Words	Word in Context
reflect (rih FLEHKT) *v.*	think about; consider	reflected reflection	In order to reflect on what had been said, I took some quiet time.
resolution (rehz uh LOO shuhn) *n.*	end of a conflict in which one or both parties is satisfied	resolved resolving	The resolution of the story helped me to see how a compromise can help many people.
team (teem) *n.*	group united in a common goal		Our team prepared a report and each member took a turn presenting it.
technology (tehk NOL uh jee) *n.*	practical application of science to business or industry	technologies	At one time, the computer was considered a new technology.
tradition (truh DIHSH uhn) *n.*	custom, as of a social group or culture	traditional	A tradition is often handed down to a new generation though storytelling.
transmit (trans MIHT) *v.*	send or give out	transmitted transmission	We were able to transmit our message over the school's radio station.
understanding (uhn duhr STAN dihng) *n.*	agreement; end of conflict	understand	The students had an excellent understanding of the author's message.
unify (YOO nuh fy) *v.*	bring together as one	unified unifying	It is important to unify details so that they support the central idea.
unique (yoo NEEK) *adj.*	one of a kind	uniqueness uniquely	Each writer has a unique way of telling a story.

Increasing Your Word Knowledge

Increase your word knowledge and chances of success by taking an active role in developing your vocabulary. Here are some tips for you.

To own a word, follow these steps:

Steps to Follow	Model
1. Learn to identify the word and its basic meaning.	The word *examine* means "to look at closely."
2. Take note of the word's spelling.	*Examine* begins and ends with an e.
3. Practice pronouncing the word so that you can use it in conversation.	The *e* on the end of the word is silent. Its second syllable gets the most stress.
4. Visualize the word and illustrate its key meaning.	When I think of the word *examine*, I visualize a doctor checking a patient's health.
5. Learn the various forms of the word and its related words.	Examination and *exam* are forms of the word *examine*.
6. Compare the word with similar words.	*Examine*, *peruse*, and *study* are synonyms.
7. Contrast the word with similar words.	When you *peruse* materials, you do a more casual kind of examination. *Study* is often used to describe preparing for a test.
8. Use the word in various contexts.	"I'd like to *examine* the footprints more closely." "I will *examine* the use of imagery in this poem."

Building Your Speaking Vocabulary

Language gives us the ability to express ourselves. The more words you know, the better able you will be get your points across. There are two main aspects of language: reading and speaking. Using the steps above will help you to acquire a rich vocabulary. Follow these steps to help you learn to use this rich vocabulary in discussions, speeches, and conversations.

Step	Tip
1. Practice pronouncing the word.	Become familiar with pronunciation guides to allow you to sound out unfamilar words. Listening to audio books as you read the text will help you learn prounciations of words.
2. Learn word forms.	Dictionaries often list forms of words following the main word entry. Practice saying word families aloud: "generate," "generated," "generation," "regenerate," "generator."
3. Translate your thoughts.	Restate your own thoughts and ideas in a variety of way, to inject formality or to change your tone, for example.
4. Hold discussions.	With a classmate, practice using academic vocabulary words in discussions about the text. Choose one term to practice at a time, and see how many statements you can create using that term.
5. Tape-record yourself..	Analyze your word choices by listening to yourself objectively. Note places your word choice could be strengthened or changed.

Truth, performed by Becca Schack

Awareness is what we need
to know what's going on
Don't leave me in the dark
all common sense gone
What we **perceive**
is not always real
What we understand
not always the deal

Come on and shed some light
Deliver more **insight**
Come on and shed some light
so we can do what's right

Can we find the **truth**
When the answers are hidden
How do we see through
Behind the eyes of deception
Reach deep inside
and you will find
what you're looking for
what you're looking for

We can spend all night
in a heated **debate**
If we don't share our ideas

how can we collaborate
Explain all the reasons why
you do the things you do
So we can **evaluate** the situation
You see it's all about communication

Continued

Factual or **fiction**

Truth or contradiction

Real or fabrication

Aware of your own creation

Can we find the **truth**

When the answers are hidden

How do we see through

Behind the eyes of deception

Reach deep inside

and you will find

what you're looking for

what you're looking for

Child, please don't be confused

Just take my hand and let me show you

It can be simple or it can be hard

The answer often lies within you

Reveal yourself

Come show me who you are

Convince me to believe

No need to go too far

In the end I will **conclude**

a resolution

I'll have made up my mind

and know just what to do

The **evidence** will show

Help us really know

What's **believable** or crazy

Is it a dream or reality

Continued

Can we find the **truth**
When the answers are hidden
How do we see through
Behind the eyes of deception
Reach deep inside
and you will find
what you're looking for
what you're looking for

Song Title: **Truth**
Artist / Performed by Becca Schack
Lyrics by Becca Schack
Music composed by Mike Pandolfo
Produced by Mike Pandolfo, Wonderful
Executive Producer: Keith London, Defined Mind

Unit 1: Fiction and Nonfiction
Big Question Vocabulary—1

The Big Question: Is there ever truth in fiction?

conclude: *v.* bring something to an end; other form: *conclusion*

convince: *v.* persuade someone to agree; sway someone's thinking; other form: *convincing*

evaluate: *v.* judge how good or successful something is; other forms: *evaluation, evaluating*

perceive: *v.* see or recognize something; discover; identify; other forms: *perception, perceptive*

reveal: *v.* uncover a secret; make something known; other forms: *revealing, revealed*

DIRECTIONS: *Review the vocabulary words and their definitions shown above. Then answer each question.*

1. Mr. Sanchez is a judge for the school talent show. As he watches each act in the show, which of these verbs **best** describes what he must do? Explain your answer. _____
   _____

2. Ms. Chang is directing the weekly meeting of the Teachers' Association. The meeting is almost over. Which verb **best** describes what she should do? Explain your answer. _____
   _____

3. The detective learned the secret identity of the Midnight Thief. He wanted to tell the newspapers the news. Which verb **best** describes what he will do? Explain your answer.
   _____

4. Joanne wants her classmates to be as concerned as she is about global warming. Which verb **best** describes what she should do? Explain your answer. _____
   _____

5. The fog made it difficult for us to see the mountain. Which verb **best** describes what we were trying to do? Explain your answer. _____
   _____

Unit 1: Fiction and Nonfiction
Big Question Vocabulary—2

 The Big Question: Is there ever truth in fiction?

awareness: *n.* a person's knowledge or understanding of a situation; other forms: *aware, unaware*

debate: *n.* a discussion between people with opposite views
   v. discuss different views on a subject; other form: *debatable*

evidence: *n.* facts, objects, or signs that prove that something is true; other form: *evident*

fiction: *n.* stories about imaginary people and events; other forms: *fictitious, fictional*

reality: *n.* what actually happens or is true; real life; other forms: *real, realism*

A. DIRECTIONS: *Review the vocabulary words listed above. On the line that precedes each question, write **Yes** or **No** to answer it. Then explain your response on the line that follows it.*

_____1. Would a book of *fiction* be the best source for facts about George Washington?

   _____

_____2. Would photographs and eyewitness reports serve as reliable *evidence* regarding what happened at a sporting event?

   _____

_____3. At a *debate*, are all participants expected to share the same opinion?

   _____

B. DIRECTIONS: *Follow each of the directions.*

1. Explain the difference between **fiction** and **reality**. Give an example of each.

   _____

   _____

   _____

2. Give three pieces of **evidence** that would raise someone's **awareness** of a fire. _____

   _____

   _____

   _____

Unit 1: Fiction and Nonfiction
Big Question Vocabulary—3

The Big Question: Is there ever truth in fiction?

believable: *adj.* able to be believed; other forms: *belief, believe, believer, believably, disbelief*

explain: *v.* describe or demonstrate something in a way that makes it clear and understandable; other form: *explanation*

factual: *adj.* based on facts; truthful; other form: *fact*

insight: *n.* personal understanding or wisdom on a subject; other form: *insightful*

truth: *n.* what can be proved, based on facts; other forms: *true, truly*

A. DIRECTIONS: *For each vocabulary word, list three things or reasons as instructed. Then, use the vocabulary word in a sentence about one of the things or reasons.*

Example: List three things that are examples of **fiction.**

a story about elves   a story about talking horses   a story about flying cats

Sentence: *In the story, the cats built an airplane and flew to a planet ruled by mice.*

---

1. List three things about cats that are *believable.*

   _____   _____   _____

   Sentence: _____

2. List three things about your school that are *factual.*

   _____   _____   _____

   Sentence: _____

3. Give three reasons for *explaining* safety rules to young children.

   _____   _____   _____

   Sentence: _____

4. List three *insights* you have about the importance of friendship.

   _____   _____   _____

   Sentence: _____

5. List three *truths* about trees.

   _____   _____   _____

   Sentence: _____

Name _____ Date _____

Unit 1: Fiction and Nonfiction
Applying the Big Question

Is there ever truth in fiction?

DIRECTIONS: *Complete the chart below to apply what you have learned about finding truth in fiction. One row has been completed for you.*

Example	Facts	Where facts are found	How the facts are revealed	How facts connect to fiction	What I learned
From Literature	Jewish families were killed and all Jews had to wear stars.	These facts were in the story "Suzy and Leah".	Suzy read Leah's journal, and Suzy's mother explained the treatment of the Jews.	The characters Suzy and Leah are fictional characters.	Some fictional stories include historical facts that can be proven.
From Literature					
From Science					
From Social Studies					
From Real Life					

Richard Peck
Listening and Viewing

Segment 1: Meet Richard Peck
- From where does Richard Peck draw his inspiration to write stories about young people?
- If you were writing a story, where might you get ideas for writing?

_____

_____

_____

_____

Segment 2: Fiction and Nonfiction
- Do you agree with Richard Peck that fiction can be "truer than fact"?
- How might a work of fiction be more convincing than a work of nonfiction, such as a newspaper article?

_____

_____

_____

_____

Segment 3: The Writing Process
- Why does Richard Peck throw out the first chapter of a book once he has written the ending?
- Which one of Richard Peck's writing methods would you use? Why?

_____

_____

_____

_____

Segment 4: The Rewards of Writing
- Why does Richard Peck believe readers "have an advantage" over people who do not read?
- How has reading helped you better understand another person, a situation, or yourself? Explain.

_____

_____

_____

_____

Learning About Fiction and Nonfiction

This chart compares and contrasts **fiction** and **nonfiction**:

Fiction	Nonfiction
tells about *made-up* people or animals, called **characters**: The characters experience a series of made-up events, called the **plot**; the plot takes place at a certain real or imagined time in a certain real or imagined location, which is the **setting**; the plot also contains a problem, or **conflict**, that characters must solve	tells about *real* people, animals, places, things, events, and ideas; presents facts and discusses ideas; may reflect the **historical context** of its time by making references to current events, society, and culture
may be told from the perspective of a character in the story (**first-person point of view**) or a narrator outside the story (**third-person point of view**)	is told from the **perspective** of the author
takes the form of short stories, novellas, novels	takes the form of biographies, autobiographies, memoirs, letters, journals, diaries, essays, articles, textbooks, and documents, such as application forms and instructions
to explain, inform, persuade, or entertain	to explain, inform, persuade, or entertain

A. DIRECTIONS: *Using clues in each title, write* fiction *or* nonfiction *on the line.*

_____ 1. "My Family Came From Mars"

_____ 2. "Historic Landings on the Moon"

_____ 3. *The Life of Thomas Jefferson*

_____ 4. *Jackie Rabbit, King of the Meadow*

_____ 5. "How to Make Oatmeal Bread"

B. DIRECTIONS: *Read this paragraph carefully, and decide whether it is fiction or nonfiction. Indicate your choice. Then, explain what hints led you to make your choice.*

The Ramirez family set off on their summer vacation yesterday. Luis was excited. It was the first trip that his family had taken since coming to the United States last year. Luis had brought along two books to read during the trip. He'd have plenty of time to read. After all, flying to a distant galaxy would take at least a week.

Fiction / Nonfiction: _____

Explanation: _____

Name _____   Date _____

"**The Three-Century Woman**" by Richard Peck
Model Selection: Fiction

Every work of **fiction** includes made-up people or animals, called **characters,** and a made-up series of events, called the **plot.** The plot may seem realistic. For example, it may be a story about students like you. On the other hand, the plot may be a fantasy. It might, for example, feature talking cats.

The plot takes place at a certain time and in a certain location, called the **setting.** The setting may or may not be real. Every plot contains a problem, or **conflict,** that one or more characters must solve.

A speaker, called the **narrator,** tells the story from a certain perspective, or **point of view.** If the narrator is a character in the story, he or she tells it from the **first-person point of view.** If the narrator is outside the story, he or she tells it from the **third-person point of view.**

Examples of fiction include novels, novellas, and short stories.

A. DIRECTIONS: *"The Three-Century Woman" is a work of fiction. Complete the following items to provide details about its characters, narrator, setting, and plot.*

1. The **characters:** _____

   _____

2. Is the **narrator** inside or outside the story? _____

3. Is the story told from the **first-person** or **third-person** point of view? _____

   _____

4. Clues that indicate the point of view: _____

   _____

5. When does the story take place? _____

   _____

6. Where does the story take place? _____

   _____

7. Is the **setting** realistic or imaginary? Explain. _____

   _____

8. Is the **plot** realistic or fantastic? _____

9. Examples of real or fantastic **plot** elements: _____

   _____

10. What **conflict,** or problem, do the characters face?

   _____

   _____

"The Fall of the *Hindenburg*" by Michael Morrison
Model Selection: Nonfiction

Nonfiction deals with *real* people, animals, places, things, events, and ideas. It may present facts or discuss ideas.

A work of nonfiction is narrated from the **point of view,** or perspective, of the author. Often nonfiction reflects the **historical context** of its time by including references to current events, society, or culture. For example, an article about the American Revolution would contain social and cultural information about the East Coast of North America in the mid-1700s.

Works of nonfiction include biographies, autobiographies, memoirs, letters, journals, diaries, essays, articles, textbooks, and various documents, such as application forms and instructions.

A. DIRECTIONS: *Answer these questions about "The Fall of the* Hindenburg."

1. What real event does the article discuss?

   _____

2. On what date, and in what location, did the event take place?

   _____

3. List three facts that the author presents.

   _____

   _____

   _____

4. What conclusions can you draw about the topic, based on your reading of the article?

   _____

   _____

5. Give an example of a detail that sets a historical context for the article.

   _____

B. DIRECTIONS: *Authors have one or more purposes for writing a piece of nonfiction. For example, an author might write to explain how to do something, to tell the story of a person's life, to inform readers about a topic, to persuade readers to share an opinion, or to share a personal experience. In your opinion, what was Michael Morrison's purpose for writing "The Fall of the Hindenburg"? Support your answer by citing facts, reasons, and examples from the article.*

_____

_____

_____

"**Papa's Parrot**" by Cynthia Rylant

Writing About the Big Question

What is the best way to find the truth?

Big Question Vocabulary

awareness	believable	conclude	convince	debate
evaluate	evidence	explain	factual	fiction
insight	perceive	reality	reveal	truth

A. *Use one or more words from the list above to complete each sentence.*

1. When a person has _____, he or she may know things that were not told to him or her.

2. It is sometimes difficult for someone to _____ strong feelings.

3. When someone acts indifferent toward me, I _____ that he or she does not like me.

4. When someone is very friendly and warm toward me, I _____ that he or she likes me.

B. *Answer the questions. Use at least one of the vocabulary words in each answer:*

1. Have you ever been unsure about how someone feels about you? Explain.

   _____

   _____

   _____

2. Was the truth about the person's feelings ever revealed? If so, how? If not, what can you do to gain insight into how the person feels about you?

   _____

   _____

   _____

C. *Complete the first sentence below. Then, answer the question to write a short paragraph connecting the sentence to the Big Question.*

   One time I learned the truth about _____ when

   _____

   How could you use that truth in a fictional story?

   _____

   _____

   _____

   _____

"Papa's Parrot" by Cynthia Rylant
Reading: Use Context Clues to Unlock the Meaning

Context, the words and phrases surrounding a word, can help you understand a word you do not know. When you come across an unfamiliar word, **use context clues to unlock the meaning.** Look for a word or words that might mean the same thing or have the opposite meaning of the unfamiliar word. In addition, you may find definitions, examples, or descriptions of the unfamiliar word. For example, in this passage from "Papa's Parrot," the italicized words are clues to the meaning of *unpack:*

New shipments of candy and nuts would be arriving. . . .

...Harry told his father that he would go to the store every day after school and <u>unpack</u> boxes. He would *sort out all the candy and nuts.*

As you read, use context clues to find possible meanings for unfamiliar words. Check the words in a dictionary after you read.

DIRECTIONS: *Read each of the following sentences or short passages from "Papa's Parrot." Look at the underlined word. Then, find other words in the passage that can be used as context clues to help you figure out the meaning of the underlined word. Write the context clue or clues on the first line. Write the meaning of the underlined word on the second line. Then, check your answer by looking up the underlined word in a dictionary.*
Hint: Sometimes the context clues appear a distance away from the unfamiliar word. For item 3, below, the context clue appears in the first paragraph of the story.

1. Harry stopped liking candy and nuts when he was around seven, but, in spite of this, he and Mr. Tillian had <u>remained</u> friends and were still friends the year Harry turned twelve.

    Context clues: _____ _____

    Meaning of word: _____

2. At home things were different. Harry and his father joked with each other at the dinner table as they always had—Mr. Tillian <u>teasing</u> Harry about his smelly socks; Harry teasing Mr. Tillian about his blubbery stomach.

    Context clues: _____

    Meaning of word: _____

3. Though his father was fat and merely owned a candy and nut shop, Harry Tillian liked his papa. . . . Harry and his father joked with each other at the dinner table as they always had—Mr. Tillian teasing Harry about his smelly socks; Harry teasing Mr. Tillian about his <u>blubbery</u> stomach.

    Context clues: _____

    Meaning of word: _____

"Papa's Parrot" by Cynthia Rylant
Literary Analysis: Narrative Writing

Narrative writing is any type of writing that tells a story. The act or process of telling a story is also called **narration.**

- A narrative is usually told in chronological order—the order in which events occur in time.
- A narrative may be fiction, nonfiction, or poetry.

When you look at events in chronological order, you see that events that occur later in a narrative often depend on events that occurred earlier. For example, in "Papa's Parrot," the part of the story in which Harry walks by his father's store and hears him talking to Rocky must follow the part in which Mr. Tillian buys Rocky in the first place.

DIRECTIONS: *Below is a list of events from "Papa's Parrot." Put the events in chronological order by writing a number from 1 to 10 on the line before the event. Remember that each event has to make sense in terms of what has already occurred in the story.*

_____ **A.** Harry stops going to the candy and nut shop when he sees his father talking to Rocky.

_____ **B.** Harry goes to the candy and nut shop to unpack boxes and feed Rocky.

_____ **C.** Harry yells at Rocky and throws peppermints at him.

_____ **D.** Mr. Tillian buys a parrot, spending more money than he can afford.

_____ **E.** Harry understands what Rocky means and goes to visit his father in the hospital.

_____ **F.** Mr. Tillian falls ill and is taken to the hospital.

_____ **G.** When they were young, Harry and his friends stopped by his father's candy and nut shop after school to buy penny candy or roasted peanuts.

_____ **H.** Mr. Tillian talks to Rocky, and the two watch television together.

_____ **I.** After Harry enters junior high school, he and his friends stop going to the candy and nut shop and spend more time playing video games and shopping for records.

_____ **J.** The parrot says, "Hello, Rocky!" and "Where's Harry?" over and over.

"Papa's Parrot" by Cynthia Rylant
Vocabulary Builder

Word List

clusters   ignored   merely   perch   resumed   shipments

A. DIRECTIONS: *Think about the meaning of the italicized Word List word in each item below. Then, answer the question, and explain your answer.*

1. After his hospital stay, Mr. Tillian *resumed* his place in the candy and nut shop. Were his customers pleased?

   _____

2. While Mr. Tillian was in the hospital, Harry *ignored* his friends. Were his friends pleased?

   _____

3. When Harry threw a cluster of peppermints at the cage, Rocky clung to his *perch*. Was Rocky scared?

   _____

4. Mr. Tillian worried about the new *shipments* of candy and nuts arriving at his shop. Who would handle them?

   _____

5. In Harry's eyes, Mr. Tillian *merely* owned a candy and nut shop. Was Harry ashamed of his father's occupation?

   _____

6. Rocky's cage was next to the sign for the maple *clusters*. What other similar items does Mr. Tillian have in his store?

   _____

B. WORD STUDY The prefix *re-* means "back" or "again." Use the context of the sentences and the meaning of the prefix to explain your answer to each question.

1. If you program a song for constant *replay*, does that mean that you like it or dislike it?

   _____

2. When a football coach *repositions* the players on the field, what is he doing?

   _____

3. If you *rethink* a decision, are you happy with the choice you made?

   _____

"**MK**" by Jean Fritz

Writing About the Big Question

What is the best way to find the truth?

Big Question Vocabulary

awareness	believable	conclude	convince	debate
evaluate	evidence	explain	factual	fiction
insight	perceive	reality	reveal	truth

A. *Use one or more words from the list above to complete each sentence*

1. In _____, an author may mix in some truth.

2. A reader can often determine which parts of a fictional story have elements of
   _____ .

3. A _____ fictional story is not always true.

B. *Answer the questions.*

1. Name a fictional book, movie, or television show that was so believable, you were
   convinced that at least part of it was based on truth.

   _____

   _____

2. Explain what elements of the fictional work were realistic.

   _____

   _____

   _____

   _____

C. *Complete the sentence below. Then, answer the question by writing a short paragraph
connecting the sentence to the Big Question.*

A story from my childhood that I would like to tell is _____

_____

If you made the story into a work of fiction, what would you change, and what
would stay the same?

_____

_____

_____

_____

_____

"MK" by Jean Fritz
Reading: Use Context Clues to Unlock the Meaning

   Context, the words and phrases surrounding a word, can help you understand a word you do not know. When you come across an unfamiliar word, **use context clues to unlock the meaning.** Look for a word or words that might mean the same thing or have the opposite meaning of the unfamiliar word. In addition, you may find definitions, examples, or descriptions of the unfamiliar word. For example, in this passage from "MK," the italicized words are clues to the meaning of *protected:*

> The women and children going to Shanghai would be <u>protected</u> *from bullets by steel barriers erected around the deck.*

   As you read, use context clues to find possible meanings for unfamiliar words. Check the words in a dictionary after you read.

DIRECTIONS: *Read each of the following sentences or short passages from "MK." Look at the underlined word. Then, find other words in the passage that can be used as context clues to help you figure out the meaning of the underlined word. Write the context clue or clues on the first line. Write the meaning of the underlined word on the second line. Then, check your answer by looking up the underlined word in a dictionary.*

1. I couldn't let on how I really felt. . . . "I'll be okay," I said, sniffing back fake tears. Sometimes it's necessary to <u>deceive</u> your parents if you love them, and I did love mine.

   Context clues: _____

   Meaning of word: _____

2. The girls were given what looked like dance cards and the boys were supposed to sign up for the talk sessions they wanted. Of course a girl could feel like a <u>wallflower</u> if her card wasn't filled up, but mine usually was.

   Context clues: _____

   Meaning of word: _____

3. It was a three-day trip across most of the <u>continent</u>, but it didn't seem long. Every minute America was under us and rushing past our windows—the Rocky Mountains, the Mississippi River, flat ranch land, small towns, forests, boys dragging school bags over dusty roads.

   Context clues: _____

   Meaning of word: _____

4. I decided that American children were <u>ignorant</u>. Didn't their teachers teach them anything?

   Context clues: _____

   Meaning of word: _____

"MK" by Jean Fritz
Literary Analysis: Narrative

Narrative writing is any type of writing that tells a story. The act or process of telling a story is also called **narration.**

- A narrative is usually told in chronological order—the order in which events occur in time.
- A narrative may be fiction, nonfiction, or poetry.

When you look at events in chronological order, you see that events that occur later in a narrative often depend on events that occurred earlier. In "MK," for example, the part of the story in which Jean takes her first steps on American soil must follow the part in which Jean and her family cross the Pacific Ocean to reach America.

DIRECTIONS: *Below is a list of ten events from "MK." Put the events in chronological order by writing a number from 1 to 10 on the line before the event. Remember that each event has to make sense in terms of what has already occurred in the story.*

_____ **A.** Paula, Jean's roommate at the Shanghai American School, cuts Jean's hair in a bob, the latest American style.

_____ **B.** Jean and most of the other passengers are seasick as they cross the Pacific Ocean on a steamer.

_____ **C.** Fletcher Barrett tells Jean that he is in love with her.

_____ **D.** In America, Jean wonders why her classmates are ignorant.

_____ **E.** Jean's mother enrolls Jean in the Shanghai American School.

_____ **F.** When Jean is almost ready to fall in love, her parents appear and tell her that the family is leaving China for America.

_____ **G.** When Jean meets her aunts and uncles and grandmother, she is thrilled to be part of a real family.

_____ **H.** Jean's mother learns that all of the American women and children in Wuhan must leave for Shanghai.

_____ **I.** In college, Jean reads about "real" Americans and makes a decision to write about them someday.

_____ **J.** When Jean first enters the Shanghai American School, she wonders why people make a fuss about football.

"MK" by Jean Fritz
Vocabulary Builder

Word List

adequate   deceive   ignorant   quest   relation   transformation

A. DIRECTIONS: *Read the incomplete paragraph below. On each line, write one of the words from the Word List. Think about the meaning of each word in the context of the paragraph.*

I was watching a quiz show one night. I tried to answer a series of questions about China. I realized I didn't know as much as I thought I did. In fact, I was (1) _____ about the country and its people. I decided to begin a search for information. My (2) _____ began at the library, where I found many books on China. Some of them were (3) _____, but others did not provide enough information to suit my purposes. Next, I checked out the Internet. There I learned about the country's topography and its rivers. A month later, I had read ten books, consulted a dozen Web sites, and watched three documentaries. I had undergone a (4) _____. I had changed from someone who knew little about China to someone who knew a great deal. I had truly learned who I was in (5) _____ to the Chinese people. I would not try to (6) _____ myself again by thinking that I was educated when I was, in fact, uneducated.

B. DIRECTIONS: *On each line, write the letter of the word whose meaning is* the same as *that of the Word List word.*

___ 1. quest
    A. trial   B. story   C. search   D. query

___ 2. adequate
    A. absent   B. enough   C. insufficient   D. compassionate

___ 3. deceive
    A. promise   B. yell   C. educate   D. mislead

C. WORD STUDY The prefix *in-* means "not." Use the context of the sentences and the meaning of the prefix to answer each question.

1. Why might an *indecisive* person take a long time in the candy aisle of a store?

_____

2. Why would it be a good idea to have safety education for *inexperienced* drivers?

_____

"Papa's Parrot" by Cynthia Rylant
"MK" by Jean Fritz

Integrated Language Skills: Grammar

Common and Proper Nouns

All nouns can be classified as either **common nouns** or **proper nouns.** A **common noun** names a person, place, or thing—such as a feeling or an idea. Common nouns are not capitalized unless they begin a sentence or are an important word in a title. In the following sentence, the common nouns are underlined.

Harry had always stopped in to see his <u>father</u> at <u>work.</u>

In that sentence, the words *father* and *work* are general names for a person and a place.

A **proper noun** names a specific person, place, or thing. Proper nouns are always capitalized. In the following sentence, the proper noun is underlined.

<u>Harry Tillian</u> liked his papa.

Harry Tillian is a proper noun because it names a specific person.

A. PRACTICE: *The following sentences are from or based on "Papa's Parrot" or "MK."*
Circle each proper noun, and underline each common noun.

1. "Rocky was good company for Mr. Tillian."
2. "New shipments of candy and nuts would be arriving. Rocky would be hungry."
3. "Harry told his father that he would go to the store every day after school and unpack boxes."
4. Jean had just finished sixth grade at the British School in Wuhan.
5. "All American women and children had to catch the . . . boat to Shanghai."
6. "Mr. Barrett met us in Shanghai and drove us to their home, where his wife was on the front porch."

B. Writing Application: *Rewrite each of the following sentences. Replace as many of the common nouns as you can with a proper noun to make the information more specific.*

1. The author lived in another country when she was young.

_____

2. The boy was disappointed when his father bought a parrot.

_____

3. The author moved to another country.

_____

4. The parrot showed by his speech that the father missed his son.

_____

"Papa's Parrot" by Cynthia Rylant
"MK" by Jean Fritz

Integrated Language Skills: Support for Writing a Brief Essay

"Papa's Parrot": Use the graphic organizer below to record details that show what Harry was like before he entered junior high school and after he entered junior high school.

Before Entering Junior High

_____
_____
_____
_____
_____
_____

After Entering Junior High

_____
_____
_____
_____
_____
_____

"MK": Use this graphic organizer to record details that show Jean's feelings about America before and after she arrives in the United States.

Before Arriving in the U.S.

_____
_____
_____
_____
_____
_____

After Arriving in the U.S.

_____
_____
_____
_____
_____
_____

Now, use your notes to draft a brief compare-and-contrast essay.

from **An American Childhood** by Annie Dillard
Writing About the Big Question

What is the best way to find the truth?

Big Question Vocabulary

awareness	believable	conclude	convince	debate
evaluate	evidence	explain	factual	fiction
insight	perceive	reality	reveal	truth

A. *Use one or more words from the list above to complete each sentence.*

1. The details in a story can make a story _____ .

2. Even when writing a work of fiction, it helps if there is _____ in the details.

3. Authors must have a(n) _____ of details in order to make people believe the story they are telling.

B. *Answer the questions.*

1. Add details to this sentence to make it more believable: *As I walked home, I was cold.*

_____

_____

_____

2. Now, add details to the same sentence to reveal that you are writing a sentence that is fantastic and not realistic.

_____

_____

_____

C. *Complete the sentence below. Then, write a short paragraph connecting the sentence to the Big Question.*

The details in a story help _____

Write a short fictional paragraph with realistic details.

_____

_____

_____

_____

_____

from **An American Childhood** by Annie Dillard
Reading: Reread and Read Ahead to Confirm Meaning

Context clues are the examples, descriptions, and other details in the text around an unfamiliar or unusual word or expression. Sometimes these clues can help you figure out what the word or expression means. When you come across an unfamiliar word, use the context clues to figure out what the word probably means. **Reread and read ahead to confirm the meaning.**

Read this example from *An American Childhood:*

> But if you flung yourself <u>wholeheartedly</u> at the back of his knees—if you gathered and joined body and soul and pointed them diving fearlessly . . .

Which context clues tell you what *wholeheartedly* means? If you look for clues before and after the word, you find the phrases "flung yourself," "joined body and soul," and "pointed them diving fearlessly." These suggest that *wholeheartedly* probably means something like "completely" or "fully"—which it does.

DIRECTIONS: *Read each quotation from* An American Childhood. *Figure out the meaning of the underlined word by looking for context clues. Write the context clue or clues on the first line. Write the meaning of the word on the second line. Then, check your definitions in a dictionary.*

1. I started making an iceball—a perfect iceball, from perfectly white snow, perfectly spherical, . . . I had just <u>embarked</u> on the iceball project when we heard tire chains come clanking from afar.

   Context clues: _____

   Meaning of word: _____

2. Wordless, we split up. We were on our turf; we could lose ourselves in the neighborhood backyards, everyone for himself. I paused and considered. Everyone had <u>vanished</u> except Mikey Fahey, who was just rounding the corner of a yellow brick house.

   Context clues: _____

   _____

   Meaning of word: _____

3. You have to <u>fling</u> yourself at what you're doing, you have to point yourself, forget yourself, aim, dive.

   Context clues: _____

   Meaning of word: _____

4. Mikey and I unzipped our jackets. I pulled off my <u>sopping</u> mittens. . . . The man's lower pants legs were wet, his cuffs were full of snow.

   Context clues: _____

   Meaning of word: _____

from **An American Childhood** by Annie Dillard
Literary Analysis: Point of View

Point of view is the perspective from which a narrative is told. Point of view affects the kinds of details that are revealed to the reader.

- **First-person point of view:** The narrator is a character who participates in the action of the story and tells the story using the words *I* and *me*. The narrator can reveal only his or her own observations, thoughts, and feelings.
- **Third-person point of view:** The narrator is not a character in the story and uses third-person pronouns such as *he, she,* and *they* to refer to the characters. The narrator may know and reveal the observations, thoughts, and feelings of more than one person or character in the narrative.

Read this example from *An American Childhood:*

It was a long time before he could speak. <u>I</u> had some difficulty at first recalling why <u>we</u> were there. <u>My</u> lips felt swollen; <u>I</u> couldn't see out of the sides of <u>my</u> eyes; <u>I</u> kept coughing.

You can see from the pronouns *I, we,* and *my* that the event is being told from the first-person point of view. The speaker is there—her lips are swollen; her eyes are clouded; she is coughing.

DIRECTIONS: *Read each quotation from* An American Childhood. *Underline each pronoun that shows that the event is told from the first-person point of view. Then, on the lines that follow, briefly describe what you learned from or about the speaker.*

1. Boys welcomed me at baseball, too, for I had, through enthusiastic practice, what was weirdly known as a boy's arm.

   What I learned: _____

   _____

2. He ran after us, and we ran away from him, up the snowy Reynolds sidewalk. At the corner, I looked back; incredibly, he was still after us. . . . All of a sudden, we were running for our lives.

   What I learned: _____

   _____

3. He chased us silently over picket fences, through thorny hedges, between houses, around garbage cans, and across streets. Every time I glanced back, choking for breath, I expected he would have quit. He must have been as breathless as we were.

   What I learned: _____

   _____

from **An American Childhood** by Annie Dillard
Vocabulary Builder

Word List

compelled   improvising   perfunctorily   righteous   strategy   translucent

A. DIRECTIONS: *Think about the meaning of the underlined Word List word in each sentence. Then, answer the question.*

1. The children came up with a <u>strategy</u> for throwing snowballs at passing vehicles. Did the children have a plan? How do you know?

   _____

2. The man <u>compelled</u> Dillard to run through the neighborhood. Did she have a choice? How do you know?

   _____

3. Dillard and Mikey were <u>improvising</u> their escape route as they went along. Had they planned an escape route? How do you know?

   _____

4. When the man finally caught the kids, he said his words <u>perfunctorily</u>. Did his words hold unique meaning? How do you know?

   _____

5. Dillard describes the man's anger as <u>righteous</u>. Did he believe he was correct to be angry? How do you know?

   _____

6. Dillard's iceball was completely <u>translucent</u>. Could you see light through it? How do you know?

   _____

B. WORD STUDY: The Latin prefix *trans-* means "over," "across," or "through." Words containing the prefix *trans-* include *transfer* ("to move from one place to another") and *translator* ("someone who converts one language to another"). Consider these meanings as you answer each question.

1. Why might you need to *transfer* your records if you change schools?

   _____

2. Why might you need a *translator* in a foreign country?

   _____

"The Luckiest Time of All" by Lucille Clifton
Writing About the Big Question

What is the best way to find the truth?

Big Question Vocabulary

awareness	believable	conclude	convince	debate
evaluate	evidence	explain	factual	fiction
insight	perceive	reality	reveal	truth

A. *Use one or more words from the list above to complete each sentence.*

1. When somebody shares his or her beliefs, we must _____ whether those beliefs are consistent with our own beliefs.

2. If we _____ that our own beliefs are different, it is okay to disagree.

3. Beliefs may not be based in _____ .

B. *Answer the questions. Use at least one of the vocabulary words in each answer.*

1. Name two objects that people believe bring them good or bad luck.

   _____   _____

2. Do you believe that an object can bring you luck? Explain.

   _____

   _____

C. *Complete the sentence below. Then, answer the question to write a short paragraph connecting the sentence to the Big Question:*

In order to be believable, character's behavior' must be _____ .

In a work of fiction, what makes a character's behaviors believable? What is the advantage of having believable characters in a story?

   _____

   _____

   _____

   _____

"The Luckiest Time of All" by Lucille Clifton

Reading: Reread and Read Ahead to Confirm Meaning

Context clues are the examples, descriptions, and other details in the text around an unfamiliar or unusual word or expression. Sometimes these clues can help you figure out what the word or expression means. When you come across an unfamiliar word or expression, use the context clues to figure out what the word probably means. **Reread and read ahead to confirm the meaning.**

In "The Luckiest Time of All," the writer sometimes uses words and phrases that may mean something different from the meanings of the individual words. Look at this example:

"Somethin like the circus. Me and Ovella wanted to join that thing and see the world. Nothin wrong at home or nothin, we just wanted to travel and see new things and have <u>high</u> times."

In another context, you would probably decide that *high* means "tall" or "rising above." In this context, notice the words and phrases around the word *high:* "somethin like the circus," "see the world," and "wanted to travel and see new things." These context clues tell you that in this selection, *high* means "exciting."

DIRECTIONS: *Read each quotation from "The Luckiest Time of All." Figure out the meaning of the underlined word or expression by looking for context clues. Write the context clue or clues on the first two lines. Write the meaning of the word or expression on the next line.*

1. We got there after a good little walk and it was the <u>world</u>, Baby, such music and wonders as we never had seen! They had everything there, or seemed like it.

   Context clues: _____

   _____

   Meaning of word: _____

2. But the stone was gone from my hand and Lord, it hit that dancin dog right on his nose! Well, he <u>lit out</u> after me, poor thing. He <u>lit out</u> after me and I flew! Round and round the Silas Greene we run.

   Context clues: _____

   _____

   Meaning of word: _____

3. I stopped then and walked slow and shy to where he had picked up that poor dog to see if he was hurt, <u>cradlin</u> him and talkin to him soft and sweet.

   Context clues: _____

   Meaning of word: _____

4. He . . . helped me find my stone. . . . We search and searched and at last he <u>spied</u> it!

   Context clues: _____

   _____

   Meaning of word: _____

"The Luckiest Time of All" by Lucille Clifton
Literary Analysis: Point of View

Point of view is the perspective from which a narrative is told. Point of view affects the kinds of details that are revealed to the reader.

- **First-person point of view:** The narrator is a character who participates in the action of the story and tells the story using the words *I* and *me*. The narrator can reveal only his or her own observations, thoughts, and feelings.
- **Third-person point of view:** The narrator is not a character in the story and uses third-person pronouns such as *he, she,* and *they* to refer to the characters. The narrator may know and reveal the observations, thoughts, and feelings of more than one person or character in the narrative.

Read this example from the beginning of "The Luckiest Time of All":

Mrs. Elzie F. Pickens was rocking slowly on the porch one afternoon when her Great-granddaughter, Tee, brought her a big bunch of dogwood blooms, and that was the beginning of a story.

"Ahh, now that dogwood reminds me of the day I met your Great-granddaddy, Mr. Pickens, Sweet Tee."

The story begins by introducing two characters, Mrs. Elzie F. Pickens and her great-granddaughter, Tee. The pronoun *her* tells you that the narrative is told from the third-person point of view. In the first paragraph of dialogue, Elzie is telling her story using the pronoun *I*, but that does not mean the story is a first-person account. It is not a first-person account because Elzie is not the narrator. The narrator is quoting Elzie as she tells her story to Tee.

DIRECTIONS: *Read each numbered passage. (Two passages are from "The Luckiest Time of All," and one is about Lucille Clifton.) Underline each pronoun that tells that the passage is told from the third-person point of view. Then, on the lines that follow, briefly describe what you learned from the passage.*

1. Tee's Great-grandmother shook her head and laughed out loud.

   What I learned: _____

2. And they rocked a little longer and smiled together.

   What I learned: _____

3. Lucille Sayles Clifton was born into a large, working-class family in New York State. Although her parents were not formally educated, she learned from their example to appreciate books and poetry.

   What I learned: _____

   _____

"The Luckiest Time of All" by Lucille Clifton
Vocabulary Builder

Word List

acquainted   hind   plaited   spied   twine   wonders

A. DIRECTIONS: *Think about the meaning of the underlined Word List word in each sentence. Then, answer the question.*

1. Are mountain climbers likely to use <u>twine</u> to attach themselves to each other while crossing a dangerous crevice? Why or why not?

_____

2. If you are <u>acquainted</u> with someone, are you likely to know where he or she lives? Why or why not?

_____

3. Are women more likely than men to have <u>plaited</u> hair? Why or why not?

_____

4. If you catch an animal by its <u>hind</u> legs, is it likely that you approached it from the front? Why or why not?

_____

5. Is it likely that it would be boring to see one of the Seven <u>Wonders</u> of the World? Why or why not?

_____

6. If you <u>spied</u> an old friend, would you likely be seeing him or her in person? Why or why not?

_____

B. WORD STUDY: The Latin prefixes *ac-/ad-* mean "motion toward," "addition to," or "nearness to." How do the meanings of the prefixes relate to the italicized words in the following sentences?

1. The key allowed me full *access* to the mansion.

_____

2. The toddler had to *adhere* to strict rules after he ran into the street.

_____

from **An American Childhood** by Annie Dillard
"The Luckiest Time of All" by Lucille Clifton
Integrated Language Skills: Grammar

Possessive Nouns

A **possessive noun** is a noun that shows ownership. Ownership is indicated by the use of the apostrophe.

- To form the possessive to a singular noun, add an apostrophe and *-s:*
  The black <u>car's</u> tires left tracks.
- To form the possessive of a plural noun that ends in *-s*, add only an apostrophe:
  All of the <u>cars'</u> tires left tracks.
- To form the possessive of a plural noun that does not end in *-s*, add an apostrophe and *-s:*
  The <u>children's</u> game had unexpected consequences.

A. PRACTICE: *Each of the following sentences is based an* An American Childhood *or* "The Luckiest Time of All." *On the line, rewrite each underlined noun as a possessive. Be sure to place the apostrophe correctly to indicate that the possessive is singular or plural.*

1. The <u>boys</u> games were more exciting to Dillard than the <u>girls</u> activities.

   _____   _____

2. The <u>snowball</u> *splat* led the <u>car</u> driver to jump out and chase the children.

   _____,   _____

3. The <u>boy</u> path took him through the <u>neighbors</u> front yard.

   _____   _____

4. Many years later the young <u>women</u> adventure would be the subject of the <u>girl</u> curiosity.

   _____   _____

B. Writing Application: *On the line after each description in brackets, write a possessive noun that matches the description. Make sure the possessives you choose make sense in the sentence.*

1. The [*belonging to the singular female adult*] _____ stone hit the [*belonging to the singular animal*] _____ nose.
2. The [*belonging to the plural male children*] _____ games included throwing snowballs at the [*belonging to the plural vehicle*] _____ windows.
3. The [*belonging to the singular adult male*] _____ breath came in gasps and his [*belonging to the legs of his clothing*] _____ cuffs were full of snow.

Name _____ Date _____

from **An American Childhood** by Annie Dillard
"The Luckiest Time of All" by Lucille Clifton
Integrated Language Skills:
Support for Writing a Description That Includes Hyperbole

To prepare to write **descriptions** that include **hyperbole,** complete the following chart, making notes about three qualities or skills a person might have.

Questions About the Quality or Skill	First Quality or Skill	Second Quality or Skill	Third Quality or Skill
What is the quality or skill?			
Who or what might have this quality or skill?			
What is exceptional about this quality or skill?			
How can I exaggerate this quality or skill?			

Now, choose one quality or skill, and use your notes to write a description of it that includes hyperbole.

from **Barrio Boy** by Ernesto Galarza
"A Day's Wait" by Ernest Hemingway

Writing About the Big Question
What is the best way to find the truth?

Big Question Vocabulary

awareness	~~believable~~	conclude	convince	debate
evaluate	evidence	~~explain~~	factual	fiction
insight	perceive	~~reality~~	~~reveal~~	~~truth~~

A. *Use one or more words from the list above to complete each sentence.*

1. The scariest stories of all deal with situations that could happen in _reality_ .

2. To _reveal_ how scary a story is, I listen to how hard my heart is pounding.

3. After my little brother watched the horror movie, I had to _explain_ to him that the "blood" was really red paint.

4. In a good detective story, the _truth_ is there all along.

B. *Answer the questions.*

1. Describe a situation that you faced that scared you at first.
   That I went rockclimbing in my sisters college and when I was almost to the top and got scared because I might fall.

2. How did you get over your fear? Use two vocabulary words in your answer.
   It was believable that I wanted to try again.

C. *Complete the sentence below. Then, answer the question to write a short paragraph connecting the sentence to the Big Question.*

The most frightening situations are those in which _People can fall_

Describe a scary fictional story that you read or a scary movie that you saw. What about it was realistic? What was unrealistic?
The book I read was called "doll bones", and I thought that the part of the book where the kids found an old doll in the cabinet was very unrealistic and the beginning of the story was realistic

"All Summer in a Day" by Ray Bradbury
Reading: Recognize Details That Indicate
the Author's Purpose

Fiction writers write for a variety of **purposes.** They may wish to entertain, to teach, to call to action, or to reflect on experiences. They may also wish to inform, to persuade, or to create a mood. **Recognizing details that indicate the author's purpose** can give you a richer understanding of a selection. For example, in this passage from "All Summer in a Day," Bradbury creates a mood:

> Margot stood alone. She was a very frail girl who looked as if she had been lost in the rain for years and the rain had washed out the blue from her eyes and the red from her mouth and the yellow from her hair. She was an old photograph dusted from an album.

DIRECTIONS: *Read these passages from "All Summer in a Day." Then, write the purpose or purposes you think the author had for writing that passage. Choose from these purposes:* to entertain, to inform, to create a mood. *A passage may have more than one purpose.*

1. It had been raining for seven years; thousands upon thousands of days compounded and filled from one end to the other with rain, with the drum and gush of water, with the sweet crystal fall of showers and the concussion of storms so heavy they were tidal waves come over the islands.

   Author's purpose: _____

2. There was talk that her father and mother were taking her back to Earth next year; it seemed vital to her that they do so, though it would mean the loss of thousands of dollars to her family.

   Author's purpose: _____

3. But they were running and turning their faces up to the sky and feeling the sun on their cheeks like a warm iron; they were taking off their jackets and letting the sun burn their arms.

   Author's purpose: _____

4. They walked slowly down the hall in the sound of cold rain. They turned through the doorway to the room in the sound of the storm and thunder, lightning on their faces, blue and terrible. They walked over to the closet door slowly and stood by it.

   Behind the closet door was only silence.

   They unlocked the door, even more slowly, and let Margot out.

   Author's purpose: _____

"All Summer in a Day" by Ray Bradbury
Literary Analysis: Setting

The **setting** of a story is the time and place of the action. In this example from "All Summer in a Day," the underlined details help establish the story's setting.

> The sun came out.
>
> It was <u>the color of flaming bronze</u> and it was <u>very large</u>. And the sky around it was <u>a blazing blue tile color</u>. And <u>the jungle burned with sunlight</u> as the children, released from their spell, rushed out, yelling, into the springtime.

- In some stories, setting is just a backdrop. The same story events might take place in a completely different setting.
- In other stories, setting is very important. It develops a specific atmosphere or mood in the story, as in the example above. There, the children joyfully rush outside to feel the sun in the springtime after seven years of constant rain. The setting may even relate directly to the story's central conflict or problem.

DIRECTIONS: *Read the name of the character or characters from "All Summer in a Day" and the passage that follows. Then, on the lines, identify the setting described in the passage and the way the character or characters feel about it. Write your response in a short sentence or two.*

1. Margot: "And once, a month ago, she had refused to shower in the school shower rooms, had clutched her hands to her ears and over her head, screaming the water mustn't touch her head."

   Setting and character's feeling about it: _____

   _____

2. Margot: "They surged about her, caught her up and bore her, protesting, and then pleading, and then crying, back into a tunnel, a room, a closet, where they slammed and locked the door. They stood looking at the door and saw it tremble from her beating and throwing herself against it."

   Setting and character's feeling about it: _____

   _____

3. The children: "The children lay out, laughing, on the jungle mattress, and heard it sigh and squeak under them, resilient and alive. They ran among the trees, they slipped and fell, they pushed each other, . . . but most of all they squinted at the sun until tears ran down their faces, they put their hands up to that yellowness and that amazing blueness and they breathed of the fresh, fresh air."

   Setting and character's feeling about it: _____

   _____

"All Summer in a Day" by Ray Bradbury
Vocabulary Builder

Word List

    intermixed   resilient   savored   slackening   tumultuously   vital

A. DIRECTIONS: *Read each sentence. If the italicized word is used correctly, write* Correct *on the line. If it is not used correctly, rewrite the sentence to correct it.*

1. The speed of the rocket was *slackening* as it prepared to land on Earth.

   _____

   _____

2. It is said that water is *vital* to life; you can live without it.

   _____

   _____

3. During the calm before the storm, the wind blew *tumultuously.*

   _____

   _____

4. Because Margot was *resilient,* she could not get used to the conditions on Venus.

   _____

   _____

5. During the parade, people were *intermixed* along the packed streets.

   _____

   _____

6. During the holiday season, we never *savored* the sweet smell of pumpkin pie as it came out of the oven.

   _____

   _____

B. WORD STUDY: The Latin roots *-vit-* or *-viv-* mean "life." Words containing *-vit-* or *-viv-* include *vitality* ("liveliness"), *survive* ("to live through something"), and *revive* ("to bring back to life"). Write two sentences in which you use all three of these words.

1. _____

   _____

2. _____

   _____

3. _____

   _____

"**Suzy and Leah**" by Jane Yolen
Writing About the Big Question
What is the best way to find the truth?

Big Question Vocabulary

awareness	believable	conclude	convince	debate
evaluate	evidence	explain	factual	fiction
insight	perceive	reality	reveal	truth

A. *Use one or more words from the list above to complete each sentence.*

1. When writing historical _____, a novelist must research in order to tell the _____ about historical events.

2. The historical facts in the story may _____ readers that the story is believable.

3. Readers must have a(n) _____ of history to know that the book is based on historical events.

4. To _____ whether historical facts are true, the reader can do research.

B. *Answer the questions.*

1. Name three things that you would need to research if you were writing a story that took place one hundred years ago and you wanted to convince your readers that the setting was real.

   _____ _____ _____

2. How is the challenge to write a believable novel that takes place in the future different from the challenge of writing a believable novel that takes place in the past? Explain using at least two vocabulary words.

   _____

   _____

   _____

   _____

C. *Complete the sentence below. Then, write a short paragraph connecting the sentence to the Big Question.*

   If I were going to write a story based on a historical event, I would write about

   _____

   What kinds of facts in your story would be true? What would be fictional?

   _____

   _____

"All Summer in a Day" by Ray Bradbury **"Suzy and Leah"** by Jane Yolen
Reading: Recognize Details That Indicate the Author's Purpose

Fiction writers may write for a variety of **purposes.** They may wish to entertain, to teach, to call to action, or to reflect on experiences. They may also wish to inform, to persuade, or to create a mood. **Recognizing details that indicate the author's purpose** can give you a richer understanding of a selection. For example, the following passage from "Suzy and Leah" is written to teach readers about the background of some Eastern European Jews:

> I have a little English. But Ruth and Zipporah and the others, though they speak Yiddish and Russian and German, they have no English at all.

DIRECTIONS: *Read these passages from "Suzy and Leah." On the line that follows each passage, write the purpose or purposes you think the author had for writing that passage. Choose from these purposes:* to entertain, to inform, to create a mood. *A passage may have more than one purpose.*

1. Leah: "Today we got cereal in a box. At first I did not know what it was. Before the war we ate such lovely porridge with milk straight from our cows. And eggs fresh from the hen's nest."

   Author's purpose: _____

2. Leah: "But they made us wear tags with our names printed on them. That made me afraid. What next? Yellow stars? I tore mine off and threw it behind a bush before we went in [to the school]."

   Author's purpose: _____

3. Suzy: "Mr. Forest . . . gave me the girl with the dark braids. . . . Gee, she's as prickly as a porcupine. I asked if I could have a different kid. . . . He wants her to learn as fast as possible so she can help the others. As if she would, Miss Porcupine."

   Author's purpose: _____

4. Leah: "One day this Suzy and her people will stop being nice to us. They will remember we are not just refugees but Jews, and they will turn on us. Just as the Germans did. Of this I am sure."

   Author's purpose: _____

5. Suzy: "[Leah's] English has gotten so good. Except for some words, like victory, which she pronounces 'wick-toe-ree.' I try not to laugh. . . . She can't dance at all. She doesn't know the words to any of the top songs."

   Author's purpose: _____

"Suzy and Leah" by Jane Yolen
Literary Analysis: Setting

The **setting** of a story is the time and place of the action. In this example from "Suzy and Leah," the underlined details help establish the story's setting:

<u>August 5, 1944</u>

Dear Diary,

Today I walked past *that* place. . . . Gosh, is it <u>ugly</u>! A line of <u>rickety wooden buildings</u> just like in the army. And <u>a fence lots higher than my head</u>. <u>With barbed wire</u> on top.

- In some stories, setting is just a backdrop. The same story events might take place in a completely different setting.
- In other stories, setting is very important. It develops a specific atmosphere or mood in the story, as in the example above. There, the reader is introduced to the refugee camp through the eyes of Suzy, who has lived a privileged life. The setting may even relate directly to the story's central conflict or problem.

DIRECTIONS: *Read the name of the character from "Suzy and Leah" and the passage that follows. Then, on the lines, identify the setting described in the passage and the way the character feels about it. Write your response in a short sentence.*

1. Suzy: "With barbed wire on top. How can anyone—even a refugee—live there?"

   Setting and character's feeling about it: _____

   _____

2. Leah: "But I say no place is safe for us. Did not the Germans say that we were safe in their camps?"

   Setting and character's feeling about it: _____

   _____

3. Leah: "Zipporah braided my hair, but I had no mirror until we got to the school and they showed us the toilets. They call it a bathroom, but there is no bath in it at all, which is strange."

   Setting and character's feeling about it: _____

   _____

4. Suzy: "[Mom] said the Nazis killed people, mothers and children as well as men. In places called concentration camps. . . . It was so awful I could hardly believe it, but Mom said it was true."

   Setting and character's feeling about it: _____

   _____

"Suzy and Leah" by Jane Yolen
Vocabulary Builder

Word List

cupboard   falsely   penned   permanent   porridge   refugee

A. DIRECTIONS: *Read each sentence. If the italicized word is used correctly, write* Correct *on the line. If it is not used correctly, rewrite the sentence to correct it.*

1. The *refugee* fled across the border.

_____

2. The *porridge* made a wonderful dessert.

_____

3. The *permanent* frown on Leah's face disappeared when Suzy offered candy.

_____

4. The teacher was correct when she *falsely* accused Sam of cheating.

_____

5. It is common to keep items like ice cream in the kitchen *cupboard*.

_____

6. It is easy to feel *penned* in when there are a lot of people in a small space.

_____

B. DIRECTIONS: *Read each sentence. If the italicized word is used correctly, write* Correct *on the line. If it is not used correctly, rewrite the sentence to correct it.*

1. The *refugee* fled across the border.

_____

2. The *porridge* made a wonderful dessert.

_____

3. The *permanent* frown on Leah's face disappeared when Suzy offered candy.

_____

_____

C. WORD STUDY: The Latin root -*man*- means "hand." Explain how the meaning of the root -*man*- relates to the following uses of the word *manual.*

1. The men performed ten long hours of <u>manual</u> labor.

_____

2. My new camera allows for both automatic and <u>manual</u> control.

_____

3. The artist showed extraordinary <u>manual</u> dexterity in her work.

_____

"Suzy and Leah" by Jane Yolen
Integrated Language Skills: Grammar

A **pronoun** is a word that takes the place of a noun or a group of words acting as a noun. A **nominative pronoun** is a pronoun used as a subject. An **objective pronoun** is a pronoun used as an object.

Suzy met Leah at the camp.	**She** met Leah at the camp.	Nominative pronoun
Suzy met **Leah** at the camp.	Suzy met **her** at the camp.	Objective pronoun

Some important nominative and objective pronouns:

Nominative	**Objective**
I	me
he	him
she	her
we	us
they	them

A. PRACTICE: *Read each sentence based on sentences in "All Summer in a Day" or "Suzy and Leah." Underline each nominative pronoun. Circle each objective pronoun.*

1. They hated her because she had seen the sun.

2. He gave her a shove, but she did not move away from him.

3. The thunder and rain chased them back inside, where they let her out of the closet.

4. When I looked back, she was gone, and I didn't see her again until the next day.

5. They didn't know how to peel oranges, so I taught them.

6. She loves Avi and tries to protect him.

B. Writing Application: *Rewrite each sentence by replacing each underlined noun with a pronoun. Be sure to see the difference between a nominative pronoun and an objective pronoun.*

1. The students wanted to see the sun, so the teacher let the students go outside.

   _____

2. Margot hoped to see the sun, but the students locked Margot in the closet.

   _____

3. William said Margot was a liar, but Margot stuck to Margot's story.

   _____

4. Leah refuses Suzy's candy because Leah doesn't want to look like an animal.

   _____

"All Summer in a Day" by Ray Bradbury
"Suzy and Leah" by Jane Yolen
Integrated Language Skills: Support for Writing a News Report

"All Summer in a Day": To prepare for your **news report** that tells about the day the sun appeared on Venus, complete this chart.

Question	Information in "All Summer in a Day"
Who sees the sun, and who does not see it?	
What happens when the sun is shining?	
When does the sun shine, and for how long?	
Where do the events take place?	
Why do the characters in the story respond to the sun the way they do?	

"Suzy and Leah": To prepare for your **news report** that tells about the refugee camp where Leah is living, complete this chart.

Question	Information in "Suzy and Leah"
Who is living in the camp that Suzy visits?	
What has brought Suzy to the camp?	
When are the events taking place?	
Where (in what country) is the camp?	
Why has the camp been set up?	

Now, use your notes to write a news report.

"**My First Free Summer**" by Julia Alvarez
Writing About the Big Question

What is the best way to find the truth?

Big Question Vocabulary

awareness	believable	conclude	convince	debate
evaluate	evidence	explain	factual	fiction
insight	perceive	reality	reveal	truth

A. *Use one or more words from the list above to complete each sentence.*

1. When an author uses autobiographical information in her writing, she _____s a personal truth.

2. When reading autobiographical fiction, the reader gains _____ into the author's real life.

3. Some works of fiction can lead to a _____ about philosophical questions.

B. *Answer the questions.*

1. Describe an event in your life that you perceived differently from someone else.

   _____

   _____

2. If you were to debate the event with the other person, would you be able to convince him or her that your version of the truth is correct? Why or why not? Use two vocabulary words in your answer.

   _____

   _____

   _____

C. *Complete the sentence below. Then, write a short paragraph connecting the sentence to the Big Question.*

   Reflecting on past events _____

   How might you incorporate an event from your life into a fictional story? Describe the event and a story you might create.

   _____

   _____

   _____

   _____

"My First Free Summer" by Julia Alvarez

Reading: Use Background Information to Determine the Author's Purpose

One way to determine the **author's purpose,** or reason, for writing a nonfiction work is to **use background information** that you already know about the author and topic. For example, knowing that an author grew up outside the United States might help you determine that she wrote an essay to inform readers about the country where she spent her childhood.

Although she was born in the United States, Julia Alvarez spent much of her childhood in the Dominican Republic. Near the beginning of her essay, she writes,

> That was the problem. English. My mother had decided to send her children to the American school so we could learn the language of the nation that would soon be liberating us.

The author's purpose for providing this background information is to inform readers of her reasons for studying English and attending an American school. Authors provide background information for other purposes as well—for example, to entertain or to create a mood.

DIRECTIONS: *Read each of these passages from "My First Free Summer." Decide whether the author's purpose is* to inform, to create a mood, *or* to entertain. *Write the purpose on the line following the passage. A passage may have more than one purpose.*

1. For thirty years, the Dominican Republic had endured a bloody and repressive dictatorship. From my father, who was involved in an underground plot, my mother knew that *los américanos* had promised to help bring democracy to the island.

   Author's purpose(s): _____

2. Meanwhile, I had to learn about the pilgrims with their funny witch hats, about the 50 states and where they were on the map, about Dick and Jane and their tame little pets, Puff and Spot, about freedom and liberty and justice for all—while being imprisoned in a hot classroom with a picture of a man wearing a silly wig hanging above the blackboard.

   Author's purpose(s): _____

3. The grounds on which the American school stood had been donated by my grandfather. . . . The bulk of the student body was made up of the sons and daughters of American diplomats and business people, but a few Dominicans—most of them friends or members of my family—were allowed to attend.

   Author's purpose(s): _____

"My First Free Summer" by Julia Alvarez

Literary Analysis: Historical Context

When a literary work is based on real events, the historical context can help you understand the action. **Historical context**—the actual political and social events and trends of the time—can explain why characters act and think the way they do. Read the following passage from "My First Free Summer." Think about what it tells you about the historical context of the selection.

> For thirty years, the Dominican Republic had endured a bloody and repressive dictatorship. From my father, who was involved in an underground plot, my mother knew that *los américanos* had promised to help bring democracy to the island.

DIRECTIONS: *Read each of these passages from "My First Free Summer." On the lines that follow, write a sentence telling how the historical context affects the action.*

1. I didn't know about my father's activities. I didn't know the dictator was bad. All I knew was that my friends who were attending Dominican schools were often on holiday to honor the dictator's birthday, the dictator's saint day, the day the dictator became the dictator, the day the dictator's oldest son was born, and so on.

   How context affects action: _____

   _____

2. But the yard replete with cousins and friends that I had dreamed about all year was deserted. Family members were leaving for the United States, using whatever connections they could drum up. The plot had unraveled. Every day there were massive arrests. The United States had closed its embassy and was advising Americans to return home.

   How context affects action: _____

   _____

3. I was about to tell her that I didn't want to go to the United States, where . . . everyone spoke English. But my mother lifted a hand for silence. "We're leaving in a few hours. I want you all to go get ready! I'll be in to pack soon." The desperate look in her eyes did not allow for contradiction. We raced off, wondering how to fit the contents of our Dominican lives into four small suitcases.

   How context affects action: _____

   _____

4. Next morning, we are standing inside a large, echoing hall as a stern American official reviews our documents. What if he doesn't let us in? What if we have to go back? I am holding my breath. My parents' terror has become mine.

   How context affects action: _____

   _____

"**My First Free Summer**" by Julia Alvarez
Vocabulary Builder

Word List

contradiction   diplomats   extenuating   repressive   summoned   vowed

A. DIRECTIONS: *Something is wrong with the following sentences. Revise each one, using the Word List word in a way that makes the sentence logical.*

1. After her first free summer, Julia *vowed* to pass all her subjects.

   Revision: _____

2. The mission of the *diplomats* was to negotiate the terms of the new car's warranty.

   Revision: _____

3. When Julia's mother *summoned* her daughters, Julia and her sister left for the beach.

   Revision: _____

4. The *repressive* government allowed complete freedom of speech and religion for all of its citizens.

   Revision: _____

5. The judge argued for a harsh sentence because of all the *extenuating* circumstances of the crime.

   Revision: _____

6. When all the witnesses offered a *contradiction* to the defendant's testimony, it was obvious that the defendant was telling the truth.

   Revision: _____

B. WORD STUDY: The Latin root *-dict-* means "to speak, assert." In the following sentences, think about the meaning of *-dict-* in each italicized word. On the line before each sentence, write *T* if the statement is true or *F* if the statement is false. Then, explain your answer.

1. _____ A *prediction* tells what happened in the past. _____

   _____

2. _____ A *dictionary* contains the roots and definitions of words. _____

   _____

3. _____ A *dictator* is the democratically elected head of a country. _____

   _____

from **Angela's Ashes** by Frank McCourt
Writing About the Big Question

What is the best way to find the truth?

Big Question Vocabulary

awareness	believable	conclude	convince	debate
evaluate	evidence	explain	factual	fiction
insight	perceive	reality	reveal	truth

A. *Use one or more words from the list above to complete each sentence.*

1. After some time has passed, it is easier to _____ important life events.

2. Though sometimes an event seems unimportant while it is happening, we may later gain _____ about its importance.

3. Often, in a memoir, the author will _____ the significance of events in his or her past.

B. *Answer the questions. Use one vocabulary word in each answer.*

1. What event in your life so far would you focus on in a short memoir?

   _____

   _____

   _____

2. If you could ask anyone to write a memoir, who would you ask, and why? What would you want them to tell about?

   _____

   _____

   _____

C. *Complete the sentence below. Then, answer the question with a short paragraph connecting the sentence to the Big Question.*

Things that don't seem important while they are happening _____

Give an example of a lesson that an author might learn from personal experience and how he or she may later use this experience in a work of fiction.

_____

_____

_____

_____

from **Angela's Ashes** by Frank McCourt

Reading: Use Background Information to Determine the Author's Purpose

One way to determine the **author's purpose,** or reason, for writing a nonfiction work is to use **background information** that you already know about the author and topic. For example, knowing that an author grew up outside the United States might help you determine that he wrote a story to inform readers about the country where he spent his youth.

Although he was born in the United States, Frank McCourt spent his childhood and teen years in Ireland. The reader learns some of this information in the excerpt from *Angela's Ashes*, which is set in the Irish hospital where the ten-year-old McCourt recovered from typhoid fever. For example, McCourt writes the following about one of the nurses in the hospital:

She's a very stern nurse from the County Kerry and she frightens me.

The author's purpose for writing this sentence is twofold: (a) to inform the reader that the story takes place in Ireland (County Kerry is a southwestern county of Ireland) and (b) to help establish a mood by portraying the harsh and frightening personality of the nurse. In addition to informing or creating a mood, an author might write a passage in order to entertain the reader.

DIRECTIONS: *Read each of these passages from the excerpt from* Angela's Ashes. *Decide whether the author's purpose is to inform, to create a mood, or to entertain. Write the purpose on the line following the passage. A passage may have more than one purpose.*

1. I have diphtheria and something else.

   What's something else?

   They don't know. They think I have a disease from foreign parts because my father used to be in Africa. I nearly died. . . .

   Author's purpose(s): _____

2. There are twenty beds in the ward, all white, all empty. The nurse tells Seamus to put me at the far end of the ward against the wall to make sure I don't talk to anyone who might be passing the door, which is very unlikely since there isn't another soul on this whole floor.

   Author's purpose(s): _____

3. [The nurse] leaves and there's silence for a while. Then Patricia whispers, Give thanks, Francis, give thanks, and say your rosary, Francis, and I laugh so hard a nurse runs in to see if I'm all right. . . .

   Author's purpose(s): _____

from **Angela's Ashes** by Frank McCourt
Literary Analysis: Historical Context

When a literary work is based on real events, the historical context can help you understand the action. Historical context—the actual political and social events and trends of the time—can explain why characters act and think the way they do. Read the following passage from the excerpt from *Angela's Ashes.* Think about what it tells you about the historical context of the selection.

> She tells Seamus this was the fever ward during the Great Famine long ago and only God knows how many died here brought in too late for anything but a wash before they were buried and there are stories of cries and moans in the far reaches of the night. She says 'twould break your heart to think of what the English did to us, that if they didn't put the blight on the potato they didn't do much to take it off.

DIRECTIONS: *Read each of these passages from* Angela's Ashes. *On the lines that follow, write a sentence telling how the historical context affects the action.*

1. Mam visits me on Thursdays. I'd like to see my father, too, but I'm out of danger, crisis time is over, and I'm allowed only one visitor. Besides, she says, he's back at work at Rank's Flour Mills and please God this job will last a while with the war on and the English desperate for flour. She brings me a chocolate bar and that proves Dad is working. She could never afford one on the dole.

   Historical context and effect on story: _____

   _____

2. [Seamus] says I'm not supposed to be bringing anything from a dipteria room to a typhoid room with all the germs flying around and hiding between the pages and if you ever catch dipteria on top of the typhoid they'll know and I'll lose my good job and be out on the street singing patriotic songs with a tin cup in my hand, which I could easily do because there isn't a song ever written about Ireland's sufferings I don't know. . . .

   Historical context and effect on story: _____

   _____

3. No pity. No feeling at all for the people that died in this very ward, children suffering and dying here while the English feasted on roast beef and guzzled the best of wine in their big houses, little children with their mouths all green from trying to eat the grass in the fields beyond, God bless us and save us and guard us from future famines.

   Historical context and effect on story: _____

   _____

from **Angela's Ashes** by Frank McCourt
Vocabulary Builder

Word List

ban   desperate   guzzle   miracle   patriotic   saluting

A. DIRECTIONS: *Write a sentence that describes each situation and shows the meaning of each vocabulary word.*

1. Why government wants to *ban* a harmful product or chemical:

   _____

   _____

2. Why someone might feel *desperate*:

   _____

   _____

3. Why one might *guzzle* a drink:

   _____

   _____

4. A situation that seems like—or calls for—a *miracle*:

   _____

   _____

5. A *patriotic* ceremony:

   _____

   _____

6. A situation that would call for *saluting*:

   _____

   _____

B. WORD STUDY: The Latin root *-sper-* means "hope." Think about the meaning of *-sper-* in each italicized word. On the line before each sentence, write *T* if the statement is true or *F* if the statement is false. Then, explain your answer.

1. _____ Someone who feels *desperate* on first seeing an exam expects to do well.

   _____

2. _____ A person who is in *despair* has a negative outlook on life.

   _____

3. _____ In a time of *prosperity*, most people are living in poverty.

   _____

"**My First Free Summer**" by Julia Alvarez
from **Angela's Ashes** by Frank McCourt
Integrated Language Skills: Grammar

A **possessive pronoun** is a pronoun that shows ownership.

The football that belongs to **me**	**my** football
The video that belongs to **you**	**your** video
The idea that belongs to **her**	**her** idea
The answer that belongs to **him**	**his** answer
The house that belongs to **them**	**their** house
The decision that belongs to **us**	**our** decision

A. PRACTICE: *Underline each possessive pronoun in the sentences below.*

1. Alvarez vowed she would learn her English.
2. My mother decided to send her children to the American school.
3. I had to learn about the pilgrims with their funny witch hats.
4. The soldiers go seat by seat, looking at our faces.
5. While in the hospital, Frank wants his father to visit him.
6. When a nurse is unkind to the children, Seamus takes their side against her.

B. Writing Application: *For each sentence below, change the underlined pronoun into a possessive pronoun.*

1. Alvarez learned <u>she</u> subjects, so she could play with <u>she</u> family that summer.

   _____

2. But, she says, "<u>I</u> family were packing <u>they</u> clothing to move to America."

   _____

3. Frank McCourt liked Patricia Madigan and appreciated <u>she</u> sense of humor.

   _____

4. Mam hopes that Frank's father can keep <u>he</u> job.

   _____

5. The nurses are cruel to Frank and Patricia and take away <u>they</u> fun.

   _____

Name _____ Date _____

"My First Free Summer" by Julia Alvarez
from Angela's Ashes by Frank McCourt
Integrated Language Skills: Support for Writing a Letter

For your letter to Julia Alvarez describing what it is like to go to school in the United States or your letter to Frank McCourt describing a favorite story or poem, gather your ideas in one of the charts below.

Letter to Julia Alvarez:

Topics for Letter	My Ideas About These Topics
School hours and holidays and the school year	
Subjects and homework	
After-school activities	
Best and worst things about school	

Letter to Frank McCourt:

Topics for Letter	My Ideas About These Topics
Title of favorite story or poem	
Details about events or characters in the story, or about descriptions or sounds in the poem	
Things you liked best about the story or poem	
A reason you might recommend the story or poem to Frank McCourt	

"Stolen Day" by Sherwood Anderson
"The Night the Bed Fell" by James Thurber

Writing About the Big Question
What is the best way to find the truth?

Big Question Vocabulary

awareness	believable	conclude	convince	debate
evaluate	evidence	explain	factual	fiction
insight	perceive	reality	reveal	truth

A. *Use one or more words from the list above to complete each sentence.*

1. When there are several different versions of _____, it does not mean that someone is not telling the _____.

2. People describe events differently when they _____ them differently.

3. Four different stories of the same event by four different witnesses can all be

   _____.

B. *Answer the questions.*

1. What are two things that you and a family member may disagree on?

   _____ _____

2. In a debate about what really happened to start an argument between you and your sibling, how do you convince your family members that your version of the truth is the correct version? Use two vocabulary words in your answer.

   _____

   _____

   _____

C. *Complete the sentence below. Then, use the writing prompt to write a short paragraph connecting the sentence to the Big Question.*

Family members may experience the same event differently because _____

_____

Write two versions of the same event. One will be your perception of the truth. The other will be a different perspective—a fictional account that someone else might think was the truth.

_____

_____

_____

_____

"**Stolen Day**" by Sherwood Anderson
"**The Night the Bed Fell**" by James Thurber
Literary Analysis: Comparing Characters

A **character** is a person or an animal that takes part in the action of a literary work. In literature, you will find characters with a range of personalities and attitudes. For example, a character might be dependable and intelligent but also stubborn. One character might hold traditional values, while another might rebel against them. The individual qualities that make each character unique are called **character traits.**

Writers use the process of **characterization** to create and develop characters. There are two types of characterization:

- **Direct characterization:** The writer directly states or describes the character's traits.
- **Indirect characterization:** The writer reveals a character's personality through his or her words and actions, and through the thoughts, words, and actions of other characters.

DIRECTIONS: *To analyze the use of characterization in "Stolen Day" and "The Night the Bed Fell," complete the following chart. Answer each question with a brief example from the story. Write* not applicable *if you cannot answer a question about one of the characters.*

Character	Words that describe the character directly	What the character says and does	How other characters talk about or act toward the character
The narrator of "Stolen Day"			
The mother in "Stolen Day"			
Briggs Beall in "The Night the Bed Fell"			
The mother in "The Night the Bed Fell"			

All-in-One Workbook
57

"**Stolen Day**" by Sherwood Anderson
"**The Night the Bed Fell**" by James Thurber
Vocabulary Builder

Word List

affects   culprit   deluge   ominous   perilous   pungent   solemn

A. DIRECTIONS: *Read each sentence, paying attention to the italicized word from the Word List. If the word is used correctly, write* Correct *on the line. If it is not used correctly, write a new sentence using the word.*

1. The girl's smile was *ominous* as she happily and gently hugged her new puppy.

_____

2. The *deluge* of rain caused the river to overflow.

_____

3. The boy was *solemn* after he heard the good news.

_____

4. A week of rainy weather often *affects* a person's mood negatively.

_____

5. The mountain climbers had the most *perilous* stretch at the tip of the peak.

_____

6. The sweet taste of peppermint ice cream was *pungent*.

_____

7. The old lady was considered the most likely *culprit* when her purse was stolen.

_____

B. DIRECTIONS: *Write the letter of the word that is most similar in meaning to the word from the Word List.*

____ 1. solemn
   A. joyful   B. silent   C. serious   D. cheerful

____ 2. perilous
   A. happy   B. tired   C. safe   D. dangerous

____ 3. pungent
   A. sharp   B. silly   C. serious   D. light

____ 4. culprit
   A. judge   B. criminal   C. jury   D. lawyer

____ 5. ominous
   A. easy   B. huge   C. threatening   D. pleasant

____ 6. deluge
   A. flood   B. water   C. storm   D. lightening

____ 7. affects
   A. enjoys   B. praises   C. allows   D. changes

All-in-One Workbook

"Stolen Day" by Sherwood Anderson
"The Night the Bed Fell" by James Thurber
Support for Writing to Compare Literary Works

Before you **write an essay comparing and contrasting** the narrator in "Stolen Day" and "The Night the Bed Fell," jot down your ideas in this graphic organizer. In the overlapping section of each set of boxes, write details that are true of both characters. In the sections on the left, write details that describe the narrator of "Stolen Day," and in the sections on the right, write details that describe the narrator of "The Night the Bed Fell,"

What are some of each character's traits?

Narrator of "Stolen Day":	Both:	Narrator of "The Night the Bed Fell":

What problems does each character face? How much responsibility does each character have in creating his problem?

Narrator of "Stolen Day":	Both:	Narrator of "The Night the Bed Fell":

What does the character learn from his situation? Which character learns more?

Narrator of "Stolen Day":	Both:	Narrator of "The Night the Bed Fell":

Now, use your notes to write an essay that compares and contrasts the two characters.

BQ Tunes

Conflict Resolution, performed by Tavi Fields

Yo'

It starts with a thought made from experience and what we are taught.

Then comes a different idea that doesn't mix in—

one against the other, now we have **competition.**

And where it goes depends on the ones involved,

the situation can remain or get solved.

It's your choice how you think about it, how you react to it—

that's your **attitude**, now don't you act foolish!

Keep your cool homie, and try to be patient.

Get your skills up, mainly your **communication.**

That's you expressing yourself and giving information.

How it's received depends on interpretation.

So choose your moves carefully and dare to be your best.

The more control you have on your end, the less stress (yeah, uh-huh)...

Sometimes we must lose in order to win in the end.

You gotta dust shoes off and get into the wind,

And let it take you farther than you can begin,

To imagine it happens again and again.

Sometimes we must lose in order to win in the end.

You gotta dust shoes off and get into the wind,

And let it take you farther than you can begin,

To imagine it happens again and again.

So we have two sides to the vision,

and when they're not similar we have **opposition.**

Then if we make it a contest that's a **challenge.**

Be careful how you handle it, it's best to find balance.

And if not, that's a **conflict**—pieces to the puzzle

are missin'. The mission to find them is the **struggle.**

The frustration naturally causes anger,

but when safety is threatened , that's **danger.**

Continued

All-in-One Workbook

Easy, self-control is a must.

If you wanna win in the end you gotta have trust

in a settlement, that's the resolution,

in other words an answer to the problem—a solution.

But you have to want it 'cause want equals desire.

It's the fire in your wishes, changing browsers into buyers.

Yo,

Sometimes we must lose in order to win in the end.

You gotta dust shoes off and get into the wind

And let it take you farther than you can begin

To imagine it happens again and again.

Sometimes we must lose in order to win in the end.

You gotta dust shoes off and get into the wind

And let it take you farther than you can begin

To imagine it happens again and again.

A lot of problems begin with **misunderstanding**—

when the point gets lost and there is confusion.

And when you make it to the end, just don't be surprised

if you have to sacrifice something 'cause that's **compromise.**

It's the solution to many **conflicts** or **disagreements**.

It's when you find middle ground, an' ease the moment.

Don't focus on the **obstacles,** the things in your way.

They'll take different forms and shapes on different days.

It's about how you get past them, that's where the lesson is.

The results, the **outcome,** that's where progression is.

And **understanding** is key to the process.

That's when you get it and eliminate the nonsense.

Word

Uh-huh, wha, yo'

Sometimes we must lose in order to win in the end.

You gotta dust shoes off and get into the wind

And let it take you farther than you can begin

To imagine it happens again and again.

Continued

All-in-One Workbook
61

Sometimes we must lose in order to win in the end.

You gotta dust shoes off and get into the wind

And let it take you farther than you can begin

To imagine it happens again and again.

Song Title: **Conflict Resolution**
Artist / Performed by Tavi Fields
Lyrics by Tavi Fields
Music composed by Mike Pandolfo, Wonderful
Produced by Mike Pandolfo, Wonderful
Executive Producer: Keith London, Defined Mind

Name _____ Date _____

Unit 2: Short Stories
Big Question Vocabulary—1

The Big Question: Does every conflict have a winner?

attitude: *n.* the opinion or feeling a person has about something

challenge: *n.* something that tests a person's strength, skill, or ability

　　　　　v. question or confront; other forms: *challenging, challenged*

communication: *n.* the act of speaking or writing to share ideas; other form: *communicate*

compromise: *v.* agree to accept less than originally wanted; negotiate

　　　　　n. an agreement in which people settle for less than they first wanted; other forms: *compromising, compromised*

outcome: *n.* final result of something; conclusion

A. DIRECTIONS: *Write the vocabulary word that best completes each group.*

1. settlement, negotiation, agreement, _____
2. test, trial, competition, _____
3. ending, resolution, answer, _____
4. conversation, correspondence, explanation, _____
5. thoughts, feelings, behavior, _____

B. DIRECTIONS: *Write a dialogue between two friends who are involved in a conflict. Through their discussion, they come to an agreement. Use all five vocabulary words.*

_____

_____

_____

_____

_____

_____

_____

_____

_____

_____

_____

_____

Unit 2: Short Stories
Big Question Vocabulary—2

The Big Question: Does every conflict have a winner?

competition: *n.* a contest between people or teams; other forms: *compete, competing, competed*

danger: *n.* a force or situation that may cause injury; hazard; other form: *dangerous*

desire: *n.* a strong hope or wish for something

 v. to want or hope for something; other forms: *desirable, desired*

resolution: *n.* the final solution to a problem or difficulty; other forms: *resolve*

understanding: *n.* knowledge about something, based on learning or experience

 adj. kind or forgiving; generous; other forms: *understand, understood*

Beth said this to Susan, Becky, and Danielle: "I can't believe that Sharon has decided to enter the race on Saturday. Everyone knows that that's *MY* race, and I'm determined to win it. I thought she was my friend, but I guess I was wrong. I hope someone trips her!"

Each of Beth's friends had a different reaction to what she said.

DIRECTIONS: *Use the word(s) given in parentheses to write what each friend said to Beth.*

Susan

(desire, competition)

Becky

(understanding, danger)

Danielle

(resolution)

Unit 2: Short Stories
Big Question Vocabulary—3

The Big Question: Does every conflict have a winner?

disagreement: *n.* a situation involving a lack of agreement, which may or may not lead to an argument; other forms: *disagree, disagreeing*

misunderstanding: *n.* a mistake caused by not understanding a situation clearly

> *v.* not understanding something correctly; other form: *misunderstand*

obstacle: *n.* something that makes it difficult for a person to succeed; barrier

opposition: *n.* a strong disagreement regarding an issue; other forms: *oppose, opposed*

struggle: *n.* a long, hard fight against something

> *v.* to fight hard to succeed in a difficult task; other forms: *struggling, struggled*

A. DIRECTIONS: *Read each passage and follow the directions after it. In your answer, use the vocabulary words in parentheses, or one of their "other forms," shown above.*

1. Ramon tells Jenna to meet him "near the supermarket." Jenna waits for him next to *Brown's Market,* but Ramon doesn't show up. He is waiting near *RightPrice Groceries.*

   Describe this situation. **(misunderstanding, obstacle)** _____

   _____

2. After a long and difficult search, Jenna finally finds Ramon, but she is angry. They argue.

   Describe what takes place. **(struggle, disagreement)** _____

   _____

3. Jenna says that Ramon should have been clearer in his directions regarding where to meet. Ramon doesn't agree.

   Describe what takes place. **(misunderstanding, opposition)** _____

   _____

4. They finally come to an agreement and settle their dispute.

   Use at least two of these vocabulary words to describe the end of the story: **(resolution, understanding, compromise, communication)** _____

   _____

Name _____ Date _____

Unit 2: Short Stories
Applying the Big Question

Does every conflict have a winner?

DIRECTIONS: *Complete the chart below to apply what you have learned about winners and losers in conflict. One row has been completed for you.*

Example	Type of Conflict	Cause	Effect	Who won or lost	What I learned
From Literature	The competition in "Amigo Brothers".	Two friends both want to win the Golden Gloves championship tournament.	They feel funny around each other at first.	Both boys won because each tried to do his best	Some conflicts do not have a loser.
From Literature					
From Science					
From Social Studies					
From Real Life					

"The Bear Boy" by Joseph Bruchac
Reading: Use Prior Knowledge to Make Predictions

Predicting means making an ~~intelligent guess~~ about what will happen next in a story based on details in the text. You can also **use prior knowledge to make predictions.** For example, if a character in a story notices animal tracks in the snow, you can predict that the animal will play a part in the story because you know from prior knowledge that animal tracks mean that the animal is nearby.

DIRECTIONS: *Fill in the following chart with predictions as you read "The Bear Boy." Use clues from the story and your prior knowledge to make predictions. Then, compare your predictions with what actually happens. An example is shown.*

Story Details and Prior Knowledge	What I Predict Will Happen	What Actually Happens
People said that someone who followed a bear's tracks might never come back, but Kuo-Haya had never been told that. I know that if people are not warned of a danger, they may do something dangerous.	Kuo-Haya will see and follow a bear's tracks.	Kuo-Haya sees and follows a bear's tracks and finds some bear cubs.
the mother Bear always protects the bear cubs.		
the father see's a Bee and realizes that bees have honey	he gets the honey for the Bear's cubs.	
the father asks the Boy to come back to the village. I know that when someones not loved for a long time.	Kuo-haya will go with the Bears and his Father	Kuo-haya will go with the Bears and his Father

"The Bear Boy" by Joseph Bruchac
Literary Analysis: Plot

Plot is the related sequence of events in a short story and other works of fiction. A plot has the following elements:

- **Exposition:** introduction of the setting (the time and place), the characters, and the basic situation
- **Rising Action:** events that introduce a **conflict,** or struggle, and increase the tension
- **Climax:** the story's high point, at which the eventual outcome becomes clear
- **Falling Action:** events that follow the climax
- **Resolution:** the final outcome and tying up of loose ends, when the reader learns how the conflict is resolved

In a story about a race, for example, the exposition would probably introduce the runners. The rising action might include a description of a conflict between two of the runners and some information about the start of the race. The climax might be the winning of the race by one of the runners. The falling action might include a meeting between the two runners, and the resolution might describe the end of their conflict.

DIRECTIONS: *Answer the following questions about the plot elements of "The Bear Boy."*

1. The exposition of "The Bear Boy" introduces characters and describes a setting. Who are the characters, and what is the setting?

   _____

   _____

2. How do you know that the father's neglect of Kuo-Haya is part of the rising action?

   _____

   _____

3. What happens in the climax of "The Bear Boy"?

   _____

   _____

4. Describe one event in the falling action of the story.

   _____

   _____

5. What happens in the resolution of "The Bear Boy"?

   _____

   _____

"The Bear Boy" by Joseph Bruchac
Vocabulary Builder

Word List

approvingly   canyon   guidance   initiation   neglected   timid

A. DIRECTIONS : *Use each vocabulary word by following the instructions below. Use the words in the same way they are used in "The Bear Boy," and write sentences that show you understand the meaning of the word.*

1. Use the word *timid* in a sentence about a rabbit.

   _____

2. Use the word *initiation* in a sentence about a ceremony.

   _____

3. Use the word *neglected* in a sentence about a garden.

   _____

4. Use the word *canyon* in a sentence about a vacation.

   _____

5. Use the word *approvingly* in a sentence about a grandmother.

   _____

6. Use the word *guidance* in a sentence about a coach.

   _____

B. WORD STUDY *The Latin suffix -ance means "the act of." Answer each of the following questions using one of these words containing -ance: compliance, dissonance, vigilance.*

1. Does *dissonance* describe a pleasing sound?

   _____

2. If I am in *compliance* with the rules, am I breaking them?

   _____

3. If people applaud my *vigilance*, do they consider me watchful?

   _____

"**Rikki-tikki-tavi**" by Rudyard Kipling
Writing About the Big Question
Does every conflict have a winner?

Big Question Vocabulary

attitude	challenge	communication	competition
~~compromise~~	~~conflict~~	~~danger~~	desire
disagreement	misunderstanding	obstacle	opposition
outcome	resolution	~~struggle~~	understanding

A. *Use one or more words from the list above to complete each sentence.*

1. People can lose perspective during an intense _struggle_.

2. Their only thought is to eliminate the _conflict_ before them.

3. As a result, they may unintentionally place others in _comprimize_.

4. This can make _danger_ of the battle more complex.

B. *Follow the directions in responding to each of the items below.*

1. List two people whom you know or learned about in school or on the news who were affected by a battle that did not directly involve them.
   reggie   _Jayden and Jaylen_.

2. Write two sentences describing the battle that affected one of these people, and explain how he or she was affected. Use at least two of the Big Question vocabulary words.
   reggie was affected because Jayden and Jaylen wouldn't give his ball back during a game of four-square.

C. *Complete the sentence below. Then, write a short paragraph in which you connect this situation to the Big Question.*

Sometimes in a battle, innocent victims _can get hurt or simply upset when a battle gets out of hand and overly competitive all because of a small problem or big problem which can lead to major violence, and major violence leads to anger and revenge which is not good because it can also hurt many people or kids all because of a mistake or small problem which can lead to extreme violence which is bad_

Name _____ Date _____

"Rikki-tikki-tavi" by Rudyard Kipling
Reading: Use Prior Knowledge to Make Predictions

Predicting means making an intelligent guess about what will happen next in a story based on details in the text. You can also **use prior knowledge to make predictions.** For example, if a story introduces a mongoose and a snake and you know that mongooses and snakes are natural enemies, you can predict that the story will involve a conflict between the two animals.

DIRECTIONS: *Fill in the following chart with predictions as you read "Rikki-tikki-tavi." Use clues from the story and your prior knowledge to make predictions. Then, compare your predictions with what actually happens. An example is shown.*

Story Details and Prior Knowledge	What I Predict Will Happen	What Actually Happens
Teddy's mother says, "Perhaps he isn't really dead." I know that Rikki-tikki is the hero of the story, and heroes rarely die during a story.	The mongoose will live.	The mongoose lives.

Name _Erika_   Date _____

*the moment the conflict can
have a positive or negitive* **"Rikki-tikki-tavi"** by Rudyard Kipling
Literary Analysis: Plot

Plot is the related sequence of events in a short story and other works of fiction. A plot has the following elements:

- **Exposition:** introduction of the setting (the time and place), the characters, and the basic situation
- **Rising Action:** events that introduce a **conflict,** or struggle, and increase the tension
- **Climax:** the story's high point, at which the eventual outcome becomes clear
- **Falling Action:** events that follow the climax _after_
- **Resolution:** the final outcome and tying up of loose ends, when the reader learns how the conflict is resolved

For example, in a story about a battle, the exposition would introduce the contestants. The rising action might explain the conflict between the contestants and describe events leading up to the battle. The climax might be the winning of the battle by one of the contestants. The falling action could include a celebration of the victory, and the resolution might tell about events that took place in the years following the battle.

DIRECTIONS: *Answer the following questions about the plot elements of "Rikki-tikki-tavi."*

1. Who are the characters, and what is the setting described in the exposition?
   Rikki-tikki-tavi, nag, nagaina, Darzee, chuchundra, Darzee's wife

2. How do you know that the appearance of Nag is part of the rising action?
   He had a fight with the mongoose.

3. What happens in the climax of "Rikki-tikki-tavi"?
   Rikki-tikki-tavi kills nag and nagaina and their eggs.

4. Describe one event in the falling action of the story.
   nag and nagaina are killed by Rikki-tikki-tavi.

5. What happens in the resolution of "Rikki-tikki-tavi"?
   The garden where nag and nagaina lived is now safe because nag and nagaina are gone.

Name _____ Date _____

Integrated Language Skills: Support for Writing an Informative Article

Use the graphic organizer below to record details from each section of "Bear Boy" or "Rikki-tikki-tavi." Your details should tell *when, how much, how often,* or *to what extent.*

Introduction

Details:

Body

Details:

Conclusion

Details:

Now, use your notes to write a short informative article about mother bears or mongooses. Write for an audience of third-graders.

"Letters from Rifka" by Karen Hesse
Writing About the Big Question

Does every conflict have a winner?

Big Question Vocabulary

attitude	challenge	communication	competition
compromise	conflict	danger	desire
disagreement	misunderstanding	obstacle	opposition
outcome	resolution	struggle	understanding

A. *Use your own words or phrases to complete the paragraph below.*

Sometimes, if a **conflict** comes too close, families _____ to leave their

_____. If their lives continue to be in **danger,** they may even emigrate to

another _____. It can be a **challenge** to maintain a positive **attitude**

when leaving everything _____.

B. *Follow the directions in responding to each of the items below.*

1. List two groups of people you learned about in school that were forced to flee their homes as a result of war.

   _____   _____.

2. Choose one of the groups listed above, and briefly explain the **conflict** that forced its members to flee. Then, explain the **struggles** they faced in their new home.

   _____

   _____

   _____

   _____

C. *Complete the sentence below. Then, write a short paragraph in which you connect this experience to the Big Question.*

   The true losers in a war are _____

   _____

   _____

   _____

   _____

   _____

   _____

from **Letters from Rifka** by Karen Hesse
Reading: Read Ahead to Verify Predictions and Reread to Look for Details

A **prediction** is an informed guess about what will happen. Use details in the text and your own knowledge and experience to make predictions as you read. Then, **read ahead to verify predictions,** to check whether your predictions are correct.

- As you read, ask yourself whether new details support your predictions. If they do not, revise your predictions based on the new information.
- If the predictions you make turn out to be wrong, **reread to look for details** you might have missed that would have helped you make a more accurate prediction.

If it had not been for your father, though, I think my family would all be dead now: Mama, Papa, Nathan, Saul, and me.

Details in this passage can help you predict that the narrator will reveal that Rifka has escaped a dangerous situation. You can read further in the excerpt from *Letters from Rifka* to check this prediction.

DIRECTIONS: *Complete the following chart. If a prediction in the second column is correct, write* Correct *in the third column. If a prediction is wrong, write* Incorrect *in the third column. Then, in the fourth column, describe what does happen, and include a detail that would have allowed an accurate prediction. The first item has been completed as an example.*

Detail in *Letters from Rifka*	Prediction	Verification of Prediction	Event in Selection and Additional Detail
1. Tovah's father helps Rifka's family.	Tovah's father is in danger.	Incorrect	Tovah's father makes it home safely: "I am sure you and Cousin Hannah were glad to see Uncle Avrum come home today."
2. Rifka is not sure she will be able to distract the guards.	Rifka will not succeed.		
3. Nathan deserts the army.	Soldiers will look for Nathan.		
4. Rifka says, "Don't we need papers?"	Papa will find the papers.		

Name _____ Date _____

from **Letters from Rifka** by Karen Hesse
Literary Analysis: Characters

A **character** is a person or an animal that takes part in the action of a literary work.

- A **character's motives** are the emotions or goals that drive him or her to act one way or another. Some powerful motives are love, anger, and hope.
- **Character traits** are the individual qualities that make each character unique. These may be things such as stubbornness, sense of humor, or intelligence.

Characters' motives and qualities are important because they influence what characters do and how they interact with other characters. As you read, think about what the characters are like and why they do what they do. For example, consider this passage:

> I am sure you and Cousin Hannah were glad to see Uncle Avrum come home today. How worried his daughters must have been after the locked doors and whisperings of last night.

This passage illustrates Rifka's character traits: her caring nature and concern for others. It also suggests a motive for her actions: She wants her family to be safe.

A. DIRECTIONS: *After each character's name, write as many adjectives as you can think of that describe that character's traits.*

1. **Rifka:** _____

_____

_____

2. **Papa:** _____

_____

_____

B. DIRECTIONS: *Each quotation on the right states or hints at a motive for one of the actions on the left. On the line before each action, write the letter of the quotation that provides the motive.*

___ 1. Rifka writes to Tovah.

___ 2. Nathan deserts the army.

___ 3. Rifka distracts guards.

___ 4. Mama insists on taking candlesticks.

___ 5. Avrum helps the family escape.

A. "I've come," he said, "to warn Saul."

B. "Soon enough they will sweep down like vultures to pick our house bare."

C. "We made it!"

D. "If it had not been for your father, . . . my family would all be dead now."

E. "I knew, no matter how frightened I was, I must not let them find Nathan."

from **Letters from Rifka** by Karen Hesse
Vocabulary Builder

Word List

distract   emerged   huddled   peasants   precaution   regiment

A. DIRECTIONS: *Think about the meaning of the underlined word in each of these sentences. Then, answer the question.*

1. What might Rifka have done to <u>distract</u> the guards?

   _____

2. If Nathan had <u>emerged</u> from under the burlap bags, what might have happened?

   _____

3. Why had the family <u>huddled</u> in Tovah's cellar through the night?

   _____

4. Aside from a desire to join his family, why might Nathan have deserted his <u>regiment</u>?

   _____

5. Why might the <u>peasants</u> ransack homes that have been deserted?

   _____

6. Why did Rifka consider shutting Tovah out of the cellar a reasonable <u>precaution</u>?

   _____

B. WORD STUDY   *The Latin root -tract- means "pull" or "drag." Answer each of the following questions using one of these words containing -tract-: attractive, protracted, retract.*

1. What are you doing when you *retract* a statement that you made?

   _____

2. What might cause a criminal trial to become *protracted*?

   _____

3. What are some things people might do to look *attractive*?

   _____

All-in-One Workbook
83

"**Two Kinds**" by Amy Tan

Writing About the Big Question

 Does every conflict have a winner?

Big Question Vocabulary

attitude	challenge	communication	competition
compromise	conflict	danger	desire
disagreement	misunderstanding	obstacle	opposition
outcome	resolution	struggle	understanding

A. *Use one or more words from the list above to complete each sentence.*

1. It can be a _____ to try to live up to someone else's expectations.

2. People should be free to pursue the goals they truly _____.

3. Through _____, they can reach a(n) _____.

4. That way, their efforts can better achieve a positive _____.

B. *Follow the directions in responding to each of the items below.*

1. Describe a time when you did not live up to someone else's expectations or they did not live up to yours. _____
_____

2. Write two or three sentences explaining how the preceding experience affected you and the other person involved. Use at least two of the Big Question vocabulary words.

_____
_____
_____

C. *Complete the sentence below. Then, write a short paragraph in which you connect this experience to the Big Question.*

When a person does not live up to someone else's expectations, the loser is _____

_____
_____
_____
_____
_____
_____

Name _____   Date _____

"Two Kinds" by Amy Tan

Reading: Read Ahead to Verify Predictions and Reread to Look for Details

A **prediction** is an informed guess about what will happen. Use details in the text and your own knowledge and experience to make predictions as you read. Then, **read ahead to verify predictions,** to check whether your predictions are correct.

- As you read, ask yourself whether new details support your predictions. If they do not, revise your predictions based on the new information.
- If the predictions you make turn out to be wrong, **reread to look for details** you might have missed that would have helped you make a more accurate prediction.

"Of course you can be prodigy, too," my mother told me when I was nine. "You can be best anything."

Details in this passage can help you predict that the narrator's mother will encourage her to become a prodigy. You can read further in "Two Kinds" to check this prediction.

DIRECTIONS: *Complete the following chart. If a prediction in the second column is correct, write* Correct *in the third column. If a prediction is wrong, write* Incorrect *in the third column. Then, in the fourth column, describe what does happen, and include a detail that would have allowed an accurate prediction. The first item has been completed as an example.*

Details in "Two Kinds"	Prediction	Verification of Prediction	Event in Selection and Additional Detail
1. The mother wants her daughter to be "a Chinese Shirley Temple."	The daughter will become the Chinese Shirley Temple.	Incorrect	The narrator fails at being Shirley Temple. "We didn't immediately pick the right kind of prodigy."
2. The daughter begins to think thoughts with "won'ts."	The daughter will rebel against her mother.		
3. The narrator must perform a simple piece "that sounded more difficult than it was."	She will perform well.		
4. The daughter sees her mother's offers of the piano "as a sign of forgiveness."	The daughter will take the piano.		

"Two Kinds" by Amy Tan
Literary Analysis: Characters

A **character** is a person or an animal that takes part in the action of a literary work.

- A **character's motives** are the emotions or goals that drive him or her to act one way or another. Some powerful motives are love, anger, and hope.
- **Character traits** are the individual qualities that make each character unique. These may be things such as stubbornness, sense of humor, or intelligence.

Characters' motives and qualities are important because they influence what characters do and how they interact with other characters. As you read, think about what the characters are like and why they do what they do. For example, consider this passage:

> She had come here in 1949 after losing everything in China: her mother and father, her family home, her first husband, and two daughters, twin baby girls. But she never looked back with regret. There were so many ways for things to get better.

This passage illustrates the mother's character traits: her strength and courage. It also suggests a motive for her actions: She wants things to get better.

A. DIRECTIONS: *After each character's name, write as many adjectives as you can think of that describe that character's traits.*

1. **The daughter:** _____

   _____

   _____

2. **The mother:** _____

   _____

   _____

B. DIRECTIONS: *Each quotation on the right states or hints at a motive for one of the actions on the left. On the line before each action, write the letter of the quotation that provides the motive.*

___ 1. Daughter wants to become a prodigy.

___ 2. Mother pushes her daughter to be a prodigy.

___ 3. Daughter refuses to play the piano.

___ 4. Mother offers her daughter the piano.

___ 5. Daughter begins to resist her mother's efforts to make her a prodigy.

A. I could sense her anger rising to its breaking point. I wanted to see it spill over.

B. I was filled with a sense that I would soon become *perfect*. My mother and father would adore me.

C. I saw the offer as a sign of forgiveness, a tremendous burden removed.

D. I won't let her change me, I promised myself. I won't be what I'm not.

E. "Only ask you be your best. For your sake."

"Two Kinds" by Amy Tan
Vocabulary Builder

Word List

conspired   debut   devastated   obedient   prodigy   reproach

A. DIRECTIONS: *Think about the meaning of the underlined word in each of these sentences. Then, answer the question.*

1. Would the daughter have been beyond <u>reproach</u> if she had become a prodigy? Why or why not?

   _____

2. How would the daughter have felt when her mother's expression <u>devastated</u> her?

   _____

3. If the mother and Old Chong <u>conspired</u> to hold a talent show, whose idea was it? How do you know?

   _____

4. What traits identify someone as a <u>prodigy</u>?

   _____

5. Where did the narrator make her musical <u>debut</u>?

   _____

6. How does an <u>obedient</u> child respond when asked to do something?

   _____

B. WORD STUDY: *The Latin root -sent- means "to feel." Answer each of the following questions using one of these words containing -sent-: sentient, sentiment, sentimental.*

1. Why would dogs be considered *sentient* creatures?

   _____

2. How might a *sentimental* person treat his spouse on Valentine's Day?

   _____

3. If someone expresses their *sentiments*, what are they doing?

   _____

from **Letters from Rifka** by Karen Hesse
"Two Kinds" by Amy Tan
Integrated Language Skills: Grammar

Regular and Irregular Verbs

A **verb** expresses an action or a state of being. Every complete sentence needs to include at least one verb. Verbs have different forms, or tenses, that tell you when the action described took place. The four main tenses are *present, present participle, past,* and *past participle.*

Most verbs are *regular;* that is, their tenses are formed in a predictable way.

> I *climb* that mountain every day.

> Last month Michael *climbed* that mountain.

> Jessica *has* often *climbed* that mountain.

Verbs that are *irregular* do not follow a predictable pattern.

> I *am* a mountain climber.

> Michael *was* a mountain climber before he broke his leg.

> Jessica *has been* a mountain climber since she learned to walk.

A. PRACTICE: *Underline the verbs in each sentence. On the line, identify each verb as* regular *or* irregular. *Then, identify the tense of each verb. The tense will be* present, present participle, past, *or* past participle.

1. Her brother ran away from the army.

    Regular/Irregular: _____; **Principal part:** _____

2. The whole family fled from their home and is starting a new life.

    Regular/Irregular: _____; **Principal part:** _____

    Regular/Irregular: _____; **Principal part:** _____

3. Rifka was courageous, and she saved her family.

    Regular/Irregular: _____; **Principal part:** _____

    Regular/Irregular: _____; **Principal part:** _____

B. Writing Application: *Write a paragraph about a time when you or someone you know faced a frightening situation. Use at least three regular verbs and three irregular verbs. Underline each regular verb once and each irregular verb twice.*

_____

_____

_____

Name _____ Date _____

from **Letters from Rifka** by Karen Hesse
"Two Kinds" by Amy Tan

Integrated Language Skills: Support for Writing a Journal Entry

For your **journal entry**, put yourself in the place of the character you have chosen. Write that character's name on the line. Jot down specific events in the story. Then, imagine what you see and what you feel, and record those ideas on this chart.

My character:

_____

Event	Details from My Point of View	My Feelings About the Event

Now, use your notes to write a journal entry about the situation.

"Seventh Grade" by Gary Soto
"Melting Pot" by Anna Quindlen
Writing About the Big Question

Does every conflict have a winner?

Big Question Vocabulary

attitude	challenge	communication	competition
compromise	conflict	danger	desire
disagreement	misunderstanding	obstacle	opposition
outcome	resolution	struggle	understanding

A. *Use one or more words from the list above to complete each sentence.*

1. People often _____ to get along when they lack _____ of one another's cultures.

2. This can be a(n) _____ to developing positive relationships.

3. Making an attempt at _____ can help everyone get along.

B. *Follow the directions in responding to each of the items below.*

1. List two different times when you experienced a conflict with another person.

   _____

   _____

2. Write two sentences explaining one of the preceding experiences, and describe how the conflict was resolved. Use at least two of the Big Question vocabulary words.

   _____

   _____

C. *Complete the sentence below. Then, write a short paragraph in which you connect this experience to the Big Question.*

When you feel a conflict with another person, it is best to _____

_____

_____

_____

_____

_____

_____

Name _____ Date _____

"Seventh Grade" by Gary Soto
"Melting Pot" by Anna Quindlen
Literary Analysis: Comparing Idioms

An **idiom** is an expression that cannot be understood by simply putting together the literal word-for-word meaning. Its meaning lies in a common use of the expression, which is often unique to a region or language.

For example, the sentence "This long line is for the birds!" contains an idiom. The phrase "for the birds" doesn't mean that the line is actually meant to be for birds. Some people use this expression to mean "not desirable" or "not good."

DIRECTIONS: *To analyze the use of idioms in "Seventh Grade" and "Melting Pot," complete the following chart. Jot down two or three idioms for each story. Then, answer the questions about each idiom.*

Story	Idioms	What is the literal, word-for-word meaning?	What is the intended common-use meaning?
"Seventh Grade"			
"Melting Pot"			

"Seventh Grade" by Gary Soto
"Melting Pot" by Anna Quindlen

Vocabulary Builder

Word List

bigots   elective   fluent   scowl

A. DIRECTIONS: *Think about the meaning of the italicized word in each sentence. Then, answer the question.*

1. Victor might have hoped that math would be an *elective* for seventh graders. Why? Explain your answer.

   _____

2. Many of the narrator's neighbors are *fluent* in Spanish. How do they speak the language?

   _____

3. New residents sometimes think the older residents are *bigots*. What does this mean?

   _____

4. Mr. Bueller is likely to *scowl* the next time a student speaks nonsense instead of French. How will Mr. Bueller look?

   _____

B. DIRECTIONS: *Write the letter of the word or phrase that is most similar in meaning to each Word Bank word.*

____ **1.** fluent
    A. soft   C. flowing
    B. quiet   D. halting

____ **2.** scowl
    A. frown   C. shovel
    B. smile   D. boat

____ **3.** bigots
    A. fanatics   C. rebels
    B. racists   D. activists

____ **4.** elective
    A. optional course   C. dismissal
    B. political process   D. requirement

Name _____ Date _____

"Seventh Grade" by Gary Soto
"Melting Pot" by Anna Quindlen

Integrated Language Skills: Support for Writing to Compare and Contrast Literary Works

Before you **write an essay comparing and contrasting** how idioms added to your interest in the stories "Seventh Grade" and "Melting Pot," jot down your ideas in this graphic organizer. For each story, choose one idiom. In the corresponding columns, write each idiom's literal and intended meanings. Then, describe how each idiom adds to our knowledge of the character or situation being described. Finally, rate the overall effectiveness of the idiom, and explain why it did or did not add interest to the story.

Story	"Seventh Grade"	"Melting Pot"
Idiom		
Literal Meaning		
Intended Meaning		
How the idiom contributes to my knowledge of the character or situation		
The overall effectiveness of the idiom in adding interest to the story		

Now, use your notes to write an essay that compares and contrasts how the idioms added to your interest in the two stories.

Name _____ Date _____

Writing About the Big Question

Does every conflict have a winner?

Big Question Vocabulary

attitude	challenge	communication	competition
compromise	conflict	danger	desire
disagreement	misunderstanding	obstacle	opposition
outcome	resolution	struggle	understanding

A. *Use one or more words from the list above to complete each sentence.*

1. We all would like to have those things that we _____ most.

2. However, a wish come true sometimes creates more _____ than joys.

3. It may even bring you into _____ with others or with your principles.

4. Your _____ toward what you want may change once you have it.

B. *Follow the directions in responding to each of the items below.*

1. List two examples of wishes that could have negative consequences if they came true.

   _____   _____

2. Write two to three sentences explaining how having one of the preceding wishes come true could turn out badly. Use at least two of the Big Question vocabulary words.

   _____

   _____

   _____

C. *Complete the sentence below. Then, write a short paragraph in which you connect this idea to the Big Question.*

   Having wishes come true can sometimes _____

   _____

   _____

   _____

   _____

   _____

Name _____ Date _____

Reading: Make Inferences by Recognizing Details

Short story writers do not directly tell you everything there is to know about the characters, setting, and events. Instead, they leave it to you to **make inferences,** or logical guesses, about unstated information.

To form inferences, you must **recognize details** in the story and consider their importance. For example, in "The Third Wish," Mr. Peters finds a swan tangled up in thorns. When he moves closer and tries to free the swan, the swan hisses at him, pecks at him, and flaps its wings in a threatening way. You can use those clues to infer that the swan does not like or trust Mr. Peters.

DIRECTIONS: *The sentences in the left-hand column of this chart offer details about characters in "The Third Wish." (Some of the items are quotations from the story; some are based on the story.) In the right-hand column, describe what the details tell you about the character.*

Detail About a Character	Inference About the Character
1. Presently, the swan, when it was satisfied with its appearance, floated in to the bank once more, and in a moment, instead of the great white bird, there was a little man all in green.	
2. Mr. Peters wishes for a wife "as beautiful as the forest." A woman appears who is "the most beautiful creature he had ever seen, with eyes as blue-green as the canal, hair as dusky as the bushes, and skin as white as the feathers of swans."	
3. But as time went by Mr. Peters began to feel that [Leita] was not happy. She seemed restless, wandered much in the garden, and sometimes when he came back from the fields he would find the house empty. She would return after half an hour with no explanation of where she had been.	
4. After Leita was returned to the form of a swan, she "rested her head lightly against [Mr. Peters's] hand. . . . Next day he saw two swans swimming at the bottom of the garden, and one of them wore the gold chain he had given Leita after their marriage; she came up and rubbed her head against his hand."	

"The Third Wish" by Joan Aiken
Literary Analysis: Conflict

Most fictional stories center on a **conflict**—a struggle between opposing forces. There are two kinds of conflict:

- When there is an **external conflict,** a character struggles with an outside force, such as another character or nature.
- When there is an **internal conflict,** a character struggles with himself or herself to overcome opposing feelings, beliefs, needs, or desires. An internal conflict takes place in a character's mind.

The **resolution,** or outcome of the conflict, often comes toward the end of the story, when the problem is settled in some way.

A story can have additional, smaller conflicts that develop the main conflict. For example, in "The Third Wish," a small external conflict occurs between Mr. Peters and the swan that is tangled up in the thorns. As Mr. Peters tries to free the bird, the swan looks at him "with hate in its yellow eyes" and struggles with him. In addition, a minor internal conflict that helps develop the main conflict is Mr. Peters's difficulty in deciding what to do with his three wishes.

DIRECTIONS: *Based on details in each of the following passages from "The Third Wish," identify the conflict as* External *or* Internal. *Then, explain your answer.*

1. [Leita] was weeping, and as he came nearer he saw that tears were rolling, too, from the swan's eyes.

   "Leita, what is it?" he asked, very troubled.

   "This is my sister," she answered. "I can't bear being separated from her."

   Type of conflict: _____

   Explanation: _____

2. "Don't you love me at all, Leita?"

   "Yes, I do, I do love you," she said, and there were tears in her eyes again. "But I miss the old life in the forest."

   Type of conflict: _____

   Explanation: _____

3. She shook her head. "No, I could not be as unkind to you as that. I am partly a swan, but I am also partly a human being now."

   Type of conflict: _____

   Explanation: _____

"The Third Wish" by Joan Aiken
Vocabulary Builder

Word List

> dabbling   malicious   presumptuous   rash   remote   verge

A. DIRECTIONS: *On the line, write the letter of the word whose meaning is* opposite *that of the Word List word.*

____ 1. malicious

    A. wicked   B. tangled   C. sour   D. kind

____ 2. presumptuous

    A. curious   B. modest   C. missing   D. hungry

____ 3. rash

    A. cautious   B. itchy   C. impure   D. hasty

____ 4. remote

    A. casual   B. close   C. faraway   D. controlled

____ 5. dabbling

    A. drooling   B. dipping   C. immersing   D. scratching

____ 6. verge

    A. edge   B. center   C. frame   D. bank

B. DIRECTIONS: *Think about the meaning of the italicized word in each sentence. Then, in your own words, answer the question that follows, and briefly explain your answer.*

1. The old King is *presumptuous* in believing that Mr. Peters will make three foolish wishes. Is the old King overconfident? How do you know?

   _____

2. The old King is a *malicious* character. How does he act toward Mr. Peters?

   _____

3. Mr. Peters lives in a *remote* valley. Is it close to town? How do you know?

   _____

Name _____ Date _____

"*Amigo Brothers*" by Piri Thomas
Writing About the Big Question

 Does every conflict have a winner?

Big Question Vocabulary

attitude	challenge	communication	competition
compromise	conflict	danger	desire
disagreement	misunderstanding	obstacle	opposition
outcome	resolution	struggle	understanding

A. *Use one or more words from the list above to complete the paragraph.*

Competition between people can be healthy, but it can also lead to
____Conflict____. If you one day find yourself in _disagreement_ with a
friend, be sure to keep the lines of _Communication_ open. If you talk things
through, you can better avoid _____ and can reach a satisfying
resolution.

B. *Follow the directions in responding to each of the items below.*

1. List two different times when you experienced a conflict with a friend.

   _____

   _____

2. Write two sentences describing one of the preceding conflicts, and explain what
   helped you resolve it. Use at least two of the Big Question vocabulary words.

   _____

   _____

   _____

   _____

C. *Complete the sentence below. Then, write a short paragraph in which you connect this
situation to the Big Question.*

When a friendship is strong enough, conflicts that arise often _____

_____

_____

_____

_____

_____

_____

Name _____ Date __11/16/15__

"**Amigo Brothers**" by Piri Thomas
Reading: Make Inferences by Recognizing Details

Short story writers do not directly tell you everything there is to know about the characters, setting, and events. Instead, they leave it to you to **make inferences,** or logical guesses, about unstated information.

To form inferences, you must **recognize details** in the story and consider their importance. For example, in "Amigo Brothers," the narrator says, "While some youngsters were into street negatives, Antonio and Felix slept, ate, rapped, and dreamt positive." You can use that clue to infer that Felix and Antonio stayed out of trouble.

DIRECTIONS: *The sentences in the left-hand column of this chart offer details about the amigo brothers. In the right-hand column, describe what the details tell you about one or both of these characters.*

Detail About a Character	Inference About the Character
1. "If it's fair, *hermano,* I'm for it." Antonio admired the courage of a tugboat pulling a barge five times its welterweight size.	Antonio is fair. He is a good sport. He is honest.
2. Tony jogged away. Felix watched his friend disappear from view, throwing rights and lefts. Both fighters had a lot of psyching up to do before the big fight.	Felix and antonio need a lot of energy for the fight
3. Felix did a fast shuffle, bobbing and weaving, while letting loose a torrent of blows that would demolish whatever got in its way. It seemed to impress the brothers, who went about their own business.	
4. [Felix] fought off a series of rights and lefts and came back with a strong right that taught Antonio respect.	
5. The announcer turned to point to the winner and found himself alone. Arm in arm the champions had already left the ring.	

Name _____ Date _____

Literary Analysis: Conflict

Most fictional stories center on a **conflict**—a struggle between opposing forces. There are two kinds of conflict:

- When there is an **external conflict,** a character struggles with an outside force such as another character or nature.
- When there is an **internal conflict,** a character struggles with himself or herself to overcome opposing feelings, beliefs, needs, or desires. An internal conflict takes place in a character's mind.

The **resolution,** or outcome of the conflict, often comes toward the end of the story, when the problem is settled in some way.

A story can have additional, smaller conflicts that develop the main conflict. In "Amigo Brothers," for example, a small external conflict occurs one morning as Felix and Antonio work out. There is tension between them, and Felix says, "Let's stop a while, bro. I think we both got something to say to each other." A minor internal conflict occurs when Felix mentions that he has stayed awake at night, "pulling punches" on Antonio. Felix struggles with the conflict between his wish not to harm his friend and his desire to win the fight.

DIRECTIONS: *Based on details in each of the following passages from "Amigo Brothers," identify the conflict as* External *or* Internal. *Then, explain your answer.*

1. He tried not to think of Felix, feeling he had succeeded in psyching his mind. But only in the ring would he really know.

    Type of conflict: Internal

    Explanation: It is in his mind.

2. He walked up some dark streets, deserted except for small pockets of wary-looking kids wearing gang colors. Despite the fact that he was Puerto Rican like them, they eyed him as a stranger to their turf.

    Type of conflict: External

    Explanation: Felix problem is real.

3. Antonio was passing some heavy time on his rooftop. How would the fight tomorrow affect his relationship with Felix? After all, fighting was like any other profession. Friendship had nothing to do with it. A gnawing doubt crept in.

    Type of conflict: Internal

    Explanation: Antonio is think about relationship.

4. Felix and Antonio turned and faced each other squarely in a fighting pose. Felix wasted no time. He came fast, head low, half hunched toward his right shoulder, and lashed out with a straight left.

    Type of conflict: External

    Explanation: They bon't cair how win.

Name _____ Date _____

"The Third Wish" by Joan Aiken
"Amigo Brothers" by Piri Thomas

Integrated Language Skills: Support for Writing an Anecdote

Use this graphic organizer to help you prepare an anecdote that tells what might have happened if either (a) Mr. Peters had not turned Leita back into a swan or (b) Antonio or Felix had been knocked out during the fight. In the first rectangle, list details about the new ending that you imagine. In the ovals below it, describe two problems, or conflicts, that might arise as a result of the new ending. Then, in the bottom rectangle, describe one way in which the main character might act to resolve the conflict.

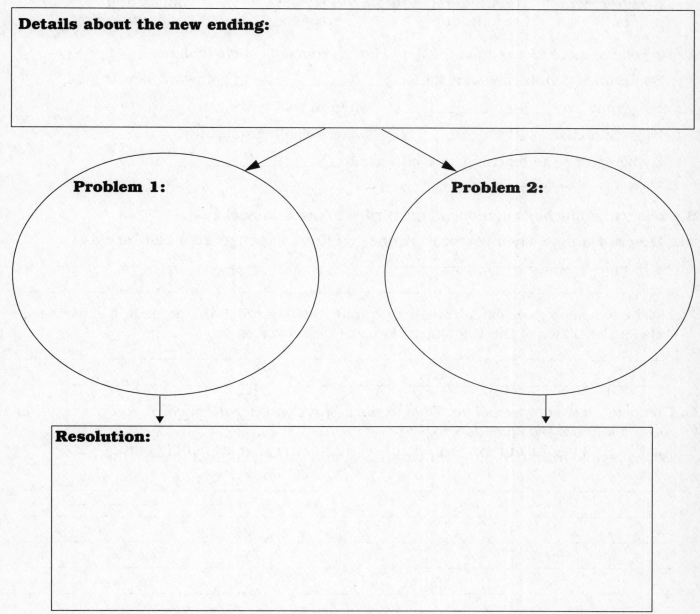

Details about the new ending:

Problem 1:

Problem 2:

Resolution:

Now, use your notes to write an anecdote telling what might have happened as a result of the new ending.

Name _____ Date _____

"Zoo" by Edward Hoch

Writing About the Big Question

Does every conflict have a winner?

Big Question Vocabulary

attitude	challenge	communication	competition
compromise	conflict	danger	desire
disagreement	misunderstanding	obstacle	opposition
outcome	resolution	struggle	understanding

A. *Use one or more words from the list above to complete each sentence.*

1. Sometimes people have a negative _____ toward new things.

2. They may see _____ when in reality they are perfectly safe.

3. In such a case, _____ is especially important.

4. By being open to learning, you can avoid _____ and
   _____.

B. *Follow the directions in responding to each of the items below.*

1. Describe a time when you or someone you know experienced a culture clash.

   _____

   _____

2. Write two sentences explaining how you (or they) handled the preceding experience.
   Use at least two of the Big Question vocabulary words.

   _____

   _____

C. *Complete the sentence below. Then, write a short paragraph in which you connect this situation to the Big Question.*

When people from two different worlds come together, conflict arises when _____

_____

_____

_____

_____

_____

_____

_____

_____

Name _____ Date _____

"Zoo" by Edward D. Hoch

Reading: Make Inferences by Reading Between the Lines and Asking Questions

An **inference** is an intelligent guess, based on what the text tells you, about things *not* stated directly in the text. Suppose a story opens with crowds forming to wait for the arrival of an interplanetary zoo. You can infer from those details that the zoo will soon arrive.

One way to make inferences is to **read between the lines by asking questions,** such as, "Why does the writer include these details?" and "Why does the writer leave out certain information?" In the opening sentence of "Zoo," for example, we learn that "the children were always good during the month of August." The next thing we learn is that the Interplanetary Zoo comes to Chicago every year around August 23. Why does the writer open his story with these details? What conclusion can be drawn about why the children are always good in August? From these details you can infer that the children are good in August because they want their parents to take them to the interplanetary zoo.

DIRECTIONS: *Read the following passages from "Zoo," and answer the questions that follow.*

1. In the following passage, what inference can you draw from the detail that the people are clutching dollars?

   Before daybreak the crowds would form, long lines of children and adults both, each one clutching his or her dollar and waiting with wonderment to see what race of strange creatures the Professor had brought this year.

   _____

   _____

2. In the following passage, what inference can you draw about the Professor from the description of his clothing?

   Soon the good Professor himself made an appearance, wearing his many-colored rainbow cape and top hat.

   _____

3. In the following passage, what inference can you draw about the horse spiders from the way they file out of their cages, listen to Hugo's parting words, and then scurry away?

   The odd horse-spider creatures filed quickly out of their cages. Professor Hugo was there to say a few parting words, and then they scurried away in a hundred different directions, seeking their homes among the rocks.

   _____

4. In the following passage, what inference can you draw from the she-creature's reaction to her mate and offspring's arrival?

   In one house, the she-creature was happy to see the return of her mate and offspring. She babbled a greeting in the strange tongue and hurried to embrace them.

   _____

"Zoo" by Edward D. Hoch
Literary Analysis: Theme

A story's **theme** is its central idea, message, or insight into life. Occasionally, the author states the theme directly. More often, however, the theme is implied.

A theme is *not* the same as the subject of a work. For example, if the subject, or topic, of a story is similarities and differences, the theme will be a message about that subject, such as "differences between groups of people can keep people from seeing the ways in which they are similar."

As you read, look at what characters say and do, where the story takes place, and objects that seem important in order to determine the theme—what the author wants to teach you about life.

DIRECTIONS: *Answer the following questions about "Zoo."*

1. What is the setting? If there is more than one setting, name and briefly describe each one.

   _____

   _____

2. What do the main characters say? Summarize the words spoken by Hugo, one of the people from Earth, the female horse spider, the male horse spider, and the little one.

   Hugo: _____

   Person from Earth: _____

   She-creature: _____

   He-creature: _____

   Little creature: _____

3. How do the characters act? Describe the actions of the people in Chicago and the actions of the horse-spider creatures.

   People in Chicago: _____

   _____

   Horse spiders: _____

   _____

4. What object or objects seem important?

   _____

5. What is the subject, or topic, of "Zoo"?

   _____

6. Based on these details, what would you say is the theme of "Zoo"?

   _____

"Zoo" by Edward D. Hoch
Vocabulary Builder

Word List

awe   babbled   expense   garments   interplanetary   wonderment

A. DIRECTIONS: *Complete each sentence with a word from the Word List.*

1. The _____ of interplanetary travel was high, but Professor Hugo earned the money back by charging admission to his zoo.

2. The crowd gazed in _____ at the terrifying yet unusual creatures.

3. Professor Hugo's _____ zoo visited Earth, Mars, Kaan, and many other planets.

4. The creature's wife _____ happily as she greeted her husband and asked him about his trip.

5. The creatures did not wear clothes, so the _____ the humans wore seemed unnatural.

6. The children's _____ only increased as the strange array of creatures paraded before them.

B. WORD STUDY *The suffix* -ment *means "the state of." Answer each of the following questions using one of these words containing* -ment: *amusements, contentment, entertainment.*

1. What type of television show would you watch for *entertainment*?

_____

2. Would you expect a child to complain about her *contentment*?

_____

3. What *amusements* might a toddler enjoy?

_____

"Ribbons" by Laurence Yep

Writing About the Big Question

Does every conflict have a winner?

Big Question Vocabulary

attitude	challenge	communication	competition
compromise	conflict	danger	desire
disagreement	misunderstanding	obstacle	opposition
outcome	resolution	struggle	understanding

A. *Use one or more words from the list above to complete each sentence.*

1. Different generations can _____ to understand one another.

2. The values of one generation can be in _____ with those of another.

3. It can be a _____ to understand one another's behaviors and beliefs.

4. Even _____ can be difficult because each may view things differently.

B. *Follow the directions in responding to each of the items below.*

1. Describe a time when you or someone you know **struggled** to **communicate** effectively with a member of another generation.

   _____

   _____

2. Explain whether both parties were able to reach an **understanding** and, if so, how. Use at least two of the Big Question vocabulary words.

   _____

   _____

C. *Complete the sentence below. Then, write a short paragraph in which you connect this situation to the Big Question.*

   Family members from different generations often do not understand _____

   _____

   _____

   _____

   _____

   _____

"**Ribbons**" by Laurence Yep

Reading: Make Inferences by Reading Between the Lines and Asking Questions

An **inference** is an intelligent guess, based on what the text tells you, about things *not* stated directly in the text. One way to make inferences is to **read between the lines by asking questions,** such as, "Why does the writer include these details?" and "Why does the writer leave out certain information?" For example, "Ribbons" opens as Stacy and Ian's grandmother arrives from Hong Kong. The narrator, Stacy, says,

> Because Grandmother's . . . expenses had been so high, there wasn't room in the family budget for Madame Oblomov's ballet school. I'd had to stop my daily lessons.

Why does the writer begin with those details? What conclusion can be drawn? From these details you can infer that Stacy feels some resentment because she has had to give up her ballet lessons so that her grandmother can come from Hong Kong.

DIRECTIONS: *Read the following passages from "Ribbons," and answer the questions.*

1. What inference can you draw from Grandmother's reaction to Stacy's hug?

   When I tried to put my arms around her and kiss her, she stiffened in surprise. "Nice children don't drool on people," she snapped at me.

   _____

2. What can you infer about Grandmother's feelings about her daughter's home?

   Grandmother was sitting in the big recliner in the living room. She stared uneasily out the window as if she were gazing not upon the broad, green lawn of the square but upon a Martian desert.

   _____

3. In the following passage, what inference can you draw from these words, spoken by Stacy's mother, about Grandmother?

   [The girls' feet] were usually bound up in silk ribbons. . . . Because they were a symbol of the old days, Paw-paw undid the ribbons as soon as we were free in Hong Kong—even though they kept back the pain.

   _____

4. In the following passage, what inference about Grandmother can you draw from this attempt to show her affection for Stacy?

   She took my hand and patted it clumsily. I think it was the first time she had showed me any sign of affection.

   _____

5. What inference can you draw from Stacy's description of the invisible ribbon?

   Suddenly I felt as if there were an invisible ribbon binding us tougher than silk and satin, stronger than steel; and it joined her to Mom and Mom to me.

   _____

"Ribbons" by Laurence Yep
Literary Analysis: Theme

A story's **theme** is its central idea, message, or insight into life. Occasionally, the author states the theme directly. More often, however, the theme is implied.

A theme is *not* the same as the subject of a work. For example, if the subject or topic of a story is cultural differences, the theme will be a message about that, such as "cultural differences can be overcome by communication."

As you read, look at what characters say and do, where the story takes place, and which objects seem important in order to determine the theme—what the author wants to teach you about life.

DIRECTIONS: *Answer the following questions about "Ribbons."*

1. What is the setting? Briefly describe it.
   _____

2. What do the main characters say? Summarize the important statements made by Grandmother, Mom, and Stacy.

   Grandmother: _____

   _____

   Mom: _____

   _____

   Stacy: _____

   _____

3. How do the characters act? Describe the important actions of Grandmother and Stacy.

   Grandmother: _____

   _____

   _____

   Stacy: _____

   _____

   _____

4. What objects seem important?
   _____

5. What is the subject, or topic, of "Ribbons"?
   _____

6. Based on your answers above, what would you say is the theme of "Ribbons"?
   _____

"Ribbons" by Laurence Yep
Vocabulary Builder

Word List

coax   exertion   furrowed   laborious   meek   sensitive

A. DIRECTIONS: *Complete each sentence with a word from the Word List.*

1. Because Grandmother's feet had been bound when she was young, she found walking and climbing stairs _____ activities.
2. Stacy loved ballet so much that she hardly realized that it was _____ until she collapsed from exhaustion after each lesson.
3. Because the binding of her feet was painful physically and emotionally, Grandmother was _____ about her feet.
4. Stacy hoped that she could _____ Grandmother into paying attention to her by explaining her love of ballet.
5. In many cultures it is expected that a daughter will be _____ and never challenge her parents' requests.
6. Unsure of what to say to her daughter, Stacy's mother _____ her brow in concentration.

B. WORD STUDY: *The suffix -ious means "full of." Answer each of the following questions using one of these words containing -ious: delicious, harmonious, industrious.*

1. How does an *industrious* worker perform her job?

   _____

2. Why would most people prefer a *harmonious* tune over a dissonant one?

   _____

3. How would a hungry child respond to a *delicious* meal?

   _____

"**Zoo**" by Edward D. Hoch
"**Ribbons**" by Laurence Yep

Integrated Language Skills: Grammar

Adverbs

An **adverb** is a word that modifies or describes a verb, an adjective, or another adverb. Adverbs provide information by answering the questions *how? when? where? how often?* or *to what extent?* Many adverbs end in the suffix *-ly.*

In the first sentence, the adverb, *always,* tells how often the children are good. In the second sentence, the adverb, *outside,* tells where the car stops:

The children were *always* <u>good</u> during the month of August.

A car <u>stopped</u> *outside.*

A. DIRECTIONS: *Underline the adverb in each sentence once, and circle the word it modifies. Then, write the question that the adverb answers.*

1. The sides slowly slid up to reveal the familiar barred cages. _____
   _____

2. The citizens of Earth clustered around as Professor Hugo's crew quickly collected the waiting dollars. _____
   _____

3. The odd horse-spider creatures filed quickly out of their cages. _____
   _____

4. The little one enjoyed it especially. _____
   _____

5. Mom bowed formally as Grandmother reached the porch. _____
   _____

B. Writing Application: *Write a sentence in response to each set of instructions. Underline the word or phrase that the adverb you use modifies.*

1. Use *quickly* in a sentence about catching a school bus.
   _____

2. Use *never* in a sentence about a food you dislike.
   _____

3. Use *gently* in a sentence about something you do.
   _____

4. Use *always* in a sentence about something else you do.
   _____

5. Use *finally* in a sentence about a process that involves several steps.
   _____

"Zoo" by Edward D. Hoch
"Ribbons" by Laurence Yep

Integrated Language Skills: Support for Writing a Letter to the Editor

Use this graphic organizer to organize your thoughts before writing your letter to the editor as a response to either "Zoo" or "Ribbons." In the top center box, write your topic (Zoo Animals or Extra Schooling). At the top of each column, list a position on the topic. Then, write down advantages and disadvantages of each position.

Topic: _____

Position:	**Position:**
Advantages: _____	Advantages: _____
Disadvantages: _____	Disadvantages: _____

Decide which position you want to take, and draft a letter to the editor of a local newspaper in support of your position. Use your notes to back up your opinion with reasons and details that will persuade readers to take your side.

"After Twenty Years" by O. Henry
"He—y, Come On O—ut!" by Shinichi Hoshi

Writing About the Big Question

Does every conflict have a winner?

Big Question Vocabulary

attitude	challenge	communication	competition
compromise	conflict	danger	desire
disagreement	misunderstanding	obstacle	opposition
outcome	resolution	struggle	understanding

A. *Use one or more words from the list above to complete each sentence.*

1. Our expectations are based on our _____ of how the world works.

2. When things take an unexpected turn, the _____ may be unwelcome.

3. It can be a _____ to accept this new turn of events.

4. On the other hand, the _____ may be a pleasant surprise.

B. *Follow the directions in responding to each of the items below.*

1. List two different times when things turned out differently from what you expected.

   _____

   _____

2. Write two sentences explaining one of the preceding experiences, and describe how you reacted at the time. Use at least two of the Big Question vocabulary words.

   _____

   _____

   _____

C. *Complete the sentence below. Then, write a short paragraph in which you connect this situation to the Big Question.*

When things turn out differently from what you expected, it can be _____

_____

_____

_____

_____

_____

"**After Twenty Years**" by O. Henry
"**He—y, Come On O—ut!**" by Shinichi Hoshi
Literary Analysis: Irony

Irony involves a contradiction or contrast of some kind. In **situational irony** (or **irony of situation**), something takes place that a character or reader does not expect to happen. For example, a student voted Most Likely to Succeed ends up going to prison.

In **verbal irony,** a writer, speaker, or character says something that deliberately contradicts or blurs what he or she actually means. Think of a man who has been dreading a reunion with his best friend from twenty years before. When they meet, he says, "I've been *so* looking forward to seeing you." That is verbal irony.

In **dramatic irony,** the reader or audience knows or understands something that a character or speaker does not. For example, readers know that the apple Snow White is about to bite into is poisoned, but Snow White does not know it. That is dramatic irony.

As you read "After Twenty Years" and "He—y, Come On O—ut!" look for situational irony in particular.

DIRECTIONS: *Answer the following questions.*

1. What is the general situation, or the plot? Describe it briefly.

   "After Twenty Years": _____

   _____

   "He—y, Come On O—ut!": _____

   _____

2. What outcome do you expect?

   "After Twenty Years": _____

   "He—y, Come On O—ut!": _____

3. What happens? How does the story end?

   "After Twenty Years": _____

   "He—y, Come On O—ut!": _____

4. What details in the story lead you to expect a certain outcome? Describe one or two details, and state what they lead you to expect.

   "After Twenty Years": _____

   _____

   "He—y, Come On O—ut!": _____

   _____

5. What is ironic about the ending of the story?

   "After Twenty Years": _____

   "He—y, Come On O—ut!": _____

"After Twenty Years" by O. Henry
"He—y, Come On O—ut!" by Shinichi Hoshi
Vocabulary Builder

Word List

apparent   destiny   intricate   plausible   proposal   simultaneously   spectators

A. DIRECTIONS: *Revise each sentence so that the italicized vocabulary word is used logically. Be sure to use the vocabulary word in your new sentence.*

1. The plot of the short story was so *intricate* that we followed it easily.

   _____

2. The *destiny* of a criminal is likely to include time spent as a police officer.

   _____

3. The two men arrived *simultaneously,* one reaching the doorway an hour after the other.

   _____

4. Because there were many *spectators* when the crime was committed, no eyewitnesses could testify at the trial.

   _____

5. The *apparent* smile on the face of the scientist was not visible to anyone.

   _____

6. The *plausible* explanation made sense to no one.

   _____

7. Because he offered no solution, everyone accepted the concessionaire's *proposal.*

   _____

B. DIRECTIONS: *Write the letter of the word whose meaning is most* similar *to that of the Word Bank word.*

____ **1.** intricate
   A. complicated   **B.** tiny   **C.** simple   **D.** intelligent

____ **2.** simultaneously
   A. genuinely   **B.** apart   **C.** together   **D.** separately

____ **3.** apparent
   A. obvious   **B.** hidden   **C.** deceptive   **D.** similar

"After Twenty Years" by O. Henry
"He—y, Come On O—ut!" by Shinichi Hoshi

Integrated Language Skills: Support for Writing to Compare Literary Works

Before you write an essay that compares your reaction to "After Twenty Years" with your reaction to "He—y, Come On O—ut!" use this graphic organizer to consider how irony is used in the two stories.

What details make the story believable or realistic?

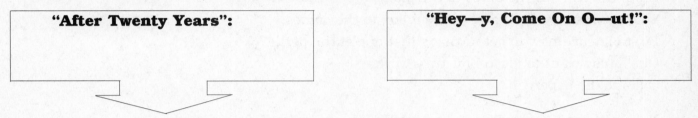

How does the believability or the realism of the story affect your response? Do you prefer a believable story to a fantasy one? Why or why not?

What is the story's message? Is the message easy to understand? Why or why not?

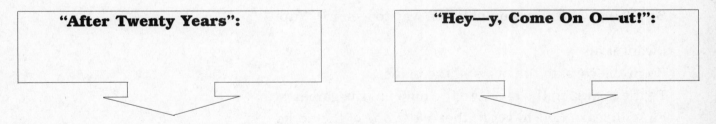

When you respond to a story, are you influenced by the difficulty of understanding its message? Why or why not?

"After Twenty Years":	"Hey—y, Come On O—ut!":

Now, use your notes to write an essay in which you compare your reactions to the use of irony in "After Twenty Years" and "He—y, Come On O—ut!"

 **BQ Tunes**

The Expert, performed by Hydra

Yeah... Unh... yea... Hydra... yea... Blitzkrieg... yea....

I want it all
From the cars, to the bikes to the planes,
To the books, to the stars, to the mike, to the games,
First I'll learn how to get it, that's just one of the perks.
Cus' I also want to learn how they work.
Call me the expert.

Nah, you can't give me a car and just hand me the keys /
I need to learn how to drive it not to crash into trees /
And aside from my safety, there's something else that's got me /
Exploring more about it that's just my **curiosity** /
So I pop open the hood and **analyze** the parts /
The radiator keeps it cool, the engine makes it start /
I want the **knowledge** to build it or tear it apart /
To repair it if it breaks down out of town in the dark /
So no Mr. Mechanic, can't overcharge me for parts /
Or sell me things I don't need please I've studied the art /
I **understand** the diagrams and the tune up charts /
So change your tune up man, I'm way too smart! Yup!

I want it all
From the cars, to the bikes to the planes,
To the books, to the stars, to the mike, to the games,
First I'll learn how to get it, that's just one of the perks.
Cus' I also want to learn how they work.
Call me the expert.

I'll learn it all
But **evaluate** things that you learn / some things are more important than others
of more concern /
I'll learn it all

Continued

All-in-One Workbook
118

Investigate to reach your objective / find out all the details like a good detective /
I'll learn it all

Inquire with those well informed on the topic / if they don't know what they're saying information is toxic

I'll learn it all

Y'all know what I mean, don't let somebody tell you what's true, find out for yourself... Feel me?

See ever since I was a freshman (yes then)

If there was something I wanted to know I'd go and ask a **question** /

Jus' because I got an answer doesn't mean I would accept them /

To be sure it was right, the truth and nothing less than /

I might set up an **experiment**, prep them and test them /

Research gave me **information** in a note book I kept them /

Examine findings carefully like a doctors dissection /

Once I knew I had the right answer I could get some rest then /

Everybody was impressed an' yeah I liked how it felt /

But the real reason I did it to get the facts for myself /

That's what's gonna help me keep putting platinum plaques on my shelf /

Discover everything I can that'll keep me on top /

If you don't seek out the knowledge you'll eventually flop /

It's better not to be so foolish / Nah, it's not the way /

Who wants to **interview** somebody with nothing to say? Huh, huh?

I want it all

From the cars to the bikes to the planes,

To the books to the stars to the mike to the games,

First I'll learn how to get it, that's just one of the perks.

Cus' I also want to learn how they work.

Call me the expert.

Continued

I want it all

From the cars to the bikes to the planes,

To the books to the stars to the mike to the games,

First I'll learn how to get it, that's just one of the perks.

Cus' I also want to learn how they work.

Call me the expert.

Song Title: **The Expert**
Artist / Performed by Hydra
Vocals: Rodney "Blitz" Willie
Lyrics by Rodney "Blitz" Willie
Music composed by Keith "Wild Child" Middleton
Produced by Keith "Wild Child" Middleton
Technical Production: Mike Pandolfo, Wonderful
Executive Producer: Keith London, Defined Mind

Unit 3: Types of Nonfiction
Big Question Vocabulary—1

The Big Question: What should we learn?

analyze: *v.* to study something's pieces and parts in order to understand it better; other forms: *analyzing, analyzed, analysis*

curiosity: *n.* a desire to learn about or know something; other form: *curious*

facts: *n.* pieces of information that are known to be true; other forms: *fact, factual*

interview: *n.* a meeting in which a person is asked questions

       v. to ask a person questions for a specific purpose; other form: *interviewed*

knowledge: *n.* information and understanding that someone gains through learning or experience; other form: *know*

DIRECTIONS: *List three items as instructed. Then answer each question.*

1. List three questions that arouse your *curiosity*.

   _____   _____   _____

   What might you do to satisfy your curiosity about one of these things? _____

   _____

2. List three famous people whom you would like to *interview*.

   _____   _____   _____

   What would be your first question to one of these people? _____

   _____

3. What *facts* would you use to help a child gain *knowledge* about your state?

   _____   _____   _____

   Which fact would be most interesting to the child? Explain. _____

   _____

4. What three steps might help a student to *analyze* a poem?

   _____   _____   _____

   Why is it important to work carefully when you *analyze* something? _____

   _____

Unit 3: Types of Nonfiction
Big Question Vocabulary—2

The Big Question: What should we learn?

discover: *v.* to uncover information that you did not know before; other forms: *discovery, discovered, discovering*

evaluate: *v.* to decide how good, useful, or successful something is; other forms: *evaluation, evaluating, evaluated*

experiment: *n.* a test that shows why things happen or why something is true

v. to perform a test to gather new information; other form: *experimenting*

explore: *v.* to discuss or think about something thoroughly; other form: *exploration*

inquire: *v.* to ask someone for information about a topic; other forms: *inquired, inquiring*

A. DIRECTIONS: *Underline the* **synonym** *(the word or phrase closest in meaning) to each vocabulary word.*

1. **discover**   a. test   b. try to see   c. find out
2. **evaluate**   a. judge   b. criticize   c. uncover
3. **experiment**   a. find   b. visualize   c. test
4. **explore**   a. overlook   b. analyze   c. decide
5. **inquire**   a. question   b. consider   c. respond

B. DIRECTIONS: *Complete each sentence by writing the correct vocabulary word in the blank space. Three possible choices are shown in parentheses.*

1. To begin his research on the rings of Saturn, Ramon went to the school librarian to _____ about the facts. *(experiment, inquire, evaluate)*

2. Cheryl performed two tests to _____ the purity of the water. *(experiment, inquire, evaluate)*

3. You can _____ many facts about animals by studying how they interact. *(experiment, discover, explore)*

4. To _____ for clues about its meaning, Jeb and I examined the strange painting carefully. *(explore, evaluate, inquire)*

5. To make his salad more delicious, the chef decided to _____ with different seasonings. *(discover, explore, experiment)*

All-in-One Workbook
122

Name _____ Date _____

Unit 3: Types of Nonfiction
Big Question Vocabulary—3

The Big Question: What should we learn?

examine: *v.* to look at something carefully in order to learn more about it; other forms: *examined, examining, examination, exam*

information: *n.* facts and details about a topic; other forms: *informative, inform*

investigate: *v.* to try to find out the truth about something, such as the details of a crime; other forms: *investigation, investigating, investigated*

question: *n.* a sentence or phrase used to ask for information

v. to have doubts about something; other forms: *questioning, questioned*

understand: *v.* to know how or why something happens or what it is like; other forms: *understood, understanding*

A. DIRECTIONS: *Review the vocabulary words and their definitions. Then write the one that belongs in each group of related words.*

1. knowledge, wisdom, truths, _____
2. check, explore, inquire, _____
3. inspect, study, watch, _____
4. know, learn, grasp, _____
5. challenge, debate, ask, _____

B. DIRECTIONS: *On the line before each sentence, write True if the statement is true, or False if it is false. If the statement is false, rewrite the sentence so that it is true.*

_____1. Most *information* is based on opinions that cannot be proved true.

_____

_____2. If you *examine* the stars through a telescope, you will see them clearly.

_____

_____3. If you don't *understand* the question, you'll probably get the right answer.

_____

_____4. A person who *investigates* a crime is often guilty.

_____

_____5. It is rude and unnecessary to *question* the claims in an advertisement.

_____

Name _____ Date _____

Unit 3: Types of Nonfiction
Applying the Big Question

What should we learn?

DIRECTIONS: *Complete the chart below to apply what you have learned about what we should learn. One row has been completed for you.*

Example	Type of knowledge	Why it is important	Effect it will have	What I learned
From Literature	Understanding different cultures, as in "Conversational Ballgames."	To be able to better relate to people who are different from us.	More tolerance and better relationships.	When with people from another culture, don't assume that your own customs are the norm.
From Literature				
From Science				
From Social Studies				
From Real Life				

Richard Mühlberger
Listening and Viewing

Segment 1: Meet Richard Mühlberger
- Why do you think Richard Mühlberger chose to write art history books?
- Do you agree with the writing advice given to Mühlberger by a fellow writer "to stick to the masters"?

_____

_____

_____

_____

Segment 2: The Essay
- According to Richard Mühlberger, what are some characteristics of essays?
- When would you write an essay, and why?

_____

_____

_____

_____

Segment 3: The Writing Process
- Why is it very important to Richard Mühlberger to write in precise, detailed language when writing about a painting?
- Why do you think Richard Mühlberger chooses to write his books in a "conversational tone"?

_____

_____

_____

_____

Segment 4: The Rewards of Writing
- What does Richard Mühlberger hope that his readers will gain by reading books about art?
- Why do you think books about art are important?

_____

_____

_____

_____

Learning About Nonfiction

An author has a specific **purpose for writing** an essay or article. Often, that purpose is to explain, to entertain, to inform, or to persuade. An essay or an article uses one or more of these **formats:**

- Expository writing: presents facts, discusses ideas, or explains a process
- Persuasive writing: attempts to persuade the reader to adopt a particular point of view or take a particular course of action
- Reflective writing: addresses an event or experience and gives the writer's insights about its importance
- Humorous writing: entertains the audience by evoking laughter
- Narrative writing: tells about real-life experiences
- Descriptive writing: appeals to the reader's senses of sight, hearing, taste, smell, and touch
- Analytical writing: breaks a large idea into parts to help the reader see how they work together as a whole

A. DIRECTIONS: *The following are titles of nonfiction essays or articles. Circle the letter of the answer choice that shows the best format for each title. Then, circle the letter of the answer choice that shows the purpose that the author probably had for writing the article.*

1. "How to Build a Doghouse"
   Format: **A.** persuasive   **B.** expository   **C.** narrative   **D.** reflective
   Purpose: **A.** to explain   **B.** to entertain

2. "Don't Throw That Cardboard and Paper in the Trash!"
   Format: **A.** persuasive   **B.** analytical   **C.** narrative   **D.** humorous
   Purpose: **A.** to entertain   **B.** to persuade

3. "Moving to Tucson Changed My Life"
   Format: **A.** persuasive   **B.** expository   **C.** analytical   **D.** reflective
   Purpose: **A.** to persuade   **B.** to share insights

B. DIRECTIONS: *Below are essay topics and their purpose. Write the format that you would use to write each essay. Explain your choice. Refer to the bulleted list above as needed for help.*

Topic: how to draw a face   Purpose: to explain
Format choice/reason: <u>expository; it explains a process</u>.

1. Topic: a strange animal   Purpose: to entertain
   Format choice/reason: _____

2. Topic: vote for a certain candidate   Purpose: to persuade
   Format choice/reason: _____

3. Topic: The Civil War   Purpose: to present ideas
   Format choice/reason: _____

"What Makes a Rembrandt a Rembrandt?" by Richard Mühlberger
Model Selection: Nonfiction

Nonfiction writing is about real people, places, objects, ideas, and experiences. Here are some common types:

Type of Nonfiction	Description
Biography	the life story of a real person, written by another person
Autobiography	the author's account of his or her own life
Media Accounts	true stories written for newspapers, magazines, television, or radio
Essays and Articles	short nonfiction works about a particular subject

Nonfiction writing must be organized to present information logically and clearly. Writers use **chronological organization** (they present details in time order); **comparison-and-contrast organization** (they show similarities and differences); **cause-and-effect organization** (they show relationships among events); and **problem-and-solution organization** (they identify a problem and present a solution).

DIRECTIONS: *On the lines below, answer these questions about "What Makes a Rembrandt a Rembrandt?"*

1. What type of nonfiction writing is "What Makes a Rembrandt a Rembrandt?" Explain.

   _____

2. How is the first paragraph in "Two Handsome Soldiers" organized? Explain.

   _____

   _____

3. What two real people are the most important in this article?

   _____

4. Why does Richard Mühlberger use an expository format for sections of "What Makes a Rembrandt a Rembrandt?"

   _____

5. Often, nonfiction writers have more than one purpose for writing an article or essay. Which *two* purposes did Richard Mühlberger have for writing this article? Check your choices.

   _____ **A.** to persuade his city to form a militia company as a social club

   _____ **B.** to entertain readers with a humorous event

   _____ **C.** to explain Rembrandt's painting techniques

   _____ **D.** to explain why Banning Cocq was a great Dutch soldier

   _____ **E.** to inform readers with facts about the painting *Night Watch*

"**Life Without Gravity**" by Robert Zimmerman
Writing About the Big Question

 What should we learn?

Big Question Vocabulary

analyze	curiosity	discover	evaluate	examine
experiment	explore	facts	information	inquire
interview	investigate	knowledge	question	understand

A. *Choose one word from the list above to complete each sentence. There may be more than one right answer.*

1. Anna's _____ about other people helped her learn about different cultures.

2. It can be fun to _____ new neighborhoods in your hometown.

3. Try to ask each new acquaintance at least one _____ about her life.

B. *Follow the directions in responding to each of the items below.*

1. List two different times that you learned something outside of school. Write your response in complete sentences.

   _____

   _____

2. Choose one of the experiences you listed in number 1. Write two sentences describing that experience. Use at least two of the Big Question vocabulary words. You may use the words in different forms (for example you can change *analyze* to *analyzing*).

   _____

   _____

C. *Complete the sentence below. Then, write a short paragraph in which you connect this sentence to the big question.*

Our assumptions about unfamiliar experiences are _____

_____

_____

"Life Without Gravity" by Robert Zimmerman

Reading: Adjust Your Reading Rate to Recognize Main Ideas and Key Points

The **main idea** is the central point of a passage or text. Most articles and essays have a main idea. Each paragraph or passage in the work also has a main idea, or **key point.**

The main idea of a paragraph is usually stated in a **topic sentence.** The paragraph then supplies **supporting details** that give examples, explanations, or reasons.

When reading nonfiction, **adjust your reading rate to recognize main ideas and key points.**

- **Skim** the article to get a sense of the main idea before you begin reading. Look over the text quickly, looking for text organization, topic sentences, and repeated words.
- **Scan** the text when you need to find answers to questions or to clarify or find supporting details. Run your eyes over the text, looking for a particular word or idea.
- **Read closely** to learn what the main ideas are and to identify the key points and supporting details.

A. DIRECTIONS: *Scan each paragraph below to find answers to the questions that follow.*

Our bodies are adapted to Earth's gravity. Our muscles are strong in order to overcome gravity as we walk and run. Our inner ears use gravity to keep us upright. And because gravity wants to pull all our blood down into our legs, our hearts are designed to pump hard to get blood up to our brains.

1. What parts of the body are discussed in this paragraph?

_____

In microgravity, you have to learn new ways to eat. Don't pour a bowl of cornflakes. Not only will the flakes float all over the place, the milk won't pour. Instead, big balls of milk will form. You can drink these by taking big bites out of them, but you'd better finish them before they slam into a wall, splattering apart and covering everything with little tiny milk globules.

2. What foods are mentioned in this paragraph?

_____

B. DIRECTIONS: *Now, read the paragraphs closely. Answer these questions.*

1. What is the main idea of the first paragraph?

_____

2. What are two details that support that main idea?

_____

3. What is the main idea of the second paragraph?

_____

4. What are two details that support that main idea?

_____

"Life Without Gravity" by Robert Zimmerman
Literary Analysis: Expository Essay

An **expository essay** is a short piece of nonfiction that explains, defines, or interprets ideas, events, or processes. The way in which the information is organized and presented depends on the specific topic of the essay. Writers organize the main points of their essays logically, to aid readers' comprehension. They may organize information in one of these ways or in a combination of ways:

- Comparison and contrast
- Cause and effect
- Chronological order
- Problem and solution

"Life Without Gravity" is an expository essay that explains an idea. It uses cause and effect to make the explanation clear. In the paragraph below, the details help readers understand some of the effects of weightlessness.

Worse, weightlessness can sometimes be downright unpleasant. Your body gets upset and confused. Your face puffs up, your nose gets stuffy, your back hurts, your stomach gets upset, and you throw up.

DIRECTIONS: *The left-hand column of the following chart names parts of the human body that are affected by weightlessness. In the right-hand column, write the effect—in your own words—as it is described in "Life Without Gravity." If one effect causes yet another effect, describe the second effect as well.*

Body Part	Effects of Weightlessness
The blood	Weightlessness causes _____ _____
The spine	Weightlessness causes _____ _____
The bones	Weightlessness causes _____ _____
The muscles	Weightlessness causes _____ _____
The stomach	Weightlessness causes _____ _____

Name _____ Date _____

"Life Without Gravity" by Robert Zimmerman
Vocabulary Builder

Word List

blander   feeble   globules   manned   readapted   spines

A. DIRECTIONS: *On the short line, write* T *if the following statement is true and* F *if it is false. Then, explain your answer in a complete sentence.*

____ 1. Animals' *spines* are very strong.

_____

____ 2. A *feeble* voice is one that can be heard across a room.

_____

____ 3. Foods made without pepper are *blander* than the same foods prepared with pepper.

_____

____ 4. All astronauts have successfully *readapted* to life on Earth.

_____

____ 5. *Manned* space flight is considered too dangerous at this time.

_____

____ 6. Floating *globules* help astronauts exercise their muscles in space.

_____

B. WORD STUDY: *The suffix -ness from Old English means "the condition or quality of being." Read the following sentences. Use your knowledge of the suffix -ness to write a full sentence to answer each question. Include the italicized word in your answer.*

1. What are some of the ways that *weightlessness* is enjoyable?

_____

2. How can living in space cause *feebleness*?

_____

3. Why is it important for astronauts to have a *willingness* to try new things?

_____

"Conversational Ballgames" by Nancy Masterson Sakamoto

Writing About the Big Question

What should we learn?

Big Question Vocabulary

analyze	curiosity	discover	evaluate	examine
experiment	explore	facts	information	inquire
interview	investigate	knowledge	question	understand

A. *Choose one word from the list above to complete each sentence. There may be more than one right answer.*

1. _____ an older person in your family to learn about history.

2. _____ is often gained after a lifetime of experience.

3. It can take time to learn to _____ someone from another culture.

B. *Follow the directions in responding to each of the items below.*

1. List two different times that you learned something about a person from another culture. Write your response in complete sentences.

   _____

   _____

2. Choose one of the experiences you listed in number 1. Write two or more sentences describing that experience. Use at least two of the Big Question vocabulary words in your answer. You may use the words in different forms (for example, you can change *analyze* to *analyzing*).

   _____

   _____

C. *Complete the sentence below. Then, write a short paragraph in which you connect this sentence to the big question.*

Cultural knowledge can _____

_____

_____

All-in-One Workbook
132

Name _____ Date _____

"Conversational Ballgames" by Nancy Masterson Sakamoto
Reading: Adjust Your Reading Rate to Recognize Main Ideas and Key Points

The **main idea** is the central point of a passage or text. Most articles and essays have a main idea. Each paragraph or passage in the work also has a main idea, or **key point.**

The main idea of a paragraph is usually stated in a **topic sentence**—a sentence that identifies the key point. The paragraph then supplies **supporting details** that give examples, explanations, or reasons.

When reading nonfiction, **adjust your reading rate to recognize main ideas and key points.**

- **Skim** the article to get a sense of the main idea before you begin reading. Look over the text quickly, looking for text organization, topic sentences, and repeated words.
- **Scan** the text when you need to find answers to questions or to clarify or find supporting details. Run your eyes over the text, looking for a particular word or idea.
- **Read closely** to learn what the main ideas are and to identify the key points and supporting details.

A. DIRECTIONS: *Scan each paragraph below to find answers to the questions that follow.*

A western-style conversation between two people is like a game of tennis. If I introduce a topic, a conversational ball, I expect you to hit it back. If you agree with me, I don't expect you simply to agree and do nothing more. I expect you to add something—a reason for agreeing, another example, or an elaboration to carry the idea further. But I don't expect you always to agree. I am just as happy if you question me, or challenge me, or completely disagree with me. Whether you agree or disagree, your response will return the ball to me.

1. What game does the author discuss in this paragraph? _____

A Japanese-style conversation, however, is not at all like tennis or volleyball. It's like bowling. You wait for your turn. And you always know your place in line. It depends on such things as whether you are older or younger, a close friend or a relative stranger to the previous speaker, in a senior or junior position, and so on.

2. What game does the author discuss in this paragraph? _____

B. DIRECTIONS: *Now, read the paragraphs closely for main ideas and supporting details.*

1. What is the main idea of the first paragraph?

_____

2. What are two details that support that main idea?

_____

3. What is the main idea of the second paragraph?

_____

4. What are two details that support that main idea?

_____

Name _____ Date _____

"Conversational Ballgames" by Nancy Masterson Sakamoto
Literary Analysis: Expository Essay

An **expository essay** is a short piece of nonfiction that explains, defines, or interprets ideas, events, or processes. The way in which the information is organized and presented depends on the specific topic of the essay. Writers organize the main points of their essays logically, to aid readers' comprehension. They may organize information in one of these ways or in a combination of ways:

- Comparison and contrast
- Cause and effect
- Chronological order
- Problem and solution

"Conversational Ballgames" is an expository essay that explains two processes. It uses comparison and contrast to make the explanation clear. In the paragraph below, the details set up the differences between Japanese and western styles of conversation.

Japanese-style conversations develop quite differently from western-style conversations. And the difference isn't only in the languages. I realized that just as I kept trying to hold western-style conversations even when I was speaking Japanese, so my English students kept trying to hold Japanese-style conversations even when they were speaking English.

DIRECTIONS: *Use this chart to compare and contrast Japanese-style conversation and western-style conversation. In the left-hand column, write five characteristics of western-style conversations as those conversations are described in "Conversational Ballgames." In the right-hand column, describe how the Japanese style differs from, or is similar to, each characteristic described on the left.*

Western-Style Conversation	Japanese-Style Conversation
1.	
2.	
3.	
4.	
5.	

"**Conversational Ballgames**" by Nancy Masterson Sakamoto
Vocabulary Builder

Word List

elaboration   indispensable   murmuring   parallel   suitable   unconsciously

A. DIRECTIONS: *Think about the meaning of the italicized word in each sentence. Then, answer the question.*

1. If two lines run *parallel* to each other, what do you know about them?

   _____

2. If a speaker is *murmuring*, what might he or she be asked to do?

   _____

3. Why might someone who is learning Japanese say that a dictionary is *indispensable*?

   _____

4. If you were engaged in a conversation about cultural differences, and someone asked you for *elaboration*, what would you do?

   _____

5. If two cultures had different ideas about *suitable* times for serious conversation, would holding a meeting be simple or difficult?

   _____

6. Why is it hard to stop doing something if you do it *unconsciously*?

   _____

B. WORD STUDY: *The suffix -able means "capable or worthy of being." Read the following sentences. Use your knowledge of the suffix -able to write a full sentence to answer each question.*

1. Does a *capable* person need help?

   _____

2. If an experience is *enjoyable*, are you eager to have it end?

   _____

3. Is a *breakable* plate a good choice for a picnic?

   _____

"**Life Without Gravity**" by Robert Zimmerman
"**Conversational Ballgames**" by Nancy Masterson Sakamoto
Integrated Language Skills: Grammar

Conjunctions

Conjunctions connect words or groups of words. **Coordinating conjunctions,** such as *but, and, nor, for, so, yet,* and *or,* connect words or groups of words that have a similar function in a sentence. They might connect two or more nouns, adjectives, adverbs, groups of words, or sentences. In the following examples, the coordinating conjunctions are in bold type. The words they connect are underlined.

Connecting nouns:	Bones **and** muscles become weak in outer space.
Connecting verbs:	How can people talk **and** eat at the same time?
Connecting adjectives:	A conversation can be interesting, exciting, **or** boring.
Connecting sentences:	Becoming an astronaut is difficult, **but** it is also rewarding.

A. PRACTICE: *Circle the coordinating conjunction in each sentence. Then, underline the words, groups of words, or sentences that the conjunction connects.*

1. Some astronauts adjust well to living without gravity, but others have problems.
2. Zero gravity is hard on the bones and the muscles.
3. Astronauts are not surprised by zero gravity, for they are trained to expect it.
4. Sakamoto had mastered Japanese, yet she was having trouble communicating.
5. In western conversations, someone may agree, question, or challenge.
6. Sakamoto learned the art of Japanese conversation, so she was able to participate fully.

B. Writing Application: *Complete the following instructions by writing sentences about "Life Without Gravity" or "Conversational Ballgames." In each sentence that you write, use the coordinating conjunction in the way described.*

1. Join two nouns with the conjunction *and.* _____

   _____

2. Join two verbs with the conjunction *or.* _____

   _____

3. Join two sentences with the conjunction *but.* _____

   _____

4. Join two groups of words with the conjunction *or.* _____

   _____

5. Join two adjectives with the conjunction *yet.* _____

   _____

"Life Without Gravity" by Robert Zimmerman
"Conversational Ballgames" by Nancy Masterson Sakamoto
Integrated Language Skills:
Support for Writing an Analogy

An **analogy** makes a comparison between two or more things that are similar in some ways, but otherwise unalike. A good analogy can spice up your writing, make the reader smile, or explain a difficult concept.

Analogies often take the form of a compound sentence with two parts joined by the phrase "is like." For example, A is like B. The two halves of the sentence usually have a parallel structure. For example,

A NOUN without a NOUN is like A NOUN without a NOUN.

___{first half}_____connector _____{second half___.

Before you write an analogy of your own, practice by completing this chart.

A	connector	B
Life without gravity	is like	French fries without ketchup.
Life without gravity	is like	spaghetti without _____.
Life without gravity	is like	(noun) _____ without _____.
	is like	
Communicating with someone from another culture	is like	hiking blindfolded.
Communicating with someone from another culture	is like	singing _____.
Communicating with someone from another culture	is like	_____.

Now, use a separate piece of paper to write three complete analogies. Use the beginning phrases provided in the chart or come up with your own.

"I Am a Native of North America" by Chief Dan George
Writing About the Big Question

What should we learn?

Big Question Vocabulary

analyze	curiosity	discover	evaluate	examine
experiment	explore	facts	information	inquire
interview	investigate	knowledge	question	understand

A. *Choose one word from the list above to fill the blanks in the sentences below. There may be more than one right answer.*

1. Many Americans wish to _____ Native American culture.

2. Like many Americans, Chief George has _____ of two cultures.

3. If you could _____ Chief George, what _____ would you ask him?

B. *Follow the directions in responding to each of the items below.*

1. List two different times that you learned something new about your own country. Write your response in complete sentences.

   _____

   _____

2. Choose one of the experiences you listed in number 1. Write two sentences describing that experience. Use at least two of the Big Question vocabulary words. You may use the words in different forms (for example you can change *analyze* to *analyzing*).

   _____

   _____

C. *Complete the sentence below. Use the completed sentence as the beginning of a short paragraph in which you discuss the big question.*

In order for people to live together in a society, they must _____

_____

_____

"**I Am a Native of North America**" by Chief Dan George
Reading: Make Connections Between Key Points and Supporting Details to Understand the Main Idea

The **main idea** is the most important thought or concept in a work or a passage of text. Sometimes the author directly states the main idea of a work and then provides key points that support it. These key points are supported in turn by details such as examples and descriptions. Other times the main idea is unstated. The author gives you *only* the key points or supporting details that add up to a main idea. To understand the main idea, **make connections between key points and supporting details.** Notice how the writer groups details. Look for sentences that pull details together.

In this passage from "I Am a Native of North America," Chief George states key points and provides details that support the main idea of the essay:

> I am afraid my culture has little to offer yours. But my culture did prize friendship and companionship. It did not look on privacy as a thing to be clung to, for privacy builds up walls and walls promote distrust. My culture lived in big family communities, and from infancy people learned to live with others.

DIRECTIONS: *Write the main idea of Chief George's essay on the line below. Then, read each passage, and write its key point and the details that support it.*

Main idea: _____

> And beyond this acceptance of one another there was a deep respect for everything in nature that surrounded them. My father loved the earth and all its creatures. The earth was his second mother. The earth and everything it contained was a gift from See-see-am . . . and the way to thank this great spirit was to use his gifts with respect.

1. **Key point:** _____
2. **Details:** _____

_____

> Love is something you and I must have. We must have it because our spirit feeds upon it. We must have it because without it we become weak and faint. Without love our self-esteem weakens. Without it our courage fails. Without love we can no longer look out confidently at the world. Instead we turn inwardly and begin to feed upon our own personalities and little by little we destroy ourselves.

3. **Key point:** _____
4. **Details:** _____

_____

"I Am a Native of North America" by Chief Dan George
Literary Analysis: Reflective Essay

A **reflective essay** is a brief prose work that presents a writer's feelings and thoughts, or reflections, about an experience or idea. The purpose is to communicate these thoughts and feelings so that readers will respond with thoughts and feelings of their own. As you read a reflective essay, think about the ideas the writer is sharing. Think about whether your responses to the experience or idea are similar to or different from the writer's.

In this passage from "I Am a Native of North America," Chief George reflects on life in apartment buildings:

> I see people living in smoke houses hundreds of times bigger than the one I knew. But the people in one apartment do not even know the people in the next and care less about them.

Chief George thinks about how neighbors do not know one another and concludes that they do not care about one another.

A. DIRECTIONS: *In the second column of the chart, summarize Chief George's thoughts about each experience described in the first column. Then, in the third column, write your response. That is, describe your own thoughts on the subject.*

Experience	Author's Thoughts	My Thoughts
1. Chief George describes his grandfather's smoke house.		
2. Chief George's father finds him killing fish "for the fun of it."		
3. Chief George sees his culture disappearing.		

B. DIRECTIONS: *Write the first paragraph of a reflective essay of your own. Include a description of an experience and your thoughts about it. Write on one of these topics:*

- the role of nature in your life
- the importance of tradition in your life
- the meaning of family in your life

_____

_____

_____

_____

_____

"I Am a Native of North America" by Chief Dan George
Vocabulary Builder

Word List

communal   distinct   hoarding   integration   justifies   promote

A. DIRECTIONS: *Use the italicized word in each sentence in a sentence of your own.*

1. Chief George seeks to *promote* a greater understanding of Native American culture.

   _____

2. Chief George suggests that *communal* living teaches people to respect one another.

   _____

3. A critical situation sometimes *justifies* a drastic solution.

   _____

4. Social scientists can identify many *distinct* cultures in North America.

   _____

5. Native American culture does not prize the *hoarding* of private possessions.

   _____

6. Many peoples see *integration* into American culture as inevitable.

   _____

B. WORD STUDY: *The Latin root -just means "law" or "right." Read the following sentences. Use your knowledge of the Latin root -just to write a full sentence to answer each question.*

1. If a decision is *unjust*, is it fair?

   _____

2. If there is no *justification* for your mistake, are you free from blame?

   _____

3. Is a *justifiable* complaint one that should be taken seriously?

   _____

Name _____ Date _____

Writing About the Big Question

What should we learn?

Big Question Vocabulary

analyze	curiosity	discover	evaluate	examine
experiment	explore	facts	information	inquire
interview	investigate	knowledge	question	understand

A. *Choose one word from the list above and use it to complete each sentence. There may be more than one right answer.*

1. Imagine the places you could _____ if you knew how to fly.

2. Children often like to _____ with different personalities.

3. Judith seems to _____ her parents' feelings very well.

B. *Follow the directions in responding to each of the items below.*

1. List two different times that you learned something new about your parents. Write your response in complete sentences.

_____

_____

2. Choose one of the experiences you listed in number 1. Write two or more sentences describing that experience. Use at least two of the Big Question vocabulary words. You may use the words in different forms (for example you can change *analyze* to *analyzing*).

_____

_____

C. *Complete the sentence below. Use the completed sentence as the beginning of a short paragraph in which you discuss the big question.*

Family connections are _____

_____

_____.

Name _____ Date _____

"Volar: To Fly" by Judith Ortiz Cofer

Reading: Make Connections Between Key Points and Supporting Details to Understand the Main Idea

The **main idea** is the most important thought or concept in a work or a passage of text. Sometimes, the author directly states the main idea of a work and then provides key points that support it. These key points are supported in turn by details such as examples and descriptions. Other times, the main idea is unstated. The author gives *only* the key points or supporting details that add up to a main idea. To understand the main idea, **make connections between key points and supporting details.** Notice how the writer groups details. Look for sentences that pull details together.

In this passage from "Volar: To Fly," Judith Ortiz Cofer states a key point and provides details that support the main idea of the essay:

> At twelve I was an avid consumer of comic books—*Supergirl* being my favorite. I spent my allowance of a quarter a day on two twelve-cent comic books or a double issue for twenty-five. I had a stack of *Legion of Super Heroes* and *Supergirl* comic books in my bedroom closet that was as tall as I.

DIRECTIONS: *Write the main point of Cofer's essay "Volar: To Fly" on the line below. Then, read each passage, and write its key point and the details that support it.*

Main idea: _____

From up there, over the rooftops, I could see everything, even beyond the few blocks of our barrio; with my X-ray vision I could look inside the homes of people who interested me. Once I saw our landlord, whom I knew my parents feared, sitting in a treasure-room dressed in an ermine coat and a large gold crown. He sat on the floor counting his dollar bills. I played a trick on him. Going up to his building's chimney, I blew a little puff of my super-breath into his fireplace, scattering his stacks of money so that he had to start counting all over again.

1. **Key point:** _____

2. **Details:** _____

I could more or less program my Supergirl dreams in those days by focusing on the object of my current obsession. This way I "saw" into the private lives of my teachers, and in the last days of my childish fantasy and the beginning of adolescence, into the secret room of the boys I liked.

3. **Key point:** _____

4. **Details:** _____

"Volar: To Fly" by Judith Ortiz Cofer
Literary Analysis: Reflective Essay

A **reflective essay** is a brief prose work that presents a writer's feelings and thoughts, or reflections, about an experience or idea. The purpose is to communicate these thoughts and feelings so that readers will respond with thoughts and feelings of their own. As you read a reflective essay, think about the ideas the writer is sharing. Think about whether your responses to the experience or idea are similar to or different from the writer's.

In this passage from "Volar: To Fly," Judith Ortiz Cofer describes the view from her kitchen window:

> The view was of a dismal alley that was littered with refuse thrown from windows. The space was too narrow for anyone larger than a skinny child to enter safely, so it was never cleaned.

Judith Ortiz Cofer considers this view and dreams of flying away from the city.

A. DIRECTIONS: *In the second column of the chart, summarize Judith Ortiz Cofer's thoughts about each experience described in the first column. Then, in the third column, write your response. That is, describe your own thoughts on the subject.*

Experience	Author's Thoughts	My Thoughts
1. Reading comic books		
2. "Seeing" her neighbors and friends in dreams		
3. Overhearing her mother's desire to fly		

B. DIRECTIONS: *Write the first paragraph of a reflective essay of your own. Include a description of an experience and your thoughts about it. Write on one of these topics:*

- the role of nature in your life
- the importance of tradition in your life
- the meaning of family in your life

_____

_____

_____

_____

_____

"Volar: To Fly" by Judith Ortiz Cofer
Vocabulary Builder

Word List

adolescence   avid   dismal   interrupted   obsession   refuse

A. DIRECTIONS: *Use the italicized word in each sentence in a sentence of your own.*

1. Before she reached *adolescence*, Judith Ortiz Cofer dreamed of flying.

   _____

2. Judith Ortiz Cofer was an *avid* reader of comic books.

   _____

3. The view out of the kitchen window was *dismal*.

   _____

4. As a child, Judith Ortiz Cofer never *interrupted* her parents' quiet time together.

   _____

5. Sometimes an *obsession* can affect our dreams.

   _____

6. *Refuse* littered the air shaft outside of Judith Ortiz Cofer's childhood apartment.

   _____

B. WORD STUDY: *The Latin root -rupt- means "break" or "burst." Read the following sentences. Use your knowledge of the Latin root -rupt- to write a full sentence to answer each question.*

1. Would a quiet conversation *disrupt* science class?

   _____

2. If a water main *ruptured*, would traffic be heavy?

   _____

3. Could a baby sleep through a *disruption*?

   _____

"I Am a Native of North America" by Chief Dan George
"Volar: To Fly" by Judith Ortiz Cofer
Integrated Language Skills: Grammar

Prepositions and Prepositional Phrases

A **preposition** relates a noun or pronoun that follows the preposition to another word in the sentence. In *The key is in the lock,* the preposition *in* relates *lock* to *key.* These are some common prepositions:

above	beyond	in	of	over	under
behind	for	inside	on	through	up
below	from	into	outside	to	with

A **prepositional phrase** begins with a preposition and ends with the noun or pronoun that follows it. In *The key is in the lock,* the prepositional phrase is *in the lock.*

A. DIRECTIONS: *The following sentences are from "I Am a Native of North America" and "Volar: To Fly." In each sentence, underline each preposition and circle the prepositional phrases.*

1. I blew a little puff of my super-breath into his fireplace.
2. I can still see him as the sun rose above the mountaintop in the early morning.
3. There was a deep respect for everything in nature.
4. In my dream I climbed the stairs to the top of our apartment building.
5. I could look inside the homes of people who interested me.
6. In the course of my lifetime I have lived in two distinct cultures.
7. I remember, as a little boy, fishing with him up Indian River.
8. I could see everything, even beyond the few blocks of our barrio.

B. Writing Application: *Write a paragraph about an artistic talent that you or someone you know possesses. Use at least three prepositional phrases. Underline each preposition, and circle the prepositional phrases.*

_____

_____

_____

_____

_____

_____

"I Am a Native of North America" by Chief Dan George
"Volar: To Fly" by Judith Ortiz Cofer

Integrated Language Skills: Support for Writing an Outline

To prepare to write an **outline** of "I Am a Native of North America" or "Volar: To Fly," create a word web. Write the main idea in the center circle. In each of the circles around it, write a key point. In the circles around each key point, write details that support the key point.

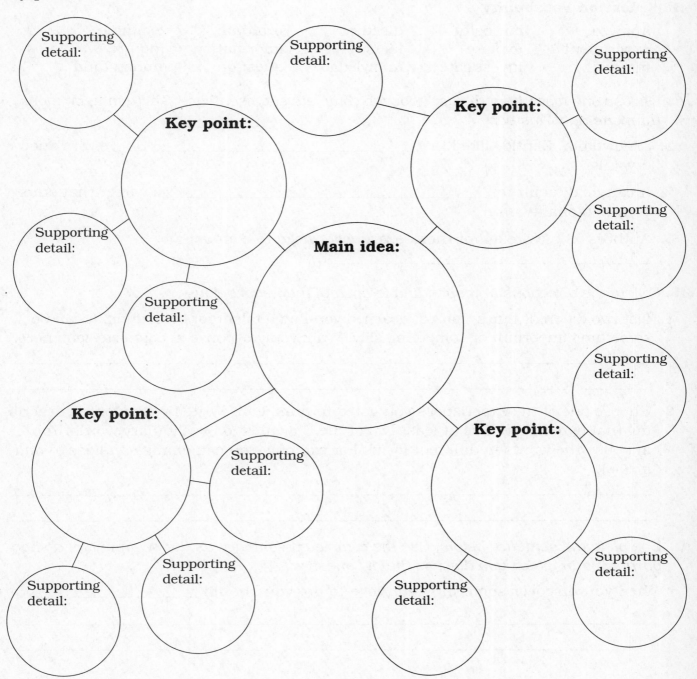

Now, use your word web to make an outline of the essay.

"A Special Gift: The Legacy of Snowflake Bentley" by Barbara Eaglesham
"No Gumption" by Russell Baker

Writing About the Big Question

What should we learn?

Big Question Vocabulary

analyze	curiosity	discover	evaluate	examine
experiment	explore	facts	information	inquire
interview	investigate	knowledge	question	understand

A. *Choose one word from the list above to complete each sentence. There may be more than one right answer.*

1. "Snowflake" Bentley liked to _____ with snow crystals.

2. It can be difficult to _____ a career that suits your personality.

3. Authors who write about themselves never need to conduct an

_____ .

B. *Follow the directions in responding to each of the items below.*

1. List two different times that you learned you had a talent for something. It can be something important or something silly. Write your response in complete sentences.

_____

_____

2. Choose one of the experiences you listed in number 1. Write two sentences describing that experience. Use at least two of the Big Question vocabulary words. You may use the words in different forms (for example you can change *analyze* to *analyzing*).

_____

_____

C. *Complete the sentence below. Use the completed sentence as the beginning of a short paragraph in which you discuss the big question.*

When you discover something you love to do, you should _____

_____

_____ .

"A Special Gift: The Legacy of 'Snowflake' Bentley" by Barbara Eaglesham
"No Gumption" by Russell Baker

Literary Analysis: Comparing Biography and Autobiography

In an **autobiography**, a person tells his or her own life story. Writers may write about their own experiences to explain their actions, to provide insight into their choices, or to show the personal side of an event.

In contrast, in a **biography**, a writer tells the life story of another person. Writers of biographies often write to analyze a person's experiences and actions. Biographies often present their subject as an example from which readers can learn a lesson.

Some biographies and autobiographies are short essays that focus on a particular episode in the subject's life.

Both biography and autobiography focus on actual events and offer insight to explain a person's actions or ideas. However, the forms have these important differences:

Biography	**Autobiography**
• More objective	• More personal
• Based on research	• Based on memory and emotion

A. Read the following sentences. Determine whether they belong to an autobiography or a biography. Use the line provided to explain your answer.

1. I was born in Detroit during the Depression.

   _____ **autobiography/biography Explanation:** _____
   _____

2. As children, my brother and I often whispered secrets late into the night.

   _____ **autobiography/biography Explanation:** _____
   _____

3. Historians agree that Jimmy Carter has been very productive since he left the presidency.

   _____ **autobiography/biography Explanation:** _____
   _____

B. Complete the following sentences:

1. Autobiographies are _____, _____, _____.
   One thing I like about autobiographies is _____.

2. Biographies are _____, _____, _____. I
   would like to read a biography of the following people: _____.

All-in-One Workbook
149

Name _____ Date _____

"A Special Gift: The Legacy of 'Snowflake' Bentley" by Barbara Eaglesham
"No Gumption" by Russell Baker
Vocabulary Builder

Word List

aptitude	crucial	evaporated	gumption
hexagons	microscope	negatives	paupers

A. DIRECTIONS: *Use the italicized word in each sentence in a sentence of your own.*

1. Russell Baker had an *aptitude* for writing.

_____

2. Baker's mother thinks gumption is *crucial* to success in life.

_____

3. The snow crystals *evaporated* quickly.

_____

4. *Gumption* may be something you are born with.

_____

5. Honeycombs are a grid of *hexagons*.

_____

6. Ordinary objects look different under the *microscope*.

_____

7. *Negatives* must not get wet.

_____

8. He achieved great success, even though his father and grandfather were *paupers*.

_____

B. DIRECTIONS: *Write the letter of the word that is most similar in meaning to the word from the Word List.*

____ 1. aptitude
   A. talent   B. desire   C. joy   D. luck

____ 2. crucial
   A. dull   B. ugly   C. minor   D. important

____ 3. evaporated
   A. vanished   B. melted   C. dried up   D. disappeared

____ 4. gumption
   A. talent   B. drive   C. personality   D. good looks

____ 5. hexagons
   A. six-sided figures   B. shapes   C. curses   D. seven-sided figures

____ 6. paupers
   A. poor people   B. dancers   C. thieves   D. leaders

"A Special Gift: The Legacy of 'Snowflake' Bentley" by Barbara Eaglesham
"No Gumption" by Russell Baker
Writing Support for Comparing Literary Works

	(Biography) "Snowflake" Bentley	(Autobiography) Russell Baker
How was each character influenced by his parents?		
What is your overall impression of the person?		
What kind of information helped you form your opinion?		
Which person do you feel you understand better?		

Now, use your notes to write an essay in which you compare and contrast what you learned about "Snowflake" Bentley with what you learned about Russell Baker.

"The Eternal Frontier" by Louis L'Amour
Writing About the Big Question

What should we learn?

Big Question Vocabulary

analyze	curiosity	discover	evaluate	examine
experiment	explore	facts	information	inquire
interview	investigate	knowledge	question	understand

A. *Choose one word from the list above to complete each sentence. There may be more than one right answer.*

1. Do you believe the desire to _____ is part of human nature?

2. Astronauts need the traits of bravery and _____.

3. I read an interesting _____ with a space shuttle astronaut.

B. *Follow the directions in responding to each of the items below.*

1. What do you think can be learned from space travel? Write at least two complete sentences, using one or more of the Big Question vocabulary words. You may use the words in different forms (for example you can change *analyze* to *analyzing*).

   _____

   _____

2. What do you think can be learned from traveling to another city, state or country? Write at least two complete sentences, using one or more of the Big Question vocabulary words. You may use the words in different forms (for example you can change *experiment* to *experiments*).

   _____

   _____

C. *Complete the sentence below. Use the completed sentence as the beginning of a short paragraph in which you discuss the big question.*

When we stop asking questions about the unknown _____

_____

_____

"The Eternal Frontier" by Louis L'Amour
Reading: Fact and Opinion

When you read nonfiction, it is important to be able to distinguish between fact and opinion. A **fact** is something that can be proved true. An **opinion** is a person's judgment or belief. It may be supported by factual evidence, but it cannot be proven.

As you read, **recognize clue words that indicate an opinion,** as in the phrases "I believe" and "in my opinion." Also look for words such as *always, never, must, cannot, best, worst,* and *all,* which may indicate a broad statement that reveals a personal judgment. Emotional statements are also often clues to opinion.

You can tell that the statement below from "The Eternal Frontier" is an opinion because it cannot be proven. Another hint is that it contains the word *must.*

What is needed now is leaders with perspective; we need leadership on a thousand fronts, but they must be men and women who can take the long view and help to shape the outlines of our future.

DIRECTIONS: *Identify each of the following quotations from "The Eternal Frontier" as a* fact *or an* opinion. *Then, briefly explain your answer. For quotations identified as opinions, point out any words or phrases that indicate it is an opinion.*

1. "All that has gone before is preliminary."

   Fact / Opinion: _____ **Explanation:** _____

   _____

2. "In 1900 there were 144 miles of surfaced road in the United States. Now there are over 3,000,000."

   Fact / Opinion: _____ **Explanation:** _____

   _____

3. "There will always be the nay-sayers, those who cling to our lovely green planet as a baby clings to its mother."

   Fact / Opinion: _____ **Explanation:** _____

   _____

4. "We have a driving need to see what lies beyond [the frontier] . . ."

   Fact / Opinion: _____ **Explanation:** _____

   _____

5. "We landed men on the moon; we sent a vehicle beyond the limits of the solar system, a vehicle still moving farther and farther into that limitless distance."

   Fact / Opinion: _____ **Explanation:** _____

   _____

6. "Nor is the mind of man bound by any limits at all."

   Fact / Opinion: _____ **Explanation:** _____

   _____

Name _____ Date _____

"The Eternal Frontier" by Louis L'Amour
Literary Analysis: Persuasive Essay

A **persuasive essay** is a piece of nonfiction that presents a series of arguments to convince readers that they should believe or act in a certain way. Below are some techniques that are often used in persuasive essays. When you read a persuasive essay, be aware of these techniques; you will need to decide whether they are powerful enough to persuade you to accept the author's ideas.

- **Appeals to authority:** using the opinions of experts and well-known people
- **Appeals to emotion:** using words that convey strong feeling
- **Appeals to reason:** using logical arguments backed by statistics and facts

DIRECTIONS: *In the left-hand column of the following chart, copy down statements from "The Eternal Frontier" that include appeals to emotion. In the right-hand column, copy down statements that include appeals to reason. Find at least two examples of each kind of appeal. (The essay does not make any appeals to authority.)*

Appeals to Emotion	Appeals to Reason

"The Eternal Frontier" by Louis L'Amour
Vocabulary Builder

Word List

antidote	atmospheric	destiny	frontier	impetus	preliminary

A. DIRECTIONS: *Answer each question in a complete sentence. In your answer, use one of the Word List words in place of the italicized word or phrase.*

1. What *unexplored region* might you want to learn more about?

   _____

2. Can you recommend a *cure* for an hour spent working in the hot sun?

   _____

3. What is the *driving force* behind studying for a test?

   _____

4. What kind of examination might be given *before* a major examination?

   _____

5. What is one important use of the gases *surrounding Earth*?

   _____

6. Do you believe humankind will find its *future* in space?

   _____

B. WORD STUDY: *The Latin root -peti- means "to ask for," "to request," or "to strive after." Read the following sentences. Use your knowledge of the Latin root -peti- to write a full sentence to answer each question. Include the italicized word in your answer.*

1. When you *petition* your principal, are you hoping for a response?

   _____

2. Can *competition* motivate a person to improve her skills?

   _____

3. Does *repetition* help you learn new words?

   _____

"**All Together Now**" by Barbara Jordan
Writing About the Big Question

What should we learn?

Big Question Vocabulary

analyze	curiosity	discover	evaluate	examine
experiment	explore	facts	information	inquire
interview	investigate	knowledge	question	understand

A. *Replace the italicized word in the sentence below with one of the vocabulary words above. The meaning of the sentence should stay the same. There may be more than one right answer.*

1. The *details* Barbara Jordan shared in her essay changed the way I saw race relations _____.

2. Barbara Jordan wants us to *study* our own circle of friends _____.

3. It is interesting to *think about* what makes people prejudiced _____.

B. *Follow the directions in responding to each of the items below.*

1. Describe one person you have met who was very different from you. Write your response in complete sentences. Use at least one of the Big Question vocabulary words. You may use the words in different forms (for example you can change *explore* to *exploration*).

_____

_____

2. Write two sentences describing what you learned from the person described in question 1. Use at least one of the Big Question vocabulary words. You may use the words in different forms (for example, you can change *analyze* to *analyzing*).

_____

_____

C. *Complete the sentence below. Use the completed sentence as the beginning of a short paragraph in which you discuss the Big Question.*

Asking questions can help _____

_____

_____

All-in-One Workbook
156

"All Together Now" by Barbara Jordan
Reading: Fact and Opinion

When you read nonfiction, it is important to be able to distinguish between fact and opinion. A **fact** is something that can be proven true. An **opinion** is a person's judgment or belief. It may be supported by factual evidence, but it cannot be proven.

As you read, **recognize clue words that indicate an opinion,** as in the phrases "I believe" and "In my opinion." Also look for words such as *always, never, must, cannot, best, worst,* and *all,* which may indicate a broad statement that reveals a personal judgment. Emotional statements are also often clues to opinion.

You can tell that this statement from "All Together Now" is an opinion because it cannot be proven. Another hint is that it contains the phrase "I don't believe":

> Frankly, I don't believe that the task of bringing us all together can be accomplished by government.

DIRECTIONS: *Identify each of the following quotations from "All Together Now" as a* fact *or an* opinion. *Then, briefly explain your answer. For quotations identified as opinions, point out any words or phrases that indicate it is an opinion.*

1. President Lyndon B. Johnson pushed through the Civil Rights Act of 1964, which remains the fundamental piece of civil rights legislation in this century.

   Fact / Opinion: _____ **Explanation:** _____

   _____

2. One thing is clear to me: We, as human beings, must be willing to accept people who are different from ourselves.

   Fact / Opinion: _____ **Explanation:** _____

   _____

3. Children learn ideas and attitudes from the adults who nurture them.

   Fact / Opinion: _____ **Explanation:** _____

   _____

4. I absolutely believe that children do not adopt prejudices unless they absorb them from their parents or teachers.

   Fact / Opinion: _____ **Explanation:** _____

   _____

5. It is possible for all of us to work on this at home, in our schools, at our jobs.

   Fact / Opinion: _____ **Explanation:** _____

   _____

Name _____ Date _____

Literary Analysis: Persuasive Essay

A **persuasive essay** is a piece of nonfiction that presents a series of arguments to convince readers that they should believe or act in a certain way. Below are some techniques that are often used in persuasive essays. When you read a persuasive essay, be aware of these techniques; you will need to decide whether they are powerful enough to persuade you to accept the author's ideas.

- **Appeals to authority:** using the opinions of experts and well-known people
- **Appeals to emotion:** using words that convey strong feeling
- **Appeals to reason:** using logical arguments backed by statistics and facts

DIRECTIONS: *In the first column of the following chart, copy statements from "All Together Now" that include appeals to authority. In the second column, copy statements that include appeals to emotion. In the third column, copy statements that include appeals to reason. Find at least one example of each kind of appeal.*

Appeals to Authority	Appeals to Emotion	Appeals to Reason

"All Together Now" by Barbara Jordan
Vocabulary Builder

Word List

culminated   equality   fundamental   legislation   optimist   tolerant

A. DIRECTIONS: *Answer each question in a complete sentence. In your answer, use one of the Word List words in place of the italicized word or phrase.*

1. In what way have civil rights *laws* changed this country?

   _____

2. What is the *basic* rule for getting along with others?

   _____

3. What happens when people are not *accepting* of others' differences?

   _____

4. Are you *someone who takes the most hopeful view of matters*?

   _____

5. Barbara Jordan's career *reached its highest point* when she was elected to the United States House of Representatives.

   _____

6. This country was founded on the idea that everyone should enjoy *the same rights*.

   _____

B. WORD STUDY: *The Latin root -leg- means "law." Use your knowledge of the Latin root -leg- to write a full sentence to answer each question. Include the italicized word in your answer.*

1. Is a thief likely to give a *legitimate* account of his actions?

   _____

2. Would you expect an honest person to do something *illegal*?

   _____

3. Is it *legal* to cross the street when the sign reads DON'T WALK?

   _____

"**The Eternal Frontier**" by Louis L'Amour
"**All Together Now**" by Barbara Jordan
Integrated Language Skills: Grammar

Subjects and Predicates

Every sentence has two parts: the **subject** and the **predicate.** The **subject** describes whom or what the sentence is about. The **simple subject** is the noun or pronoun that states exactly whom or what the sentence is about. The **complete subject** includes the simple subject and all of its modifiers.

The **predicate** is a verb that tells what the subject does, what is done to the subject, or what the condition of the subject is. The **simple predicate** is the verb or verb phrase that tells what the subject of the sentence does or is. It includes the simple predicate and any modifiers or complements.

In the following example, the simple subject and the simple predicate are in bold type. The complete subject is underlined once, and the complete predicate is underlined twice.

Louis L'Amour, a writer of novels about the American West, **has written** a persuasive essay about the importance of space exploration.

A. PRACTICE: *In each sentence, underline the simple subject once and the simple predicate twice.*

1. Louis L'Amour writes about the importance of space travel.

2. In L'Amour's view, outer space is the next frontier.

3. All of humankind longs for exploration and discovery.

4. According to Barbara Jordan, we can win the fight against prejudice.

5. Little children do not hate other people.

6. People learn to hate from parents and teachers.

B. WRITING APPLICATION: *In a paragraph of at least four sentences, describe a place you would like to explore. Underline each simple subject once and each simple predicate twice.*

_____

_____

_____

_____

_____

_____

_____

"The Eternal Frontier" by Louis L'Amour
"All Together Now" by Barbara Jordan
Integrated Language Skills:
Support for Writing a Persuasive Essay

Prepare to write a brief **persuasive essay** on one of the following topics:

- A letter to community leaders telling them how people in the community can promote tolerance
- A letter to government leaders advising them about space travel.

Organize your thoughts by completing the chart below. In the left-hand column, write down the goals you would like to see achieved by government or your community. In this column, explain any challenges elected officials or community members might face in trying to achieve the goal.

In the right-hand column, describe the persuasive technique you will use to make each point. Your choices are to:

- **Appeal to authority** by using opinions of experts and well-known people

- **Appeal to reason** by using logical arguments backed by facts.

- **Appeal to emotion** by using words that convey strong feelings

Points	Persuasive Techniques

Now, use the ideas you have gathered to write your persuasive letter.

"The Real Story of a Cowboy's Life" by Geoffrey C. Ward
Writing About the Big Question

 What should we learn?

Big Question Vocabulary

analyze	curiosity	discover	evaluate	examine
experiment	explore	facts	information	inquire
interview	investigate	knowledge	question	understand

A. *Replace the italicized word in the sentence below with one of the vocabulary words above. The meaning of the sentence should stay the same. There may be more than one right answer.*

1. It was a good idea to *ask* cowboys about what their lives were really like

    _____.

2. It is difficult to *estimate* how many cattle were on the range at once

    _____.

3. This essay helped me *find out about* another way of life

    _____.

B. *Follow the directions in responding to each of the items below.*

1. Write about a job that you'd like to know more about and explain why. Write your response in complete sentences. Use at least one of the Big Question vocabulary words. You may change the form of the word (for example, you can change *information* to *inform*.)

    _____

    _____

2. Write about a job that you'd never want to do and explain why. Write your response in complete sentences. Use at least one of the Big Question vocabulary words. You may change the form of the word (for example, you can change *discover* to *discovery*.)

    _____

    _____

C. *Complete the sentence below. Use the completed sentence as the beginning of a short paragraph in which you discuss the big question.*

Talking to people who participated in an event can _____

_____

_____

"The Real Story of a Cowboy's Life" by Geoffrey C. Ward
Reading: Use Resources to Check Facts

A **fact** is information you can prove. An **opinion** is a judgment.

Fact:	The big herds . . . carried with them a disease . . . that devastated domestic livestock.
Opinion:	The settlers' hostility was entirely understandable.

Be aware that some writers present opinions or beliefs as facts. To get to the truth, **use resources to check facts.**

Resource	Characteristics
almanac	a collection of facts and statistics on the climate, planets, stars, people, places, events, and so on, updated yearly
atlas	a collection of maps
biographical dictionary	an alphabetical listing of famous or historically significant persons with identifying information and dates of birth and death
dictionary	an alphabetical listing of words with their pronunciation and definition
encyclopedia	an alphabetically organized collection of articles on a broad range of subjects
reliable Web sites	Internet pages and articles on an extremely wide variety of topics, sponsored by individuals, companies, governments, and organizations

DIRECTIONS: *Read these passages from "The Real Story of a Cowboy's Life." Then, identify each one as a* fact *or an* opinion. *If the statement is a fact, indicate the best resource for checking it.*

1. Most Texas herds numbered about 2,000 head with a trail boss and about a dozen men in charge though herds as large as 15,000 were also driven north with far larger escorts.

   Fact/opinion: _____ **Resource:** _____

2. Regardless of its ultimate destination, every herd had to ford a series of rivers—the Nueces, the Guadalupe, the Brazos, the Wichita, the Red.

   Fact/opinion: _____ **Resource:** _____

3. After you crossed the Red River and got out on the open plains . . . it was sure a pretty sight to see them strung out for almost a mile, the sun shining on their horns.

   Fact/opinion: _____ **Resource:** _____

4. Initially, the land immediately north of the Red River was Indian territory, and some tribes charged tolls for herds crossing their land payable in money or beef.

   Fact/opinion: _____ **Resource:** _____

"The Real Story of a Cowboy's Life" by Geoffrey C. Ward
Literary Analysis: Word Choice and Diction

A writer's **word choice** and **diction** are important elements of his or her writing. The specific words a writer uses can make writing difficult or easy to read, formal or informal. Diction includes not only the vocabulary the writer uses but also the way in which the sentences are put together. Here are some questions writers consider when deciding which words to use:

- What does the audience already know about the topic? If an audience is unfamiliar with a topic, the writer will have to define technical vocabulary or use simpler language.
- What feeling will this work convey? Word choice can make a work serious or funny, academic or personal. The length and style of the sentences can make a work simple or complex.

In this passage from "The Real Story of a Cowboy's Life," notice that the author uses both technical vocabulary (*point, swing, drag*) and informal language ("eating dust"):

> The most experienced men rode "point" and "swing," at the head and sides of the long herd; the least experienced brought up the rear, riding "drag" and eating dust.

DIRECTIONS: *Read each passage. Then, on the lines that follow, write down examples of technical vocabulary, formal language, and informal language. If there are no examples of a particular kind of language, write* none.

1. If . . . the cattle started running you'd hear that low rumbling noise along the ground and the men on herd wouldn't need to come in and tell you, you'd know—then you'd jump for your horse and get out there in the lead, trying to head them and get them into a mill before they scattered. It was riding at a dead run in the dark, with cut banks and prairie dog holes all around you, not knowing if the next jump would land you in a shallow grave.

   Technical vocabulary: _____

   Informal language: _____

   Formal language: _____

2. The big herds ruined their crops, and they carried with them a disease, spread by ticks and called "Texas fever," that devastated domestic livestock. Kansas and other territories along the route soon established quarantine lines, called "deadlines," at the western fringe of settlement, and insisted that trail drives not cross them.

   Technical vocabulary: _____

   Informal language: _____

   Formal language: _____

"The Real Story of a Cowboy's Life" by Geoffrey C. Ward
Vocabulary Builder

Word List

discipline   diversions   emphatic   gauge   longhorns   ultimate

A. DIRECTIONS: *Write the correct word from the Word List on each line.*

1. The teammates want to win the next match, but their _____ goal is to win the championship.

2. The fair offered games, rides, and a few other _____.

3. The cowboys tried to _____ the mood of the cattle by the way the animals moved and the cries they uttered.

4. Bosses like Charles Goodnight needed to impose _____ along the trail.

5. Settlers had an _____ message for cowboys: STAY OUT!

6. _____ are a type of cattle popular in Texas.

B. WORD STUDY: *The Latin root -vers- means "to turn." Use your knowledge of the Latin root -vers- to write a full sentence to answer each question. Include the italicized word in your answer.*

1. If you *reverse* direction do you go the opposite way?

   _____

2. If you behave in a *subversive* manner are you being supportive?

   _____

3. Can a *versatile* employee handle many different responsibilities?

   _____

"**Rattlesnake Hunt**" by Marjorie Kinnan Rawlings
Writing About the Big Question

What should we learn?

Big Question Vocabulary

analyze	curiosity	discover	evaluate	examine
experiment	explore	facts	information	inquire
interview	investigate	knowledge	question	understand

A. *Choose one word from the list above to complete each sentence. There may be more than one right answer.*

1. Journalists often _____ dozens of experts before writing an article.

2. Sometimes it's impossible to _____ why something frightens us.

3. The scientist did an _____ to learn how many rattlesnakes he could catch.

B. *Follow the directions in responding to each of the items below.*

1. Write about a time when you learned about something that frightens you. Write your response in complete sentences. Use at least one of the Big Question vocabulary words. You may use the words in different forms (for example you can change *analyze* to *analyzing*).

_____

_____

2. Write about a common fear you find difficult to understand. Write your response in complete sentences. Use at least one of the Big Question vocabulary words. You may use the words in different forms (for example you can change *analyze* to *analyzing*).

_____

_____

C. *Complete the sentence below. Use the completed sentence as the beginning of a short paragraph in which you discuss the big question.*

The more we understand something, _____

_____

_____

"Rattlesnake Hunt" by Marjorie Kinnan Rawlings
Reading: Use Resources to Check Facts

A **fact** is information you can prove. An **opinion** is a judgment.

Fact: Ross Allen is a young herpetologist from Florida.

Opinion: "The scientific and dispassionate detachment of the material and the man made a desirable approach to rattlesnake territory."

Be aware that some writers present opinions or beliefs as facts. To get to the truth, **use resources to check facts.** You can confirm whether a statement is accurate by using one of these resources:

Resource	Characteristics
almanac	a collection of facts and statistics on the climate, planets, stars, people, places, events and so on, updated yearly
atlas	a collection of maps
geographical dictionary	an alphabetical listing of places with statistical and factual information about them and perhaps some maps
dictionary	an alphabetical listing of words with their pronunciations and definitions
encyclopedia	an alphabetically organized collection of articles on a broad range of subjects
reliable Web sites	Internet pages and articles on an extremely wide variety of topics, sponsored by individuals, companies, governments, and organizations

DIRECTIONS: *Read these passages from and about "Rattlesnake Hunt." Then, identify each one as a* fact *or an* opinion. *If the statement is a fact, indicate the best resource for checking it.*

1. Big Prairie, Florida, is south of Arcadia and west of the northern tip of Lake Okeechobee.

   Fact/opinion: _____ **Resource:** _____

2. Snakes take on the temperature of their surroundings. They can't stand too much heat for that reason, and when the weather is cool, as now, they're sluggish.

   Fact/opinion: _____ **Resource:** _____

3. Snakes are not cold and clammy.

   Fact/opinion: _____ **Resource:** _____

4. The next day was magnificent. The air was crystal, the sky was aquamarine.

   Fact/opinion: _____ **Resource:** _____

5. A rattler will lie quietly without revealing itself if a man passes by and it thinks it is not seen.

   Fact/opinion: _____ **Resource:** _____

"**Rattlesnake Hunt**" by Marjorie Kinnan Rawlings
Literary Analysis: Word Choice and Diction

A writer's **word choice** and **diction** are important elements of his or her writing. The specific words a writer uses can make writing difficult or easy to read, formal or informal. Diction includes not only the vocabulary the writer uses but also the way in which the sentences are put together. Here are some questions writers consider when deciding which kinds of words to use:

- What does the audience already know about the topic? If an audience is unfamiliar with a topic, the writer will have to define technical vocabulary or use simpler language.
- What feeling will this work convey? Word choice can make a work serious or funny, academic or personal. The length or style of the sentences can make a work simple or complex.

In this passage from "Rattlesnake Hunt," note that the author uses formal language and difficult vocabulary, but she also uses the informal word *varmints*:

> The scientific and dispassionate detachment of the material and the man made a desirable approach to rattlesnake territory. As I had discovered with the insects and varmints, it is difficult to be afraid of anything about which enough is known.

DIRECTIONS: *Read each passage. Then, on the lines that follow, write down examples of technical vocabulary, formal language, and informal language. If there are no examples of a particular kind of language, write* none.

1. They lived in winter, he said, in gopher holes, coming out in the midday warmth to forage, and would move ahead of the flames and be easily taken.

   Technical vocabulary: _____

   Informal language: _____

   Formal language: _____

2. After the rattlers, water snakes seemed innocuous enough. We worked along the edge of the stream and here Ross did not use his L-shaped steel.

   Technical vocabulary: _____

   Informal language: _____

   Formal language: _____

3. Yet having learned that it was we who were the aggressors; that immobility meant complete safety; that the snakes, for all their lightning flash in striking, were inaccurate in their aim, ... suddenly I understood that I was drinking in freely the magnificent sweep of the horizon, with no fear of what might be at the moment under my feet.

   Technical vocabulary: _____

   Informal language: _____

   Formal language: _____

"Rattlesnake Hunt" by Marjorie Kinnan Rawlings
Vocabulary Builder

Word List

adequate   arid   desolate   forage   mortality   translucent

A. DIRECTIONS: *Write* true *if a statement is true and* false *if it is false. Then, explain your answer.*

1. If a region is *arid*, crops will grow there easily.

   True/false: _____ **Explanation:** _____

   _____

2. If a character in a book faces his *mortality*, he believes he will live forever.

   True/false: _____ **Explanation:** _____

   _____

3. If a scene in a movie is set in a *desolate* location, the mood will likely be lonely.

   True/false: _____ **Explanation:** _____

   _____

4. If you will be around dangerous animals, it is important to take *adequate* precautions.

   True/false: _____ **Explanation:** _____

   _____

5. *Forage* can be an important part of cattle's diet.

   True/false: _____ **Explanation:** _____

   _____

6. Windows are never *translucent*.

   True/false: _____ **Explanation:** _____

   _____

B. WORD STUDY: *The Latin root* -sol- *means "alone." Use your knowledge of the Latin root* -sol- *to write a full sentence to answer each question. Include the italicized word in your answer.*

1. How many people can play a game of *solitaire*?

   _____

2. If you seek *solitude*, do you want others around?

   _____

3. Would many people play a *solo* at one time?

   _____

"The Real Story of a Cowboy's Life" by Geoffrey C. Ward
"Rattlesnake Hunt" by Marjorie Kinnan Rawlings
Integrated Language Skills: Grammar

Compound Subjects and Predicates

A **compound subject** contains two or more subjects that share the same verb. A **compound predicate** contains two or more verbs that share the same subject. Both compound subjects and compound predicates are joined by conjunctions such as *and, or, but,* and *nor.*

Compound subject:	Discipline *and* planning were essential to the success of a cattle drive.
Compound predicate:	"The snake did not coil, *but* lifted its head *and* whirred its rattles lightly."

A. PRACTICE: *In these sentences, underline the compound subjects once and the compound predicates twice.*

1. On trail rides, cowboys keep the herd together and guide them along the trail.
2. Trail bosses and cowboys work together to keep the cattle safe.
3. Sometimes bosses pay homesteaders or face their anger.
4. Most trail bosses forbid gambling and punish cowboys for drinking.
5. Rattlesnakes warn intruders but strike quickly.
6. Snakes and other reptiles are cold-blooded.
7. Sun and warm temperatures bring snakes out of hiding.
8. Snake catchers must move carefully or suffer the consequences.

B. Writing Application: *Imagine that you are describing an attempt at catching a rattlesnake. Follow these instructions.*

1. Write a sentence with a compound predicate; use *walked* and *searched.*

   _____

   _____

2. Write a sentence with a compound subject; use *insects* and *snakes.*

   _____

   _____

3. Write a sentence with a compound predicate; use *hissed* and *rattled.*

   _____

   _____

4. Write a sentence with a compound predicate; use *found* and *caught.*

   _____

   _____

"The Real Story of a Cowboy's Life" by Geoffrey C. Ward
"Rattlesnake Hunt" by Marjorie Kinnan Rawlings

Integrated Language Skills: Support for Writing an Adaptation

Prepare to write an **adaptation** of one of the incidents described in "Rattlesnake Hunt" or "The Real Story of a Cowboy's Life," by completing the following graphic organizer. First note the incident you plan to adapt and the audience you plan to present your adaptation to. For examples, tell the incident to a group of kinder-gartners or a class of students learning English. Then, in the first column of the chart, copy down the incident. In the second column, write your adaptation, keeping your audience in mind. Finally, look carefully at your adaptation. See if you can simplify it even further. In the last column, note your revisions.

Incident: _____

Audience: _____

Passage	Adaptation	Revision of Adaptation

Now, use your notes to write a final draft of your adaptation.

"Alligator" by Bailey White
"The Cremation of Sam McGee" by Robert Service
Writing About the Big Question

What should we learn?

Big Question Vocabulary

analyze	curiosity	discover	evaluate	examine
experiment	explore	facts	information	inquire
interview	investigate	knowledge	question	understand

A. *Choose one word from the list above to complete each sentence. There may be more than one right answer.*

1. I think _____ made the alligator visit shore.

2. The characters in "The Cremation of Sam McGee" hoped to _____ gold.

3. I would like to _____ the Yukon.

B. *Follow the directions in responding to each of the items below.*

1. Write about what makes you laugh. Write your response in complete sentences. Use at least one of the Big Question vocabulary words. You may use the words in different forms (for example you can change *analyze* to *analyzing*).

   _____

   _____

2. Explain one way you think laughter is important. Write your response in complete sentences. Use at least one of the Big Question vocabulary words. You may use the words in different forms.

   _____

   _____

C. *Complete the sentence below. Use the completed sentence as the beginning of a short paragraph in which you discuss the big question.*

   The funniest things happen when _____

   _____

   _____ .

Name _____ Date _____

"Alligator" by Bailey White
"The Cremation of Sam McGee" by Robert Service
Literary Analysis: Comparing Humorous Essays

Humorous essays are works of nonfiction meant to amuse readers. To entertain, authors may use one or more of these comic techniques:

- presenting an illogical, inappropriate, improper, or unusual situation
- contrasting reality with characters' mistaken views
- exaggerating the truth or exaggerating the feelings, ideas, and actions of characters

While most humorists want to entertain the reader, many also want to convey a serious message.

Writers of humorous essays often develop the humor through the characters they present. For example, humorous characters are central to "Alligator" and "The Cremation of Sam McGee."

DIRECTIONS: *Explain your answers to the following questions, using examples from the selections.*

Question	"Alligator"	"The Cremation of Sam McGee"
1. Does the essay describe illogical, inappropriate, improper, or unusual situations?		
2. Does the writer contrast reality with characters' mistaken views?		
3. Does the writer exaggerate the truth or the feelings, ideas, and actions of characters?		
4. Which character did you find the most humorous? How is that character's appearance described? How are his or her actions described? What does the character say, or what do other characters say about him or her, to add to the humor?		

"Alligator" by Bailey White
"The Cremation of Sam McGee" by Robert Service
Vocabulary Builder

Word List

bellow   cattails   exultant   loathed   whimper

A. DIRECTIONS: *Read each sentence, paying attention to the italicized word from the Word List. Then, explain whether the sentence makes sense. If it does not make sense, rewrite the sentence using the Word List word correctly, or write a new sentence using the word.*

1. On our trip to the desert, we found *cattails* growing everywhere.

   Explanation: _____

   New sentence: _____

2. The crowds in the arena *bellow* when the referee makes an unfair call.

   Explanation: _____

   New sentence: _____

3. When she discovered she had come in last place, the student was *exultant*.

   Explanation: _____

   New sentence: _____

4. We hated to hear our dog *whimper* when we left him home alone.

   Explanation: _____

   New sentence: _____

5. Maria *loathed* eating things she found delicious.

   Explanation: _____

   New sentence: _____

B. DIRECTIONS: *Write the letter of the word that is most similar in meaning to the word from the Word List.*

____ **1.** exultant
   A. depressed   B. overjoyed   C. safe   D. dangerous

____ **2.** cattails
   A. plants   B. clothes   C. cat   D. pattern

____ **3.** bellow
   A. write   B. shout   C. whisper   D. read

____ **4.** whimper
   A. sing   B. shout   C. whine   D. drive

____ **5.** loathed
   A. hated   B. loved   C. cherished   D. ignored

"Alligator" by Bailey White
"The Cremation of Sam McGee" by Robert Service
Integrated Language Skills:
Support for Writing to Compare Literary Works

To prepare to write an essay **comparing humorous essays,** complete this graphic organizer.

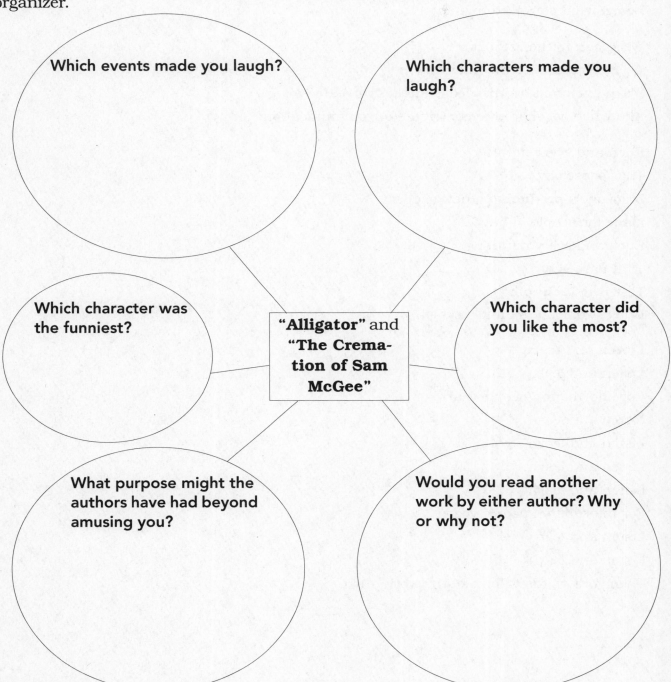

Which events made you laugh?

Which characters made you laugh?

Which character was the funniest?

"Alligator" and **"The Cremation of Sam McGee"**

Which character did you like the most?

What purpose might the authors have had beyond amusing you?

Would you read another work by either author? Why or why not?

Now, use your notes to write an essay explaining why you found "Alligator" funnier than "The Cremation of Sam McGee" or why you found "The Cremation of Sam McGee" funnier than "Alligator."

Listen & Learn, performed by Nina Zeitlin

Listen, can you hear me?
Learn what you need to know

We **speak** to the listener
We **communicate** the information
We're **enriched** by knowledge (makes us better)
And when we share, we contribute to communication

Each and every minute
That passes by
Someone's **producing** a new gadget
Made for people to buy
Each and every minute
That passes by
This new **technology**
Enters someone's mind's eye

Listen and **learn**
Listen and learn
For information people yearn
Listen and learn
Listen and learn
Listen and learn
Listen and learn
For information people yearn
Listen and learn
Listen and learn
Then your words will make the world turn

Continued

To play our favorite music

To **transmit** the words we say

Show an **entertaining** movie, or my favorite TV show

On whatever media we chose today (we chose today)

Teach ourselves how to use it

To learn and to be **informed**

To speak and to **express** ourselves

Choosing one from the other, we might be torn but

Listen and **learn**

Listen and learn

For information people yearn

Listen and learn

Listen and learn

Listen and learn

Listen and learn

For information people yearn

Listen and learn

Listen and learn

Then your words will make the world turn

There will always be something new

People **react,** they respond to the next big thing

Who's **producing** the greatest **media** toy? (**media** toy)

No matter what form of communication this year brings, ya gotta…

Listen and **learn**

Listen and learn

For information people yearn

Listen and learn

Listen and learn

Listen and learn

Listen and learn

Continued

For information people yearn

Listen and learn

Listen and learn

Then your words will make the world turn

Song Title: **Listen & Learn**

Artist / Performed by Nina Zeitlin

Guitar: Josh Green

Drums/Bass: Mike Pandolfo

Keys: Mike Pandolfo & Nina Zeitlin

Conga: Vlad Gutkovich

Lyrics by Nina Zeitlin

Music composed by Mike Pandolfo & Nina Zeitlin

Produced by Mike Pandolfo, Wonderful

Executive Producer: Keith London, Defined Mind

Unit 4: Poetry
Big Question Vocabulary—1

The Big Question: What is the best way to communicate?

communicate: *v.* to exchange information with others; other forms: *communication, communicating, communicated*

elaborate: *v.* to give more details or information about a topic

> *adj.* having a lot of small parts or details put together in a complicated way; other forms: elaborated, elaborating, elaboration

entertain: *v.* to amuse or interest others in a way that makes them happy; other forms: *entertainment, entertaining, entertained*

generate: *v.* to create or develop new ideas on a topic; other forms: *generated, generator*

listen: *v.* to pay attention to what someone is saying; other forms: *listening, listened, listener*

A. DIRECTIONS: *Read each sentence carefully. Each one describes an action that is the* **opposite** *of the action that a vocabulary word describes. Identify each vocabulary word. Write it on the line following the word* **Opposite.**

> **Example:** He wanted to *open* the door.   Opposite:_____ shut _____

1. I decided to *ignore* what he said.   **Opposite:** _____
2. Let's *simplify* this complicated issue.   **Opposite:** _____
3. He will bore the audience with that performance.   **Opposite:** _____
4. She wanted to *conceal* her ideas.   **Opposite:** _____
5. He wanted us to *use his old plans and ideas.*   **Opposite:** _____

B. DIRECTIONS: *Complete each sentence by adding the correct vocabulary word.*

1. The school principal asked the students to _____ new ideas about improving school safety.
2. If you don't _____ carefully, you won't hear the beautiful, soft call of the Baltimore oriole.
3. I didn't understand the math problem, so I asked the teacher to _____ on the directions.
4. To _____ with each other effectively, you must speak clearly and listen carefully.
5. Using rich, vivid words and humorous situations will help you to _____ your readers.

Unit 4: Poetry
Big Question Vocabulary—2

The Big Question: What is the best way to communicate?

contribute: *v.* to share or give something of value to others; other form: *contribution*

express: *v.* to use words or actions to show thoughts and feelings; other forms: *expression, expressing, expressed*

learn: *v.* to gain knowledge and understanding of information; other forms: *learning, learned*

produce: *v.* to create something; other forms: *production, producing, produced, producer*

teach: *v.* to help someone learn by giving them information; other forms: *teacher, taught*

DIRECTIONS: *List three things as instructed. Then, use the vocabulary word in a sentences about one of the things. You may use one of its other forms, as shown above.*

1. List three ways that a person might use to *express* happiness.

   _____   _____   _____

   Sentence: _____

2. List three things that grandparents and other older people can *teach* young people.

   _____   _____   _____

   Sentence: _____

3. List three things that a person might *produce* with a pencil and paper.

   _____   _____   _____

   Sentence: _____

4. List three ways that a person might *contribute* to his or her neighborhood or community.

   _____   _____   _____

   Sentence: _____

5. List three things that you consider to be the most important things for a young child to *learn*.

   _____   _____   _____

   Sentence: _____

Unit 4: Poetry
Big Question Vocabulary—3

The Big Question: What is the best way to communicate?

enrich: *v.* to improve the quality of something; other forms: *enrichment, enriching, enriched*

inform: *v.* to share facts or information with someone; other forms: *information, informed*

media: *n.* institutions or items that present news and other information, including newspapers, magazines, television programs, and Internet sources; other form: *medium*

technology: *n.* machines and equipment that are based on modern knowledge about science; other forms: *technological, technologies*

transmit: *v.* to send a message or signal, through such sources as radios, televisions, or the Internet; other forms: *transmission, transmitting, transmitted*

A. DIRECTIONS: *Give an example of each of the following.*

1. a *technology* that you use at school: _____

2. something that you *transmitted* to someone electronically: _____

3. a way to *enrich* a friendship: _____

4. a fact that you'd like to *inform* people about: _____

5. a specific form of the *media* that you respect as a news source: _____

B. DIRECTIONS: *Imagine that you are a scientist who just discovered life on another planet. On the lines below, write a summary of your findings, telling how you made your discovery, what messages the people sent to you and how they sent them, and why you feel your discovery might improve life on Earth. Use each of the vocabulary words.*

_____

_____

_____

_____

_____

_____

_____

_____

Name _____ Date _____

Unit 4: Poetry
Applying the Big Question

What is the best way to communicate?

DIRECTIONS: *Complete the chart below to apply what you have learned about communication. One row has been completed for you.*

Example	Type of communication	Purpose	Pros	Cons	What I learned
From Literature	Writing about meaningful family lessons.	To share an important life lesson.	Conveys a personal story to a broader audience.	The audience for poetry is smaller than media, such as TV.	A metaphor's lesson can apply many people.
From Literature					
From Science					
From Social Studies					
From Real Life					

Pat Mora
Listening and Viewing

Segment 1: Meet Pat Mora
- Why does Pat Mora use both English and Spanish when she writes?
- What are some reasons that it is important to read literature by or about people of many different cultures?

_____

_____

_____

_____

Segment 2: Poetry
- Why does Pat Mora write the last line of "The Desert Is My Mother" in Spanish?
- What effect do the Spanish lines in this poem have on you as a reader?

_____

_____

_____

_____

Segment 3: The Writing Process
- How does Pat Mora prepare to begin writing?
- Which one of her writing strategies would you use, and why?

_____

_____

_____

_____

Segment 4: The Rewards of Writing
- How are poetry readings particularly rewarding to Pat Mora?
- Has a certain piece of literature had a strong impact on you as a reader? Explain.

_____

_____

_____

_____

Learning About Poetry

Poetry is the most musical, and often the most imaginative, of all literary forms. A common characteristic of poetry is **figurative language,** which is writing or speech that is not meant to be taken literally, or as though it is realistic.

FIGURATIVE LANGUAGE	• **metaphor:** describes one thing as if it were something else *(You are the sunshine of my life.)*
	• **simile:** uses *like* or *as* to compare two unlike things *(Your smile is as bright as the sun.)*
	• **personification:** gives human qualities to a nonhuman thing *(The sun smiled on our picnic.)*
	• **symbol:** something that represents something else *(The flag is a symbol of our country; a dove is a symbol of peace.)*

A. DIRECTIONS: *On the lines, write the letter of the type of figurative language used in each line of poetry.*

___ 1. bubbly and bright like a mountain stream

    A. simile

___ 2. a bright lantern that welcomed me home

    B. metaphor

___ 3. your eyes are moonlight to my earth

    C. symbol

___ 4. the apple pie that means "home"

    D. personification

B. DIRECTIONS: *Follow each direction by writing an original phrase or sentence.*

1. Use a metaphor to write about the moon.

_____

2. Use a simile to write about a dog.

_____

3. Use personification to write about a clock.

_____

4. Write a sentence containing a symbol.

_____

The Poetry of Pat Mora
Model Selection: Poetry

In addition to figurative language, Pat Mora's three poems contain examples of **sound devices,** or writing or speech that adds a musical quality.

SOUND DEVICES	• **alliteration:** repetition of consonant sounds at the beginning of words (*a busy bee*)
	• **repetition:** use of a sound, word, or group of words more than once (*the beat of the drum and the beat of my heart*)
	• **onomatopoeia:** use of words that imitate sounds (*quack, bang*)
	• **rhyme:** repetition of sounds at the ends of words (*sit, lit, hit*)
	• **meter:** arrangement of stressed and unstressed syllables (*The day began at eight o'clock.*)

A. DIRECTIONS: *Answer these questions about the characteristics in Pat Mora's poems.*

1. In the first stanza of "Maestro," what verb is an example of onomatopoeia?

   _____

2. What example of repetition appears in the first five lines of "Bailando"?

   _____

3. What type of sound device is represented by the word *whispers*?

   _____

4. What type of sound device is represented by the phrase *the snow's silence*?

   _____

B. DIRECTIONS: *In these poems, Pat Mora speaks of family members. On the lines below, write your own short poem about a family member or friend. Include at least two examples of figurative language and sound devices.*

_____

_____

_____

_____

_____

"The Rider" by Naomi Shihab Nye, **"Seal"** by William Jay Smith, **Haiku** by Buson

Writing About the Big Question

What is the best way to communicate?

Big Question Vocabulary

communicate	contribute	enrich	entertain	express
inform	learn	listen	media	produce
react	speak	teach	technology	transmit

A. *Use one or more words from the list above to complete each sentence.*

1. Helping others to _____ new skills is a good way to communicate.

2. One way to communicate what you know is to _____ a skill to someone else.

3. When you _____ your knowledge to others, they find out about you as well as your subject.

4. You can use _____ such as computers to communicate your knowledge.

B. *Answer each question with a complete sentence.*

1. Write down two things you have taught another person. Use at least two of the Big Question vocabulary words.

_____

_____

2. Write two sentences explaining how you communicated the knowledge you taught.

_____

_____

C. *In "Poetry Collection 1," three poets use different forms to share their thoughts or observations. Complete these sentences:*

Through poetry, writers **communicate** _____.
I most enjoy reading poems that **express** _____.

Poetry Collection: Naomi Shihab Nye, William Jay Smith, Buson
Reading: Ask Questions to Draw a Conclusion

Drawing conclusions means arriving at an overall judgment or idea by pulling together several details. By drawing conclusions, you recognize meanings that are not directly stated. **Asking questions** can help you identify details and make connections that lead to a conclusion. You might ask yourself questions such as these:

- What details does the writer include and emphasize?
- How are the details related?
- What do the details mean all together?

Consider, for example, this haiku by Buson:

After the moon sets,

slow through the forest, shadows

drift and disappear

What do the details suggest? The moon has set, so it must be morning. Why, though, do "shadows / drift and disappear"? Is it because it has grown darker or because it has grown lighter, because the sun is rising? The reader might conclude that Buson's haiku vividly evokes the darkness that precedes dawn.

DIRECTIONS: *Complete the following chart. First, ask a question about the poem. Then, record the details that prompted the question. Finally, write a conclusion that you can draw based on the question and the related details.*

Poem	Question	Details Relating to Question	Conclusion
"The Rider"			
"Seal"			
"O foolish ducklings"			
"Deep in a windless wood"			

Name _____ Date _____

Literary Analysis: Forms of Poetry

There are many different **forms of poetry.** A poet will follow different rules depending on the structure of a poem. These are the three forms represented by the poems in this collection:

- A **lyric poem** expresses the poet's thoughts and feelings about a single image or idea in vivid, musical language.
- In a **concrete poem,** the poet arranges the letters and lines to create a visual image that suggests the poem's subject.
- **Haiku** is a traditional form of Japanese poetry that is often about nature. In a traditional haiku, the first line always has five syllables, the second line always has seven syllables, and the third line always has five syllables.

DIRECTIONS: *Write your responses to the following questions.*

1. If you were to rewrite "The Rider" as a concrete poem, what shape would you use to express the main idea of the poem? Why?

   _____

   _____

2. If you were to rewrite "Seal" as a haiku, what seven-syllable line might you write that contained the phrase "Quicksilver-quick"?

   _____

3. If you were to rewrite one of Buson's haiku as a lyric poem, on what single image would you focus? Why?

   _____

   _____

4. If you were to rewrite "The Rider" as a haiku, what would one of your lines be?

   _____

5. If you were to rewrite "Seal" as a lyric poem, how would you change it? Why?

   _____

   _____

Poetry Collection: Naomi Shihab Nye, William Jay Smith, Buson
Vocabulary Builder

Word List

luminous   minnow   swerve   translates   utter   weasel

A. DIRECTIONS: *Provide an explanation for your answer to each question.*

1. Would you be able to see *luminous* stars in a clear night sky?

   _____

   _____

2. If someone did not *utter* a word, would she be likely to win a debate?

   _____

   _____

3. Would you be likely to see a *weasel* in the Large Mammals section of a zoo?

   _____

   _____

4. Would a driver likely go into a *swerve* to avoid hitting something in the road?

   _____

   _____

5. Would you find a *minnow* in a forest?

   _____

   _____

6. If someone *translates* a poem into English, could you read it?

   _____

   _____

B. WORD STUDY: *The Latin root* -lum- *means "light." Write a sentence that answers each question, using the italicized word.*

1. If a soccer field is *illuminated*, what time of day is the game probably being played?

   _____

2. What part of the ocean is a *bioluminescent* fish likely to live in?

   _____

3. If someone is a *luminary* in the field of medicine, what do people probably think of the person?

   _____

"Winter" by Nikki Giovanni, **"Forsythia"** by Mary Ellen Solt, **Haiku** by Matsuo Bashō

Writing About the Big Question

What is the best way to communicate?

Big Question Vocabulary

communicate	contribute	enrich	entertain	express
inform	learn	listen	media	produce
react	speak	teach	technology	transmit

A. *Use one or more words from the list above to complete each sentence.*

1. One of the most direct ways to get to know someone is to _____ to the person in a conversation.

2. When you have a conversation, is it important to _____ to what the other person says.

3. The way you _____ to someone's statements may show in your face or body.

4. You can use facial expressions and body language to _____ your feelings.

B. *Answer each question with a complete sentence.*

1. Describe a facial expression and what it can communicate to another person. Use a Big Question vocabulary word in your description.

   _____

   _____

2. Describe an example of body language and what it can communicate to another person. Use a Big Question vocabulary word in your description.

   _____

   _____

C. *In "Poetry Collection 2," each poem describes an aspect of nature. Complete this sentence:*

Descriptive language can **contribute** to _____

_____

_____.

Poetry Collection: Nikki Giovanni, Mary Ellen Solt, Bashō
Reading: Ask Questions to Draw a Conclusion

Drawing conclusions means arriving at an overall judgment or idea by pulling together several details. By drawing conclusions, you recognize meanings that are not directly stated. **Asking questions** can help you identify details and make connections that lead to a conclusion. You might ask yourself questions such as these:

- What details does the writer include and emphasize?
- How are the details related?
- Taken together, what do all the details mean?

Consider, for example, this haiku by Bashō:

On sweet plum blossoms

The sun rises suddenly.

Look, a mountain path!

What do those details mean? As the sun rises, it shines on a blossoming plum tree. You can conclude that it is a spring morning.

DIRECTIONS: *Complete the following chart. First, ask a question about the poem. Then, record the details that prompted the question. Finally, write a conclusion that you can draw based on the question and the related details.*

Poem	Question	Details Relating to Question	Conclusion
"Winter"			
"Forsythia"			
"Has spring come indeed?"			
"Temple bells die out"			

Name _____ Date _____

Poetry Collection: Nikki Giovanni, Mary Ellen Solt, Bashō
Literary Analysis: Forms of Poetry

There are many different **forms of poetry.** A poet will follow different rules, depending on the structure of a poem. These are the three forms represented by poems in this collection:

- A **lyric poem** expresses the poet's thoughts and feelings about a single image or idea in vivid, musical language.
- In a **concrete poem,** the poet arranges the letters and lines to create a visual image that suggests the poem's subject.
- **Haiku** is a traditional form of Japanese poetry that is often about nature. In a traditional haiku, the first line always has five syllables, the second line always has seven syllables, and the third line always has five syllables.

DIRECTIONS: *Write your answers to the following questions.*

1. If you were to rewrite one of Bashō's haiku as a concrete poem, what shape would you use to express the main idea? Why?

   _____

   _____

   _____

2. If you were to rewrite "Winter" as a haiku, what seven-syllable line might you write that contained the phrase "Bears store fat"?

   _____

3. If you were to rewrite "Forsythia" as a lyric poem, on what single idea would you focus? Why?

   _____

   _____

   _____

4. If you were to rewrite "Forsythia" as a haiku, what would one of your lines be?

   _____

5. If you were to rewrite one of Bashō's haiku as a lyric poem, how would you change it? Why?

   _____

   _____

   _____

Poetry Collection: Nikki Giovanni, Mary Ellen Solt, Bashō
Vocabulary Builder

Word List

burrow   forsythia   fragrant   telegram

A. DIRECTIONS: *Provide an explanation for your answer to each question.*

1. Would you see a *forsythia* flowering in the fall?

   _____

2. Would a *telegram* be likely to include a long description?

   _____

3. Would an animal *burrow* in the sand to escape an enemy?

   _____

4. Would a bouquet of roses smell *fragrant*?

   _____

B. WORD STUDY: *The Greek root -gram- means "write, draw, or record." Write a sentence that answers each question, using the italicized word.*

1. What could an *electrocardiogram* show about your heart?

   _____

2. What does a *grammarian* study?

   _____

3. What might be an *anagram* of the word "bat"?

   _____

Poetry Collections: Naomi Shihab Nye, William Jay Smith, Buson;
Nikki Giovanni, Mary Ellen Solt, Bashō

Integrated Language Skills: Grammar

Infinitives and Infinitive Phrases

An **infinitive** is a verb that acts as a noun, an adjective, or an adverb. An infinitive usually begins with the word *to.*

Some dogs like *to swim.* (infinitive as a noun serving as the object of the verb *like*)

To travel is my objective. (infinitive as a noun serving as the subject of the sentence)

Paris is the city *to visit.* (infinitive as an adjective modifying the noun *city*)

Everyone waited *to hear.* (infinitive as an adverb modifying the verb *waited*)

An **infinitive phrase** is an infinitive plus its own modifiers or complements.

Some dogs like *to swim all year round.* (phrase serving as object of the verb *like*)

To travel in Europe is my objective. (phrase serving as subject of the sentence)

Paris is the city *to visit in the spring.* (phrase modifying the noun *city*)

Everyone waited *to hear the news.* (phrase modifying the verb *waited*)

A. PRACTICE: *Underline the infinitive in each sentence, and circle any infinitive phrases.*

1. In "Winter," the speaker goes outside to air her quilts.
2. To create a poem that looks like a forsythia bush was the aim of Mary Ellen Solt.
3. In "The Rider," the roller skater wants to escape his loneliness.
4. In one of Buson's haiku, "not one leaf dares to move."
5. In "Seal," the seal loves to swim fast.

B. Writing Application: *Review the poems in these collections. Then, write a sentence that captures your reaction to each poem and includes an infinitive or an infinitive phrase.*

1. **"The Rider":** _____

_____

2. **"Seal":** _____

_____

3. **One of Buson's haiku:** _____

_____

4. **"Winter":** _____

_____

5. **"Forsythia":** _____

_____

6. **One of Bashō's Haiku:** _____

_____

Name _____ Date _____

Poetry Collections: Naomi Shihab Nye, William Jay Smith, Buson; Nikki Giovanni, Mary Ellen Solt, Bashō

Integrated Language Skills: Support for Writing a Lyric Poem, Concrete Poem, or Haiku

In the chart below, write details that you might use in your poem.

Subject: _____

Vivid Descriptions	Action Words	Thoughts	Feelings

Now, use the details you have collected to draft a **lyric poem, concrete poem,** or **haiku.**

"Life" by Naomi Long Madgett, "The Courage that My Mother Had" by Edna St. Vincent Millay, "Loo-Wit" by Wendy Rose

Writing About the Big Question

What is the best way to communicate?

Big Question Vocabulary

communicate	contribute	enrich	entertain	express
inform	learn	listen	media	produce
react	speak	teach	technology	transmit

A. *Use one or more words from the list above to complete each sentence.*

1. The _____, such as newspapers and television, is a useful way to communicate.

2. News articles can _____ you about important events and issues.

3. Stories about other cultures can _____ your understanding about how others live.

4. Reading and listening to the news can _____ a greater understanding of the world.

B. *Answer each question with a complete sentence.*

1. Write two things you have learned about other cultures from newspapers or television. Use two Big Question vocabulary words in your response.

   _____

   _____

2. Explain how your knowledge of other cultures has helped you understand the world more fully. Use two Big Question vocabulary words in your response.

   _____

   _____

C. *In Poetry Collection 3, each poem includes one or more comparisons between objects or ideas. Complete this sentence:*

When you make connections between unrelated things, you **enrich**

_____ and **learn** _____.

Poetry Collection: Naomi Long Madgett, Wendy Rose, Edna St. Vincent Millay

Reading: Connect the Details to Draw a Conclusion

A **conclusion** is a decision or an opinion that you reach after considering the details in a literary work. **Connecting the details** can help you draw conclusions as you read. For example, if the speaker in a poem uses the words *spits, growls, snarls, trembling, shudder, unravel,* and *dislodge,* you might conclude that he or she is expressing dissatisfaction, anger, or some aspect of violence. As you read, identify important details. Then, look at the details together and draw a conclusion about the poem or the speaker.

DIRECTIONS: *In the first column of the chart below are details from the poems in this collection. Consider each set of details, and use them to draw a conclusion about the poem. Write your conclusion in the second column.*

Details	Conclusion
"Life": • The speaker says that life is a toy. • The toy ticks for a while, amusing an infant. • The toy, a watch, stops running.	_____ _____ _____ _____
"Loo-Wit": • The old woman is "bound" by cedar. • Huckleberry "ropes" lie around her neck. • Machinery operates on her skin.	_____ _____ _____ _____
"The Courage That My Mother Had": • The speaker's mother had courage. • The speaker has a brooch her mother wore. • The speaker wants her mother's courage.	_____ _____ _____ _____

All-in-One Workbook
197

Poetry Collection: Naomi Long Madgett, Wendy Rose, Edna St. Vincent Millay

Literary Analysis: Figurative Language

Figurative language is language that is not meant to be taken literally. Writers use figures of speech to express ideas in vivid and imaginative ways. Common figures of speech include the following:

- A **simile** compares two unlike things using a word such as *like* or *as*.
- A **metaphor** compares two unlike things by stating that one thing is another thing. In an **extended metaphor,** several related comparisons extend over a number of lines.
- **Personification** gives human characteristics to a nonhuman subject.
- A **symbol** is an object, a person, an animal, a place, or an image that represents something else.

Look at this line from "Life." What figure of speech does the speaker use?

Life is but a toy that swings on a bright gold chain.

The speaker uses a metaphor to compare life to a toy, one "that swings on a bright gold chain."

DIRECTIONS: *As you read the poems in this collection, record the similes, metaphors, extended metaphors, personification, and symbols.*

Poem	Passage	Figurative Language
"Life"		
"Loo-Wit"		
"The Courage That My Mother Had"		

Poetry Collection: Naomi Long Madgett, Wendy Rose, Edna St. Vincent Millay
Vocabulary Builder

Word List

    crouches   dislodge   fascinated   granite   prickly   unravel

A. DIRECTIONS: *Read each sentence, paying attention to the italicized word. Then, explain whether the sentence makes sense. If it does not make sense, rewrite the sentence or write a new sentence, using the italicized word correctly.*

1. The angry woman *crouches* as she stretches herself on her bumpy bed.

   Explanation: _____

   New sentence: _____

2. If you *dislodge* the stones, they may start an avalanche.

   Explanation: _____

   New sentence: _____

3. Anita was so *fascinated* by the movie that she fell asleep.

   Explanation: _____

   New Sentence: _____

4. The sweater was so well made that it began to *unravel*.

   Explanation: _____

   New sentence: _____

5. The rough wool sweater felt *prickly* and uncomfortable.

   Explanation: _____

   New Sentence: _____

6. The piece of *granite* dissolved in the hard rain.

   Explanation: _____

   New Sentence: _____

B. WORD STUDY: *The Latin suffix* -ly *means "like; in the manner of." Answer each question, using the italicized word with the suffix added.*

1. How can you tell if someone is *brave*?

   _____

2. What might a person who is *ambitious* do at work?

   _____

3. Why is it important to be *careful* when you are hiking?

   _____

"**Mother to Son**" by Langston Hughes, "**The Village Blacksmith**" by Henry Wadsworth Longfellow, "**Fog**" by Carl Sandburg

Writing About the Big Question

What is the best way to communicate?

Big Question Vocabulary

communicate	contribute	enrich	entertain	express
inform	learn	listen	media	produce
react	speak	teach	technology	transmit

A. *Use one or more words from the list above to complete each sentence.*

1. Some people like to _____ others through music, dance, or acting.

2. The arts are a good way to _____ your thoughts and feelings.

3. When you _____ to a musician or actor, you can hear the feelings of both the performer and the composer or playwright.

4. A performer can _____ thoughts and feelings in the audience, too.

B. *Answer each question with a complete sentence.*

1. Describe two times when you have listened to a musical or dramatic piece that moved you.

   _____

   _____

2. Explain how you reacted to one of the preceding experiences. Tell what feelings or thoughts it produced in you.

   _____

   _____

C. *In Poetry Collection 4, the poets use evocative language to make their poems memorable. Complete this sentence:*

Words that **express** strong emotions _____.

_____

_____

_____

_____

_____

Poetry Collection: Langston Hughes, Henry Wadsworth Longfellow, Carl Sandburg
Reading: Connect the Details to Draw a Conclusion

A **conclusion** is a decision or an opinion that you reach after considering the details in a literary work. **Connecting the details** can help you draw conclusions as you read. For example, if the speaker in a poem uses the words *tacks*, *splinters*, *boards*, *bare*, and *dark*, you might conclude that he or she wishes to create an image of hardship. As you read, identify important details. Then, look at the details together and draw a conclusion about the poem or the speaker.

DIRECTIONS: *In the first column of the chart below are details from the poems in this collection. Consider each set of details, and use them to draw a conclusion about the poem. Write your conclusion in the second column.*

Details	Conclusion
"Mother to Son": • The speaker describes the staircase she has climbed: it had tacks, splinters, bare boards, and places with no light. • The speaker is still climbing.	_____ _____ _____ _____ _____ _____
"The Village Blacksmith": • On the blacksmith's brow is "honest sweat." • The blacksmith "owes not any man." • The blacksmith works long and hard.	_____ _____ _____ _____ _____ _____
"Fog": • The fog arrives "on little cat feet." • The fog sits "on silent haunches." • The fog looks "over harbor and city / . . . and then moves on."	_____ _____ _____ _____ _____

Poetry Collection: Langston Hughes, Henry Wadsworth Longfellow, Carl Sandburg
Literary Analysis: Figurative Language

Figurative language is language that is not meant to be taken literally. Writers use figures of speech to express ideas in vivid and imaginative ways. Common figures of speech include the following:

- A **simile** compares two unlike things using a word such as *like* or *as.*
- A **metaphor** compares two unlike things by stating that one thing is another thing. In an **extended metaphor,** several related comparisons extend over a number of lines.
- **Personification** gives human characteristics to a nonhuman subject.
- A **symbol** is an object, a person, an animal, a place, or an image that represents something else.

Look at this line from "The Village Blacksmith." What figure of speech does the speaker use?

And the muscles of his brawny arms

Are strong as iron bands.

The speaker uses a simile to compare the blacksmith's muscles to iron bands.

DIRECTIONS: *As you read the poems in this collection, record the similes, metaphors, extended metaphors, personification, and symbols you find in the poems.*

Poem	Passage	Figurative Language
"Mother to Son"		
"The Village Blacksmith"		
"Fog"		

Poetry Collection: Langston Hughes, Henry Wadsworth Longfellow, Carl Sandburg
Vocabulary Builder

Word List

brawny   crystal   haunches   parson   sinewy   wrought

A. DIRECTIONS: *Read each sentence, paying attention to the italicized word. Then, explain whether the sentence makes sense. If it does not make sense, rewrite the sentence or write a new sentence, using the italicized word correctly.*

1. The cheetah sprang from its *haunches* to bring down the fleeing antelope.

   Explanation: _____

   New sentence: _____

2. Because the blacksmith was *brawny*, he easily lifted the heavy sledgehammer.

   Explanation: _____

   New sentence: _____

3. The *sinewy* construction worker could carry only the lightest loads.

   Explanation: _____

   New sentence: _____

4. The *crystal* vase shattered when it hit the ground.

   Explanation: _____

   New Sentence: _____

5. The *parson* had always been too shy to speak in public.

   Explanation: _____

   New Sentence: _____

6. The bracelet was *wrought* from white gold.

   Explanation: _____

   New Sentence: _____

B. WORD STUDY: *The Latin suffix -y means "marked by, having." Answer each question, using the italicized word with the suffix added.*

1. How does a person who feels *anger* behave?

   _____

2. How would someone who learns with *ease* probably do in school?

   _____

3. Why is it important not to make a *mess* on a test paper?

   _____

Poetry Collections: Naomi Long Madgett, Wendy Rose, Edna St. Vincent Millay;
Langston Hughes, Henry Wadsworth Longfellow, Carl Sandburg

Integrated Language Skills: Grammar

Appositives and Appositive Phrases

An **appositive** is a noun or pronoun that is placed after another noun or pronoun to identify, rename, or explain it. In the following sentence, the appositive is underlined:

> In "Fog," the poet compares an animal, a <u>cat</u>, to fog.

An **appositive phrase** is a noun or pronoun, along with any modifiers, that is placed after another noun or pronoun to identify, rename, or explain it. In the following sentence, the appositive is underlined; the words that make up the appositive phrase are in italics:

> Longfellow made the village blacksmith, *an honest and reliable <u>man</u>*, into a hero.

A. PRACTICE: *In each sentence, underline the appositive phrase. Then, circle the noun that the appositive phrase identifies or explains.*

1. Loo-Wit, a volcano, is about to erupt.
2. Death, an old man, lets the watch run down.
3. The speaker in "The Courage That My Mother Had" mentions New England, a region in the northeast.
4. The speaker in "The Courage That My Mother Had" compares her mother's courage to granite, a hard rock.
5. The village blacksmith weeps when he hears the voice of his daughter, a singer in the choir.
6. In "Mother to Son," a poem by Langston Hughes, a mother gives advice to her son.

B. Writing Application: *Use each phrase in brackets as an appositive phrase in the sentence that follows it. Set off each phrase with commas or dashes.*

1. [a beautiful golden pin] In "The Courage That My Mother Had," the speaker's mother has given the speaker a brooch.

   _____

   _____

2. [a blanket of white mist] In "Fog," fog covers a harbor.

   _____

3. [a symbol of an easy life] The mother in "Mother to Son" speaks of the crystal stair.

   _____

   _____

Name _____ Date _____

Poetry Collections: Naomi Long Madgett, Wendy Rose, Edna St. Vincent Millay; Langston Hughes, Henry Wadsworth Longfellow, Carl Sandburg

Integrated Language Skills: Support for Writing an Extended Metaphor

Use the word web below to collect ideas for an **extended metaphor** about a quality or an idea, such as love, loyalty, life, or death. Decide on the quality or idea, and then decide what you will compare it to. It may be an object, an animal, or an idea. Write your ideas in the center of the web. Then, complete the web by writing down ideas that relate to your central idea. Use vivid images and descriptive language. Your extended metaphor may include similes, metaphors, personification, and symbols.

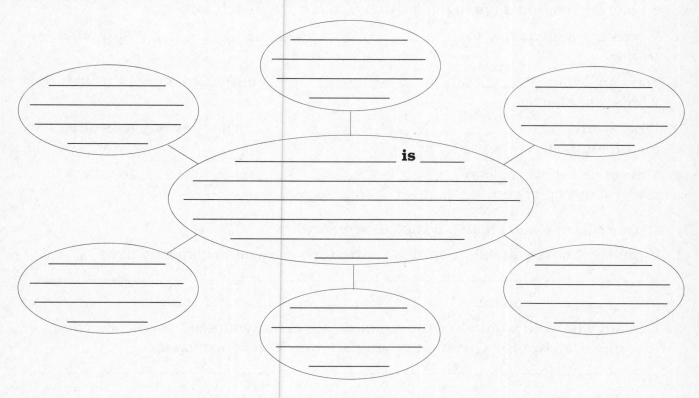

Now, use your notes to write an extended metaphor about a quality or an idea. Be sure to use vivid images and descriptive language.

"The Highwayman" by Alfred Noyes and **"How I Learned English"** by Gregory Djanikian

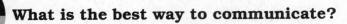

Writing About the Big Question

What is the best way to communicate?

Big Question Vocabulary

communicate	contribute	enrich	entertain	express
inform	learn	listen	media	produce
react	speak	teach	technology	transmit

A. *Use one or more words from the list above to complete each sentence.*

1. Words are a great way to _____ with other people.

2. You can _____ yourself to others through the words you choose.

3. When you _____, what you say tells others about yourself.

4. Your choice of words can _____ to others' understanding of you.

B. *Answer each question with a complete sentence.*

1. Write the words you might speak to introduce yourself to someone new.

   _____

   _____

2. Explain what you would like to communicate about yourself to someone you have just met. Use two Big Question vocabulary words in your response.

   _____

   _____

C. *In each of these narrative poems, people communicate in an unconventional way. Complete this sentence:*

_____ can be more expressive than words.

Poetry by Alfred Noyes and Gregory Djanikian
Literary Analysis: Comparing Narrative Poems

Narrative poetry combines elements of fiction and poetry to tell a story. Like short stories, narrative poetry usually includes characters, setting, plot, conflict, and point of view. Like other poems, narrative poetry uses sound devices, such as rhythm and rhyme, to bring out the musical qualities of the language. It also uses figurative language to create memorable images, or word pictures.

Narrative poetry is well suited to a wide range of stories. For example, narrative poems may tell romantic tales about knights and ladies, heroic deeds, amazing events, or larger-than-life characters. In contrast, the form may be used to relate everyday stories about ordinary people.

The poems presented in this collection blend elements of fiction and poetry in a memorable way. As you read these poems, look for ways in which each one blends the elements of narration and poetry.

DIRECTIONS: *Complete this chart about the narrative poems in this collection. In the second column, briefly describe the poem's plot and conflict. In the third column, describe the sound devices and/or figurative language in the poem.*

Poem	Plot and Conflict	Poetic Devices
"The Highwayman"		
"How I Learned English"		

Poetry by Alfred Noyes and Gregory Djanikian
Vocabulary Builder

Word List

    bound   strive   torrent   transfixed   whimper   writhing

A. DIRECTIONS: *Pay attention to the way the italicized vocabulary word is used in each sentence. Decide whether each statement is true or false. Write* T *or* F. *Then, explain your answer.*

1. If a dog were *bound* to a tree, it would be free to roam.

    T / F: _____ **Explanation:** _____

2. Someone *writhing* in pain is lying still.

    T / F: _____ **Explanation:** _____

3. A *torrent* of rain is likely to cause a river to overflow its banks.

    T / F: _____ **Explanation:** _____

4. If children *whimper,* they are probably content.

    T / F: _____ **Explanation:** _____

5. Someone *transfixed* by fear is running to escape danger.

    T / F: _____ **Explanation:** _____

6. People who *strive* are usually very lazy.

    T / F: _____ **Explanation:** _____

B. WORD STUDY: *Change each underlined word into another form from its word family. Answer the question using the new word.*

1. What can cause a small waterfall to become a *torrent*?

    _____

2. Why are people often *transfixed* when they watch a scary movie?

    _____

3. Why should a wound be *bound*?

    _____

Name _____ Date _____

Poetry by Alfred Noyes and Gregory Djanikian

Integrated Language Skills: Support for Writing to Compare Literary Works

Use this chart to take notes for an essay comparing and contrasting the stories that are told in the narrative poems in this collection.

Point of Comparison	"The Highwayman"	"How I Learned English"
Who narrates the poem? Is it a character in the poem or someone outside the poem?		
Is there any suspense? If so, when does it occur, and why?		
How do the poetic elements increase my interest in or my appreciation of the story?		

Now, use your notes to write an essay comparing and contrasting the poems' stories.

"Sarah Cynthia Sylvia Stout Would Not Take the Garbage Out" by Shell Silverstein,
"Weather" by Eve Merriam, **"One"** by James Berry

Writing About the Big Question

What is the best way to communicate?

Big Question Vocabulary

communicate	contribute	enrich	entertain	express
inform	learn	listen	media	produce
react	speak	teach	technology	transmit

A. *Use one or more words from the list above to complete each sentence.*

1. _____ has made it much faster and easier for
people to communicate.

2. It is possible to _____ messages almost
instantly.

3. One problem with this form of communication is that people don't see or
_____ directly with each other.

4. They cannot see how others _____ to what they say.

B. *Answer each question with a complete sentence.*

1. Think of a time when you sent a message using technology, such as instant
messaging or text messaging, that cause a problem. Describe how the other person
reacted to the message.

_____

_____

2. Explain how the other person would have reacted differently if you had spoken
directly with him or her.

_____

_____

C. *In "Poetry Collection 1," the poems have a pleasing musical quality. Complete this
sentence:*

The use of musical language can **produce** _____.

Poetry Collection: Shel Silverstein, Eve Merriam, James Berry

Reading: Read Aloud According to Punctuation in Order to Paraphrase

When you **paraphrase,** you restate something in your own words. To paraphrase a poem, you must first understand it. **Reading aloud according to punctuation** can help you identify complete thoughts in a poem and therefore grasp its meaning. Because poets do not always complete a sentence at the end of a line, pausing simply because a line ends can interfere with your understanding of the meaning. Follow these rules when you read aloud:

- Keep reading when a line has no end punctuation.
- Pause at commas, dashes, and semicolons.
- Stop at end marks, such as periods, question marks, or exclamation points.

As you read poetry, allow the punctuation to help you paraphrase the poet's ideas.

DIRECTIONS: *The following items are from "Sarah Cynthia Sylvia Stout Would Not Take the Garbage Out," "Weather," or "One." Read each item aloud, following the rules above. Then, paraphrase the lines. That is, restate them in your own words.*

1. Dot a dot dot dot a dot dot
   Spotting the windowpane.

   _____

   _____

2. Nobody can get into my clothes for me
   or feel my fall for me, or do my running.
   Nobody hears my music for me, either.

   _____

   _____

   _____

3. Poor Sarah met an awful fate,
   That I cannot right now relate
   Because the hour is much too late.
   But children, remember Sarah Stout
   And always take the garbage out!

   _____

   _____

   _____

   _____

   _____

Literary Analysis: Sound Devices

Sound devices create musical effects that appeal to the ear. Here are some common sound devices used in poetry:

- **Onomatopoeia** is the use of words whose sounds suggest their meaning:

  The explosion made a thunderous <u>boom</u>. The snake uttered a <u>hiss</u>.

- **Alliteration** is the repetition of sounds at the beginnings of words:

  <u>She</u> <u>s</u>ells <u>s</u>ea <u>sh</u>ells by the <u>s</u>ea <u>sh</u>ore.

- **Repetition** is the repeated use of words, phrases, and/or rhythms:

  I said, "Come," / I said, "Sit," / My dog would have none of it.

In the last example, there is repetition of both the words (*I said*) and the rhythm. In poetry, a line may contain more than one sound device.

DIRECTIONS: *The following items are from "Sarah Cynthia Sylvia Stout Would Not Take the Garbage Out," "Weather," or "One." Read each item, and decide which sound devices the lines contain. Then, identify the sound devices in each line by writing* Onomatopoeia, Alliteration, *and/or* Repetition. *An item may contain more than one sound device.*

1. Prune pits, peach pits, orange peel

   _____

2. Crusts of black burned buttered toast

   _____

3. A spatter a scatter a wet cat a clatter
   A splatter a rumble outside.

   _____

4. And mirrors can show me multiplied
   Many times

   _____

5. Umbrella umbrella umbrella umbrella
   Bumbershoot barrel of rain.

   _____

6. Sarah Cynthia Sylvia Stout
   Would not take the garbage out!

   _____

7. Slosh a galosh slosh a galosh
   Slither and slather and glide

   _____

Poetry Collection: Shel Silverstein, Eve Merriam, James Berry
Vocabulary Builder

Word List

curdled   expectancy   rancid   slather   stutter   withered

A. DIRECTIONS: *Read each item, and think about the meaning of the italicized word from the Word List. Then, answer the question, and explain your answer.*

1. The *withered* flowers had been in the vase for a week. Were the flowers brightly colored?

   _____

2. The hungry twins found *rancid* cheese in the refrigerator. Would they have thrown it out or eaten it?

   _____

3. The suspect began to *stutter* when he was questioned. Was he nervous? How can you tell?

   _____

4. The milk has *curdled* in the bottle. Would you drink it?

   _____

5. The girl stared out the window with *expectancy*. Why was she probably looking out?

   _____

6. At the beach, Nora was careful to *slather* on sunscreen. Was this a good idea?

   _____

B. WORD STUDY: *The Latin suffix -ancy mean "the state of being." Decide whether each statement is true or false. Write T or F. Then, explain your answer.*

1. The baby was still in its *infancy*.

   T / F: _____ **Explanation:** _____

2. Someone who shows *hesitancy* is sure of himself or herself.

   T / F: _____ **Explanation:** _____

3. A diamond is likely to shine with great *brilliancy*.

   T / F: _____ **Explanation:** _____

"**Full Fathom Five**" by William Shakespeare, "**Onomatopoeia**" by Eve Merriam,
"**Train Tune**" by Louise Bogan

Writing About the Big Question

What is the best way to communicate?

Big Question Vocabulary

communicate	contribute	enrich	entertain	express
inform	learn	listen	media	produce
react	speak	teach	technology	transmit

A. *Use one or more words from the list above to complete each sentence.*

1. When you have a problem with a friend, you can _____ your opinion by talking it over.

2. It is important to _____ to your friend's opinions, too.

3. Listening well and speaking honestly can _____ a friendship.

B. *Answer each question with a complete sentence.*

1. Describe two occasions when you have expressed an opinion to a friend. Use two of the Big Question vocabulary words.

   _____

   _____

2. Choose one of the discussions above. Explain how the discussion helped to enrich your friendship.

   _____

   _____

C. *In "Poetry Collection 2," each poem uses sound to create an image or to bring about a certain mood. Complete this sentence:*

When you really **listen**, you can _____.

Poetry Collection: William Shakespeare, Eve Merriam, Louise Bogan
Reading: Read Aloud According to Punctuation in Order to Paraphrase

When you **paraphrase,** you restate something in your own words. To paraphrase a poem, you must first understand it. **Reading aloud according to punctuation** can help you identify complete thoughts in a poem and therefore grasp its meaning. Because poets do not always complete a sentence at the end of a line, pausing simply because a line ends can interfere with your understanding of the meaning. Follow these rules when you read aloud:

- Keep reading when a line has no end punctuation.
- Pause at commas, dashes, and semicolons.
- Stop at end marks, such as periods, question marks, or exclamation points.

As you read poetry, allow the punctuation to help you paraphrase the poet's ideas.

DIRECTIONS: *The following items are from "Full Fathom Five," "Onomatopoeia," or "Train Tune." Read each item aloud, following the rules above. Then, paraphrase the lines. That is, restate them in your own words.*

1. spurts,
   finally stops sputtering
   and plash!
   gushes rushes splashes
   clear water dashes.

   _____

   _____

   _____

2. Back through lightning
   Back through cities
   Back through stars
   Back through hours

   _____

   _____

   _____

3. Sea nymphs hourly ring his knell;
   Ding-dong.
   Hark! Now I hear them ding-dong bell.

   _____

   _____

   _____

Poetry Collection: William Shakespeare, Eve Merriam, Louise Bogan
Literary Analysis: Sound Devices

Sound devices create musical effects that appeal to the ear. Here are some common sound devices used in poetry:

- **Onomatopoeia** is the use of words whose sounds suggest their meaning:

  The saw cut through the tree with a <u>buzz</u>. The librarian <u>murmured</u> her answer.

- **Alliteration** is the repetition of sounds at the beginnings of words:

  <u>P</u>eter <u>P</u>iper <u>p</u>icked a <u>p</u>eck of <u>p</u>ickled <u>p</u>eppers.

- **Repetition** is the repeated use of words, phrases, and/or rhythms:

  <u>The leaves blew</u> up, / <u>The leaves blew</u> down, / <u>The leaves blew</u> all around the town.

In the last example, there is repetition of both the words (*The leaves blew*) and the rhythm. In poetry, a line may contain more than one sound device.

DIRECTIONS: *The following items are from "Full Fathom Five," "Onomatopoeia," or "Train Tune." Read each item, and decide which sound devices the lines contain. Then, identify the sound devices in each line by writing* Onomatopoeia, Alliteration, *and/or* Repetition. *An item may contain more than one sound device.*

1. Full fathom five thy father lies

   _____

2. The rusty spigot
   sputters,
   utters
   a splutter

   _____

3. Back through clouds
   Back through clearing
   Back through distance
   Back through silence

   _____

4. finally stops sputtering
   and plash!
   gushes rushes splashes
   clear water dashes

   _____

5. Nothing of him that doth fade
   But doth suffer a sea change
   Into something rich and strange.

   _____

Poetry Collection: William Shakespeare, Eve Merriam, Louise Bogan
Vocabulary Builder

Word List

fathoms   garlands   groves   smattering   spigot   sputters

A. DIRECTIONS: *Read each item, and think about the meaning of the italicized word from the Word List. Then, answer the question, and explain your answer.*

1. If a plumber says you need a new *spigot,* should you purchase a device to keep water from running down the drain?

   _____

2. If a person *sputters* as she speaks, is she likely to be calm?

   _____

3. If there are orange *groves* on your property, are there trees on your property?

   _____

4. If you are measuring the depths of a lake, would you measure in *fathoms*?

   _____

5. If you were hit by a *smattering* of raindrops, would you need to change your clothes?

   _____

6. If someone decorates her house with *garlands,* would it probably smell good?

   _____

B. WORD STUDY: *The Latin suffix* -less *means "without." Decide whether each statement is true or false. Write T or F. Then, explain your answer.*

1. You could trust someone who is *careless* with your most prized possession.

   T / F: _____ **Explanation:** _____

2. A movie that seems *endless* is very long or very dull.

   T / F: _____ **Explanation:** _____

3. A *joyless* person is almost always happy.

   T / F: _____ **Explanation:** _____

   _____

Poetry Collections: Shel Silverstein, Eve Merriam, James Berry;
William Shakespeare, Eve Merriam, Louise Bogan

Integrated Language Skills: Grammar

Independent and Subordinate Clauses

A **clause** is a group of words with its own subject and verb. There are two types of clauses: independent clauses and subordinate clauses. An **independent clause** expresses a complete thought and can stand alone as a sentence.

A **subordinate clause** (also called a **dependent clause**) has a subject and a verb, but it does not express a complete thought. Therefore, it cannot stand alone as a sentence. The following sentence contains both an independent clause and a subordinate clause. The subject in each clause is underlined once, and the verb is underlined twice. The subordinate clause appears in italics:

> Shel Silverstein was a cartoonist and a writer, *though he also composed songs.*

A subordinate clause may appear either before or after the independent clause:

> *Though he also composed songs,* Shel Silverstein was a cartoonist and a writer.

A. DIRECTIONS: *In each sentence, underline the independent clause once and the subordinate clause twice.*

1. Eve Merriam's lifelong love was poetry even though she wrote fiction, nonfiction, and drama.
2. Because language and its sound gave Eve Merriam great joy, she tried to communicate her enjoyment by writing poetry for children.
3. Berry moved to the United States when he was seventeen.
4. If Berry had not lost his job as a telegraph operator, he might not have become a writer.
5. Because he did not play ball or dance when he was young, Shel Silverstein began to draw and write.
6. Silverstein began to draw cartoons after he served in the military.

B. Writing Application: *Rewrite each sentence by adding a subordinate clause.*

1. Sarah Stout was a stubborn young woman.

   _____

2. The rain spotted the windowpane.

   _____

3. Anyone can dance like me.

   _____

4. The drowned man's bones had turned to coral.

   _____

Poetry Collections: Shel Silverstein, Eve Merriam, James Berry;
William Shakespeare, Eve Merriam, Louise Bogan

Integrated Language Skills: Support for Writing a Poem Called "Alliteration"

Use this chart as you draft a **poem** called "Alliteration."

"Alliteration": A Poem
Alliteration, defined by the textbook: "Alliteration is the repetition of sounds at the beginning of words."
Alliteration, defined in my own words: _____   _____   _____
Example of alliteration: <u>P</u>eter <u>P</u>iper <u>p</u>icked a <u>p</u>eck of <u>p</u>ickled <u>p</u>eppers.
My own example of alliteration: _____   _____   _____   _____   _____
My poem, combining my definition of alliteration with my examples of alliteration: _____   _____   _____   _____   _____   _____   _____   _____   _____

Look over your poem to be sure your examples work. Do they contain words that begin with the same sound? Then, check your definition. Does it correctly define alliteration? Revise your poem before creating your final draft.

"Annabel Lee" by Edgar Allan Poe, **"Martin Luther King"** by Raymond R. Patterson,
"I'm Nobody" by Emily Dickinson

Writing About the Big Question

What is the best way to communicate?

Big Question Vocabulary

communicate	contribute	enrich	entertain	express
inform	learn	listen	media	produce
react	speak	teach	technology	transmit

A. *Use one or more words from the list above to complete each sentence.*

1. An argument with someone can _____ feelings of anger, or it can work out problems.

2. Arguing can actually be a good way to _____.

3. When you argue, you need to _____ yourself clearly.

4. Use positive words and a calm tone of voice when you _____.

B. *Answer each question with a complete sentence.*

1. Describe an argument you have had in which you were able to communicate with the other person. Use at least two Big Question vocabulary words.

   _____

   _____

2. Explain how you expressed yourself in the argument, describing the words you used and your tone of voice.

   _____

   _____

C. *In "Poetry Collection 1," the poets present people and ideas about which they feel passionate. Complete these sentences:*

Words can be used to **produce** _____.
The way people **react** can _____.

Poetry Collection: Edgar Allan Poe, Raymond Richard Patterson, Emily Dickinson

Reading: Reread in Order to Paraphrase

To **paraphrase** means to restate or explain something in your own words. When you paraphrase lines of poetry, you make the meaning clear to yourself. If you are unsure of a poem's meaning, **reread** the parts that are difficult. Follow these steps:

- Look up unfamiliar words, and replace them with words you know.
- Restate the line or passage using your own everyday words.
- Reread the passage to make sure that your version makes sense.

Look at these lines from the poem "Martin Luther King":

He came upon an age / Beset by grief, by rage

The first line tells you that King "came upon an age." If you look up "come upon" in a dictionary, you will learn that it means "meet by chance." In this case, you might use a looser definition: "happen to live in." *Age* can refer to the number of years a person has lived or to a period in history. In this case, it refers to a period of history when African Americans did not have the same rights as white Americans.

If you looked up *beset*, you would discover that one of its meanings is "troubled." You probably know that *grief* is a synonym for *sorrow* or *sadness* and that *rage* is a synonym for *anger*. Now you have all the ingredients for a paraphrase of the line. It might look like this:

He happened to live at a time that was troubled by sorrow and anger.

DIRECTIONS: *Read these passages from "Annabel Lee," "Martin Luther King," and "I'm Nobody." Following the process described above, write a paraphrase of each passage.*

1. "A wind blew out of a cloud by night / Chilling my Annabel Lee; /
   So that her highborn kinsmen came / And bore her away from me, /
   To shut her up in a sepulcher / In this kingdom by the sea."

   _____

   _____

   _____

2. "He came upon an age / Beset by grief and rage—
   His love so deep, so wide / He could not turn aside."

   _____

   _____

   _____

3. "How dreary to be Somebody! / How public like a Frog /
   To tell your name the livelong June / To an admiring Bog!"

   _____

   _____

Poetry Collection: Edgar Allan Poe, Raymond Richard Patterson, Emily Dickinson

Literary Analysis: Rhythm, Meter, and Rhyme

Rhythm and rhyme make poetry musical. **Rhythm** is a poem's pattern of stressed (´) and unstressed (˘) syllables.

Meter is a poem's rhythmical pattern. It is measured in *feet,* or single units of stressed and unstressed syllables. In the examples below, stressed and unstressed syllables are marked, and the feet are separated by vertical lines (|). The first line of "Annabel Lee" contains four feet, and the second line contains three feet. The two lines of "Martin Luther King" contain three feet each.

Rhyme is the repetition of sounds at the ends of lines. The two words that rhyme in the lines from "Martin Luther King" are underlined.

It was MAN | -y and MAN | -y a YEAR | a-GO. | / In a KING | -dom BY | the SEA.

He CAME | up-ON | an AGE | be-SET | by GRIEF, | by RAGE.

A. DIRECTIONS: *Mark the stressed (´) and unstressed (˘) syllables in these lines. Then, show the meter by drawing a vertical rule after each foot.*

1. But our love it was stronger by far than the love / Of those who were older than we

2. His passion, so profound, / He would not turn around.

B. DIRECTIONS: *The words that end each line of "Annabel Lee" and "Martin Luther King" are listed in the following items. In each item, circle each word that rhymes with another word. Then, draw lines to connect all the words that rhyme with each other in that item.*

1. ago sea know Lee thought me

2. child sea love Lee Heaven me

3. ago sea night Lee came me sepulcher sea

4. Heaven me know sea chilling Lee

5. love we we above sea soul Lee

6. dreams Lee Lee side bride sea sea

7. age rage / wide aside / profound around / Earth worth / be free

Poetry Collection: Edgar Allan Poe, Raymond Richard Patterson, Emily Dickinson
Vocabulary Builder

Word List

banish   coveted   envying   kinsmen   passion   profound

A. DIRECTIONS: *Read each sentence, and think about the meaning of the italicized word from the Word List. Then, answer the question, and explain your answer.*

1. The speaker in "Annabel Lee" says that the angels *coveted* the love between him and Annabel Lee. Did the angels criticize their love?

   _____

2. The speaker in "Martin Luther King" says that King's feeling was *profound*. Did King feel very strongly?

   _____

3. The speaker in "I'm Nobody" says that "they" will *banish* her if they find out that she is a Nobody. Will "they" accept her in their social circle?

   _____

4. The speaker in "Annabel Lee" says the angels were *envying* the love he and Annabel shared. Did the angels want love for themselves?

   _____

5. Annabel Lee's *kinsmen* took her away from the speaker. Were they related to her?

   _____

6. The speaker of "Martin Luther King" says that King felt a deep *passion*. Was King's feeling one of despair?

   _____

B. WORD STUDY: *The Latin prefix im- means "in, into, toward." Use the meaning of the italicized word in each question to write an answer.*

1. If someone had a tooth *implanted*, what would the result be?

   _____

2. What would it look like if you *imprinted* a picture on a T-shirt?

   _____

3. If your car is *impounded*, what has happened to it?

   _____

All-in-One Workbook
223

"Jim" by Gwendolyn Brooks, **"Father William"** by Lewis Carroll,
"Stopping by Woods on a Snowy Evening" by Robert Frost

Writing About the Big Question

What is the best way to communicate?

Big Question Vocabulary

communicate	contribute	enrich	entertain	express
inform	learn	listen	media	produce
react	speak	teach	technology	transmit

A. *Use one or more words from the list above to complete each sentence.*

1. When you take part in a poetry slam, you can _____
an audience with poetry.

2. You _____ yourself through your poetry to the
audience.

3. Your audience can _____ about you as they
_____ to your poems.

B. *Answer each question with a complete sentence.*

1. Describe a poem you have listened to or read that you found moving or entertaining.

_____

_____

2. Explain why the poem entertained you, and explain what you learned from it. Use at
least two Big Question vocabulary words in your response.

_____

_____

C. *In "Poetry Collection 2," each poem uses rhythm and rhyme to create a musical quality.
Complete this sentence:*

Messages that **entertain** as well as **inform** _____.

Poetry Collection: Gwendolyn Brooks, Lewis Carroll, Robert Frost
Reading: Reread in Order to Paraphrase

To **paraphrase** means to restate or explain something in your own words. When you paraphrase lines of poetry, you make the meaning clear to yourself. If you are unsure of a poem's meaning, **reread** the parts that are difficult. Follow these steps:

- Look up unfamiliar words, and replace them with words you know.
- Restate the line or passage using your own everyday words.
- Reread the passage to make sure that your version makes sense.

Look at these lines from "Father William":

"In my youth," said his father, "I took to the law

And argued each case with my wife;

And the muscular strength which it gave to my jaw

Has lasted the rest of my life."

The first line tells you that Father William "took to the law." If you look up *law* in a dictionary, you will learn that one of its meanings is "the legal profession." Father William is saying that he was a lawyer. That knowledge will help you understand the second line: Father William prepared for his legal cases by arguing them with his wife. You probably know or can guess that *muscular* has to do with muscles. Now you have all the ingredients to write a paraphrase of the verse. It might look like this:

"When I was young," Father William said, "I was a lawyer

And I talked over every case with my wife;

And as a result, I developed strong jaw muscles

That I still have today."

DIRECTIONS: *Read these passages from "Jim," "Father William," and "Stopping by Woods on a Snowy Evening." Following the process described above, write a paraphrase of each passage.*

1. The sun should drop its greatest gold / On him.

   _____

2. "In my youth," said the sage, as he shook his gray locks, / "I kept all my limbs very supple / By the use of this ointment—one shilling the box—/ Allow me to sell you a couple?"

   _____

   _____

   _____

3. He gives his harness bells a shake / To ask if there is some mistake. / The only other sound's the sweep / Of easy wind and downy flake.

   _____

   _____

   _____

Poetry Collection: Gwendolyn Brooks, Lewis Carroll, Robert Frost
Literary Analysis: Rhythm, Meter, and Rhyme

Rhythm and rhyme make poetry musical. **Rhythm** is a poem's pattern of stressed (´) and unstressed (˘) syllables.

Meter is a poem's rhythmical pattern. It is measured in *feet*, or single units of stressed and unstressed syllables. In the examples below, stressed and unstressed syllables are marked, and the feet are separated by vertical lines (|). The first line of "Father William" contains four feet, and the second line contains three feet. The two lines of "Stopping by Woods on a Snowy Evening" contain four feet each.

"You are OLD, | Fa-ther WILL- | iam," the YOUNG | man SAID, |

And your HAIR | has be-COME | ver-y WHITE" |

Rhyme is the repetition of sounds at the ends of lines. The two words that rhyme in the lines from "Stopping by Woods on a Snowy Evening" are underlined.

My LIT- | tle HORSE | must THINK | it <u>QUEER</u> |

to STOP | with-OUT | a FARM- | house <u>NEAR</u> |

A. DIRECTIONS: *Mark the stressed (´) and unstressed (˘) syllables in these lines. Then, show the meter by drawing a vertical rule after each foot.*

1. "You are old," said the youth, "as I mentioned before. / And have grown most

   uncommonly fat."

2. He gives his harness bells a shake / To ask if there is some mistake. / The only

   other sound's the sweep / Of easy wind and downy flake.

B. DIRECTIONS: *The words that end each verse of "Jim," "Father William," and "Stopping by Woods on a Snowy Evening" are listed in the following items. In each item, circle each word that rhymes with another word. Then, draw lines to connect all the words that rhyme with each other in that item.*

1. boy Jim gold him / sick in bread medicine / room see baseball Terribly

2. said white head right / son brain none again before fat door that

3. locks supple box couple / weak suet beak do it law wife jaw life

4. suppose ever nose clever / enough airs stuff downstairs

5. know though here snow / queer near lake year

6. shake mistake sweep flake / deep keep sleep sleep

Poetry Collection: Gwendolyn Brooks, Lewis Carroll, Robert Frost
Vocabulary Builder

Word List

downy   harness   incessantly   sage   supple   uncommonly

A. DIRECTIONS: *Read each item, and think about the meaning of the italicized word from the Word List. Then, answer the question, and explain your answer.*

1. Father William stands on his head *incessantly*. Does he stand on his head for an hour at a time, taking breaks when he gets tired?

   _____

2. Father William is a *sage*. Would he be likely to do well on a quiz show?

   _____

3. Father William used an ointment to keep his joints *supple*. Was he likely to have had trouble bending down to tie his shoes?

   _____

4. The snow falls in *downy* flakes. Is the snow heavy?

   _____

5. The horse wears a *harness* with bells. Does the harness keep it warm?

   _____

6. Father William has grown *uncommonly* fat. Is it usual for someone to become so fat?

   _____

B. WORD STUDY: *The Latin prefix* un- *means "not." Answer each question by adding* un- *to each italicized word and using the new word in your response.*

1. What would happen if you were not *prepared* for a test?

   _____

2. Is a fantasy movie likely to have only *realistic* characters?

   _____

3. Is it hard to sleep in a *comfortable* bed?

   _____

Poetry Collections: Edgar Allan Poe, Raymond Richard Patterson, Emily Dickinson;
Gwendolyn Brooks, Lewis Carroll, Robert Frost

Integrated Language Skills: Grammar

Sentence Structure

A **simple sentence** is an independent clause. That is, it is a group of words that has a subject and a verb and can stand by itself as a complete thought.

A **compound sentence** consists of two or more independent clauses that are joined by a conjunction such as *and, but, or,* or *for.*

> Lewis Carroll was a mathematician, <u>but</u> he also wrote stories and poetry.

A **complex sentence** contains one independent clause and one or more subordinate clauses. In this sentence, the subordinate clause is underlined:

> <u>Although he was a mathematician</u>, Lewis Carroll also wrote novels.

A. DIRECTIONS: *Identify each sentence below by writing* Simple, Compound, *or* Complex.

1. Gwendolyn Brooks lived in an area of Chicago known as Bronzeville, and one of her volumes of poetry is called *A Street in Bronzeville.*

    _____

2. Although she was primarily a poet, Brooks published a novel, *Maud Martha.*

    _____

3. Gwendolyn Brooks served as the poet laureate of Illinois.

    _____

4. Lewis Carroll's *Alice's Adventures in Wonderland* has been translated into more than thirty languages.

    _____

5. Carroll liked to write nonsense verse, and he invented nonsense characters, such as the Snark, the Jabberwock, and the twins Tweedledee and Tweedledum.

    _____

B. Writing Application: *Write a short paragraph in which you describe your reaction to one of the poems in these collections. Tell what you liked most about the poem and why it appeals to you. Use at least one simple sentence, one compound sentence, and one complex sentence. Label your sentences by writing* Simple, Compound, *or* Complex *in parentheses after each one.*

_____

_____

_____

_____

_____

Poetry Collections: Edgar Allan Poe, Raymond Richard Patterson, Emily Dickinson; Gwendolyn Brooks, Lewis Carroll, Robert Frost

Integrated Language Skills: Support for Writing a Paraphrase

Use these charts to draft a **paraphrase** of one of the six poems you have read. In the first chart, write down unfamiliar words from the poem, their dictionary definition, and the definition restated in your own words. In the second chart, write each line of the poem in the first column. In the second column, restate the meaning of the line in your own words. If you are paraphrasing "Father William," finish your paraphrase on a separate sheet of paper.

Title of poem: _____

Word to Look Up	Dictionary Definition	Definition in My Own Words

Poem, Line by Line	Paraphrase, Line by Line

Now, read over your paraphrase to make sure it has the same meaning as the original. Make your revisions as you prepare your final draft.

Poetry by Walt Whitman and E. E. Cummings

Writing About the Big Question

What is the best way to communicate?

Big Question Vocabulary

communicate	contribute	enrich	entertain	express
inform	learn	listen	media	produce
react	speak	teach	technology	transmit

A. *Use one or more words from the list above to complete each sentence.*

1. You can _____ with others by speaking, writing, or through the arts.

2. All communication helps you _____ about other people.

3. Communication can _____ your life and the lives of others.

B. *Respond to each item with a complete sentence.*

1. Describe your favorite way to communicate and tell when you are likely to use it. Use at least two Big Question vocabulary words.

   _____

   _____

   _____

2. Explain why you prefer to communicate in the way you have chosen. Tell how it helps you express yourself and learn about other people.

   _____

   _____

   _____

C. In the poetry of Whitman and Cummings, the writers use imagery to paint vivid pictures in the minds of readers. Think about the Big Question as you complete the sentence.

Descriptive words can enrich a piece of writing because _____ .

_____

_____

_____

Name _____ Date _____

Literary Analysis: Comparing Imagery

In poetry, an **image** is a word or phrase that appeals to one or more of the five senses. Writers use **imagery** to bring poetry to life with descriptions of how their subjects look, sound, feel, taste, and smell.

Both "Miracles" and "in Just—" contain images that appeal to the senses. For example, "wade with naked feet along the beach" appeals to the sense of touch, and "the little lame balloonman" appeals to sight.

DIRECTIONS: *Read each image in the first column, and mark an X in the column or columns to indicate the sense or senses that the image appeals to. The first fifteen images are from "Miracles"; the last nine are from "in Just—."*

Image	Sight	Hearing	Touch	Taste	Smell
1. "walk the streets of Manhattan"					
2. "dart my sight over the roofs"					
3. "stand under trees in the woods"					
4. "talk by day with any one I love"					
5. "sit at table at dinner with the rest"					
6. "look at strangers opposite me"					
7. "honeybees busy around the hive"					
8. "animals feeding in the fields"					
9. "birds, or . . . insects in the air"					
10. "the sundown"					
11. "stars shining so quiet and bright"					
12. "thin curve of the new moon"					
13. "fishes that swim the rocks"					
14. "the motion of the waves"					
15. "the ships with men in them"					
16. "the world is mud-luscious"					
17. "little lame balloonman whistles"					
18. "eddieandbill come running"					
19. "from marbles and piracies"					
20. "the world is puddle-wonderful"					
21. "queer old balloonman whistles"					
22. "bettyandisbel come dancing"					
23. "from hop-scotch and jump-rope"					

Poetry by Walt Whitman and E. E. Cummings
Vocabulary Builder

Word List

distinct   exquisite

A. DIRECTIONS: *Complete these word maps by writing synonyms, antonyms, and an example sentence for each vocabulary word.*

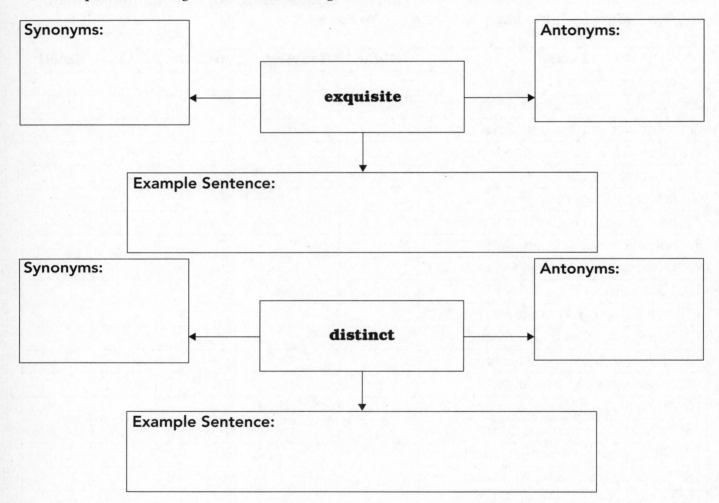

Synonyms:

Antonyms:

exquisite

Example Sentence:

Synonyms:

Antonyms:

distinct

Example Sentence:

B. DIRECTIONS: *Write the letter of the word or words whose meaning is most nearly* the same as *the word from the Word List.*

____ 1. exquisite
     A. quaint   B. significant   C. costly   D. beautiful

____ 2. distinct
     A. blurry   B. separate   C. similar   D. pure

Name _____ Date _____

Poetry by Walt Whitman and E. E. Cummings

Integrated Language Skills: Support for Writing to Compare Literary Works

Use the following graphic organizers as you prepare to write an essay recommending either "Miracles" or "in Just—" to someone your age.

Imagery from "Miracles" that appeals to me:		
Sight	**Hearing**	**Touch**

Imagery from "in Just—" that appeals to me:		
Sight	**Hearing**	**Touch**

Which poem's imagery is fascinating or strange? What about it is fascinating or strange?

_____

_____

Which poem is more musical? Why?

_____

Which poem's images do I find more meaningful? Why?

_____

_____

_____

Now, use your notes to write an essay about the poem that you would recommend.

All-in-One Workbook
© Pearson Education, Inc. All rights reserved.
233

True Identity, performed by Carolyn Sills and the Boss Tweed Band

People make **assumptions**, think their opinion must be true,
that your **image**, or how you present yourself, is the actual you.
So if you think that their opinion is **biased** or personally skewed,
just be yourself so they can rightfully **define** and describe you.

You can't **ignore**, or not acknowledge, who you are.
Your looks and your **appearance** will only take you so far.
So **appreciate** and be grateful for what makes you one of a kind
and show the world, reveal to them, what's really on your mind

Your **reaction** or response to life's daily ins and outs
is all some people need to think they know what you're all about.
So if you want to **reflect** or show how you truly are inside,
make use of your features and characteristics, to imitate is simply to hide.

You can't **ignore**, or not acknowledge, who you are.
Your looks and **appearance** will only take you so far.
So **appreciate** and be grateful for what makes you one of a kind
and show the world, reveal to them, what's really on your mind

How other people see things, **perceptions**, can hold true
if you refuse to concentrate or focus on the real you.

So if you think they have the wrong **perspective** or point of view,
Just make sure that your identity, your true self, is shining through.

Continued

You can't **ignore**, or not acknowledge, who you are.

Your looks and **appearance** will only take you so far.

So **appreciate** and be grateful for what makes you one of a kind

and show the world, **reveal** to them, what's really on your mind

and show the world, **reveal** to them, what's really on your mind

and show the world, **reveal** to them, what's really on your mind

---

Song Title: **True Identity**
Artist / Performed by Carolyn Sills and the Boss Tweed Band
Vocals & Bass Guitar: Carolyn Sills
Guitar: Gerard Egan
Drums: Vlad Gutkovich
Lyrics by Carolyn Sills
Music composed by Carolyn Sills & the Boss Tweed Band

Unit 5: Drama
Big Question Vocabulary—1

The Big Question: Do others see us more clearly than we see ourselves?

appreciate: *v.* to understand something's importance or value; other form: *appreciation*

assumption: *n.* a decision that something is true, without definite proof; other form: *assume*

bias: *n.* the act of favoring one group of people over another; other form: *biased*

define: *v.* to describe something correctly and thoroughly; other forms: *definition, defined*

reveal: *v.* to expose something that has been hidden or secret; other forms: *revealed, revealing*

A. DIRECTIONS: *In the chart, write a synonym and an antonym for each vocabulary word. Choose your answers from the words and phrases in the box. You will not use all of them.*

theory	fairness	distort	be thankful	be happy	be ungrateful	hide
characterize	uncover	proof	pride	concentrate	prejudice	

Word	Synonym	Antonym
1. appreciate		
2. assumption		
3. bias		
4. define		
5. reveal		

B. DIRECTIONS: *Write a humorous short story about a man who receives a large parrot for a pet. At first he is unhappy because he doesn't like birds. However, the parrot is so clever that the man changes his mind. Use all five vocabulary words.*

_____

_____

_____

_____

_____

_____

Unit 5: Drama
Big Question Vocabulary—2

The Big Question: Do others see us more clearly than we see ourselves?

appearance: *n.* the way a person looks to other people; other forms: *appear, appearing*

focus: *v.* to direct one's attention to one specific thing; other forms: *focusing, focused*

identify: *v.* to recognize and correctly name something; other forms: *identification, identified*

ignore: *v.* to act as if something has not been seen or heard; other forms: *ignoring, ignorant*

perspective: *n.* a special way to think about something, usually influenced by one's personality and experiences

A. DIRECTIONS: *Write the vocabulary word that best completes each group of related words.*

1. avoid, neglect, forget, _____

2. attitude, viewpoint, thoughts, _____

3. looks, image, personality, _____

4. concentrate, stare, study, _____

5. classify, define, describe, _____

B. DIRECTIONS: *On the line before each sentence, write* True *if the statement is true, or* False *if it is false. If the statement is false, rewrite the sentence so that it is true.*

_____1. A person's *appearance* is his or her innermost thoughts.

_____

_____2. If the fire alarm goes off, the best course of action is to *ignore* it.

_____

_____3. To board an airplane, you must carry a suitcase in order to *identify* yourself.

_____

_____4. Activities that require you to *focus* carefully include sleeping and daydreaming.

_____

_____5. A person's *perspective* is often based on opinions and attitudes.

_____

Unit 5: Drama
Big Question Vocabulary—3

The Big Question: Do others see us more clearly than we see ourselves?

characteristic: *n.* a special quality or feature that is typical of someone or something

image: *n.* the way a person appears to others; other forms: *images, imagination, imagine*

perception: *n.* the unique way you think about someone or something; other form: *perceive*

reaction: *n.* a response to someone or something in the form of thoughts, words, or actions; other forms: *react, reactionary*

reflect: *v.* to express or show through gestures or actions; other forms: *reflection, reflected*

Karen said this to Mario, Heidi, and Ramon: "I saw a really strange looking man on the subway. He gave me a spooky feeling. Maybe he was a magician. Anyway, he was carrying a huge bag. I peeked inside and almost fainted with shock. It was a painting—a painting of ME!"

Each of Karen's friends had a different reaction to what she said.

DIRECTIONS: *Use the word(s) shown to write what each friend said to Karen.*

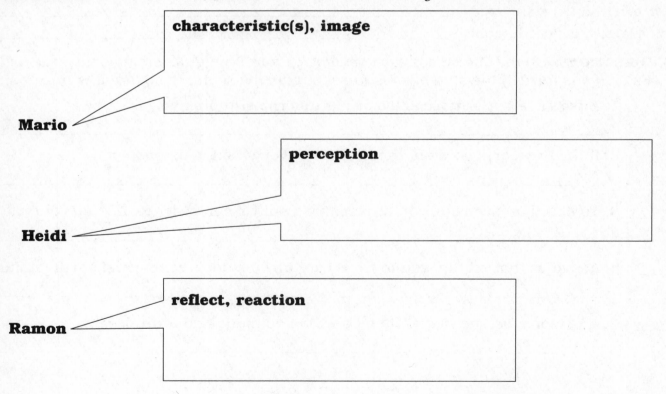

characteristic(s), image

Mario

perception

Heidi

reflect, reaction

Ramon

Name _____ Date _____

Unit 5: Drama
Applying the Big Question

Do others see us more clearly than we see ourselves?

DIRECTIONS: *Complete the chart below to apply what you have learned about how people form impressions of others. One row has been completed for you.*

Example	Who/What is Judged	Who does the Judging	Is the judgment fair	What I learned
From Literature	Goodman in "The Monsters . . .	His neighbors	No, it is based on the fact that he is an "oddball"	Fear can change the way people see others
From Literature				
From Science				
From Social Studies				
From Real Life				

Laurence Yep
Listening and Viewing

Segment 1: Meet Laurence Yep
- Why did Laurence Yep identify with the themes he encountered in science fiction?
- Does it surprise you that he chose to write science fiction? Why or why not?

_____

_____

_____

_____

Segment 2: Drama
- According to Yep, what are the differences between a drama and a novel?
- Which form, the drama or the novel, might be more difficult to write? Why?

_____

_____

_____

_____

Segment 3: The Writing Process
- Why does Yep adjust his drafts as he writes?
- What method of Yep's would you be most inclined to try in your own writing? Why?

_____

_____

_____

_____

Segment 4: The Rewards of Writing
- What does Yep think literature can do for young readers?

_____

_____

_____

_____

Learning About Drama

Drama is a story told in dialogue by performers in front of an audience. The **playwright** is the author of a drama, which may also be called a *play.* The play itself is written in segments, called **acts.** Acts are often divided into **scenes.**

A playwright uses **characterization** to create believable characters. To advance the action, the playwright creates **dramatic speech.** Two types of dramatic speech are **dialogue,** conversation between two or more characters, and **monologue,** a long speech by a single character. A monologue often reveals a character's thoughts and feelings.

Stage directions describe the scenery and tell how the characters move and speak. The **set** is the construction onstage that suggests the time and place of the action (the setting). **Props** are small movable items that make the set look realistic.

Two types of drama are comedy and tragedy. A **comedy** has a happy ending. It often features ordinary characters in funny situations. In a **tragedy,** the events lead to the downfall of the main character. The main character may be an ordinary person, but the traditional tragic hero is a man of great significance, such as a king.

A. DIRECTIONS: *Read the following excerpt from a drama. Then, answer the questions.*

[*The* FISCHERS' *kitchen, 7* A.M. MRS. FISCHER *sits at kitchen table, reading a newspaper. The door opens.* BECKY *rushes in. She wears school clothes and carries a book bag.*]

BECKY. Mom! I overslept! I'll miss the tryouts for the play. Why didn't you wake me?

MRS. FISCHER [*getting up from the table*]. Calm down. Let me make you some breakfast.

BECKY [*almost shouting*]. Breakfast? I'm already late!

MRS. FISCHER [*patiently*]. No, dear, you're early. It's Saturday. Tryouts aren't until Monday.

1. Describe the set. _____

2. What props are used? _____

3. Quote a stage direction that tells how a character speaks.

_____

4. Quote a stage direction that tells how a character moves.

_____

5. Is the passage a dialogue or a monologue? Explain.

_____

6. Is this scene more likely from a comedy or a tragedy? Explain. _____

_____

from **Dragonwings** by Laurence Yep
Model Selection: Drama

Dragonwings is a **drama,** or *play,* a story told in dialogue and meant to be performed by actors before an audience. Laurence Yep is the **playwright,** the author of the play. A play is written in segments. You have read just one segment, a **scene.** In a full-length work, several scenes usually make up an **act,** and several acts make up the play.

To advance the action, Yep wrote **dramatic speech.** Most of the excerpt from *Dragonwings* contains **dialogue,** conversation between several characters. One section might be considered a **monologue,** a long speech by a single character. A monologue often reveals a character's thoughts and feelings.

Stage directions describe the scenery and sound effects and tell how the characters move and speak. The **set** is the construction onstage that suggests the time and place of the action (the setting). **Props** are small movable items that make the set look realistic.

In a drama, as the **main character** develops, the audience should identify with his or her emotions. The **climax** of a drama, the moment of greatest tension, concerns the main character in some way. With the climax comes some insight or revelation.

A. DIRECTIONS: *Answer these questions about Scene 9 of* Dragonwings.

1. What is the setting? _____

2. What props is Moon Shadow most likely using during his opening speech?

   _____

3. Describe one sound effect that is used. _____

4. After Windrider takes off in the airplane, Moon Shadow speaks these lines:

   I thought he'd fly forever and ever. Up, up to heaven and never come down. But then . . . Dragonwings came crashing to earth. Father had a few broken bones, but it was nothing serious. Only the aeroplane was wrecked. . . . Father didn't say much, just thought a lot I figured he was busy designing the next aeroplane. . . .

   What type of dramatic speech would you call this passage? Explain your answer.

   _____

5. Who is the main character? How can you tell?

   _____

B. DIRECTIONS: *What is the climax of events in Scene 9 of* Dragonwings? *What insight does Windrider gain in response to the climax? What insight does Moon Shadow gain?*

_____

_____

_____

"A Christmas Carol: Scrooge and Marley, *Act 1*" by Israel Horowitz

Writing About the Big Question

Do others see us more clearly than we see ourselves?

Big Question Vocabulary

appearance	appreciate	assumption	bias	characteristic
define	focus	identify	ignore	image
perception	perspective	reaction	reflect	reveal

A. *Choose one word from the list above to complete each sentence. There may be more than one right answer.*

1. Over time, Betsy learned to _____ her mother's fashion advice.

2. Sometimes you know what a word means, but find it hard to _____.

3. Eric's hard work in the gym helped quicken his _____ time.

B. *Follow the directions in responding to each of the items below.*

1. List two different times when you learned something new about yourself. Write your response in complete sentences.

   _____

   _____

2. Choose one of the experiences you listed in number 1. Write three or more sentences describing that experience. Use at least two of the Big Question vocabulary words. You may use the words in different forms (for example you can change *reflect* to *reflection*).

   _____

   _____

C. *Complete the sentence below. Use the completed sentence as the topic sentence in a short paragraph about the big question.*

The way we treat others reveals _____

_____

_____

A Christmas Carol: Scrooge and Marley, *Act I,* by Israel Horovitz
Reading: Preview a Text to Set a Purpose for Reading

When you **set a purpose for reading,** you decide what you want to get from a text. Setting a purpose gives you a focus as you read. These are some of the reasons you might have for reading something:

- to learn about a subject
- to be entertained
- to gain understanding
- to prepare to take action or make a decision
- to find inspiration
- to complete a task

In order to set a purpose, **preview a text** before you read it. Look at the title, the pictures, the captions, the organization, and the beginnings of passages. If you already have a purpose in mind, previewing will help you decide whether the text will fit that purpose. If you do not have a purpose in mind, previewing the text will help you determine one.

DIRECTIONS: *Read the passages from Act I of* A Christmas Carol: Scrooge and Marley *indicated below, and then complete each item.*

1. Following the list of "The People of the Play," read the information labeled "The Place of the Play." Where is the play set?

   _____

2. Read the information labeled "The Time of the Play." When does the play take place?

   _____

3. What purpose or purposes might you set based on that information?

   _____

   _____

4. The illustrations that accompany the text of Act I of the play are photographs from a production of the play. Look at those photographs now, but ignore the one of the ghostly character in chains. How are the characters dressed?

   _____

5. Based on that information, what purpose might you set for reading Act I of the play?

   _____

6. Read the opening lines of Act I, Scene 1, spoken by a character called Marley. Then, look at the photograph of the ghostly character in chains. What purpose might you set based on that information?

   _____

A Christmas Carol: Scrooge and Marley, *Act I,* by Israel Horovitz
Literary Analysis: Dialogue

Dialogue is a conversation between characters. In a play, the characters are developed almost entirely through dialogue. Dialogue also advances the action of the plot and develops the conflict.

In the script of a dramatic work, you can tell which character is speaking by the name that appears before the character's lines. In this example of dialogue, you are introduced to two of the characters in *A Christmas Carol: Scrooge and Marley:*

> **NEPHEW.** [*Cheerfully; surprising* SCROOGE] A merry Christmas to you, Uncle! God save you!
>
> **SCROOGE.** Bah! Humbug!
>
> **NEPHEW.** Christmas a "humbug," Uncle? I'm sure you don't mean that.
>
> **SCROOGE.** I do! Merry Christmas? What right do you have to be merry? What reason have you to be merry? You're poor enough!

In just a few words apiece, the characters establish a conflict between them. The nephew thinks Christmas is a joyful holiday, and Scrooge thinks it is nonsense. This conflict will reappear throughout the play until it is resolved. Those lines of dialogue also give you a look at the character traits of Scrooge and his nephew. Scrooge is quarrelsome and unpleasant; the nephew is upbeat and friendly.

DIRECTIONS: *Answer the following questions about this passage from* A Christmas Carol: Scrooge and Marley, *Act I, Scene 2.*

> **PORTLY MAN.** . . . [*Pen in hand; as well as notepad*] What shall I put you down for, sir?
>
> **SCROOGE.** Nothing!
>
> **PORTLY MAN.** You wish to be left anonymous?
>
> **SCROOGE.** I wish to be left alone! [*Pauses; turns away; turns back to them*] Since you ask me what I wish, gentlemen, that is my answer. I help to support the establishments that I have mentioned; they cost enough: and those who are badly off must go there.
>
> **THIN MAN.** Many can't go there; and many would rather die.
>
> **SCROOGE.** If they would rather die, they had better do it, and decrease the surplus population. . . .

1. How many characters are speaking? Who are they?

   _____

2. What is Scrooge like in this scene?

   _____

3. How is he different from the men he is talking to?

   _____

   _____

4. Based on the identification of the characters, whom would you expect to speak next?

   _____

A Christmas Carol: Scrooge and Marley, *Act 1,* by Israel Horovitz
Vocabulary Builder

Word List

conveyed   destitute   gratitude   implored   morose   void

A. DIRECTIONS: *Think about the meaning of the italicized word from the Word List in each sentence. Then, answer the question, and explain your answer.*

1. Marley *implored* Scrooge to pay attention to him. Did Marley ask casually?

   _____

2. Scrooge was *morose.* Did he enjoy celebrating Christmas?

   _____

3. Are the *destitute* able to save money?

   _____

4. Scrooge looked into the *void.* Did he see anything?

   _____

5. In Act I, Scene 3, of *A Christmas Carol: Scrooge and Marley,* has Scrooge *conveyed* his fear?

   _____

6. Do Fezziwig's employees feel *gratitude?*

   _____

B. WORD STUDY: *The Latin root -grat- means "thankful, pleasing." Read the following sentences. Use your knowledge of the root -grat- to write a full sentence to answer each question. Include the italicized word in your answer.*

1. If you are *grateful,* is it likely that someone has done something nice for you?

   _____

2. Is *gratitude* an unhappy emotion?

   _____

3. Would you value a *gratifying* friendship?

   _____

A Christmas Carol: Scrooge and Marley, *Act I,* by Israel Horovitz
Integrated Language Skills: Grammar

Interjections

An **interjection** is a part of speech that exclaims and expresses a feeling, such as pain or excitement. It may stand on its own or it may appear within a sentence, but it functions independently of the sentence—it is not related to it grammatically. If an interjection stands on its own, it is set off with a period or an exclamation point. If it appears in a sentence, it is set off with commas.

Wow, look at that sunset!

My pants are covered with mud. Yuck!

Boy, do my legs ache after climbing all those stairs.

Here are some common interjections:

Boy	Hmmm	Oh	Ugh	Whew	Yikes
Hey	Huh	Oops	Well	Wow	Yuck

A. DIRECTIONS: *Rewrite each item. Punctuate the sentence or pair of sentences to set off the interjections. Some sentences or pairs of sentences may be written in more than one way.*

1. Oops the cat spilled his food all over the floor

   _____

2. Ouch I dropped the hammer on my foot

   _____

3. I worked for two hours in the hot sun Whew

   _____

4. Hmmm I think this CD costs way too much

   _____

5. Hey do not go near that downed electric wire

   _____

B. WRITING APPLICATION: *Write three sentences using interjections. Be sure to punctuate the sentences correctly.*

1. _____

2. _____

3. _____

A Christmas Carol: Scrooge and Marley, *Act I,* by Israel Horovitz
Integrated Language Skills: Support for Writing a Letter

Use this form to prepare to **write a letter** to Scrooge.

Salutation
   State your main point: Scrooge is missing out in life by being cranky and negative with the people around him.
   State a specific thing that Scrooge is missing out on. Include a detail from the play or from your experience to support your point.
   State another specific thing that Scrooge is missing out on. Include a detail from the play or from your experience to support your point.
   Conclude with a summary or a request that Scrooge change his behavior.
Closing,
Signature

Dear _____,
_____
_____
_____
_____
_____
_____
_____
_____
_____
_____
_____
_____
_____
_____
_____
_____
_____
_____
_____
_____
_____
_____
                              _____
                              _____

Now, prepare a final draft of your letter.

Name _____ Date _____

"A Christmas Carol: Scrooge and Marley, *Act 2*" by Israel Horowitz

Writing About the Big Question

Do others see us more clearly than we see ourselves?

Big Question Vocabulary

appearance	appreciate	assumption	bias	characteristic
define	focus	identify	ignore	image
perception	perspective	reaction	reflect	reveal

A. *Choose one word from the list above to complete each sentence. There may be more than one right answer.*

1. Do you think someone's _____ can tell you something about their personality?

2. The players felt that the coach had a _____ against short players.

3. Luke found it difficult to _____ on his work in the noisy classroom.

B. *Follow the directions in responding to each of the items below.*

1. Make a list of four or more different ways people can communicate. For example, people can communicate by *telephone*. Write your response in a complete sentence.

   _____

   _____

2. Choose one of the means of communication you listed in question 1. Write three or more sentences describing the good and bad points of communicating that way. Use at least two of the Big Question vocabulary words. You may use the words in different forms (for example you can change *reflect* to *reflection*).

   _____

   _____

C. *Complete the sentence below. Then, write a short paragraph in which you connect this sentence to the big question.*

   In order to change, we must first identify _____

   _____

   _____

A Christmas Carol: Scrooge and Marley, *Act II,* by Israel Horovitz
Reading: Adjust Your Reading Rate to Suit Your Purpose

Setting a purpose for reading is deciding before you read what you want to get out of a text. The purpose you set will affect the way you read.

Adjust your reading rate to suit your purpose. When you read a play, follow these guidelines:

- Read stage directions slowly and carefully. They describe action that may not be revealed by the dialogue.
- Read short lines of dialogue quickly in order to create the feeling of conversation.
- Read longer speeches by a single character slowly in order to reflect on the character's words and look for clues to the message.

DIRECTIONS: *Read the following passages, and answer the questions that follow each one.*

MAN # 1. Hey, you, watch where you're going.

MAN # 2. Watch it yourself, mate!

[PRESENT *sprinkles them directly, they change.*]

MAN # 1. I pray go in ahead of me. It's Christmas. You be first!

MAN # 2. No, no. I must insist that YOU be first!

1. How would you read the preceding dialogue? Why?

   _____

2. How would you read the stage directions? Why?

   _____

3. What important information do the stage directions contain? How does it affect your understanding of the lines that follow it?

   _____

   _____

   _____

PRESENT. Mark my words, Ebenezer Scrooge. I do not present the Cratchits to you because they are a handsome, or brilliant family. They are not handsome. They are not brilliant. They are not well-dressed, or tasteful to the times. Their shoes are not even waterproofed by virtue of money or cleverness spent. So when the pavement is wet, so are the insides of their shoes and the tops of their toes. They are the Cratchits, Mr. Scrooge. They are not highly special. They are happy, grateful, pleased with one another, contented with the time and how it passes. They don't sing very well, do they? But, nonetheless, they do sing . . . [*Pauses*] think of that, Scrooge. Fifteen shillings a week and they do sing . . . hear their song until its end.

4. How would you read the preceding passage? Why?

   _____

   _____

A Christmas Carol: Scrooge and Marley, *Act II*, by Israel Horovitz
Literary Analysis: Stage Directions

Stage directions are the words in the script of a drama that are not spoken by characters. When a play is performed, you can see the set, the characters, and the movements, and you can hear the sound effects. When you read a play, you get this information from the stage directions. Stage directions are usually printed in italic type and set off by brackets or parentheses.

DIRECTIONS: *Read the following passages, and answer the questions that follow each one.*

[BOB CRATCHIT *enters, carrying* TINY TIM *atop his shoulder. He wears a threadbare and fringe-less comforter hanging down in front of him.* TINY TIM *carries small crutches and his small legs are bound in an iron frame brace.*]

1. Who appears in this scene?

   _____

2. What does the description of Bob Cratchit reveal about the Cratchit family?

   _____

3. What does the description of Tiny Tim reveal about him?

   _____

   _____

SCROOGE. Specter, something informs me that our parting moment is at hand. I know it, but I know not how I know it.

[FUTURE *points to the other side of the stage. Lights out on* CRATCHITS. FUTURE *moves slowing, gliding . . .* FUTURE *points opposite.* FUTURE *leads* SCROOGE *to a wall and a tombstone. He points to the stone.*]

Am I that man those ghoulish parasites so gloated over?

4. Who appears in this scene? How do you know?

   _____

   _____

5. What do the stage directions reveal that the dialogue does not reveal?

   _____

   _____

   _____

A Christmas Carol: Scrooge and Marley, *Act II,* by Israel Horovitz
Vocabulary Builder

Word List

astonish   audible   compulsion   intercedes   meager   severe

A. DIRECTIONS: *Think about the meaning of the italicized word from the Word List in each sentence. Then, answer the question, and explain your answer.*

1. Scrooge's new attitude will *astonish* his family. Will they be surprised by it?

_____

2. Scrooge has a *compulsion* to go with each of the ghosts. Can he easily resist going?

_____

3. Mrs. Cratchit's judgment of Scrooge is *severe.* Does she think highly of him?

_____

4. Scrooge paid Cratchit a *meager* salary. Was the salary generous?

_____

5. The actor's voice is *audible* when he whispers. Can the audience hear him?

_____

6. The Ghost of Christmas Future *intercedes* on Scrooge's behalf. Does the ghost help Scrooge?

_____

B. WORD STUDY: *The Latin prefix* inter- *means "between, among." Read the following sentences. Use your knowledge of the prefix* inter- *to write a full sentence to answer each question. Include the italicized word in your answer.*

1. Have your parents ever *interceded* on your behalf?

_____

2. If a ball is *intercepted*, does it reach its destination?

_____

3. Is a highway *intersection* a place where two roads meet?

_____

A Christmas Carol: Scrooge and Marley, *Act II*, by Israel Horovitz
Integrated Language Skills: Grammar

Double Negatives

Double negatives occur when two negative words appear in a sentence, but only one is needed. Examples of negative words are *nothing, not, never,* and *no.* You can correct a double negative by revising the sentence.

Incorrect	Correct
I do <u>not</u> have <u>no</u> homework tonight.	I do <u>not</u> have <u>any</u> homework tonight.
You <u>never</u> said <u>nothing</u> about that movie.	You <u>never</u> said <u>anything</u> about that movie.

A. DIRECTIONS: *Put a checkmark (✓) next to each sentence that uses a negative word correctly. Put an ✗ next to each sentence that contains a double negative.*

____ 1. Do not ever say nothing to Mom about the surprise party.

____ 2. You never told me anything about your new coach.

____ 3. The team never had time to make a comeback.

____ 4. We do not have no reason to get up early tomorrow.

____ 5. They did not have no money for the movie.

B. Writing Application: *Rewrite each sentence to eliminate the double negative.*

1. We do not have no bread for sandwiches.

   _____

2. The spy never had no intention of giving himself up.

   _____

3. This article does not have nothing to do with our assignment.

   _____

4. They are not going to no championship game tonight.

   _____

5. Our dog will not ever eat no food she does not like.

   _____

A Christmas Carol: Scrooge and Marley, *Act II*, by Israel Horovitz
Integrated Language Skills: Support for Writing a Tribute

To prepare to write a **tribute,** or an expression of admiration, to the changed Ebenezer Scrooge, answer the following questions.

What is Scrooge like before the change?

_____

_____

What anecdotes—brief stories that make a point—illustrate Scrooge's character before the change?

_____

_____

_____

_____

What causes Scrooge to change?

_____

_____

What is Scrooge like after the change?

_____

_____

What anecdotes illustrate Scrooge's character after the change?

_____

_____

_____

_____

Now, write a draft of your tribute to Scrooge. Be sure to explain how Scrooge has changed and why his new behavior deserves to be honored. Use this space to write your first draft.

_____

_____

_____

_____

from **A Christmas Carol: Scrooge and Marley,** *Act I, Scenes 2 & 5* by Israel Horovitz

Writing About the Big Question

Do others see us more clearly than we see ourselves?

Big Question Vocabulary

appearance	appreciate	assumption	bias	characteristic
define	focus	identify	ignore	image
perception	perspective	reaction	reflect	reveal

A. *Choose one word from the list above to complete each sentence. There may be more than one right answer.*

1. The wrong _____ will lead to the wrong conclusion.

2. It is important to _____ on life's big events.

3. Her family members tried not to _____ the plans for the surprise party.

B. *Follow the directions in responding to each of the items below.*

1. Think of at least three adjectives or descriptive phrases that you feel describe you well. List the adjectives or phrases in a complete sentence.

_____

_____

2. Write at least two sentences describing an article of clothing that makes you feel special. Write your response in complete sentences. Use at least one of the Big Question vocabulary words. You may use the words in different forms (for example, you can change *reveal* to *reveals*).

_____

_____

C. *Complete the sentence below. Then, write a short paragraph in which you connect this sentence to the Big Question.*

Over time, people change _____

_____

_____

from **A Christmas Carol: Scrooge and Marley,** *Act 1, Scenes 2 & 5* by Israel Horovitz
Literary Analysis: Comparing Characters

A **character** is a person who takes part in a literary work. Like main characters in stories and novels, main characters in dramas have traits that make them unique. These may include qualities such as dependability, intelligence, selfishness, and stubbornness. The characters in dramas have motives, or reasons, for behaving the way they do. For example, one character may be motivated by compassion, while another may be motivated by guilt.

When you read a drama, pay attention to what each character says and does, and note the reactions those words and actions spark in others. Notice what those words and actions reveal about the character's traits and motives.

In drama, one way to develop a character is through a **foil,** a character whose behavior and attitude contrast with those of the main character. With a foil, audiences can see good in contrast with bad or generousness in contrast with selfishness.

DIRECTIONS: *Answer the following questions to compare the older Scrooge with Fezziwig.*

Question	Scrooge	Fezziwig
1. What does the character say?		
2. What does the character do?		
3. How does the character react to Christmas?		
4. What do other characters say to or about him?		
5. What adjectives describe the character?		

from A Christmas Carol: Scrooge and Marley, *Act I, Scenes 2 & 5* by Israel Horovitz
Vocabulary Builder

Word List

    fiddler   snuffs   suitors

A. DIRECTIONS: *Complete the word maps by writing a definition, synonyms, and an example sentence for each word from the Word List.*

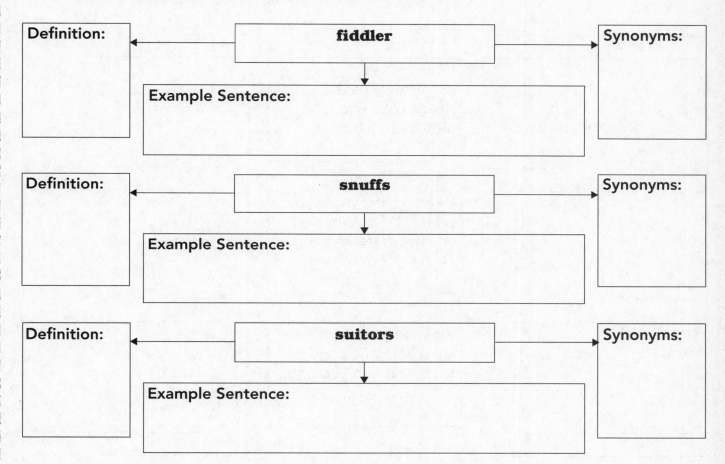

Definition:

fiddler

Synonyms:

Example Sentence:

Definition:

snuffs

Synonyms:

Example Sentence:

Definition:

suitors

Synonyms:

Example Sentence:

B. DIRECTIONS: *Write the letter of the word whose meaning is* most like *that of the word from the Word List.*

_____ 1. fiddler
    A. crab   B. musician   C. violinist   D. tinkerer

_____ 2. snuffs
    A. sniffs   B. erases   C. blots   D. extinguishes

_____ 3. suitors
    A. boyfriends   B. tailors   C. lawyers   D. apprentices

from **A Christmas Carol: Scrooge and Marley,** *Act I, Scenes 2 & 5* by Israel Horovitz

Support for Writing to Compare Literary Works

Use this graphic organizer to gather notes for an essay in which you compare and contrast Fezziwig and Scrooge.

Scrooge   **Fezziwig**

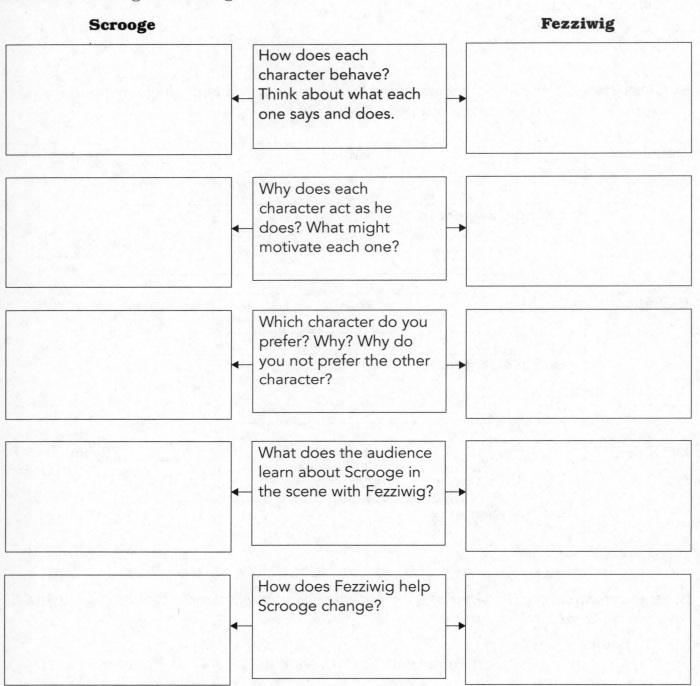

How does each character behave? Think about what each one says and does.

Why does each character act as he does? What might motivate each one?

Which character do you prefer? Why? Why do you not prefer the other character?

What does the audience learn about Scrooge in the scene with Fezziwig?

How does Fezziwig help Scrooge change?

Now, use your notes to write an essay comparing and contrasting Fezziwig and Scrooge. Be sure to discuss how each character's actions and words help the playwright make a point about Scrooge and his behavior.

Name _____ Date _____

"**The Monsters Are Due on Maple Street**" by Rod Serling
Writing About the Big Question

Do others see us more clearly than we see ourselves?

Big Question Vocabulary

appearance	appreciate	assumption	bias	characteristic
define	focus	identify	ignore	image
perception	perspective	reaction	reflect	reveal

A. *Choose one word from the list above to complete each sentence. There may be more than one right answer.*

1. Most people have one _____ that is more noticeable than the others.

2. Sometimes it is hard to _____ your talents.

3. It is dangerous to _____ your shortcomings.

B. *Follow the directions in responding to each of the items below.*

1. List at least four ways that kids project an image to others.

   _____

   _____

2. Do you think school uniforms are a good idea? Write three or more sentences explaining your position. Use at least two of the Big Question vocabulary words. You may use the words in different forms (for example, you can change *reflect* to *reflection*).

   _____

   _____

C. *Complete the sentence below. Then, write a short paragraph in which you connect this sentence to the Big Question.*

   When we are afraid, our reactions can sometimes _____

   _____

   _____

"The Monsters Are Due on Maple Street" by Rod Serling

Reading: Distinguish Between Important and Unimportant Details to Write a Summary

A **summary** is a brief statement that presents only the main ideas and most important details. Summarizing helps you review and understand what you are reading. To summarize, you must first **distinguish between important and unimportant details.** Ask yourself questions like these:

- Is the detail necessary to an understanding of the literary work?
- Would the work hold together without the inclusion of this information?

As you read, pause periodically to recall and restate only the key events and important details.

DIRECTIONS: *Read these summaries of portions of "The Monsters Are Due on Maple Street." Then, answer the questions that follow each summary.*

It is an ordinary September evening on Maple Street when a roar is heard and a flash is seen. The power goes off, and telephones and portable radios stop working. One neighbor leaves to see what is happening on another street. Another neighbor says that he will go downtown to find out what is going on. For no explainable reason, his car will not start. He and a third neighbor decide to walk downtown. Tommy, a fourteen-year-old boy who wears eyeglasses, tells the men not to go. Tommy tells the crowd that what is happening is like every story about aliens he has read. He says that before they land, aliens send a family that looks human to live in a community and prepare for the aliens' arrival.

1. What is the main idea of the preceding summary?

   _____

2. Which detail in the preceding summary is unnecessary?

   _____

After Les Goodman's car starts on its own, the neighbors become suspicious of Goodman. A neighbor says that she has seen him standing on his porch in the middle of the night, looking at the sky. Goodman explains that he often has insomnia. He compares his neighbors to frightened rabbits. He says that they are letting a nightmare begin.

3. What is the main idea of the preceding summary?

   _____

   _____

4. Which detail in the preceding summary is unimportant? How do you know it is unimportant?

   _____

"The Monsters Are Due on Maple Street" by Rod Serling
Literary Analysis: A Character's Motives

A character's motives are the reasons for his or her actions. Motives are usually related to what a character wants, needs, or feels. Powerful motives include love, anger, fear, and greed. As you read, think about what motivates each character.

DIRECTIONS: *Read the following passages from "The Monsters Are Due on Maple Street." Then, answer the questions that follow, about the characters' motives.*

STEVE. It isn't just the power failure, Charlie. If it was, we'd still be able to get a broadcast on the portable.

[*There's a murmur of reaction to this.* STEVE *looks from face to face and then over to his car.*]

STEVE. I'll run downtown. We'll get this all straightened out.

1. What are Steve's motives for volunteering to go downtown?

_____

_____

GOODMAN. I just don't understand it. I tried to start it and it wouldn't start. You saw me. All of you saw me.

[*And now, just as suddenly as the engine started, it stops and there's a long silence that is gradually intruded upon by the frightened murmuring of the people.*]

GOODMAN. I don't understand. I swear . . . I don't understand. What's happening?

DON. Maybe you better tell us. Nothing's working on this street. Nothing. No lights, no power, no radio. . . . Nothing except one car—yours!

[*The people pick this up and now their murmuring becomes a loud chant filling the air with accusations and demands for action. Two of the men . . . head toward* GOODMAN, *who backs away, backing into his car and now at bay.*]

GOODMAN. Wait a minute now. You keep your distance—all of you. So I've got a car that starts by itself—well, that's a freak thing. I admit it. But does that make me some kind of a criminal or something? I don't know why the car works—it just does!

2. Which speaker appears to be motivated by confusion? _____

3. Which speaker appears to be motivated by suspicion? _____

4. What emotion or emotions appear to be motivating Goodman after the crowd has accused him? _____

5. Why might Goodman be feeling this emotion? _____

_____

"The Monsters Are Due on Maple Street" by Rod Serling
Vocabulary Builder

Word List

defiant   flustered   metamorphosis   persistently   sluggishly   transfixed

A. DIRECTIONS: *Read each sentence, and think about the meaning of the italicized word from the Word List. Then, answer the question, and explain your answer.*

1. Would you expect a *flustered* person to speak clearly?

   _____

2. If a heavy rain fills a riverbed, will the river move *sluggishly*?

   _____

3. If someone *persistently* asks a question, would you assume that she is eager to know the answer?

   _____

4. Would a *defiant* child be likely to refuse to do his chores?

   _____

5. If a rude person undergoes a *metamorphosis*, is she likely to continue to be rude?

   _____

6. If a person is *transfixed* by a performance, does he find it interesting?

   _____

B. WORD STUDY: *The Latin root -sist- means "stand." Read the following sentences. Use your knowledge of the root -sist- to write a full sentence to answer each question. Include the italicized word in your answer.*

1. Is an *assistant* someone who competes with you?

   _____

2. If you *insist* on doing something, are you expressing yourself in a firm manner?

   _____

3. Is a *persistent* person going to give up easily?

   _____

All-in-One Workbook
262

"The Monsters Are Due on Maple Street" by Rod Serling
Integrated Language Skills: Grammar

Sentence Functions and Endmarks

Sentences are classified into four categories, according to their function.

Category, Function, and Endmark	Example
A **declarative sentence** makes a statement. It ends with a period. (.)	Monsters are due on Maple Street.
An **interrogative sentence** asks a question. It ends with a question mark. (?)	What is going on?
An **imperative sentence** gives a command. It ends with a period or an exclamation point. (. or !)	Do not leave town. Watch out!
An **exclamatory sentence** calls out or exclaims. It ends with an exclamation point. (!)	Hey! How frightened we were!

Note that the subject of an imperative sentence is always the word *you*, and it is never stated: *(You) do not leave town. (You) watch out!*

Also note that in your writing, you should use exclamatory sentences as if they were a powerful spice. For the greatest effect, use them sparingly.

A. DIRECTIONS: *Add the correct endmark to each sentence. Then, identify the sentence as* declarative, interrogative, imperative, *or* exclamatory.

1. Where did you go on your field trip on Saturday _____ _____
2. We drove to a quarry and looked for fossils _____ _____
3. What cool fossils _____ _____
4. This one is a trilobite _____ _____
5. Don't drop it _____ _____
6. Next time we go, you should come with us _____ _____
7. Will you tell me when you plan to go again _____ _____

B. Writing Application: *Write a short dialogue between two characters. Use at least one of each kind of sentence. Label your sentences* dec *for declarative,* int *for interrogative,* imp *for imperative, and* exclam *for exclamatory.*

_____

_____

_____

_____

"The Monsters Are Due on Maple Street" by Rod Serling
Integrated Language Skills: Support for Writing a Summary

A **summary** is a brief statement that presents only the main ideas and most important details of a literary work. Summarizing helps you review and understand what you are reading.

To summarize, you must first distinguish between important and unimportant details. Ask yourself questions like the following:

- Is this detail necessary for my understanding of the literary work?

- Would the literary work hold together without this information?

Use the following chart to take notes for your summary of Act 1 or Act 2 of the screenplay. Fill in the left-hand column first. Finish this column by stating the theme, or underlying meaning, of the act. Then, go through the right-hand column, and verify that each fact you are including reflects the act's meaning.

	Supports Underlying Meaning?
Main Idea #1:	(Y/N)
Supporting Detail:	(Y/N)
Supporting Detail:	(Y/N)
Supporting Detail:	(Y/N)
Main Idea #2	(Y/N)
Supporting Detail:	(Y/N)
Supporting Detail:	(Y/N)
Supporting Detail:	(Y/N)
Underlying Meaning:	

Now, write a draft of your summary. Include only those ideas and supporting details that reflect the underlying meaning of the screenplay.

from **Grandpa and the Statue** by Arthur Miller
"My Head Is Full of Starshine" by Peg Kehret
Writing About the Big Question
Do others see us more clearly than we see ourselves?

Big Question Vocabulary

appearance	appreciate	assumption	bias	characteristic
define	focus	identify	ignore	image
perception	perspective	reaction	reflect	reveal

A. *Choose one word from the list above to complete each sentence. There may be more than one right answer.*

1. Some musicians work very hard to create the right _____ for their band.

2. An older person's _____ on a problem may be different from a child's.

3. What we see, smell, taste, hear and feel adds up to our _____ of the world.

B. *Follow the directions in responding to each of the items below.*

1. List at least two different ways people may get the wrong impression of another person. Write your response in complete sentences.

   _____

   _____

2. If you could see yourself as others do, would you want to? Write at least three sentences explaining your position. Use at least two of the Big Question vocabulary words. You may use the words in different forms (for example, you can change *reflect* to *reflection*).

   _____

   _____

C. *Complete the sentence below. Then, write a short paragraph in which you connect this sentence to the Big Question.*

   The best way to understand a person is to _____

   _____

   _____

from **Grandpa and the Statue** by Arthur Miller
"My Head Is Full of Starshine" by Peg Kehret
Literary Analysis: Comparing Dramatic Speeches

Dramatic speeches are performed by actors in a drama or play. Whether spoken by a character who is onstage alone or given by a character who is part of a larger scene, these speeches move the action of the story forward and help define the conflict in a play. There are two main types of dramatic speeches:

- **Monologues** are long, uninterrupted speeches that are spoken by a single character. They reveal the private thoughts and feelings of the character.
- **Dialogues** are conversations between characters. They reveal characters' traits, develop conflict, and move the plot forward.

Grandpa and the Statue is a dialogue, and "My Head Is Full of Starshine" is a monologue. As you read these selections, consider what you learn about the characters. Also, think about how other key information is revealed.

DIRECTIONS: *Answer the following questions about the excerpts from* Grandpa and the Statue *and "My Head Is Full of Starshine."*

1. In the excerpt from *Grandpa and the Statue,* what does the audience learn about Monaghan's character?

   _____

   _____

2. What conflict is revealed in Monaghan and Sheean's dialogue in the excerpt from *Grandpa and the Statue?*

   _____

   _____

3. In the excerpt from *Grandpa and the Statue,* what does Monaghan reveal about himself in the speech about his experiences when he first came to America?

   _____

   _____

4. How does the reader learn about the writer's tendency to daydream in "My Head Is Full of Starshine"?

   _____

   _____

5. What does the writer reveal about her feelings toward having library fines in "My Head Is Full of Starshine"?

   _____

   _____

All-in-One Workbook
266

from Grandpa and the Statue by Arthur Miller
"My Head Is Full of Starshine" by Peg Kehret
Vocabulary Builder

Word List

peeved   potential   practical   rummaging

A. DIRECTIONS: *Read each sentence, paying attention to the italicized word from the Word List. Then, answer each question, and explain your answer.*

1. If you accidentally threw away a diamond ring, might you be *rummaging* through the trash?

   _____

2. Is a *practical* person one who daydreams and puts things off until the last minute?

   _____

3. Is a relaxed, easygoing person likely to be easily *peeved*?

   _____

4. Is someone with great *potential* as an athlete likely to compete in the Olympics someday?

   _____

B. DIRECTIONS: *Write the letter of the word whose meaning is* most like *that of the word from the Word List.*

____ 1. peeved
   A. outgoing   B. happy   C. realistic   D. annoyed

____ 2. practical
   A. happy   B. realistic   C. strong   D. imaginative

____ 3. rummaging
   A. reselling   B. organizing   C. searching   D. destroying

____ 4. potential
   A. capability   B. intelligence   C. sharpness   D. volume

Name _____ Date _____

from **Grandpa and the Statue** by Arthur Miller
"My Head Is Full of Starshine" by Peg Kehret
Support for Writing to Compare Dramatic Speeches

Use this graphic organizer to take notes for your essay comparing and contrasting the dramatic speech by Monaghan in the excerpt from *Grandpa and the Statue* with the one by the speaker in "My Head Is Full of Starshine."

Which ideas in the speech are familiar to you? _____
_____
_____
_____
_____
_____

With which ideas in the speech do you agree or disagree? _____
_____
_____
_____
_____
_____

Which character do you relate to more? Why?
_____
_____
_____
_____
_____
_____
_____
_____
_____

The speaker in "My Head Is Full of Starshine"

Monaghan in *Grandpa and the Statue*

From which character do you think you learn more? Why? _____
_____
_____
_____
_____
_____
_____
_____
_____

Which ideas in the speech are familiar to you? _____
_____
_____
_____
_____
_____

With which ideas in the speech do you agree or disagree? _____
_____
_____
_____
_____
_____

Now, use your notes to write a draft of an essay comparing and contrasting the two speeches.

Solidarity, performed by the Fake Gimms

We have a **common** goal to achieve
Yea, what we want is the same.
We share a place, our home, our **community**.
We have a stake in the game.

It's bigger than you.
It's bigger than me, too.

Just a single **individual** trying to succeed.
It's not so easy by yourself,
You've got to work as a **team**.

It's bigger than you.
It's bigger than me, too.

Part of the **culture** stems from **tradition**.
The ways that we're defined.
These are the things that bring us together,
The things that **unify**.

It's bigger than you.
It's bigger than me, too.

Our **duty** and obligation,
Stand as one, a **group** of many in solidarity.
A **family** with a **unique** plan.
More effective than a single man.
To make a change when it matters.
Now.

Now.

I am a product of my surroundings,
Of my **environment**.
I have a **custom** and it defines how I live.

All-in-One Workbook
269

It's bigger than you.

It's bigger than me, too.

Ethnicity and identity might show them where we're from,

But **diversity** and difference will serve to make us strong.

It's bigger than you.

It's bigger than me, too.

Song Title: **Solidarity**

Artist / Performed by the Fake Gimms

Vocals & Guitar: Joe Pfeiffer

Guitar: Greg Kuter

Bass Guitar: Jared Duncan

Drums: Tom Morra

Lyrics by the Fake Gimms

Produced by the Fake Gimms

Studio Production: Mike Pandolfo, Wonderful

Executive Producer: Keith London, Defined Mind

Unit 6: Themes in the Oral Tradition
Big Question Vocabulary—1

The Big Question: Community or individual: Which is more important?

common: *adj.* shared with others, such as mutual ideas or interests

community: *n.* a town or neighborhood in which a group of people live; other forms: *communal, communities*

culture: *n.* the ideas, beliefs, and customs that are shared by people in a society; other forms: *cultural, cultured*

individual: *n.* a person; other form: *individually*

unique: *adj.* single, one of a kind

A. DIRECTIONS: *Follow each direction.*

1. Explain the difference between something that is **common** and something that is **unique**. Provide an example of each. _____
   _____

2. Explain the relationship between an **individual** and his or her **community.** _____
   _____

3. Provide three examples of **culture**—ideas, beliefs, or customs shared by people living in your community or in the United States at large.
   _____
   _____
   _____

B. DIRECTIONS: *Provide an example of each of the following.*

1. a common interest shared by you and a friend: _____
   _____

2. a community in which you would like to live someday: _____
   _____

3. a foreign culture of your family, neighbors, or friends: _____
   _____

4. an individual whom you admire: _____
   _____

5. a characteristic or feature that makes you unique: _____
   _____

All-in-One Workbook
271

Name _____ Date _____

Unit 6: Themes in the Oral Tradition
Big Question Vocabulary—2

The Big Question: Community or individual: Which is more important?

custom: *n.* a tradition shared by people from the same culture; other form: *customary*.

diversity: *n.* a variety of different ideas, cultures, or objects; other form: *diverse*

environment: *n.* the setting in which an individual lives; other form: *environmental*

group: *n.* several people or things that are together; other forms: *grouping, grouped*

duty: *n.* conduct due to parents and superiors; tasks, conduct, service, or functions that arise from one's position; other form: *dutiful*

DIRECTIONS: *Answer each question.*

1. Many snakes and colorful birds reside in a rain forest. Which vocabulary word **best** describes where they live? Explain your answer. _____
   _____

2. Sally takes care of her sisters every day when she comes home from school. Which vocabulary word **best** describes this situation? Explain your answer. _____
   _____

3. Every May 1, my sister and I make May baskets. Then we deliver them to our neighbors. Which vocabulary word **best** describes this annual event? Explain your answer.
   _____

4. Everyone interested in running the marathon got together to share their ideas about training. Which vocabulary word **best** describes these individuals? Explain your answer.
   _____

5. The restaurant serves Italian, Spanish, English, African, and German foods. Which vocabulary word **best** describes the menu? Explain your answer. _____
   _____

Unit 6: Themes in the Oral Tradition
Big Question Vocabulary—3

The Big Question: Community or individual: Which is more important?

ethnicity: *n.* the race or national group to which an individual belongs; other form: *ethnic*

family: *n.* a group of people who are related to each other; other forms: *families, familiar*

team: *n.* a group of people who work together to achieve a common goal

tradition: *n.* a belief or custom that has existed for a long time; other form: *traditional*

unify: *v.* to combine two or more things to form a single unit; other form: *unified*

DIRECTIONS: *Answer each question.*

1. Which vocabulary word is an **antonym** for the word *separate* ? Explain their opposite meanings.

_____

2. Chico and Manny's family came to this country from Spain. Which vocabulary word **best** describes their family's roots? Explain your answer. _____

3. The students in my class broke into small groups to create radio plays. Which vocabulary word **best** describes each group? Explain your answer. _____

_____

4. On Valentine's Day each year, my mother and her friend Mrs. Ortiz make delicious heart-shaped cookies. Which vocabulary word **best** describes this annual event? Explain your answer. _____

_____

5. I have four brothers and fifteen cousins. Which vocabulary word **best** describes this group? Explain your answer. _____

_____

Unit 6: Themes in the Oral Tradition
Applying the Big Question

Community or individual—which is more important?

DIRECTIONS: *Complete the chart below to apply what you have learned about the importance of the community and the individual. One row has been completed for you.*

Example	What does the individual want?	What does the community want?	Who won or lost	What I learned
From Literature	Ixtla wants to marry Popo	Ixtla to rule the kingdom	Nobody, because Ixtla dies of a broken heart	Sometimes individuals cannot be forced to do what others wish of them
From Literature				
From Science				
From Social Studies				
From Real Life				

Jon Scieszka
Listening and Viewing

Segment 1: Meet Jon Scieszka
* How did Jon Scieszka choose his audience? Scieszka reads all different types of literature.
* How do you think this helps him come up with writing ideas?

_____

_____

_____

_____

Segment 2: Themes in the Oral Tradition
* Why is Jon Scieszka "amazed" by fairy tales, myths, and legends?
* Why do you think that the retelling of these stories over time is important?

_____

_____

_____

_____

Segment 3: The Writing Process
* Who is Lane Smith, and how is he involved in Jon Scieszka's writing process?
* Why are illustrations important in fairy tales, myths, and fables like the stories that Jon Scieszka writes?

_____

_____

_____

_____

Segment 4: The Rewards of Writing
* Why is being a writer rewarding to Jon Scieszka?
* Why do you think that reading is a valuable activity for young people in today's age of technology?

_____

_____

_____

_____

Learning About the Oral Tradition

The sharing of stories, cultures, and ideas by word of mouth is called the **oral tradition.** Here are common elements of the oral tradition.

- The **theme** is a central idea, message, or insight that a story reveals.
- A **moral** is a lesson about life that is taught by a story.
- **Heroes** and **heroines** are larger-than-life figures whose virtues and deeds are often celebrated in stories from the oral tradition.
- **Storytelling** calls on the talents and personality of the teller to bring the narrative to life. Storytelling techniques include **hyperbole,** or the use of exaggeration or overstatement, and **personification,** the giving of human characteristics to a non-human subject.

Many stories have been written down for readers. Categories of stories in the oral tradition that have been committed to paper include the following.

- **Myths** are ancient tales that describe the actions of gods, goddesses, and the heroes who interact with them.
- **Legends** are traditional stories about the past. They are based on real-life events or people, but they are more fiction than fact.
- **Folk tales** tell about ordinary people. These stories reveal the traditions and values of a culture and teach a lesson about life.
- **Tall tales** are folk tales that contain hyperbole.
- **Fables** are brief animal stories that contain personification. Fables often end with a moral or lesson.
- **Epics** are long narrative poems about a hero who engages in a dangerous journey.

A. DIRECTIONS: *The following items are elements of stories in the oral tradition. Decide which of the two terms matches the preceding description. Underline your choice.*

1. A woman spins cloth out of gold.   hyperbole   personification
2. The god Apollo drives his chariot across the sky.   myth   legend
3. Baseball great Babe Ruth hits the ball into another state.   fable   legend
4. The sun refuses to shine on an evil character's birthday.   personification   theme
5. It is best to be prepared.   moral   hero

B. DIRECTIONS: *On the lines below, write a plot summary for an original fable. Include one or more animal characters, and include an example of personification. End your fable with a moral. Use a separate sheet of paper if more space is needed.*

_____

_____

_____

"Grasshopper Logic," "The Other Frog Prince," and "duckbilled platypus vs. beefsnakstik®" by Jon Scieszka and Lane Smith

Model Selection: The Oral Tradition

Jon Scieszka entertains readers with his comical versions of traditional **fairy tales** and **fables. Fables** are brief animal stories that contain personification. Fables often end with a moral or lesson. These three short selections are humorous examples of stories in the **oral tradition**—the sharing of stories, cultures, and ideas by word of mouth. Elements of the oral tradition include the following.

- The **theme** is a central idea, message, or insight that a story reveals.
- A **moral** is a lesson about life that is taught by a story. An example of a moral is "Hard work leads to success."
- **Hyperbole** is a deliberate exaggeration or overstatement. It is often used to create humor. For example, a man might be as strong as an ox.
- **Personification** is the granting of human characteristics to a nonhuman subject. This would include a talking fox or an angry tree.

A. DIRECTIONS: *Answer the following questions.*

1. Give an example of hyperbole from "Grasshopper Logic." Tell why it is a hyperbole.

   _____

   _____

2. How does the ending of "The Other Frog Prince" differ from the ending of the traditional "Frog Prince" fairy tale?

   _____

   _____

3. What types of characters are in "duckbilled platypus vs. beefsnakstik®," and in what specific ways are they examples of personification?

   _____

   _____

B. DIRECTIONS: *On the lines below, describe the specific ways in which the grasshopper and his mother talk and act like humans.*

_____

_____

_____

_____

_____

_____

"Icarus and Deadalus" by Josephine Preston Peabody

Writing About the Big Question

Community or individual: Which is more important?

Big Question Vocabulary

common	community	culture	custom	diversity
duty	environment	ethnicity	family	group
individual	team	tradition	unify	unique

A. *Use one or more words from the list above to complete each sentence.*

1. I used a lot of paper printing drafts of a _____ research project.

2. My teammate was concerned about the impact on the _____ .

3. We decided it was our _____ to recycle.

4. That way we could balance our _____ needs with those of the earth.

B. *Follow the directions in responding to each of the items below.*

1. Describe a time when you became so focused on getting what you wanted that you failed to consider the consequences of your actions.

_____

_____

2. Write two sentences explaining how the preceding experience affected those around you, such as friends or family. Use at least two of the Big Question vocabulary words.

_____

_____

_____

C. *Complete the sentence below. Then, write a short paragraph in which you connect this experience to the big question.*

When an individual becomes too focused on his or her own desires, _____

_____

_____

_____

_____

_____

"Icarus and Daedalus" by Josephine Preston Peabody

Reading: Ask Questions to Analyze Cause-and-Effect Relationships

A **cause** is an event, an action, or a feeling that produces an **effect,** or result. In some literary works, multiple causes result in one single effect. In other works, a single cause results in multiple effects. Effects can also become causes for events that follow. The linking of causes and effects propels the action forward.

As you read, **ask questions** such as "What happened?" and "What will happen as a result of this?" **to analyze cause-and-effect relationships.**

DIRECTIONS: *Use the following graphic organizer to analyze some of the cause-and-effect relationships in "Icarus and Daedalus." The first response has been filled in as an example. Where there is no box in which to write the question you would ask yourself, ask the question mentally, and then write the effect in the next box.*

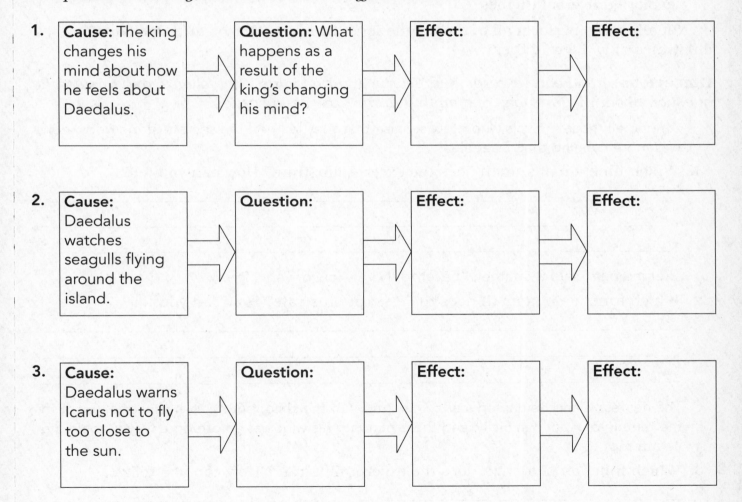

1. **Cause:** The king changes his mind about how he feels about Daedalus.

   Question: What happens as a result of the king's changing his mind?

   Effect:

   Effect:

2. **Cause:** Daedalus watches seagulls flying around the island.

   Question:

   Effect:

   Effect:

3. **Cause:** Daedalus warns Icarus not to fly too close to the sun.

   Question:

   Effect:

   Effect:

"Icarus and Daedalus" by Josephine Preston Peabody
Literary Analysis: Myth

Since time began, people have tried to understand the world around them. Ancient peoples created **myths**—stories that explain natural occurrences and express beliefs about right and wrong. Every culture has its own collection of myths, or *mythology*. In many myths, gods and goddesses have human traits, and human heroes have superhuman traits. Myths explore universal themes and explain the world in human terms.

Most myths perform some of the following functions:

- explain natural occurrences
- express beliefs about right and wrong
- show gods or goddesses with human traits
- show human heroes with superhuman traits
- explore universal themes

Not all myths perform all of those functions, however. "Icarus and Daedalus" illustrates only a few of them.

DIRECTIONS: *Read each excerpt from "Icarus and Daedalus" that follows, and answer the question about the functions of a myth that the excerpt illustrates.*

Among all those mortals who grew so wise that they learned the secrets of the gods, none was more cunning than Daedalus.

1. Which function of a myth does the excerpt illustrate? How can you tell?

   _____

   _____

   _____

"Remember," said the father, "never to fly very low or very high."

2. Which function of a myth does the excerpt illustrate? How can you tell?

   _____

   _____

   _____

The nearest island he named Icaria, in memory of the child; but he, in heavy grief, went to the temple of Apollo in Sicily, and there hung up his wings as an offering. Never again did he attempt to fly.

3. Which function of a myth does the excerpt illustrate? How can you tell?

   _____

   _____

   _____

Name _____   Date _____

"Icarus and Daedalus" by Josephine Preston Peabody
Vocabulary Builder

Word List

aloft   captivity   liberty   reel   sustained   vacancy

A. DIRECTIONS: *Write the letter of the word that means* the same or about the same as *the word from the Word List.*

____ 1. vacancy
   A. property   C. emptiness
   B. appointment   D. discount

____ 2. sustained
   A. supported   C. deprived
   B. starved   D. competed

____ 3. liberty
   A. dependence   C. history
   B. freedom   D. agreement

____ 4. aloft
   A. in the air   C. trapped
   B. still   D. on the ground

____ 5. reel
   A. punch   C. unravel
   B. sing   D. stagger

____ 6. captivity
   A. exterior   C. resort
   B. prison   D. arrangement

B. WORD STUDY: *The Latin root -vac- means "empty." Answer each of the following questions using one of these words containing -vac-: vacancy, vacuous, vacuum.*

1. Why would you look for a *vacancy* sign if you needed to rent a room?

   _____

2. What has been done to a jar that is *vacuum* packed?

   _____

3. Why would a *vacuous* TV show not be worth watching?

   _____

All-in-One Workbook
281

"Demeter and Persephone" by Anne Terry White
Writing About the Big Question

Community or individual: Which is more important?

Big Question Vocabulary

common	community	culture	custom	diversity
duty	environment	ethnicity	family	group
individual	team	tradition	unify	unique

A. *Use one or more words from the list above to complete each sentence.*

1. Zach and his dad had a _____ of washing their cars on Sunday.

2. However, their local _____ was experiencing a water shortage.

3. They had a _____ to consider the impact of their actions on others.

4. They decided to forgo the carwash for the _____ good of the town.

B. *Follow the directions in responding to each of the items below.*

1. Describe a time when you or someone you know was faced with a decision that would affect a large number of people. _____

   _____

2. Write two sentences explaining the decision and how it affected those involved. Use at least two of the Big Question vocabulary words.

   _____

   _____

C. *Complete the sentence below. Then, write a short paragraph in which you connect this situation to the big question.*

When making a decision that will affect the greater community, it is one's duty to

_____

_____

_____

_____

_____

_____

Name _____ Date _____

"Demeter and Persephone" by Anne Terry White
Reading: Ask Questions to Analyze Cause-and-Effect Relationships

A **cause** is an event, an action, or a feeling that produces an **effect,** or result. In some literary works, multiple causes result in one single effect. In other works, a single cause results in multiple effects. Effects can also become causes for events that follow. The linking of causes and effects propels the action forward.

As you read, **ask questions** such as "What happened?" and "What will happen as a result of this?" **to analyze cause-and-effect relationships.**

DIRECTIONS: *Use the following graphic organizer to analyze some of the cause-and-effect relationships in "Demeter and Persephone." The first response has been filled in as an example. Where there is no box in which to write the question you would ask yourself, ask the question mentally, and then write the effect in the next box.*

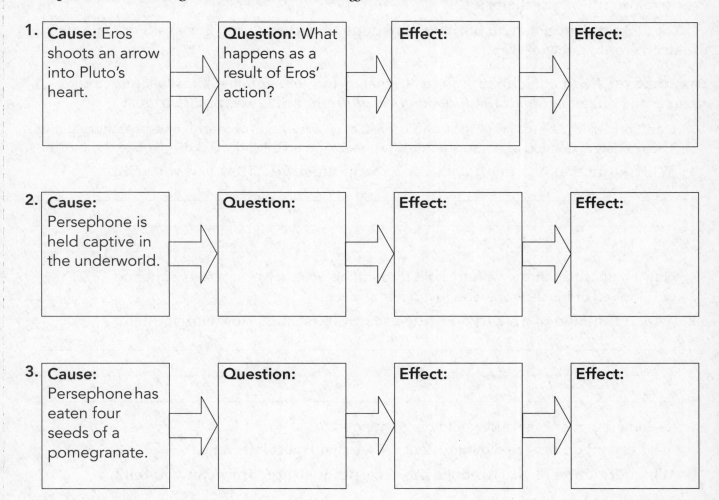

1. **Cause:** Eros shoots an arrow into Pluto's heart. → **Question:** What happens as a result of Eros' action? → **Effect:** → **Effect:**

2. **Cause:** Persephone is held captive in the underworld. → **Question:** → **Effect:** → **Effect:**

3. **Cause:** Persephone has eaten four seeds of a pomegranate. → **Question:** → **Effect:** → **Effect:**

"Demeter and Persephone" by Anne Terry White
Literary Analysis: Myth

Since time began, people have tried to understand the world around them. Ancient peoples created **myths**—stories that explain natural occurrences and express beliefs about right and wrong. Every culture has its own collection of myths, or *mythology.* In many myths, gods and goddesses have human traits, and human heroes have superhuman traits. Myths explore universal themes and explain the world in human terms.

Most myths perform some of the following functions:

- explain natural occurrences
- express beliefs about right and wrong
- show gods or goddesses with human traits
- show human heroes with superhuman traits
- explore universal themes

Not all myths perform all of those functions, however. "Demeter and Persephone" illustrates only a few of them.

DIRECTIONS: *Read each excerpt from "Demeter and Persephone" that follows, and answer the question about the function of a myth that the excerpt illustrates.*

Deep under Mt. Aetna, the gods had buried alive a number of fearful, fire-breathing giants. The monsters heaved and struggled to get free. And so mightily did they shake the earth . . .

1. Which function of a myth does the excerpt illustrate? How can you tell?

   _____

   _____

   _____

Now an unaccustomed warmth stole through his veins. His stern eyes softened. . . . The god looked at Persephone and loved her at once.

2. Which function of a myth does the excerpt illustrate? How can you tell?

   _____

   _____

   _____

It seemed that all mankind would die of hunger.
"This cannot go on," said mighty Zeus. "I see that I must intervene."

3. Which function of a myth does the excerpt illustrate? How can you tell?

   _____

   _____

   _____

Name _____ Date _____

"Demeter and Persephone" by Anne Terry White
Vocabulary Builder

Word List

abode   defies   dominions   intervene   monarch   realm

A. DIRECTIONS: *Revise each sentence so that it makes sense.*

1. Zeus is pleased when a god or goddess <u>defies</u> his orders.

   _____

2. When the world is calm and at peace, Zeus is likely to <u>intervene</u>.

   _____

3. The <u>monarch</u> bowed before his subjects.

   _____

4. Pluto rules supreme outside his <u>dominions</u>.

   _____

5. Within the <u>realm</u> of fantasy, imagination is restrained.

   _____

6. With its cheerful fire and sweet scent, the Queen's <u>abode</u> gave her a sense of danger.

   _____

B. WORD STUDY: *The Latin root -dom- means "master" or "building." Answer each of the following questions using one of these words containing -dom-: domicile, dominant, domesticate.*

1. What do people do in a *domicile*?

   _____

2. If you are a *dominant* figure in politics, what kind of position would you hold?

   _____

3. What happens when you *domesticate* an animal?

   _____

"Icarus and Daedalus" by Josephine Preston Peabody
"Demeter and Persephone" by Anne Terry White

Integrated Language Skills: Grammar

Punctuation: Colons

A **colon** looks like two periods, one above the other (:). Colons are used to introduce a list that follows an independent clause.

> To make wings, Daedalus gathered the following materials: feathers, wax, and thread.

A. PRACTICE: *Each of the following sentences is missing a colon. Rewrite the sentences, and insert a colon in the correct place.*

1. All of the characters in "Demeter and Persephone" are gods or goddesses Aphrodite, Eros, Pluto, Persephone, Demeter, Zeus, and Hermes.

   _____

   _____

2. Daedalus warns Icarus not to do these things fly too low, fly too high, and fly too far from him.

   _____

   _____

B. Writing Application: *Write two sentences about Greek mythology. In each sentence, use a colon to introduce a list.*

_____

_____

_____

_____

_____

_____

_____

_____

_____

_____

_____

_____

_____

Name _____ Date _____

"Icarus and Daedalus" by Josephine Preston Peabody
"Demeter and Persephone" by Anne Terry White
Integrated Language Skills: Support for Writing a Myth

Use the following graphic organizer to take notes for a **myth** you will write to explain a natural phenomenon. You do not have to respond to each prompt in the chart in the order in which it appears, but you should probably decide on the phenomenon you want to explain before you decide on anything else. You might describe the problem and the resolution next and then work on the characters. Coming up with the title may be the last thing you do.

Natural phenomenon that myth will explain:
Title of myth:
Names and traits of characters—how they look, what they do, what they say to one another:
Problem to be solved and creative way in which it will be solved:

Now, write the first draft of your myth.

"Tenochtitlan: Inside the Aztec Capital" by Jacqueline Dineen

Writing About the Big Question

Community or individual: Which is more important?

Big Question Vocabulary

common	community	culture	custom	diversity
duty	environment	ethnicity	family	group
individual	team	tradition	unify	unique

A. *Use one or more words from the list above to complete each sentence.*

1. Gary's volunteer _____ was made up of twenty workers.

2. Each worker contributed something _____ to the project.

3. As they worked together, they developed a strong sense of _____.

4. The work was hard, but they stayed focused on their _____ goal.

B. *Follow the directions in responding to each of the items below.*

1. List two different times when you worked with others on a school or community project.

   _____.

   _____.

2. Write two sentences explaining how your involvement in one of the preceding projects made you feel. Use at least two of the Big Question vocabulary words.

   _____

   _____

   _____

   _____

C. *Complete the sentence below. Then, write a short paragraph in which you connect this situation to the big question.*

   Protecting a community sometimes requires that individuals _____

   _____

   _____

   _____

   _____

Name _____ Date _____

"**Tenochtitlan: Inside the Aztec Capital**" by Jacqueline Dineen
Reading: Reread to Look for Connections That Indicate Cause-and-Effect Relationships

A **cause** is an event or a situation that produces an **effect,** or the result produced. In a story or an essay, each effect may eventually become a cause for the next event. This series of events results in a cause-and-effect chain, which propels the action forward.

As you read, think about the causes and effects of events. If you do not see a clear cause-and-effect relationship in a passage, **reread to look for connections** in the text. Look for words and phrases that identify cause-and-effect relationships—for example, *because, due to, for that reason, therefore,* and *as a result.*

DIRECTIONS: *Read the following sequences of events. Underline any words or phrases that help you identify a cause-and-effect relationship. Then, identify each event as a* cause, *an* effect, *or both* cause and effect.

_____ 1. The Aztecs were excellent engineers.

_____ 2. Therefore, they were able to build three causeways linking the island city to the mainland.

_____ 3. Because of their skill as engineers, they were also able to build bridges that could be removed.

_____ 4. As a result, they could prevent their enemies from reaching the city.

_____ 5. The land around Lake Texcoco was dry.

_____ 6. Because the land was dry, the Aztecs built ditches to irrigate the land.

_____ 7. As they dug, they piled up the earth from the ditches in shallow parts of the lake, thus forming swamp gardens.

_____ 8. Because they had formed swamp gardens, they had land on which to grow crops.

_____ 9. Because they had land on which to grow crops, a portion of the population was able to grow its own food.

_____ 10. Two of the lakes that fed into Lake Texcoco contained salt water.

_____ 11. For that reason, the Aztecs built an embankment to keep out the salt water.

_____ 12. The embankment also protected the city from floods.

"Tenochtitlan: Inside the Aztec Capital" by Jacqueline Dineen
Literary Analysis: Legends and Facts

A **legend** is a traditional story about the past. Legends are based on facts that have grown into fiction over generations of retelling. Legends usually include these elements: a larger-than-life hero or heroine; fantastic events; roots, or a basis, in historical facts; and actions and events that reflect the culture that created the legend.

A **fact** is something that can be proved true. We uncover facts about ancient cultures by studying a variety of sources: written material, paintings, objects, and excavated ruins. When historians are unable to prove a theory about the past, they may speculate, or make a guess, based on the available evidence.

DIRECTIONS: *Read each excerpt from "Tenochtitlan: Inside the Aztec Capital." Then, circle whether the statement describes a* fact *or a* speculation, *and explain how you know.*

1. The Aztecs . . . built three causeways over the swamp to link the city with the mainland.

   Fact / Speculation: _____

   _____

2. These bridges could be removed to leave gaps, and this prevented enemies from getting to the city.

   Fact / Speculation: _____

   _____

3. The Spaniards' first view of Tenochtitlan was described by one of Cortés's soldiers, Bernal Diaz.

   Fact / Speculation: _____

   _____

4. Tenochtitlan was built in a huge valley, the Valley of Mexico.

   Fact / Speculation: _____

   _____

5. Archaeologists think that when Tenochtitlan was at its greatest, about one million people lived in the Valley of Mexico.

   Fact / Speculation: _____

   _____

6. Historians are not sure how many people in Tenochtitlan were farmers, but they think it may have been between one third and one half of the population.

   Fact / Speculation: _____

   _____

"Tenochtitlan: Inside the Aztec Capital" by Jacqueline Dineen
Vocabulary Builder

Word List

causeways   goblets   irrigation   nobility   outskirts   reeds

A. DIRECTIONS: *Read each item, and think about the meaning of the underlined word from the Word List. Then, answer each question, and explain your answer.*

1. Poorer people lived on the <u>outskirts</u> of Tenochtitlan. Did they live near the Temple Mayor?

   _____

   _____

2. <u>Reeds</u> were cut down in the swamps, dried, and woven into baskets. Are reeds trees?

   _____

   _____

3. The host passed <u>goblets</u> to his guests. Was he serving food?

   _____

   _____

4. People used <u>causeways</u> to travel to the mainland. Did they travel through tunnels?

   _____

   _____

5. The Aztecs dug <u>irrigation</u> ditches around their chinampas. Did these ditches carry water?

   _____

   _____

6. The <u>nobility</u> lived in homes near the city center. Would their homes be smaller than the farmers' homes?

   _____

   _____

B. WORD STUDY: *The prefix* out- *means "outside" or "more than." Answer each of the following questions using one of these words containing* out-: *outcast, outlaw, outplays.*

1. Why would you expect an *outcast* to have few friends?

   _____

2. Why might an *outlaw* be wanted by the police?

   _____

3. What happens when an opposing team *outplays* your team?

   _____

"Popocatepetl and Ixtlaccihuatl" by Juliet Piggott Wood
Writing About the Big Question

Community or individual: Which is more important?

Big Question Vocabulary

common	community	culture	custom	diversity
duty	environment	ethnicity	family	group
individual	team	tradition	unify	unique

A. *Use one or more words from the list above to complete each sentence.*

1. Cassie's coach begins each new season with a special _____.

2. She always hosts a _____ dinner the night before the first game.

3. Cassie doesn't want to go this year, but she feels it is her _____.

4. The coach sees the dinner as a way to _____ the team.

B. *Follow the directions in responding to each of the items below.*

1. List two examples that show the value of tradition or community involvement.

   _____

   _____

2. Write two sentences describing one of the preceding examples and explain how it benefits those involved. Use at least two of the Big Question vocabulary words.

   _____

   _____

   _____

   _____

C. *Complete the sentences below. Then, write a short paragraph in which you connect this idea to the big question.*

   Tradition and **duty** to one's **community** should _____

   _____

   _____

   _____

   _____

   _____

"Popocatepetl and Ixtlaccihuatl" by Juliet Piggott Wood

Reading: Reread to Look for Connections That Indicate Cause-and-Effect Relationships

A **cause** is an event or a situation that produces an **effect,** or the result produced. In a story or an essay, each effect may eventually become a cause for the next event. This series of events results in a cause-and-effect chain, which propels the action forward.

As you read, think about the causes and effects of events. If you do not see a clear cause-and-effect relationship in a passage, **reread to look for connections** in the text. Look for words and phrases that identify cause-and-effect relationships—for example, *because, due to, for that reason, therefore,* and *as a result.*

DIRECTIONS: *Read the following sequences of events. Underline any words or phrases that help you identify a cause-and-effect relationship. Then, identify each event as a* cause, *an* effect, *or both* cause and effect.

_____ 1. The Emperor wants Ixtla to rule the empire after he dies.

_____ 2. Therefore, Ixtla becomes more serious and more studious.

_____ 3. Ixtla also studies harder because she has fallen in love.

_____ 4. The Emperor becomes ill.

_____ 5. As a result, he rules the empire less effectively.

_____ 6. Because the empire has grown weaker, enemies are emboldened to surround it.

_____ 7. Because enemies surround the empire, the Emperor commands his warriors to defeat them.

_____ 8. Jealous warriors tell the Emperor that Popo has been killed in battle.

_____ 9. The Emperor tells Ixtla that Popo has died.

_____ 10. Because she is heartbroken and does not want to marry anyone but Popo, Ixtla grows sick and dies.

_____ 11. When Popo learns the circumstances of Ixtla's death, he kills the warriors who lied to the Emperor.

_____ 12. Popo grieves for Ixtla.

_____ 13. Therefore, Popo instructs the warriors to build two pyramids.

_____ 14. Popo stands atop the second pyramid, holding a burning torch.

_____ 15. Over time, the pyramids became mountains.

"Popocatepetl and Ixtlaccihuatl" by Juliet Piggott Wood

Literary Analysis: Legends and Facts

A **legend** is a traditional story about the past. A legend generally starts out as a story based on **fact**—something that can be proved true. Over the course of many generations, however, the story is retold and transformed into fiction. It becomes a legend.

Every culture has its own legends to immortalize real people who were famous in their time. Most legends include these elements:

- a larger-than-life hero or heroine
- fantastic events
- roots, or a basis, in historical facts
- actions and events that reflect the culture that created the legend

A powerful Aztec emperor wants to pass his kingdom on to his daughter, Ixtlaccihuatl, or Ixtla. Ixtla studies hard so that she will be worthy of this role. She loves Popocatepetl, or Popo, a brave and strong warrior in the service of the emperor. The emperor, Ixtla, and Popo are three larger-than-life characters who will form the basis of the legend.

DIRECTIONS: *Read each excerpt from "Popocatepetl and Ixtlaccihuatl." On the line, identify the element or elements of a legend that the passage reflects, and briefly explain how you recognized the element.*

1. The pass through which the Spaniards came to the ancient Tenochtitlan is still there, as are the volcanoes on each side of that pass. Their names have not been changed. The one to the north is Ixtlaccihuatl and the one on the south of the pass is Popocatepetl.

   Element of legend: _____

   Explanation: _____

2. There was once an Aztec Emperor in Tenochtitlan. He was very powerful. Some thought he was wise as well, whilst others doubted his wisdom.

   Element of legend: _____

   Explanation: _____

3. As time went on natural leaders emerged and, of these, undoubtedly Popo was the best. Finally it was he, brandishing his club and shield, who led the great charge of running warriors across the valley, with their enemies fleeing before them.

   Element of legend: _____

   Explanation: _____

4. So Popocatepetl stood there, holding the torch in memory of Ixtlaccihuatl, for the rest of his days.
   The snows came and, as the years went by, the pyramids of stone became high white-capped mountains.

   Element of legend: _____

   Explanation: _____

"Popocatepetl and Ixtlaccihuatl" by Juliet Piggott Wood
Vocabulary Builder

Word List

decreed   feebleness   relish   routed   shortsightedness   unanimous

A. DIRECTIONS: *Answer each question after thinking about the meaning of the underlined word from the Word List. Then, explain your answer.*

1. When the Emperor <u>decreed</u> that the triumphant warrior would marry his daughter, did he ask a question?

_____

2. Would the story have ended happily if the warriors' support for Popo had been <u>unanimous</u>?

_____

3. Would the Emperor have shown <u>shortsightedness</u> by considering the needs of his kingdom after his death?

_____

4. When the warriors <u>routed</u> the enemy, did the battles continue?

_____

5. Did the Emperor's <u>feebleness</u> inspire him to lead his warriors into battle?

_____

6. Did Ixtla <u>relish</u> the idea of marrying Popo?

_____

B. WORD STUDY: *The Latin prefix* uni- *means "having or consisting of only one." Answer each of the following questions using one of these words containing* uni-: *unicycle, unicorn, unite.*

1. Why would it be challenging to balance on a *unicycle*?

_____

2. What is a *unicorn* said to have on its forehead?

_____

3. If two separate groups *unite*, what do they form?

_____

"Tenochtitlan: Inside the Aztec Capital" by Jacqueline Dineen
"Popocatepetl and Ixtlaccihuatl" by Juliet Piggott Wood
Integrated Language Skills: Grammar

Commas and Semicolons

A **comma** (,) is used in the following ways:

Function	Example
to separate two independent clauses that are joined by a conjunction	One mountain is called Popocatepetl, and the other one is called Ixtlaccihuatl.
to separate three or more words, phrases, or clauses in a series	There were goblets for pulque and other drinks, graters for grinding chilis, and storage pots of various designs.
after an introductory word, phrase, or clause	Unfortunately, some warriors were jealous of Popo. On an island in a swampy lake, the Aztecs built a city. As the city grew, more and more land was drained.

The **semicolon** (;) looks like a period above a comma. It has two main uses:

Function	Example
to join independent clauses that are not joined by a conjunction	One mountain is called Popocatepetl; the other one is called Ixtlaccihuatl.
to separate items in a series when one or more of the items itself contains a comma	The three main characters in the legend are the Emperor; his daughter, Ixtla; and Popo, a warrior.

A. PRACTICE: *Each sentence is missing one or more commas or semicolons. Rewrite each sentence with the correct punctuation.*

1. The family consisted of a couple their married children and their grandchildren.

   _____

2. Aztec houses were very plain everyone slept on mats of reeds.

   _____

B. WRITING APPLICATION: *Write two sentences about the Aztecs. In one, use one or more semicolons, and in the other, use one or more commas.*

_____

_____

_____

_____

Name _____ Date _____

Integrated Language Skills: Support for Writing a Description

Use this chart to take notes as you prepare to write a **description** of Tenochtitlan or Ixtla. Write down as many details as you can to describe the various aspects of the city or of Ixtla's character. Include verbs and adjectives that appeal to the five senses: sight, touch, taste, smell, and hearing.

Background information about Tenochtitlan (When was it built? Where was it located?) or about Ixtla (Who is she? What is she like? What is expected of her?):
Physical description of Tenochtitlan or Ixtla:
Activities in which Ixtla or the residents of Tenochtitlan take part:

Now, use your notes to write a draft of a description of the city of Tenochtitlan or the character of Ixtla. Be sure to use vivid verbs and adjectives that will make your description interesting to your readers. Use words that appeal to the senses of sight, touch, taste, smell, and hearing.

"To the Top of Everest" by Samantha Larson
"The Voyage from Tales from the Odyssey" by Mary Pope Osborne
Writing About the Big Question

Community or individual: Which is more important?

Big Question Vocabulary

common	community	culture	custom	diversity
duty	environment	ethnicity	family	group
individual	team	tradition	unify	unique

A. *Use one or more words from the list above to complete each sentence.*

1. The _____ of rock climbers prepared for their journey.

2. They had a _____ goal of reaching the summit.

3. They were awed by the _____ of flora and fauna around them.

4. They felt fortunate to be in such a beautiful _____ .

B. *Follow the directions in responding to each of the items below.*

1. List two times when you traveled to a new place. _____.
   _____

2. Write two sentences describing one of the preceding experiences, and explain how it affected your view of the world. Use at least two of the Big Question vocabulary words.

   _____

   _____

C. *Complete the sentence below. Then, write a short paragraph in which you connect this idea to the big question.*

Travel enriches an individual's view of the world. A community of travelers

_____

_____

_____

_____

_____

_____

Name _____ Date _____

"To the Top of Everest" by Samantha Larson
"The Voyage from Tales from the Odyssey" by Mary Pope Osborne
Literary Analysis: Comparing Universal Themes

A universal theme is a message about life that is expressed regularly in many different cultures and time periods. Universal themes include the importance of courage, the power of love, and the danger of greed. Universal themes are often found in epics, or stories or long poems about the adventures of a larger-than-life hero. Epic tales usually focus on the hero's bravery, strength, and success in battle or adventure. In addition to telling the story of a hero, an epic is a portrait of the culture that produced it. The following **epic conventions** are traditional characteristics of this form of literature:

- An epic involves a dangerous journey, or *quest,* that the hero must take.
- Gods or powerful characters help the hero.
- The setting of an epic is broad, covering several nations or even the universe.
- The style is serious and formal.

Because epics have become an important part of the literature of different cultures, they often inspire the works of later generations. For example, it is not unusual to find an allusion, or reference, to the ancient Greek epic the *Odyssey* in a contemporary adventure story. As you read "To the Top of Everest" and "The Voyage from Tales from the Odyssey," look for the use of epic conventions in the stories.

DIRECTIONS: *Use the following chart to compare "To the Top of Everest" and "The Voyage from Tales of the Odyssey." If the information to answer a question does not appear in the selection, write* information not mentioned.

Questions	"To the Top of Everest"	"The Voyage from Tales from the Odyssey"
1. What is the setting?		
2. What dangerous journey is undertaken?		
3. Who helps along the journey?		
4. What is the character's attitude?		
5. What obstacles must be overcome?		
6. What is the outcome?		

"To the Top of Everest" by Samantha Larson
"The Voyage from Tales from the Odyssey" by Mary Pope Osborne
Vocabulary Builder

Word List

designated   impervious   inflicted   saturation

A. DIRECTIONS: *Think about the meaning of each italicized word from the Word List. Then, explain whether the sentence makes sense. If it does not make sense, write a new sentence. In the new sentence, use the italicized word correctly.*

1. Jenna *inflicted* comfort with her gentle touch.

   Explanation: _____

   New sentence: _____

2. The leaky bottle resulted in the *saturation* of Emma's cotton bib.

   Explanation: _____

   New sentence: _____

3. We *designated* our star player as our choice for team captain.

   Explanation: _____

   New sentence: _____

4. Her proud smile suggested she was *impervious* to our compliments.

   Explanation: _____

   New sentence: _____

B. DIRECTIONS: *Write the letter of the word that means the same or about the same as the word from the Word List.*

____ 1. designated
   A. designed   C. described
   B. arranged   D. marked

____ 2. impervious
   A. unaffected   C. lazy
   B. angry   D. bored

____ 3. inflicted
   A. stopped   C. caused
   B. soothed   D. increased

"To the Top of Everest" by Samantha Larson
"The Voyage from Tales from the Odyssey" by Mary Pope Osborne
Support for Writing to Compare Universal Themes

Use this graphic organizer to take notes for an **essay** in which you compare and contrast the themes of "To the Top of Everest" and "The Voyage from Tales from the Odyssey."

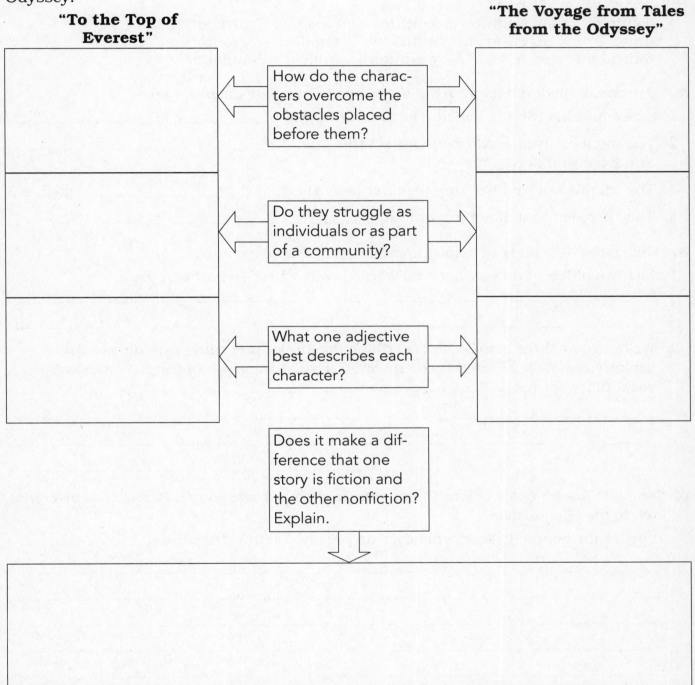

"To the Top of Everest"

"The Voyage from Tales from the Odyssey"

How do the characters overcome the obstacles placed before them?

Do they struggle as individuals or as part of a community?

What one adjective best describes each character?

Does it make a difference that one story is fiction and the other nonfiction? Explain.

Now, use your notes to write an essay comparing and contrasting the themes of "To the Top of Everest" and "The Voyage from Tales from the Odyssey."

"**Sun and Moon in a Box**" by Ricahrd Erdoes and Alfonso Ortiz

Writing About the Big Question

Community or individual: Which is more important?

Big Question Vocabulary

common	community	culture	custom	diversity
duty	environment	ethnicity	family	group
individual	team	tradition	unify	unique

A. *Use one or more words from the list above to complete each sentence.*

1. Jesse and his friends joined a local fundraising _____ .

2. The money raised would help protect the _____
   and local wildlife.

3. The friends enjoyed working together toward a _____ goal.

4. They decided to make it an annual _____ .

B. *Follow the directions in responding to each of the items below.*

1. List two different times when you worked with others as part of a team.

   _____

   _____

2. Write two or three sentences describing one of the preceding experiences and
   explaining how it affected those involved. Use at least two of the Big Question
   vocabulary words. _____

   _____

   _____

   _____

C. *Complete the sentence below. Then, write a short paragraph in which you connect this
idea to the big question.*

   In order for people to work together as part of a team, they must _____

   _____

   _____

   _____

   _____

   _____

   _____

   _____

Name _____   Date _____

"Sun and Moon in a Box" by Richard Erdoes and Alfonso Ortiz

Reading: Use Prior Knowledge to Compare and Contrast

A **comparison** tells how two or more things are alike. A **contrast** tells how two or more things are different. When you **compare and contrast,** you recognize similarities and differences. You can often understand an unfamiliar concept by **using your prior knowledge to compare and contrast.** For example, you may understand an ancient culture better if you look for ways in which it is similar to and different from your own culture. You also might find similarities and differences between a story told long ago and one that is popular today. To compare and contrast stories, ask questions such as "What does this event bring to mind?" or "Does this character make me think of someone I know or have read about?"

DIRECTIONS: *Read each passage from "Sun and Moon in a Box." In the second column of the chart, write a question that will help you compare or contrast the passage to something else you have read or to something or someone you know or know about. In the third column, write the answer to your question. The first item has been completed as an example.*

Passage from "Sun and Moon in a Box"	Question Based on My Prior Knowledge	Comparison or Contrast
1. Coyote and Eagle were hunting. Eagle caught rabbits. Coyote caught nothing but grasshoppers. Coyote said, "Friend Eagle, my chief, we make a great hunting pair."	How are these characters like Wile E. Coyote and Road Runner in the cartoons I used to watch?	Road Runner is a bird, but not an eagle, and Wile E. Coyote tries to catch him. Here, the coyote and the eagle seem to be friends.
2. Whenever [the Kachinas] wanted light they opened the lid and let the sun peek out. Then, it was day. When they wanted less light, they opened the box just a little for the moon to look out.		
3. After a while Coyote called Eagle, "My chief, let me have the box. I am ashamed to let you do all the carrying." "No," said Eagle, "You are not reliable. You might be curious and open the box."		
4. [Coyote] sat down and opened the box. In a flash, . . . icy winds made all living things shiver. Then, before Coyote could put the lid back, . . . snow fell down from heaven and covered the plains and the mountains.		

"Sun and Moon in a Box" by Richard Erdoes and Alfonso Ortiz
Literary Analysis: Cultural Context

Stories such as fables, folk tales, and myths are influenced by cultural context. **Cultural context** is the background, customs, and beliefs of the people who originally told them. Knowing the cultural context of a work will help you understand and appreciate it. You can keep track of the cultural context of a work by considering these elements: the *title* of the selection, the *time* in which it takes place, the *place* in which it takes place, the *customs* of the characters, the *beliefs* that are expressed or suggested.

Consider this passage from "Sun and Moon in a Box":

Now, at this time, the earth was still soft and new. There was as yet no sun and no moon.

The passage tells you that the folk tale is set in the distant past, before Earth looked as it does today and before there was a sun and a moon. From the cultural context, you can infer that the people who told the tale believed there was a time when Earth existed, but the sun and the moon as yet did not.

DIRECTIONS: *Read each passage from "Sun and Moon in a Box." In the second column of the chart, indicate which element of the cultural context—*time, place, customs, *or* beliefs—*the passage illustrates. Then, explain your choice. Tell why you think the example shows the element you have chosen.*

Passage from "Sun and Moon in a Box"	Element of Cultural Context and Explanation
1. [Eagle and Coyote] went toward the west. They came to a deep canyon.	
2. Whenever [the Kachinas] wanted light they opened the lid and let the sun peek out. . . . When they wanted less light, they opened the box just a little for the moon to look out.	
3. "Let us steal the box," said Coyote. "No, that would be wrong," said Eagle. "Let us just borrow it."	
4. Eagle grabbed the box and . . . Coyote ran after him on the ground. After a while Coyote called Eagle: "My chief, let me have the box. I am ashamed to let you do all the carrying."	

"Sun and Moon in a Box" by Richard Erdoes and Alfonso Ortiz
Vocabulary Builder

Word List

cunning   curiosity   pestering   regretted   relented   reliable

A. DIRECTIONS: *Circle* T *if the statement is* true *or* F *if it is* false. *Then, explain your answer.*

1. A car that starts only half the time is *reliable*.

   T / F _____

   _____

2. A teacher who refuses her students' pleas to make a test easier has *relented*.

   T / F _____

   _____

3. Someone who always gets caught cheating is *cunning*.

   T / F _____

   _____

4. A man who thoroughly disliked a movie, probably *regretted* going to see it.

   T / F _____

   _____

5. Parents would be charmed by a child who is *pestering* them.

   T / F _____

   _____

6. A gossipy neighbor's *curiosity* naturally leads him to mind his own business.

   T / F _____

   _____

B. WORD STUDY: *The Latin suffix* -ity *means "state, quality, or condition of." Answer each of the following questions using one of these words containing* -ity: *elasticity, sincerity, predictability.*

1. How might you test an object's *elasticity*?

   _____

2. What might lead you to question a person's *sincerity*?

   _____

3. Why might you appreciate a coworker's *predictability*?

   _____

"How the Snake Got Poison" by Zora Neale Hurston
Writing About the Big Question

Community or individual: Which is more important?

Big Question Vocabulary

common	community	culture	custom	diversity
duty	environment	ethnicity	family	group
individual	team	tradition	unify	unique

A. *Use one or more words from the list above to complete each sentence.*

1. As an _____ , Snake had the right to protect himself.

2. However, he presented a threat to members of the larger _____.

3. They lived in an _____ of fear and anxiety.

4. For the _____ good of all involved, compromise was necessary.

B. *Follow the directions in responding to each of the items below.*

1. List a time when your needs or the needs of someone you know were in conflict with the needs of family, neighbors, classmates, or any larger community.

_____

_____

2. Write two sentences explaining the preceding experience and describe how the situation was resolved. Use at least two of the Big Question vocabulary words.

_____

_____

_____

C. *Complete the sentence below. Then, write a short paragraph in which you connect this situation to the big question.*

When the needs of the **individual** and the needs of the larger **group** are in conflict,

_____

_____

_____

_____

_____

Name _____ Date _____

"How the Snake Got Poison" by Zora Neale Hurston
Reading: Use Prior Knowledge to Compare and Contrast

A **comparison** tells how two or more things are alike. A **contrast** tells how two or more things are different. When you **compare and contrast,** you recognize similarities and differences. You can often understand an unfamiliar concept by **using your prior knowledge to compare and contrast.** For example, you may understand an ancient culture better if you look for ways in which it is similar to and different from your own culture. You also might find similarities and differences between a story told long ago and one that is popular today. To compare and contrast stories, ask questions such as "What does this event bring to mind?" or "Does this character make me think of someone I know or have read about?"

DIRECTIONS: *Read each passage from "How the Snake Got Poison." In the second column of the chart, write a question that will help you compare or contrast the passage to something else you have read or to something or someone you know or know about. In the third column, write the answer to your question. The first item has been completed as an example.*

Passage from "How the Snake Got Poison"	Question Based on My Prior Knowledge	Comparison or Contrast
1. "Ah ain't so many, God, you put me down here on my belly in de dust and everything trods upon me and kills off my generations. Ah ain't got no kind of protection at all."	How does this snake compare with Nag and Nagaina in the story "Rikki-tikki-tavi"?	Like this snake, Nag and Nagaina can talk. They also have a problem protecting themselves and their unborn children.
2. "God, please do somethin' 'bout dat snake. He' layin' in de bushes there wid poison in his mouf and he's strikin' everything dat shakes de bushes. He's killin' up our generations."		
3. "Lawd, you know Ah'm down here in de dust. Ah ain't got no claws to fight wid, and Ah ain't got no feets to git me out de way. All Ah kin see is feets comin' to tromple me. Ah can't tell who my enemy is. . . ."		
4. "Well, snake, I don't want yo' generations all stomped out and I don't want you killin' everything else dat moves. Here take dis bell and tie it to yo' tail."		

"How the Snake Got Poison" by Zora Neale Hurston
Literary Analysis: Cultural Context

Stories such as fables, folk tales, and myths are influenced by cultural context. **Cultural context** is the background, customs, and beliefs of the people who originally told them. Knowing the cultural context of a work will help you understand and appreciate it. You can keep track of the cultural context of a work by considering these elements: the *title* of the selection, the *time* in which it takes place, the *place* in which it takes place, the *customs* of the characters, the *beliefs* that are expressed or suggested.

Consider this passage from "How the Snake Got Poison":

Well, when God made de snake he put him in de bushes to ornament de ground.

The passage tells you that the folk tale is set in the distant past. From the cultural context, you can infer that the people who told the tale held beliefs about the purpose of the snake in nature.

DIRECTIONS: *These passages from "How the Snake Got Poison" illustrate the folk tale's cultural context by suggesting beliefs held by the people who told the tale. In the second column of the chart, tell what belief the passage illustrates.*

Passage from "How the Snake Got Poison"	Suggested Belief
1. God . . . said, "Ah didn't mean for nothin' to be stompin' you snakes lak dat. You got to have some kind of a protection. Here, take dis poison and put it in yo' mouf and when they tromps on you, protect yo'self."	
2. "Snake, . . . Ah didn't mean for you to be hittin' and killin' everything dat shake de bush. I give you dat poison and tole you to protect yo'self when they tromples on you. But you killin' everything dat moves."	
3. "Here take dis bell and tie it to yo' tail. When you hear feets comin' you ring yo' bell and if it's yo' friend, he'll be keerful. If it's yo' enemy, it's you and him."	

"How the Snake Got Poison" by Zora Neale Hurston
Vocabulary Builder

Word List

immensity   ornament   suit   varmints

A. DIRECTIONS: *Circle* T *if the statement is* true *or* F *if it is* false. *Then, explain your answer.*

1. Colored lights and Chinese lanterns will *ornament* a backyard party.

   T / F _____

   _____

2. An *immensity* can easily be fenced in.

   T / F _____

3. A bright green dress *suits* a rosy complexion.

   T / F _____

   _____

4. Gardeners hope their gardens will attract *varmints*.

   T / F _____

   _____

B. WORD STUDY: *The Latin suffix* -ity *means "state, quality, or condition of." Answer each of the following questions using one of these words containing* -ity: *marketability, integrity, enmity.*

1. Why should a company consider the *marketability* of its products?

   _____

2. Why might a politician who lacks *integrity* lose an election?

   _____

3. How would you respond to someone who treats you with *enmity*?

   _____

"Sun and Moon in a Box" by Richard Erdoes and Alfonso Ortiz
"How the Snake Got Poison" by Zora Neale Hurston
Integrated Language Skills: Grammar

Capitalization is the use of uppercase letters (*A, B, C,* and so on). Capital letters signal the beginning of a sentence or a quotation and identify proper nouns and proper adjectives. **Proper nouns** include the names of people, geographical locations, specific events and time periods, organizations, languages, and religions. **Proper adjectives** are derived from proper nouns.

Use of Capital Letter	Example
Sentence beginning	**T**he coyote was a bad swimmer. **H**e nearly drowned.
Quotation	The snake said, "**Y**ou know I'm down here in the dust."
Proper nouns	They traveled through the **S**outhwest.
Proper adjectives	Coyote might have run as far as the **M**exican border.

A. PRACTICE: *Rewrite each sentence below. Use capitalization correctly.*

1. the character named coyote suggested that they steal the box.

   _____

2. the folk tale takes place in the american southwest, perhaps in present-day arizona or new mexico.

   _____

   _____

3. coyote said to eagle, "this is a wonderful thing."

   _____

4. "i do not trust you," eagle said many times. "you will open that box."

   _____

B. Writing Application: *Write a short episode telling what Coyote might have done after he let the sun and the moon escape from the box. Include at least one quotation, one proper noun, and one proper adjective. Use capitalization correctly.*

   _____

   _____

   _____

   _____

   _____

"Sun and Moon in a Box" by Richard Erdoes and Alfonso Ortiz
"How the Snake Got Poison" by Zora Neale Hurston

Integrated Language Skills: Support for Writing a Plot Summary

Use this chart to take notes for a **plot summary** of "Sun and Moon in a Box" or "How the Snake Got Poison." .

Plot Summary

Setting:	
Major character 1:	**Major character 2:**

Main event from beginning of folk tale:	Main event from middle of folk tale:	Main event from end of folk tale:

Final outcome:

Now, use your notes to write your **plot summary.** Be sure to include all the information called for on the chart.

"The People Could Fly" by Virginia Hamilton

Writing About the Big Question

Community or individual: Which is more important?

Big Question Vocabulary

common	community	culture	custom	diversity
duty	environment	ethnicity	family	group
individual	team	tradition	unify	unique

A. *Use one or more words from the list above to complete each sentence.*

1. America has not always embraced the _____ of its population.

2. Some people were discriminated against because of their _____.

3. When people came together as a _____ , they made a difference.

4. There was power in their _____ that could not be denied.

B. *Follow the directions in responding to each of the items below.*

1. List two different groups of people who struggled against oppression.

_____   _____

2. Write two sentences describing what helped unify one of the preceding groups in their efforts. Use at least two of the Big Question vocabulary words.

_____

_____

_____

C. *Complete the sentence below. Then, write a short paragraph in which you connect this situation to the big question.*

In order to unify people who share a common struggle, _____

_____

_____

_____

_____

_____

_____

_____

"The People Could Fly" by Virginia Hamilton
Reading: Use a Venn Diagram to Compare and Contrast

When you **compare and contrast,** you recognize similarities and differences. You can compare and contrast elements in a literary work by **using a Venn diagram** to examine character traits, situations, and ideas. First, reread the text to locate the details you will compare. Then, write the details on a diagram like the ones shown below. Recording these details will help you understand the similarities and differences in a literary work.

DIRECTIONS: *Fill in the Venn diagrams as directed to make comparisons about elements of "The People Could Fly."*

1. Compare Toby and Sarah. Write characteristics of Toby in the left-hand oval and characteristics of Sarah in the right-hand oval. Write characteristics that they share in the overlapping part of the two ovals.

Toby   **Both**   **Sarah**

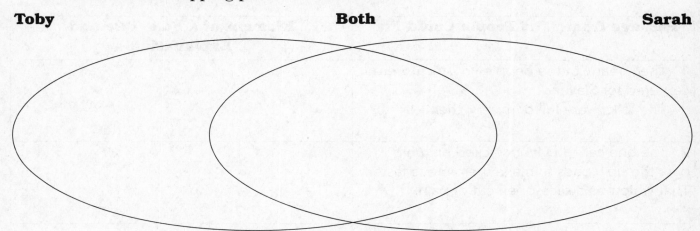

2. Compare the enslaved people with the Overseer and Driver. Write characteristics of the enslaved people in the left-hand oval and characteristics of the Overseer and Driver in the right-hand oval. Write characteristics that they share in the overlapping part of the two ovals.

Enslaved People   **Both**   **Overseer and Driver**

"The People Could Fly" by Virginia Hamilton
Literary Analysis: Folk Tale

A **folk tale** is a story that is composed orally and then passed from person to person by word of mouth. Although folk tales originate in this **oral tradition,** many of them are eventually collected and written down. Similar folk tales are told by different cultures throughout the world. Such folk tales have common character types, plot elements, and themes. Folk tales often teach a lesson about life and present a clear separation between good and evil. Folk tales are part of the oral tradition that also includes fairy tales, legends, myths, fables, tall tales, and ghost stories.

DIRECTIONS: *Read each passage from "The People Could Fly." In the second column of the chart, indicate whether the passage* teaches a lesson about life *or whether it* clearly presents good, clearly presents evil, *or presents a clear distinction between the two. Then, explain your choice. Tell why you think the example shows the element you have chosen.*

Passage from "The People Could Fly"	Element of a Folk Tale and Explanation
1. Then, many of the people [in Africa] were captured for Slavery. . . . The folks were full of misery, then.	
2. The one called Driver cracked his whip over the slow ones to make them move faster. That whip was a slice-open cut of pain.	
3. The . . . woman fell to the earth. The old man that was there, Toby, came and helped her to her feet.	
4. A young man slave fell from the heat. The Driver come and whipped him. Toby come over and spoke words to the fallen one.	
5. "Take us with you!" . . . Toby couldn't take them with him. Hadn't the time to teach them to fly. They must wait for a chance to run.	
6. The slaves who could not fly told about the people who could fly to their children. When they were free.	

"The People Could Fly" by Virginia Hamilton
Vocabulary Builder

Word List

croon   hoed   mystery   scorned   shed   shuffle

A. DIRECTIONS: *Write the letter of the word or group of words that means* the opposite of *the vocabulary word.*

___ 1. scorned
   A. commanded   B. resigned   C. appreciated   D. hired

___ 2. croon
   A. sing softly   B. speak quietly   C. speak haltingly   D. sing loudly

___ 3. shuffle
   A. jump   B. walk quickly   C. drag   D. pull into

___ 4. mystery
   A. ritual   B. secret   C. explanation   D. magic

___ 5. shed
   A. put on   B. pull down   C. take off   D. drop

___ 6. hoed
   A. dug   B. straightened   C. released   D. planted

B. WORD STUDY: *The Greek root* -myst- *means "a secret rite." Answer each of the following questions using one of these words containing* -myst-: *mystified, mystical, mystic.*

1. How would you reply if you were *mystified* by a friend's request?

   _____

   _____

2. When might an ancient artifact be considered a *mystical* object?

   _____

   _____

3. Why might someone seek guidance from a *mystic?*

   _____

   _____

Name _____ Date _____

"All Stories Are Anansi's" by Harold Courlander
Writing About the Big Question

Community or individual: Which is more important?

Big Question Vocabulary

common	community	culture	custom	diversity
duty	environment	ethnicity	family	group
individual	team	tradition	unify	unique

A. *Use one or more words from the list above to complete each sentence.*

1. The two con men targeted a _____ of small-town residents.

2. They worked as a _____ to gain the residents' trust.

3. They offered a free seminar and created a friendly _____ .

4. Once they had what they wanted, both _____ disappeared.

5. After that, the _____ was wary of strangers offering free advice.

B. *Follow the directions in responding to each of the items below.*

1. List two people you have heard or read about who exploited others for personal gain.

   _____   _____

2. Write two sentences describing one of the preceding incidents and how it affected those involved. Use at least two of the Big Question vocabulary words.

   _____

   _____

   _____

C. *Complete the sentence below. Then, write a short paragraph in which you connect this situation to the big question.*

When an individual exploits others for personal gain, _____

_____

_____

_____

_____

_____

Name _____   Date _____

Reading: Use a Venn Diagram to Compare and Contrast

When you **compare and contrast,** you recognize similarities and differences. You can compare and contrast elements in a literary work by **using a Venn diagram** to examine character traits, situations, and ideas. First, reread the text to locate the details you will compare. Then, write the details on a diagram like the ones shown below. Recording these details will help you understand the similarities and differences in a literary work.

DIRECTIONS: *Fill in the Venn diagrams as directed to make comparisons about elements of "All Stories Are Anansi's."*

1. Compare Anansi and Onini, the great python. Write characteristics of Anansi in the left-hand oval and characteristics of Onini in the right-hand oval. Write characteristics that they share in the overlapping part of the two ovals.

Anansi   **Both**   **Onini**

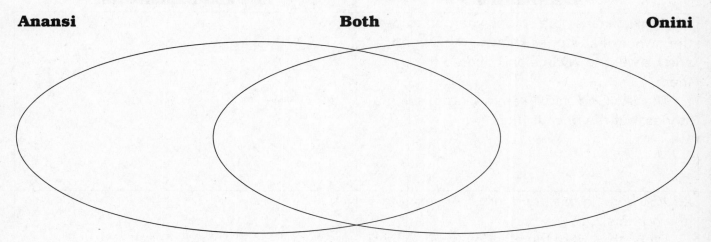

2. Compare Mmoboro, the hornets, with Osebo, the leopard. Write characteristics of the hornets in the left-hand oval and characteristics of the leopard in the right-hand oval. Write characteristics that they share in the overlapping part of the two ovals.

Hornets   **Both**   **Leopard**

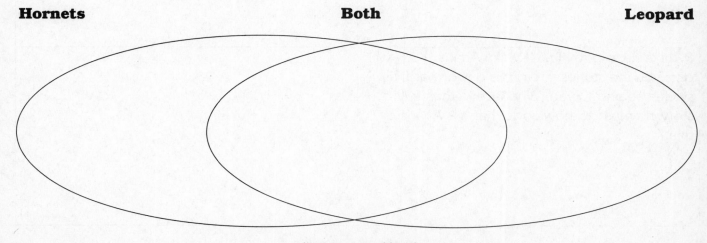

"**All Stories Are Anansi's**" by Harold Courlander
Literary Analysis: Folk Tale

A **folk tale** is a story that is composed orally and then passed from person to person by word of mouth. Although folk tales originate in this **oral tradition,** many of them are eventually collected and written down. Similar folk tales are told by different cultures throughout the world. Such folk tales have common character types, plot elements, and themes. Folk tales often teach a lesson about life and present a clear separation between good and evil. Folk tales are part of the oral tradition that also includes fairy tales, legends, myths, fables, tall tales, and ghost stories.

DIRECTIONS: *Read each passage from "All Stories Are Anansi's." In the second column of the chart, indicate what value or lesson about life the passage teaches. Then, explain your choice.*

Passage from "All Stories Are Anansi's"	Value or Lesson About Life and Explanation
1. Kwaku Anansi, the spider, yearned to be the owner of all stories known in the world, and he went to Nyame and offered to buy them. The Sky God said: "I am willing to sell the stories, but the price is high."	
2. "Go here, in this dry gourd," Anansi told [the hornets]. . . . When the last of them had entered, Anansi plugged the hole with a ball of grass, saying: "Oh, yes, but you are really foolish people!"	
3. Nyame said to him: "Kwaku Anansi, . . . I will give you the stories. From this day onward, all stories belong to you. Whenever a man tells a story, he must acknowledge that it is Anansi's tale."	

"All Stories Are Anansi's" by Harold Courlander
Vocabulary Builder

Word List

acknowledge   dispute   gourd   opinion   python   yearned

A. DIRECTIONS: *Write the letter of the word that means* the same or about the same as *the vocabulary word.*

____ **1.** yearned
   A. rejected   **B.** questioned   **C.** desired   **D.** ignored

____ **2.** gourd
   A. cup   **B.** fork   **C.** platter   **D.** knife

____ **3.** acknowledge
   A. taunt   **B.** challenge   **C.** credit   **D.** dismiss

____ **4.** python
   A. panther   **B.** snake   **C.** cougar   **D.** spider

____ **5.** opinion
   A. statement   **B.** fact   **C.** statistic   **D.** belief

____ **6.** dispute
   A. argument   **B.** lie   **C.** error   **D.** agreement

B. WORD STUDY: *The root* -know- *means "to understand." Answer each of the following questions using one of these words containing* -know-: *unknowingly, acknowledge, knowledgeable.*

1. How might you *unknowingly* hurt a friend's feelings?

_____

_____

2. How would you *acknowledge* a friend's presence?

_____

_____

3. Why would you ask a *knowledgeable* person a difficult question?

_____

_____

All-in-One Workbook
319

"**The People Could Fly**" by Virginia Hamilton
"**All Stories Are Anansi's**" by Harold Courlander
Integrated Language Skills: Grammar

Abbreviations

An **abbreviation** is a shortened form of a word or phrase. Most abbreviations end with a period, but many do not, and some may be written either with or without a period. Most dictionaries have entries for abbreviations, so look them up if you are not sure of the correct form. Note which abbreviations are written with periods, which ones are not, and which ones appear in capital letters in these lists:

Titles of persons: Mr. Ms. Mrs.

Days of the week: Sun. Mon. Tues. Wed. Thurs. Fri. Sat. Sun.

Months of the year: Jan. Feb. Mar. Apr. Aug. Sept. Oct. Nov. Dec.

Times of day: a.m. p.m.

Street designations: Ave. Blvd. Pl. St.

State postal abbreviations: AL AK AZ AR CA CO CT DE FL GA HI ID IL IN IA KS KY LA ME MD MA MI MN MS MO MT NE NV NH NJ NM NY NC ND OH OK OR PA RI SC SD TN TX UT VT VA WA WV WI WY

Organizations: NAACP UN YMCA

Units of measure: in. ft. yd. lb. qt. gal. *but* mm cm m mg g ml dl l

A. PRACTICE: *Rewrite each sentence below, and abbreviate the words in italics.*

1. James lives at 115 Elm *Street*, Pleasant Valley, *Nebraska.*

   _____

2. The gardener said that if your yard measures 50 *feet* (16.6 *yards*) by 40 *feet* (13.3 *yards*), you will need 2 *pounds* of fertilizer.

   _____

   _____

3. *Mister* Raymond works for the *United Nations.*

   _____

B. Writing Application: *Compose an e-mail message to a friend. Tell about something you have done recently. Use at least five abbreviations. If you are not sure of the correct form, look up the abbreviation in a dictionary.*

_____

_____

_____

_____

_____

Name _____ Date _____

Integrated Language Skills: Support for Writing a Review

Use this chart to take notes for a **review** of "The People Could Fly" or "All Stories Are Anansi's."

Notes for Review

Element of the Tale	My Opinion of the Element	Details From the Tale That Support My Opinion
Characters		
Description		
Dialogue		
Plot		

Now, write a draft of your review. Tell readers whether or not you think they will enjoy the folktale. Remember to support your opinions with details from the tale.

"The Fox Outwits the Crow" by William Cleary
Writing About the Big Question

 Community or individual: Which is more important?

Big Question Vocabulary

common	community	culture	custom	diversity
duty	environment	ethnicity	family	group
individual	team	tradition	unify	unique

A. *Use one or more words from the list above to complete each sentence.*

1. People enjoyed listening to Leslie's _____ singing voice.

2. She frequently sang at _____ gatherings.

3. She felt it was her _____ to share her gift with others.

4. She did not want to use her talent for _____ gain.

B. *Follow the directions in responding to each of the items below.*

1. List two works of literature from which you have learned something significant.

   _____   _____

2. Write two sentences describing one of the works and what it taught you. Use at least two of the Big Question vocabulary words.

   _____

   _____

   _____

   _____

C. *Complete the sentence below. Then, write a short paragraph in which you connect this experience to the big question.*

   One of the purposes of literature is to teach individuals how to _____

   _____

   _____

   _____

   _____

   _____

"The Fox Outwits the Crow" by William Cleary
"The Fox and the Crow" by Aesop
Literary Analysis: Comparing Tone

The **tone** of a literary work is the writer's attitude toward his or her subject and characters. The tone can often be described by a single adjective, such as *formal, playful,* or *respectful.* To determine the tone of each selection, notice the words and phrases that the authors use to express their ideas.

The theme is a central message in a literary work. A theme can usually be expressed as a general statement about life. Although a theme may be stated directly in the text, it is more often presented indirectly. To figure out the theme of a work, look at what it reveals about people or life.

A. DIRECTIONS: *Compare the tone of the two selections by completing this chart. Choose one adjective to describe each passage. Use* serious, formal, informal, *or* playful.

"The Fox Outwits the Crow"	Adjective	"The Fox and the Crow"	Adjective
1. One day a young crow snatched a fat piece of cheese. . . .		A Fox once saw a Crow fly off with a piece of cheese in its beak. . . .	
2. A fox . . . got a whiff of the cheese, / The best of his favorite hors d'oeuvres, . . .		"That's for me, as I am a Fox," said Master Reynard, . . .	
3. Hey, you glamorous thing, / Does your voice match your beautiful curves?		"I feel sure your voice must surpass that of other birds, just as your figure does."	

B. DIRECTIONS: *Answer the following questions to determine the theme of each work.*

1. What are the characters' key traits?

   Poem: _____

   Fable: _____

2. What is the main conflict in the story?

   Poem: _____

   Fable: _____

3. What happens as a result?

   Poem: _____

   Fable: _____

4. What general statement about life does this outcome suggest?

   Poem: _____

   Fable: _____

"The Fox Outwits the Crow" by William Cleary
"The Fox and the Crow" by Aesop
Vocabulary Builder

Word List

flatterers   glossy   hors d'oeuvres   malice   surpass   whiff

A. DIRECTIONS: *Circle* T *if the statement is true or* F *if the statement is false. Then, explain your answer.*

1. A true bloodhound can follow someone's trail after getting only a *whiff* of the person's odor.

   T / F _____

2. *Flatterers* are honest and sincere.

   T / F _____

3. Something that is *glossy* has a rough finish.

   T / F _____

4. Most people would feel *malice* toward someone who has harmed them.

   T / F _____

5. *Hors d'oeuvres* are served after the main course.

   T / F _____

6. For a person to *surpass* expectations, he or she must do better than expected.

   T / F _____

B. DIRECTIONS: *For each pair of words in CAPITAL LETTERS, write the letter of the pair of words that best expresses a* similar *relationship.*

____ **1.** OUTDO : SURPASS ::
   A. lose : win
   B. talk : remember
   C. work : play
   D. throw : toss

____ **2.** WHIFF : SCENT ::
   A. sight : hearing
   B. good : bad
   C. love : adoration
   D. eyes : nose

____ **3.** MALICE : GOODWILL ::
   A. stroll : walk
   B. painter : artist
   C. large : humongous
   D. blame : praise

Name _____ Date _____

"The Fox Outwits the Crow" by William Cleary
"The Fox and the Crow" by Aesop

Support for Writing to Compare Reactions to Tone and Theme

Use this graphic organizer to take notes for an essay that compares your reaction to the tone and theme in "The Fox Outwits the Crow" with your reaction to the tone and theme in "The Fox and the Crow."

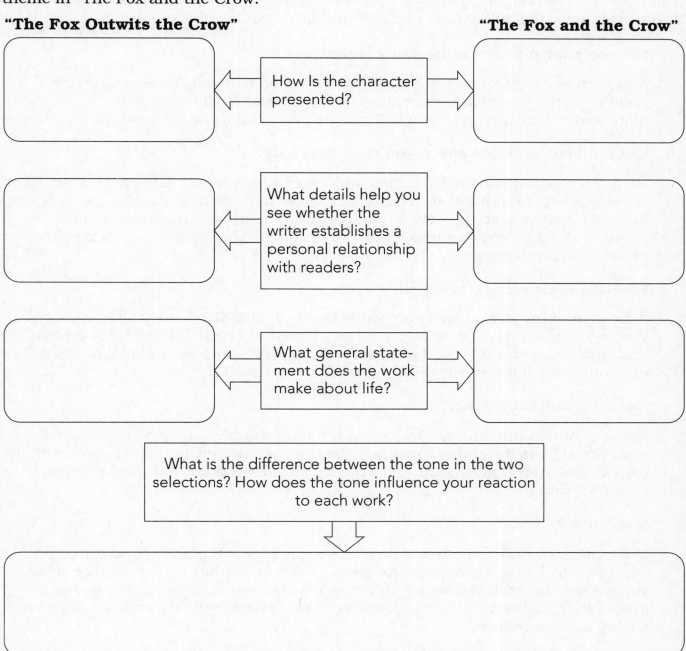

"The Fox Outwits the Crow"　　　　　　　　　　**"The Fox and the Crow"**

How Is the character presented?

What details help you see whether the writer establishes a personal relationship with readers?

What general state-ment does the work make about life?

What is the difference between the tone in the two selections? How does the tone influence your reaction to each work?

Now, use your notes to write an essay in which you compare your reaction to the tone and theme of "The Fox Outwits the Crow" with your reaction to the tone and theme of "The Fox and the Crow."

Tips for Improving Your Reading Fluency

You've probably heard the expression "Practice makes perfect." Through your own experiences, you know that practice improves all types of skills. If you play a guitar, you know that practicing has made you a better player. The same is true for sports, for crafts, and for reading. The following tips will help you to practice skills that will lead to reading **fluency**—the ability to read easily, smoothly, and expressively.

Choose your practice materials carefully.

Make reading fun! Make a list of subjects that interest you. Then, search for reading materials—books, magazines, newspapers, reliable Web sites. As you learn more about your interests, you will also be practicing your reading skills.

Choose your practice space and time carefully.

Help your concentration skills. Find a quiet, comfortable place to read—away from the television and other distractions. Get in the habit of treating yourself to an hour of pleasure reading every day—apart from homework and other tasks. Reading about interesting topics in a quiet, comfortable place will provide both pleasure and relaxation.

Practice prereading strategies.

A movie preview gives viewers a good idea about what the movie will be about. Before you read, create your own preview of what you plan to read. Look at pictures and captions, subheads, and diagrams. As you scan, look for unfamiliar words. Find out what those words mean before you start reading.

Use punctuation marks.

Think of punctuation marks as stop signs. For example, the period at the end of a sentence signals the end of a complete thought. From time to time in your reading, stop at that stop sign. Reread the sentence. Summarize the complete thought in your own words.

Read aloud.

Use your voice and your ears as well as your eyes. Read phrases and sentences expressively. Pause at commas and periods. Show emphasis in your voice when you come to an exclamation point. Let your voice naturally rise at the end of a question. If possible, record your reading. Then listen to the recording, noting your pacing and expression.

Pause to ask questions.

Stop reading after a short amount of time (for example, five minutes) or at the end of a meaty paragraph. Look away from the text. Ask yourself questions—What are the main ideas? What message does the author want me to get? What might happen next? If the answers seem unclear, reread—either silently or aloud. Find the answers!

Use what you know.

As you read an informational article, think about what you already know about the topic. Use your knowledge and ideas as background information. Doing so will help you to understand new ideas. As you read fiction or a personal narrative, think about your own experiences. If you have been in a situation that is similar to that of a fictional character, you will be better able to understand his or her feelings, actions, and goals.

Talk about it.

Ask a friend or family member to read what you have read. Take turns reading aloud together, listening to both content and expression. Then discuss what you read. Share, compare, and contrast your ideas. Doing so will reinforce your knowledge of the content of what you read, and may provide new and interesting perspectives about the topic.

Reading Fluency Assessment Passage 1

Nonverbal communication is vital to expressing people's true thoughts and feelings. We watch how others move and stand when they speak; we hear the tone of their voice and notice their facial expressions and body language. All of this information is extremely important. Just think about it—has a person's[50] exquisite smile ever meant more to you than a hundred words that this individual might have spoken?

Signing is another critical form of communication. For those who can neither hear nor communicate verbally, signing is a powerful tool for listening and speaking. Many parents today are teaching their very young[100] children to sign so that they can communicate before they are able to talk.

Going beyond these forms of daily nonverbal communication are art forms created to speak to us without words. For example, the ancient art of drumming is considered a universal form of communication. As you listen to[150] people playing in a drum circle, you can feel their emotions. A drumbeat can sound serious or humorous, powerful or lighthearted. Drummers can tell entire stories. A drumbeat can take you to the top of a mountain or to the depths of the brilliant ocean.

Other art forms work wordlessly,[200] too: Rather than hearing a message, you see it. For example, a mime is a person who acts out complete scenes while remaining mute. Often appearing in slippered feet, mimes try to avoid creating any sounds. Even when a scene calls for jostling or other usually noisy encounters, a mime[250] succeeds in showing the action quietly. Watching a mime perform is like seeing a woodpecker at work through a soundproof window. You can hear what is happening but only in your mind. Through the silence, you can think more deeply about the action you see.[295]

950L

Check Your Understanding

1. Which of the following is not a form of nonverbal communication?

   a. signing
   b. smiling
   c. singing
   d. miming

2. Name two emotions that can be created by a drumbeat.

   _____

   _____

Reading Fluency Assessment Passage 2

Shoes protect our feet, but how they look has always seemed to matter as much as their ability to save our feet from cold, injury, and dirt. The first shoes were simply animal skins wrapped around the feet. Around the 1400s, however, shoes were becoming quite fancy.

Men who were[50] rich wore shoes with very long, pointed toes. Ribbons tied around the knees were used to hold the toes off the ground. After a day of trying to walk in such shoes, the wearers no doubt headed home quickly to their sore and aching feet!

Workers wore less complex shoes,[100] often with leather or wood bottoms strapped on to the feet with leather ties. At home, people might have worn soft fabric slippers. They would keep them on even after saying good-night and going to bed. What could feel better than toasty warm feet while you sleep?

In the 1850s,[150] an American shoemaker developed a machine that could sew the upper parts of shoes to their soles. He sold the rights of ownership to the machine to a factory owner, whereupon the first mass-produced shoes could be made. Since then, we have had shoes for every type of activity. We[200] have sports shoes, work shoes, and dress shoes. If you want, you can even find a pair of shoes to match your purse. In fact, our society might be described as shoe crazy. You can see people with one pair of shoes on their feet and another pair slung across[250] their shoulders.

Shoe fashion is big business today. Colors, styles, and materials are offered in huge variety. When you watch the brunettes and redheads on fashion show runways, be sure to look at their feet. These models will be wearing the latest shoe fashions to match their outfits.[298]

950L

Check Your Understanding

1. Describe two kinds of early shoes.

   _____

   _____

2. What happened when an American shoemaker sold his machine to a factory owner?

   _____

   _____

Reading Fluency Assessment Passage 3

As the sun sinks slowly behind the horizon each evening, darkness creeps across the land. For many animals, this hour is the time to wake up and become active. As you prepare for bed, these nighttime animals begin a busy day.

In a forest setting, as a person peers into[50] the growing gloom and hustles home before nightfall, small animals like the raccoon begin prowling around. These animals are on their nightly search for food. Red foxes, mule deer, and badgers join the raccoons on the hunt. All are as quiet as possible as they do not want to be[100] heard by those they hunt. Others are quiet to protect themselves from animals that hunt them.

The peacefulness of the night is rarely disturbed by loud animal sounds. If forest animals do make noise, they usually are raising an alarm. An enemy or a fire may have been sighted.

The[150] moon begins to gleam, revealing other creatures of the night. Bats whirr and swoop, feasting on mosquitoes. A barn owl glides gracefully through the night air, its white face shining. Its dive toward the ground will scatter all small animals aware of the owl's presence. They are afraid of becoming the[200] mighty bird's evening meal.

You might, one night, also spot a flying squirrel soaring through the trees until morning. It watches the action above and below its path. The flying squirrel's cousin, the tree squirrel, is active during the day and peacefully sleeps the night away in a snug nest.[250]

So, as you drift off into the land of dreams tonight, imagine creatures large and small roaming the night. If you listen very closely, you may hear the quiet whoosh of a squirrel or the soft patter of a fox.[299]

960L

Check Your Understanding

1. Why might animals make a loud noise at night.

_____

2. Name three animals that hunt for food at night in the forest.

_____

_____

_____

Reading Fluency Assessment Passage 4

In a wealthy British home during the 1800s, dozens of servants worked to make the household run smoothly. Male servants held the highest rank. The head female housekeeper was viewed as slightly inferior to the butler.

Truly, the head housekeeper ran the house. She handled everything from financial matters to[50] the supervision of cooking and cleaning. If any servants were viewed as lax in their duties, they would have to answer to the housekeeper. Yet, the butler was viewed as the "boss" of the servants. Why, then, was the housekeeper usually the one with the keys to every lock in[100] the house?

Discrepancies between male and female servants were also obvious in the kitchen. A male chef was considered much more desirable than a female cook. However, male chefs had to be paid higher wages. As a result, most cooks were female. Still, their employers liked to be able to[150] say that male chefs had trained the female cooks.

Sometimes, ladies of the house would insist on a French maid. However, an English maid who could speak a few French phrases was also acceptable. Young women training to be rich ladies' maids often heard potential employers say, "She curtsies nicely,[200] but does she speak French?" Learning how to say French words with a flawless accent greatly increased a young woman's chances of being hired.

Several funny movies have been made about the typical wealthy, hard-working Englishman who constantly had to deal with the problems of keeping his estate running. With[250] a look of confusion on his face, the man confronts his wife's complaints about nannies, maids, and footmen. In the England of the 1800s, wealthy men preferred to focus on business. They left all matters concerning the home to their wives. In this respect, then, the movies are true.[299]

970L

Check Your Understanding

1. In the 1800s, the head housekeeper held the highest rank among servants.

   True / False? Explain:

   _____

2. Why were most cooks female in the 1800s?

   _____

   _____

Reading Fluency Assessment Passage 5

Maya Ying Lin, the college student and architect who designed the Vietnam Veterans Memorial, had a strong idea about fitting the Wall into its surroundings. Her plans found an appropriate way to connect this new structure to the land and to the other memorials around it. Her ideas for the[50] site seemed as perfect as anyone could have hoped to see.

What Lin and others could not possibly have known was the deep level of emotion the memorial would stir in visitors. The coordinators of the effort hoped that the Wall would help to heal the political division caused by the Vietnam War. They have been thrilled with the results. Visitors[100] often let their feeling show, and many are stunned by the impact the memorial has on them.

Visitors bring things to leave behind at the Wall. Together, these objects are a huge tribute to the men and women who served our country. More than fifty thousand objects have been left[150] at the Wall. They are collected twice daily by the National Park Service. When the weather is bad, the objects are picked up more often, ensuring that the less durable items are not damaged. The items are carefully entered into the Vietnam Veterans Memorial Collection. Exceptions are flags and living[200] things, such as plants. The flags are given to hospitals for former soldiers and groups like the Boy Scouts or Girl Scouts. The flags are also given to people who are attending special events at the memorial.

The things often left are writings, such as poems or letters. Bracelets worn[250] to remember missing soldiers are numerous, too. Rubbings of the names carved into the wall are often left too. Things that soldiers owned and photographs are also among the most commonly deposited mementoes.[283]

970L

Check Your Understanding

1. How do visitors to the wall respond?

_____

2. Which items are not entered into the Vietnam Veterans Memorial Collection?

   a. flags
   b. photographs
   c. poems

Reading Fluency Assessment Passage 6

When Fredrick Douglass was born, no one could have predicted that he would lead a life of greatness. Born in 1818 into slavery on a plantation in Maryland, he was sent by his owner to Baltimore at the age of eight.

Douglass might have grown into a sullen, illiterate young man, but[50] an unexpected gift filled him with hope. He learned to read, in defiance of the law. After years of being treated cruelly, Frederick, at eighteen, planned an escape. His plan was discovered, and he was imprisoned. Once out of jail, Frederick's dream of freedom became possible, and he fled north to[100] New Bedford, Massachusetts.

Douglass became active in anti-slavery organizations. At one abolitionists' meeting, he met the great speaker William Lloyd Garrison. Garrison's unconcealed hatred for slavery and his fiery speech greatly inspired Douglass.

A few days later, Douglass himself gave a speech at an anti-slavery convention. One observer wrote, "Flinty[150] [hard] hearts were pierced, and cold ones melted by his eloquence." Douglass's speech so stirred listeners that he was asked to become a lecturer. It was the start of a career that took him to many places in the North and to Europe.

Douglass also published an autobiography. Because it[200] gave details of his former life, he had to increase his vigilance for possible capture by his former owner. He soon left the country for a two-year speaking tour in the British Isles.

Douglass returned from Europe with enough money to buy his freedom and start his own anti-slavery paper,[250] the *North Star*. After the Civil War, he began fighting for civil rights for freed slaves and for women and later served in several government positions. Thus Douglass defied his those who believed he was not destined for greatness.[288]

980L

Check Your Understanding

1. Name two of young Douglass's acts that were against the law.

_____

_____

2. Why did Frederick Douglass leave the United States for two years?

_____

Reading Fluency Assessment Passage 7

Over the centuries, wigs have been popular accessories. Since the earliest times wigs were used to enhance beauty. In ancient Egypt, both men and women of nobility wore wigs of human hair adorned with flowers and gold ornaments on special occasions. Paintings of the dead wearing wigs prove that wigs[50] were important to the Egyptians. They believed that everything needed in the afterlife must be buried with the dead.

The expression blonds have more fun may have originated in ancient Rome. Many Roman women believed that blond hair was more desirable than their own dark locks. The solution? Wigs were[100] fashioned from the hair of blond captives. Apparently, the Romans were slaves to fashion. A sculpture of one noblewoman was fitted with a sequence of different marble wigs, each succeeding the other as styles changed.

Throughout history, the wearing of wigs was a sign of prosperity. Only wealthy people and[150] members of the royalty could afford the elaborate headpieces that were fashionable. Unlike modern men's hairpieces, the wigs popular in 17th-century were not meant to disguise hair loss. It did not take much scrutiny to recognize that a king's long and curly locks were not his own.

In the 1700s, [200] wigs for women were designed with support wires that raised the hairdo three feet in the air. Some included cages with miniature ships or live birds. It would take an agile woman to move easily in such a headpiece without tipping over!

These days, wigs are mainly worn by entertainers[250] and those who have lost their hair due to illness. Some people donate their hair for wigs that are donated to cancer patients.[273]

990L

Check Your Understanding

1. In the 17th century, wigs were

   a. thought of as fashion accessories.

   b. primarily used to disguise hair loss.

   c. made out of marble and feathers.

2. Why might the expression *blondes have more fun* have originated in ancient Rome?

   _____

   _____

Reading Fluency Assessment Passage 8

Anyone who feels a moral duty to help those less fortunate will be drawn to the ideas of Make a Difference Day. This national day of helping others is run each October by USA WEEKEND Magazine. The magazine has an alliance with the Points of Light Foundation and the actor[50] Paul Newman, among others. They holds the event to encourage people to commit to a specific project that will help others.

Paul Newman and his nonprofit company pledge $100,000 to the program each year. The money that has been promised will be divided among ten participants whose good deeds are[100] chosen as the best of the year. More times than not, the winners pass on the cash they have received to the very people they helped on Make a Difference Day. The virtue of these acts is impressive. Such good deeds surely encourage others to join the program.

Over the[150] years, millions of people have taken part in Make a Difference Day. The effort might be one person spending a couple of hours reading to others. It might involve a whole town joining together to collect and deliver food to the needy. Truly, every deed is remarkable. Despite our busy[200] lives, surely we all can get behind the simple idea of the event. "Put your own cares on hold for one day to care for someone else." Before next October rolls around, get involved in your own pursuit of a solution to a problem in your neighborhood.

Make a Difference[250] Day is held on the last Saturday of the month. Make plans early to spend a few hours that day on the project of your choice. The sick, the poor, and other needy members of society will appreciate your help.[290]

1000L

Check Your Understanding

3. What do the sponsors of Make a Difference Day hope to achieve?

_____

_____

4. More times than not, what do winners of their part of the $10,000 prize do with the money?

_____

_____

Reading Fluency Assessment Passage 9

Billy was a daydreamer.

It started when he was in preschool. Billy would start doing a jigsaw puzzle, but his mind would begin to wander even before he inserted the first puzzle piece into the rectangular frame. At first, his thoughts would drift aimlessly, in no apparent direction. Then his[50] eyes would close, and a story would start to take shape in his mind. Soon Billy would be off on a great adventure in some distant land that was far more exciting than Miss Hannah's Preschool.

That's when Miss Hannah would tap him on the shoulder and ask why he[100] wasn't completing his puzzle like the other children.

When he got older, Billy learned to daydream with his eyes open. He would sit in class, carelessly doodling in his notebook, when suddenly his mind would drift. For a few fleeting moments, Billy would enjoy leading a squad of fearless soldiers[150] into battle or piloting a space shuttle through the treacherous rings of Saturn.

Then, like clockwork, the teacher would barge in, saying in a stern voice, "Time to rejoin the real world," and the whole class would laugh.

Billy didn't care, though. Sometimes, when his parents were bickering, Billy would[200] escape into a private world where people never argued or raised their voices. In Billy's daydreams, everyone got along.

When he reached high school, Billy began to write down some of his daydreams as stories. His teachers had to admit that the stories were good, even if Billy did have[250] trouble paying attention in class.

In his sophomore year, Billy suggested that he and other student authors begin a school literary magazine. In it, they would have the opportunity to share their daydreams with others. Before long, this particular daydream of Billy's became a reality![295]

1000L

Check Your Understanding

1. Students in Billy's classes often laughed at him because he

   a. wanted to start a literary magazine.

   b. got into trouble because he daydreamed.

   c. thought that everyone should get along.

   d. made funny doodles in his notebooks.

2. What traits and habits probably helped Billy to write great stories?

   _____

   _____

Reading Fluency Assessment Passage 10

People call swirling wind storms by many names, such as whirlwind, twister, tornado, and cyclone. This violent storm can occur at any time of the year, but they are most common during the spring and early summer. May and June are the most common months, but tornadoes occurring during April[50] are the deadliest. These storms have brought fatal consequences to an average of nearly thirty people a year.

Tornadoes occur mainly in the central and southern United States. This region is known as "tornado alley." It lies between the Rocky Mountains and the Appalachians, and runs from Iowa and Nebraska[100] down to the Gulf of Mexico. If you live in this region, you have probably experienced all kinds of extreme weather.

The level of destruction caused by a tornado depends on the speed of the winds. A level F0 tornado, with winds of 40–72 miles per hour, usually causes[150] light damage. Branches might be ripped from trees, and trees with shallow roots may topple over. Damage to signs, traffic signals, and chimneys might occur.

Almost half of all tornadoes fall into the F1 category. With winds of 73–112 miles per hour, this tornado usually causes moderate damage. Mobile[200] homes can be knocked off their foundations. Cars might be flipped over. Roofing materials might be damaged.

A level F2 tornado, with winds of 113–157 miles per hour, causes considerable damage. Solid, old trees are uprooted easily. Some homes are completely destroyed. Roofs are ripped off buildings. Train cars[250] can be knocked over.

Tornadoes labeled F3, F4, and F5 range from "severe" to "devastating" to "incredible damage." Only about one percent are classified as F5. The winds of one of these tornadoes can toss cars through the air and turn houses to piles of sticks and stones.[298]

1000L

Check Your Understanding

1. The worst tornadoes

   a. often occur in September.

   b. occur in the northeastern part of the United States.

   c. are classified as F5.

   d. are classified as F1.

2. What is the difference between a cyclone and a tornado?

   _____

   _____

Reading Fluency Assessment Passage 11

Long before the invention of airplanes and steam engines, people relied on wind power to travel great distances over the water. While sailboats are still used for fishing and for recreation today, sailing ships no longer play a prominent role in transportation and commerce.

Every sailing ship has a hull,[50] rigging, and at least one mast to support its sails. The hull is the framework upon which the ship is built. The rigging allows the crew to raise and lower the sails on the masts. Traditionally, a vessel with fewer than three masts was called a *boat* rather than a[100] *ship*.

Sailing across the ocean has always been a treacherous undertaking. A severe storm can blow a sailing ship off course. It can even lead to shipwreck. Seasickness can transform an otherwise pleasant ocean crossing into a nauseating experience. Although gazing at the beautiful, starry sky is a fine distraction[150] on a balmy evening, boredom can become another hazard. Passengers can grow restless on long and uneventful voyages.

Sailors on a traditional sailing ship had many projects at hand. All crew members would alternate hours, working four hours on and four hours off around the clock. They would take turns[200] steering the ship and navigating. Another daily responsibility was keeping the ship adequately maintained. Rigging and sails often needed repairs, and masts needed oiling. As guardians of the ship's safety, the sailors in charge of keeping lookout had one of the most important jobs of all.

Attacks by pirates were[250] not uncommon and, after many weeks at sea, sailors sometimes reported seeing such fantastic creatures as mermaids and sea serpents. Often, these sightings would turn out to be whale sharks or giant squid. Other times, they proved to be no more than figments of a bored sailor's imagination.[298]

1030L

Check Your Understanding

1. Sailing ships no longer play a prominent role in long-distance travel because

   a. airplanes and other modern vessels have replaced them.

   b. they required too much maintenance.

   c. people became bored during long voyages.

   d. people were scared of sharks and giant squids.

2. Describe the work of crew members on traditional sailing ships.

   _____

   _____

Reading Fluency Assessment Passage 12

In 1965, the first close-up picture of the planet Mars was revealed below its hazy pink sky. Since then, spacecraft traveling by and landing on the planet have shown us an amazing world. Exploration of Mars has brought us increasing knowledge of this cold, rocky wasteland.

Clues hint at past[50] conditions quite different from those today. For example, at one time, volcanoes erupted on Mars.

The big question today for most scientists is whether life ever existed on Mars. Operations managers at the United States space agency have developed a strategy called "follow the water" to answer such questions. Scientists[100] gather data from features such as the polar ice caps and dry riverbeds with the hope that their work will show that water once may have covered parts of the planet. Furthermore, they dream of discovering hot springs or pockets of water beneath the Martian surface.

Advancement in computer technology[150] enables Scientists to receive and study data from a Mars explorer that moves along the surface. If the explorer stops working properly, they can remotely correct its programs.

One problem that equipment on Mars has had is dust from the planet's surface. Dust forms a layer on the spacecraft's solar[200] panels. The panels sunlight and change it to the electricity the spacecraft needs. If the spaceship does not get enough power, the situation could turn critical resulting in an early-ending mission. Perhaps software engineers will develop a program to fix the problem. Imagine a robotic arm that can dust[250] off the panels.

Will people ever travel to Mars? Scientists need to know a lot more than they do now before sending humans there. If humans do walk on Mars, might they be able to discover more than any robot can? Maybe in your lifetime you'll find out![298]

1030L

Check Your Understanding

1. To determine if life existed on Mars, scientists are first looking for

   a. volcanic rock
   b. water
   c. dust particles

2. What feature of Mars causes problems for the equipment?

_____

Part 1
INTRODUCTION

Part 1 will give you an overview of California standards for English-Language Arts content for Grade 7. This part contains the following:

- an explanation of the purpose of the California English-Language Arts content standards;
- scoring rubrics to show you how your test results will be evaluated; and
- advice on how to approach the different types of questions you will encounter on standardized tests.

California English-Language Arts Content Standards Review

The purpose of the California English-Language Arts content standards is to help you by defining the language arts knowledge, concepts, and skills that you should acquire at each grade level.

The skills that fall under Language Arts are reading, writing, listening, and speaking. These skills are interrelated, so it is helpful for you to learn them together. Mastering reading, writing, listening, and speaking skills presented in these California standards will help you do well in other school subjects.

These language arts skills will also add to the quality of your life. For example, learning the skills in the English-Language Arts content standards can help you go on to higher education and enter the workplace as a capable communicator.

Grade Seven Scoring Rubrics

In grade seven, you will be required to produce five types of writing: narrative, persuasive essays, summaries, responses to literature, and research reports. Use the rubrics on the following pages to evaluate and improve your writing. The stronger your writing is, the higher the score you will receive. Although you will not be tested on all of these types of writing, using these self-scoring rubrics will make you a better writer and a better test taker.

Fictional or Autobiographical Narrative Writing Scoring Rubric

	Genre	Organization and Focus	Sentence Structure	Conventions
4	• Provides a *thoroughly developed* plot line, including major and minor characters and a *definite* setting. • Includes *appropriate* strategies (e.g., dialogue; suspense; narrative action).	• *Clearly* addresses the writing task. • Demonstrates a *clear* understanding of purpose and audience. • Maintains a *consistent* point of view, focus, and organizational structure, including the *effective* use of transitions. • Includes a *clearly presented* central idea with *relevant* facts, details, and/or explanations.	• Includes sentence *variety*.	• Contains *some errors* in the conventions of the English language (grammar, punctuation, capitalization, spelling). These errors do **not** interfere with the reader's understanding of the writing.

(continued on next page)

Fictional or Autobiographical Narrative Writing Scoring Rubric *(continued)*

3	• Provides an *adequately developed* plot line, including major and minor characters and a *definite* setting. • Includes *appropriate* strategies (e.g., dialogue; suspense; narrative action).	• Addresses *most* of the writing task. • Demonstrates a *general* understanding of purpose and audience. • Maintains a *mostly consistent* point of view, focus, and organizational structure, including use of isolated and/or single word transitions. • Presents a central idea with *mostly relevant* facts, details, and/or explanations.	• Includes *some* sentence *variety.*	• Contains *errors* in the conventions of the English language (grammar, punctuation, capitalization, spelling). These errors do **not** interfere with the reader's understanding of the writing.
2	• Provides a *minimally developed* plot line, including characters and a setting. • *Attempts* to use strategies but with *minimal* effectiveness (e.g., dialogue; suspense; narrative action).	• Addresses *some* of the writing task. • Demonstrates *little* understanding of purpose and audience. • Maintains an *inconsistent* point of view, focus, and/or organizational structure, which may include *ineffective or awkward* transitions that do not unify important ideas. • *Suggests* a central idea with *limited* facts, details, and/or explanations.	• Includes *little* sentence variety.	• Contains *many errors* in the conventions of the English language (grammar, punctuation, capitalization, spelling). These errors **may** interfere with the reader's understanding of the writing.
1	• *Lacks* a developed plot line. • *Fails* to use strategies (e.g., dialogue; suspense; narrative action).	• Addresses *only one* part, if any, of the writing task. • Demonstrates no understanding of purpose and audience. • *Lacks* a point of view, focus, organizational structure, and transitions that unify important ideas. • *Lacks* a central idea but may contain *marginally related* facts, details, and/or explanations.	• Includes *no* sentence variety.	• Contains *serious errors* in the conventions of the English language (grammar, punctuation, capitalization, spelling). These errors interfere with the reader's understanding of the writing.

Response to Literature Writing Scoring Rubric

	Genre	Organization and Focus	Sentence Structure	Conventions
4	• Develops interpretations that demonstrate a *thoughtful*, comprehensive grasp of the text. • Organizes *accurate* and *coherent* interpretations around *clear* ideas, premises, or images from the literary work. • Provides *specific* textual examples and details to support the interpretations.	• *Clearly* addresses the writing task. • Demonstrates a *clear* understanding of purpose and audience. • Maintains a *consistent* point of view, focus, and organizational structure, including the *effective* use of transitions. • Includes a *clearly presented* central idea with *relevant* facts, details, and/or explanations.	• Includes sentence *variety*.	• Contains *some errors* in the conventions of the English language (grammar, punctuation, capitalization, spelling). These errors do **not** interfere with the reader's understanding of the writing.
3	• Develops interpretations that demonstrate a comprehensive grasp of the text. • Organizes accurate and *reasonably* coherent interpretations around *clear* ideas, premises, or images from the literary work. • Provides textual examples and details to support the interpretations.	• Addresses *most* of the writing task. • Demonstrates a *general* understanding of purpose and audience. • Maintains a *mostly consistent* point of view, focus, and organizational structure, including use of isolated and/or single word transitions. • Presents a central idea with *mostly relevant* facts, details, and/or explanations.	• Includes some sentence *variety*.	• Contains *errors* in the conventions of the English language (grammar, punctuation, capitalization, spelling). These errors do **not** interfere with the reader's understanding of the writing.

(continued on next page)

Response to Literature Writing Scoring Rubric *(continued)*

2	• Develops interpretations that demonstrate a *limited* grasp of the text. • Includes interpretations that *lack* accuracy or coherence as related to ideas, premises, or images from the literary work. • Provides *few, if any*, textual examples and details to support the interpretations.	• Addresses *some* of the writing task. • Demonstrates *little* understanding of purpose and audience. • Maintains an *inconsistent* point of view, focus, and/or organizational structure, which may include *ineffective or awkward* transitions that do not unify important ideas. • *Suggests* a central idea with *limited* facts, details, and/or explanations.	• Includes *little* sentence variety.	• Contains *many errors* in the conventions of the English language (grammar, punctuation, capitalization, spelling). These errors **may** interfere with the reader's understanding of the writing.
1	• Demonstrates *little* grasp of the text. • *Lacks* an interpretation or *may* be a simple retelling of the passage. • *Lacks* textual examples and details.	• Addresses *only one* part, if any, of the writing task. • Demonstrates *no* understanding of purpose and audience. • *Lacks* a point of view, focus, organizational structure, and transitions that unify important ideas. • *Lacks* a central idea but may contain *marginally related* facts, details, and/or explanations.	• Includes *no* sentence variety.	• Contains *serious errors* in the conventions of the English language (grammar, punctuation, capitalization, spelling). These errors **interfere** with the reader's understanding of the writing.

Persuasive Writing Scoring Rubric

	Genre	Organization and Focus	Sentence Structure	Conventions
4	• *Authoritatively* defends a clear position with precise and relevant evidence and *convincingly* addresses the reader's concerns, biases, and expectations.	• *Clearly* addresses the writing task. • Demonstrates a *clear* understanding of purpose and audience. • Maintains a *consistent* point of view, focus, and organizational structure, including the *effective* use of transitions. • Includes a *clearly presented* central idea with *relevant* facts, details, and/or explanations.	• Includes sentence *variety*.	• Contains *some errors* in the conventions of the English language (grammar, punctuation, capitalization, spelling). These errors do **not** interfere with the reader's understanding of the writing.
3	• *Generally* defends a position with relevant evidence and addresses the reader's concerns, biases, and expectations.	• Addresses *most* of the writing task. • Demonstrates a *general* understanding of purpose and audience. • Maintains a *mostly consistent* point of view, focus, and organizational structure, including use of isolated and/or single word transitions. • Presents a central idea with *mostly relevant* facts, details, and/or explanations.	• Includes some sentence *variety*.	• Contains *errors* in the conventions of the English language (grammar, punctuation, capitalization, spelling). These errors do **not** interfere with the reader's understanding of the writing.
2	• Defends a position with *little*, *if any*, evidence and *may* address the reader's concerns, biases, and expectations.	• Addresses *some* of the writing task. • Demonstrates *little* understanding of purpose and audience. • Maintains an *inconsistent* point of view, focus, and/or organizational structure, which may include *ineffective or awkward* transitions that do not unify ideas. • *Suggests* a central idea with *limited* facts, details, and/or explanations.	• Includes *little* sentence variety.	• Contains *many errors* in the conventions of the English language (grammar, punctuation, capitalization, spelling). These errors **may** interfere with the reader's understanding of the writing.

(continued on next page)

Persuasive Writing Scoring Rubric *(continued)*

1				
	• *Fails* to defend a position with *any* evidence and *fails* to address the reader's concerns, biases, and expectations.	• Addresses *only one* part, if any, of the writing task. • Demonstrates *no* understanding of purpose and audience. • *Lacks* a point of view, focus, organizational structure, and transitions that unify important ideas. • *Lacks* a central idea but may contain *marginally* related facts, details, and/or explanations.	• Includes *no* sentence variety.	• Contains *serious errors* in the conventions of the English language (grammar, punctuation, capitalization, spelling). These errors interfere with the reader's understanding of the writing.

Summary Writing Scoring Rubric

	Genre	Organization and Focus	Sentence Structure	Conventions
4	• Summarizes text with clear identification of the main idea(s) and most significant details, in the student's own words, and clearly reflects underlying meaning.	• *Clearly* addresses the writing task. • Demonstrates a *clear* understanding of purpose and audience. • Maintains a *consistent* point of view, focus, and organizational structure, including the *effective* use of transitions. • Includes a *clearly presented* central idea with *relevant* facts, details, and/or explanations.	• Includes sentence *variety*.	• Contains *some errors* in the conventions of the English language (grammar, punctuation, capitalization, spelling). These errors do **not** interfere with the reader's understanding of the writing.
3	• Summarizes text with the main idea(s) and important details, mostly in the student's own words, and generally reflects underlying meaning.	• Addresses most of the writing task. • Demonstrates a *general* understanding of purpose and audience. • Maintains a *mostly consistent* point of view, focus, and organizational structure, including use of isolated and/or single word transitions. • Presents a central idea with *mostly relevant* facts, details, and/or explanations.	• Includes some sentence *variety*.	• Contains *errors* in the conventions of the English language (grammar, punctuation, capitalization, spelling). These errors do **not** interfere with the reader's understanding of the writing.

(continued on next page)

Summary Writing Scoring Rubric (*continued*)

2	• Summarizes text with some of the main idea(s) and details, which may be superficial, minimal use of the student's own words, and minimal reflection of underlying meaning.	• Addresses *some* of the writing task. • Demonstrates *little* understanding of purpose and audience. • Maintains an *inconsistent* point of view, focus, and/or organizational structure, which may include *ineffective or awkward* transitions that do not unify important ideas. • *Suggests* a central idea with *limited* facts, details, and/or explanations.	• Includes *little* sentence variety.	• Contains *many errors* in the conventions of the English language (grammar, punctuation, capitalization, spelling). These errors **may** interfere with the reader's understanding of the writing.
1	• Summarizes text with few, if any, of the main idea(s) and/or details, little or no use of the student's own words, little or no reflection of underlying meaning.	• Addresses *only one* part, if any, of the writing task. • Demonstrates *no* understanding of purpose and audience. • *Lacks* a point of view, focus, organizational structure, and transitions that unify important ideas. • *Lacks* a central idea but may contain *marginally related* facts, details, and/or explanations.	• Includes *no* sentence variety.	• Contains *serious errors* in the conventions of the English language (grammar, punctuation, capitalization, spelling). These errors interfere with the reader's understanding of the writing.

Tackling Test Questions

Multiple-Choice Questions

A multiple-choice item is a question that has different answer choices provided for you. The multiple-choice questions offer four answer choices.

There are different types of Language Arts multiple-choice questions. Questions may test your knowledge of vocabulary, reading comprehension, literary analysis, writing strategies, or English-language conventions.

The following is an example of a multiple-choice question that tests vocabulary knowledge.

---

6. Which familiar word is the *best* replacement for the underlined word in the following sentence?

You may find it <u>perplexing</u> *when you first try to understand how a bank works. Once you read more about the subject, however, it will become easier to understand.*

A. unlikely   C. unnecessary

B. confusing   D. empty

This is an example of a reading comprehension multiple-choice question.

---

4. Which choice *best* describes the narrator's perspective in the following passage?

Yesterday, I was a boy of twelve. Today, I am a man of thirteen. I must put away my toys and take responsibility for my share of the work around this place. As my mother tells me, "Life is not a free ride; everyone must pay."

A. a boy who wants to grow up   C. a boy who does not want to grow up

B. a mother speaking to her son   D. a man looking back on his childhood

---

The following is an example of a multiple-choice question that tests literary analysis skills.

---

3. Which of the following sentences does *not* work with the others to develop consistent character?

A. Jed rarely spoke, and when he did, he chose his words with care.

B. Jed dressed for comfort, not for looks.

C. Some people were afraid of Jed, but his friends knew they could trust him.

D. At parties, Jed liked to sing funny songs in a goofy, high voice.

Here is an example of a writing strategies multiple-choice question.

---

1. Read the following passage. Then, choose the letter of the sentence that would require a citation in a research paper.

World War II was the bloodiest conflict in the history of humankind. The war officially began when Germany invaded Poland on September 1, 1939. In a quick, devastating attack, known as a *blitzkrieg*, German forces used swiftly moving armored columns with close air support to overwhelm the inadequately prepared Polish Army. According to Walter Cronkite, the Poles were completely powerless in the face of the *blitzkrieg*.

   A. World War II officially began on September 1, 1939.
   B. Germany attacked Poland in the first official battle of World War II.
   C. According to Walter Cronkite, the Poles were completely powerless in the face of the *blitzkrieg*.
   D. German forces used swiftly moving armored columns with close air support.

The following is an example of a multiple-choice question that tests English-language conventions.

---

3. In which one of the following sentences does the adverb modify an adjective?

   A. He painted gracefully.
   B. The colors were astonishingly vibrant.
   C. The colors blended well.
   D. The museum visitors looked for the painting eagerly.

Here are tips on tackling multiple-choice questions on tests.

- First, answer those questions to which you immediately know the answer.
- For questions that require more thought, eliminate answer options that you know are wrong.
- If you have considered a question and all of its answers but still have not chosen a response, make a guess. It is important to respond to every question.
- If you have answered all the questions and still have time left, check your work.

Writing Prompt Questions

A writing prompt item has an explanation of a writing activity that may or may not be based on a selection. The prompt identifies the form your writing should take, and it describes what ideas you should include in your writing. It is important to read the writing prompt carefully.

Read the example writing prompt test item below.

Writing Task 3:

You have learned about many important inventions that have been developed throughout history. These inventions have had major impacts on the way people live. Think about an invention you have studied and the influence it has had on society.

Write a composition in which you discuss an important invention. Write about the invention's initial impact and its impact on today's world. Support your assertion that the invention is important with details and examples.

Checklist for Your Writing

The following checklist will help you do your best work. Make sure you read the description of the task carefully.

- Use specific details and examples to fully support your ideas.
- Organize your writing with a strong introduction, body, and conclusion.
- Choose specific words that are appropriate for your audience and purpose.
- Vary your sentences to make your writing interesting to read.
- Check for mistakes in grammar, spelling, punctuation, and sentence formation.

By reading the writing prompt carefully, you can understand that you are being asked to write a persuasive essay. The prompt provides you with the general topic for this essay ("the importance of an invention"). The bulleted "Checklist for Your Writing" gives you further information about form ("strong introduction, body, and conclusion") and ideas that should be included in your essay.

It is important that you do not rush through your task. Instead, after reading the writing prompt carefully, you should pick out key words in order to make sure you write about the assigned topic exactly as stated. Then, take time to plan your essay by writing a list or an outline. This will help you write a well-organized, logical essay.

As you write, pay special attention to the first couple of sentences and the last couple of sentences of your essay. The beginning and end of it will likely have the most impact on the test scorer. If you finish your essay and have time left over, read over your work and neatly edit it.

Part 2
INTRODUCTION

Part 2 will give you practice working with the California standards for English-Language Arts content for Grade 7. This part contains two types of exercises: Daily Standards Reviews and Writing Support for Essays (Narrative, Persuasive, and Expository).

- **Daily Standards Reviews** cover all California reading, writing, speaking, and listening standards. There are two pages for each standard. The first page states and defines the standard, gives examples, and provides a way to understand the skill. The second page provides test practice questions to ensure that the standard's skills have been mastered.

- **Writing Support for Essays** covers all writing standards that are tested on the standardized California tests. Practice writing prompts are provided for Written and Oral English Language Conventions skills and Writing Strategies skills. Scoring rubrics are presented and used for testing practice.

Reading

> **Vocabulary and Concept Development**
> **1.1** Identify idioms, analogies, metaphors, and similes in prose and poetry.

Explanation

Figures of speech and other types of descriptive language are used in literature to illustrate ideas through comparisons and contrasts.

a. An idiom is an expression. Its literal meaning differs from its meaning in casual conversation. Idioms can add realism to dialogue in a story and can contribute to characterization.

b. An analogy compares two unlike things, such as a heart and a pump. Analogies help readers to understand unknown concepts by comparing them to known things.

c. A metaphor is a figure of speech that implies or directly states that two unlike things are similar. Writers use metaphors to call attention to certain qualities of one or both things that are being compared. A metaphor does not use *like* or *as* to make the comparison.

d. A simile is a figure of speech that uses *like* or *as* to compare two unlike things.

Examples

The following are examples of an idiom, an analogy, a metaphor, and a simile.

- Idiom: *Who let the cat out of the bag?*
- Analogy: *Your smile lights up the room, just as the sun brightens the sky.*
- Metaphor: *All the world's a stage.*
- Simile: *The world is like a stage.*

Understand the Skill

List examples of each type of descriptive language included on this page, but do not label them. Mix up the order. Exchange lists with a partner and identify the examples as an idiom, an analogy, a metaphor, or a simile.

Choose the letter of the best answer to each question.

1. Which of the following uses *like* or *as* in a sentence?

   A. analogy
   B. simile
   C. metaphor
   D. idiom

2. What does the idiom "pound the pavement" mean in the following statement?

   Marge was determined to find a summer job, so she went out on Monday morning to pound the pavement. She went to every store in town.

   A. to go on a shopping spree
   B. to bang rocks on the sidewalk
   C. to work diligently to find a job
   D. to buy various items in a store

3. Which of the following sentences contains a metaphor?

   A. The snow fell like stuffing from a burst pillow.
   B. When he opened the door, everyone looked up.
   C. Cotton candy looks like clouds at sunset.
   D. When he opened the door, a lightning bolt of fur and claws streaked out.

4. Which one of the following sentences contains an analogy?

   A. Tiny tubes in a tree bring sugar to the leaves, just as blood vessels carry nutrients in the body.
   B. She wolfed down her dinner.
   C. I felt as drained as a wrung-out sponge.
   D. On the outside, the ride looks like a big rocket ship, but inside, it looks more like an ordinary Ferris wheel.

5. What type of element is found in the following sentence?

   She's the apple of my eye.

   A. idiom
   B. simile
   C. metaphor
   D. gerund

6. Which of the following sentences contains a simile?

   A. The trees are sentinels on the prairie land.
   B. The harbor seals barked like an unruly church choir.
   C. It's raining cats and dogs.
   D. Pink stone walls surround the gray rocky castle.

Reading

Vocabulary and Concept Development
1.2 Use knowledge of Greek, Latin, and Anglo-Saxon roots and affixes to understand content-area vocabulary.

Explanation

Many words in the English language have Greek, Latin, or Anglo-Saxon roots and affixes. Readers who recognize the meanings of roots and affixes can more easily determine the meanings of unknown words.

a. A root is the main part of a word. It can also be the word itself.

b. An affix is either a prefix or a suffix. A prefix is attached to the beginning of a word. A suffix is attached to the end of a word.

Examples

Origin	Common Roots	Common Prefixes	Common Suffixes
Greek	*photo* (light) *bio* (life) *psyche* (mind/soul) *chron* (time)	*micro-* (small) *anti-* (against) *thermo-* (heat) *auto-* (self)	*-ist* (one who studies, practices, or makes) *-logy* (the study of) *-path* (feeling, suffering)
Latin	*retro* (backwards) *sol* (sun) *ego* (I) *aqua* (water)	*bi-* (two) *trans-* (across) *sub-* (under, below) *non-* (not)	*-ous* (full of) *-able* (capable or worthy of) *-fy* (to make or cause)
Anglo-Saxon	*dear* (valued) *ward* (guard) *spell* (recite) *drink* (swallow)	*a-* (on, in) *mis-* (wrong) *un-* (not)	*-ness* (state of being) *-ful* (full of, having) *-less* (without)

Understand the Skill

Look at the following examples to help you understand this concept.

bio- + -logy = biology (the study of life)

un- + necessary = unnecessary (not necessary)

Study the word roots and affixes shown on this page, and then combine the elements to form new words. Use a dictionary for help.

Choose the letter of the best answer to each question.

1. Which affix could be added to the word *likely* to create a word that means "not expected to happen"?

   A. *un-*
   B *-hood*
   C. *-ment*
   D. *im-*

2. Which word indicates the state of being ready?

   A. readily
   B. readiest
   C. readiness
   D. readying

3. What is the meaning of the word *appropriateness*?

   A. the opposite of appropriate
   B. the quality of being appropriate
   C. the least appropriate
   D. the appropriate individual

4. What is the meaning of the word *psychologist*?

   A. one who studies the mind
   B. the study of the mind
   C. one who studies life
   D. one who is capable of studying

5. Which prefix could be added to the word *organism* to indicate that it is small?

   A. *bio-*
   B. *macro-*
   C. *-ology*
   D. *micro-*

6. A *biyearly* event happens how often?

   A. once a year
   B. twice a year
   C. yearly
   D. every ten years

Reading

> **Vocabulary and Concept Development**
> **1.3** Clarify word meanings through the use of definition, example, restatement, or contrast.

Explanation

The meanings of unknown words can often be determined by using definition, example, restatement, or contrast.

a. A definition gives the meaning of a word. Some words have more than one meaning. Dictionaries, glossaries, and other sources can be used to find definitions.

b. An example offers additional details about the meaning of a word. It is especially helpful with words that have multiple meanings.

c. Restatement involves simplifying or clarifying the definition of a word. It can also involve using the word in a different, more familiar context.

d. Contrast uses opposites to clarify word meaning. An unknown word is contrasted with a familiar word that is its opposite in meaning.

Examples

The following are examples of a definition, an example, restatement, and contrast.

- Definition: *I like nonfiction books because real-life stories appeal to me.*
- Example: *The canine dashed off, and like a good dog, fetched the stick.*
- Restatement: *Miranda saw the analogy, or relationship, between the two.*
- Contrast: *I thought it would improve her mood, not make her glum.*

Understand the Skill

Working with a partner, scan through magazine articles and list unfamiliar words. Use the techniques described on this page to determine the meanings of the words.

Choose the letter of the best answer to each question.

1. Which word in the following sentence helps to clarify the meaning of *attire*? Blue and gold shirts were the <u>attire</u> of the day when our school held the Friday football pep rally.

    A. football
    B Friday
    C. blue
    D. shirts

2. Which one of the following is the *best* definition of *indispensable*?

    Joe thought his team didn't need him to play first base, but his teammates thought Joe was <u>indispensable</u>.

    A. not needed
    B. absolutely necessary
    C. a baseball player
    D. lacking confidence

3. In the following sentence, which type of clue helps clarify the meaning of the word *abridged*?

    I have read only the <u>abridged</u>, or shortened, version of the book.

    A. contrast
    B. restatement
    C. example
    D. definition

4. Which of the following is the correct definition of the underlined word in this sentence?

    Irene, our friend, is a <u>somnambulist</u>, which means she walks in her sleep.

    A. someone who drives an ambulance
    B. our friend
    C. someone who is asleep
    D. someone who walks while asleep

5. Based on its use in the following sentence, what is the meaning of the word *sage*?

    She grows <u>sage</u> in her herb garden, and she uses the leaves to season the soup.

    A. a flower
    B. a garden
    C. an herb
    D. a type of soup

6. Which familiar word is the *best* replacement for the underlined word in the following sentence?

    You may find it <u>perplexing</u> when you first try to understand how a bank works. Once you read more about the subject, however, it will become easier to understand.

    A. unlikely
    B. confusing
    C. unnecessary
    D. empty

Reading

TESTED

> **Structural Features of Informational Materials**
> **2.1** Understand and analyze the differences in structure and purpose between various categories of informational materials (e.g., textbooks, newspapers, instructional manuals, signs).

Explanation

Informational materials are nonfiction works that offer information about specific topics. The writer's goal is to inform the reader through the use of facts and detailed explanations.

   a. A textbook provides information about a particular academic subject. The book may be written by one or several authors, all experts in their field of study. Most textbooks include assessments, or tests, to gauge the reader's knowledge of the subject.

   b. A newspaper provides information about local, state, national, and global events. Newspaper articles state the facts and often include quotes from concerned parties; they provide an unbiased view of an event by giving both sides of the argument. Most newspapers have editorial pages. Newspaper editorials offer opinions of events or people. Editorials are not unbiased.

   c. Instructional manuals provide detailed, step-by-step information about a process or type of technology. They are often included with consumer products and may be written in several different languages. Instructional manuals are particularly useful to consumers who are using a product for the first time.

   d. Signs are used by local, state, and national governments to inform the public. Road signs, for example, direct travelers and give information about driving laws and road conditions. Signs may use symbols rather than words to provide information. Signs also are used by businesses to advertise their products or services, or to give hours of operation.

Example

The following is an example of text from an instructional manual to help you understand this concept.

> *Step 1: Turn on the computer.*
> *Step 2: Place the disk labeled "Printer Start-up" into the computer's DVD slot.*

Understand the Skill

Select two types of informational materials from the list on this page. Scan through the materials, and then give a brief oral summary explaining how they offer information.

Choose the letter of the best answer to each question.

1. In which of the following would you *most* likely find a writer's point of view or position on a current event or issue?

   A. encyclopedia

   B science textbook

   C. newspaper editorial page

   D. newspaper article

2. The author of a textbook would *most* likely include which of the following in the book?

   A. opinions

   B. facts and details

   C. quotes

   D. a position

3. Which of the following types of information is usually *not* supplied by signs?

   A. rules

   B. warnings

   C. hours of operation

   D. arguments for or against a particular action

4. What is the *most* likely purpose for reading a traffic sign?

   A. to learn an author's point of view

   B. to understand both sides of an argument

   C. to get very particular information

   D. to be entertained

5. Which of the following new products would *most* likely be accompanied by an instructional manual?

   A. a book

   B. a camera

   C. a sofa

   D. a pair of shoes

6. Who would *most* likely write an instructional manual?

   A. a manufacturer

   B. a reporter

   C. a city mayor

   D. a textbook author

Reading

TESTED

> **Structural Features of Informational Materials**
> **2.2** Locate information by using a variety of consumer, workplace, and public documents.

Explanation

Information about a wide variety of topics can be found in consumer, workplace, and public documents.

a. Consumer documents can inform or entertain the public.

b. Workplace documents provide information about businesses.

c. Public documents inform the public and give basic information to improve life.

d. When accessing information, take into consideration the source. Magazines, for example, tend to be more biased than newspapers. Public documents are usually the most reliable source of information. Research to find out which source can provide the needed information. For example, information about an environmental issue can be found in state or federal environmental protection agencies, or from newspapers and magazines.

Examples

Consumer Documents	Workplace Documents	Public Documents
Internet	Internet	Internet
Instructional manuals	Annual business reports	Universities
Warranties		Local government agencies
Newspapers		State government agencies
Magazines		Federal government
Nonfiction books		agencies

Understand the Skill

Suppose that you are assigned to write a brief biography of your favorite author. Detail how you would go about finding the information.

Choose the letter of the best answer to each question.

1. Which of the following public documents would you use to find the standards for safe drinking water?

   A. income tax chart

   B telephone book

   C. document from the Department of Education

   D. document from the Environmental Protection Agency

2. What is an instruction manual?

   A. step-by-step instructions for assembling and operating a device

   B. a document that uses symbols to explain rules and laws

   C. a map that shows how to get from one location to another

   D. directions that cannot be understood by seventh-grade students

3. Which of the following explain why local, state, or federal agencies print government documents?

   A. to give basic information to improve life

   B. to get votes for candidates

   C. to entertain a variety of people

   D. to gain support for a bill

4. For which of the following research topics might you consult government publications?

   A. ancient history

   B. farming statistics

   C. antique collections

   D. celebrity birthdays

5. Which consumer document would explain a manufacturer's responsibility if a product is defective?

   A. nonfiction book

   B. newspaper

   C. warranty

   D. magazine

6. Which document would you access to find out how many products a certain company sold last year?

   A. the company's instructional manual

   B. documents from the county commissioner's office

   C. documents from the U.S. Department of Health

   D. the company's annual business report

Reading

Structural Features of Information
2.3 Analyze text that uses the cause-and-effect organizational pattern.

Explanation

Authors often use organizational patterns to help clarify their messages. Readers can better understand an author's purpose by identifying and analyzing the patterns he or she uses in the text. One such pattern is cause-and-effect. A cause is the reason for an event. An effect is the event that results from the cause. Cause-and-effect statements are often characterized by words such as:

- because
- so
- as a result of
- therefore
- thus
- consequently
- subsequently

Examples

The following are examples of a cause-and-effect organizational pattern to help you understand this concept.

- *I missed the bus because I overslept. (Cause: I overslept; Effect: I missed the bus.)*
- *It snowed all night. Therefore, school was cancelled. (Cause: It snowed all night; Effect: School was cancelled.)*

Understand the Skill

As a class, look through your science textbooks for examples of cause-and-effect organizational patterns. Take turns sharing examples with the class. Identify the cause and the effect in the examples.

Choose the letter of the best answer to each question.

1. What is the effect in a cause-and-effect organizational pattern?

   A. a surprise that occurs in a text

   B the event that results from a cause

   C. the reason for an event

   D. the visual images in a text

2. What is the cause in the following cause-and-effect statement?

   Jim studied hard and attended all of his classes, so he was not surprised when he received an "A" in biology class.

   A. receiving an "A" in biology class

   B. being surprised

   C. Jim's good luck

   D. studying hard and attending classes

3. Which of the following would you expect to find in an article that has a cause-and-effect organization?

   A. an explanation of how one behavior affects another

   B. a request for a donation

   C. step-by-step directions

   D. guidelines for evaluating a service

Read the following passage. Then, use the information to answer questions 4 and 5.

Many reptiles in the northern United States spend winters in a sleepy state resembling hibernation. As summer changes to autumn, the days grow cooler and shorter. When the average temperature outdoors drops, a reptile's body releases certain chemicals. These chemicals tell its body to slow down. The reptile eats less and less. Sometime in the mid-fall, the reptile is ready to dig itself under the forest leaf litter or the muddy bottom of a pond, where it will sleep away the winter. Hibernation helps it survive the winter months, when food may be scarce.

4. Which of the following causes a reptile to go into hibernation?

   A. shortages of food

   B. sleepiness

   C. changes in temperature

   D. digging under the leaf litter

5. Which of the following *directly* causes a hibernating reptile to stop eating?

   A. cooler temperatures

   B. the release of certain chemicals

   C. shortages of food

   D. digging in mud

Reading

Comprehension and Analysis of Grade-Level-Appropriate Text
2.4 Identify and trace the development of an author's argument, point of view, or perspective in text.

Explanation

An author may want to get across a particular message to readers or take a position on an issue. He or she may do this by writing a logical argument or by using opinions. Sometimes the arguments or opinions are given through a narrator's point of view.

   a. An argument is a type of text in which the author uses reasoning to try to sway the reader. In a written argument, details and facts often lead up to and support the main idea. An author's argument can be determined by identifying the main idea and supporting details.

   b. An author can take a positive or negative point of view on a subject. A positive point of view is favorable, while a negative point of view is unfavorable. An author's point of view may not involve logical arguments. Instead, emotions and opinions can characterize viewpoints.

   c. Perspective refers to the narrator's role in a text. He or she may speak directly to the reader, using the word *I*. Or, the narrator may speak through the thoughts and words of characters, using the words *he* or *she*.

Examples

The following are examples of an argument, point of view, and perspective to help you understand this concept.

- Argument: *Since we started the tutoring program, math scores have risen by 20 percent. Therefore, the tutoring program should be continued.*

- Negative point of view: *I hate cold temperatures and snow. Winter is my least favorite season.*

- Perspective: *She watched as her brother got on the plane. The plane hadn't left yet, and she missed him already.*

Understand the Skill

Write a positive point of view about a subject of your choice.

Choose the letter of the best answer to each question.

1. Which statement reflects an author's positive point of view?

   A. There is too much crime in cities today.

   B   You can't go outside anymore without worrying about crime.

   C. Citizen groups are effective in combating crime in the cities.

   D. Someone should do something about the crime rate in cities.

2. Which statement reflects an author's negative point of view?

   A. Climbing mountains is a great challenge and test of will.

   B. The climb is the reward, not the view from the top.

   C. Injury is just one of the risks mountain climbers face.

   D. With a guide and preparation, anyone can climb mountains.

3. What is the *best* way to identify an author's argument?

   A. Notice descriptive words.

   B. Read the first and last paragraphs.

   C. Scan rapidly through the text.

   D. Identify the facts and details that lead to a main point.

4. What is the author's argument in the following passage?

   Our committee believes that carpools help to protect the environment. Carpooling cuts down on the number of cars on the road and decreases the consumption of gasoline. Also, if there are not as many cars driving, there would be less pollution.

   A. People should use public transportation.

   B. People should carpool to help the environment.

   C. People should care about the environment.

   D. Cars are deadly.

5. What message is the author trying to convey in the following passage?

   The force of gravity is very great at first, but the rumbling and shaking of the craft is beyond anything we expected. Rather suddenly, the pressure pulling us tight into our seats is gone and all is silent. Earth recedes until it looks like a classroom globe.

   A. the experience of being a person on the ground watching a spacecraft liftoff

   B. the amazing experience of being an astronaut on a spacecraft liftoff

   C. the frightening experience of being an astronaut

   D. the appearance of Earth from space

6. Which choice *best* describes the narrator's perspective in the following passage?

   Yesterday, I was a boy of twelve. Today, I am a man of thirteen. I must put away my toys and take responsibility for my share of the work around this place. As my mother tells me, "Life is not a free ride; everyone must pay."

   A. a boy who wants to grow up

   B. a mother speaking to her son

   C. a boy who does not want to grow up

   D. a man looking back on his childhood

Reading

> **Comprehension and Analysis of Grade-Level-Appropriate Text**
> **2.5** Understand and explain the use of a simple mechanical device by following technical directions.

Explanation

Technical directions are written guidelines that explain how to use a mechanical device, such as a bicycle or tool. To best understand technical directions, read through the document and picture each step in your mind.

 a. How-to essays tell readers how to make or use a device. These types of essays may be found in newspapers, magazines, books, or on the Internet.

 b. Instructional manuals for using a device are usually included with the product. Instructional manuals have several components, including step-by-step instructions, warranty information, and diagrams that show each part of the device.

Examples

The following is an example of text for technical directions to help you understand this concept.

 1. *Check for missing parts and have tools at hand.*
 2. *Read through all the directions.*
 3. *Follow the instructions in proper order.*
 4. *If you have difficulties, reread the directions.*

Understand the Skill

Write a four-step list of technical directions for using a toaster.

Choose the letter of the best answer to each question.

1. What is the writer's purpose in a how-to essay?

   A. to persuade the reader to do something
   B   to entertain the reader
   C. to give the reader insight into life
   D. to explain how to do or how to make something

2. What is the first thing you do before you begin to ride a bike?

   A. begin to pedal
   B. turn around
   C. press the brakes
   D. sit on the seat

3. Which of the following topics would *best* be explained with step-by-step directions?

   A. my favorite person
   B. how to assemble a bicycle
   C. why we need a skateboard park
   D. the architecture of our new library

4. If you wanted to know the name of a certain part of your new microscope, which section of the technical directions would be *most* useful to you?

   A. step-by-step instructions
   B. troubleshooting guide
   C. diagram
   D. safety warning

5. Which of the following would you *most* likely find in technical directions?

   A. rising action
   B. setting, including time and place
   C. a street map
   D. a list of needed materials

6. Which of the following is the *best* reading strategy when reading technical directions?

   A. paraphrase the figurative language
   B. read through the entire directions, visualizing each step
   C. compare and contrast characters
   D. understand the author's point of view

Reading

TESTED

Explanation

Authors should support nonfiction writing with plenty of accurate evidence. The author's purpose often determines the type of evidence included in the work. Arguments, for example, should include facts and details that can be verified, or proven true. When reading a nonfiction work, be aware of instances of bias, stereotyping, or generalizations. These things cannot be proven true, and they undermine an author's argument.

a. Bias results when an author has a particular opinion or point of view about a subject. The author's opinion can be found in his or her work, unsupported by facts. Biased statements may include such words as *I believe, I strongly feel that*, or *In my opinion.*

b. Stereotyping is a judgment, good or bad, made about a particular group based on limited observation. Stereotyping can involve race, gender, age, nationality, or other characteristics.

c. A generalization is a sweeping statement about a subject that cannot be backed up by facts. An author may base the generalization on one experience and carry it over to include all similar experiences.

Examples

The following are examples of bias, stereotyping, and a generalization to help you understand these concepts.

- Bias: *I believe that our educational system is in good shape.*
- Stereotyping: *Teenagers don't like to work.*
- Generalization: *All dogs have fleas.*

Understand the Skill

Search through magazines or newspaper articles for examples of bias, stereotyping, or generalizations. Share your examples with the class.

Choose the letter of the best answer to each question.

1. What is a stereotype?

   A. a sound system that includes a CD player
   B a character with two strong personality traits
   C. the judgment of one person based on a conversation with that person
   D. the categorizing of a whole group of people based on limited observation

2. Which of the following is sometimes used as a basis for forming a stereotype?

   A. race
   B. gender
   C. age
   D. all of the above

3. Which of the following *most* strongly influences the types of evidence an author includes in an essay?

   A. author's popularity
   B. author's place of birth
   C. author's purpose for writing
   D. author's ability to use figurative language

4. Which of the following is an example of bias?

   A. Dogs are much friendlier than cats.
   B. I own two dogs, and one is very active.
   C. I often walk my dog along the river because he enjoys swimming.
   D. My friend's cat is black with gray stripes.

5. Which of the following can weaken an author's message?

   A. inaccurate data
   B. bias
   C. stereotyping
   D. all of the above

6. Which of the following is an example of a fact?

   A. I think students call in sick just to miss a day of school.
   B. Taking vitamin C might help cure a cold.
   C. In one year, about 61 million Americans will suffer from colds.
   D. These tissues are the best to use when you have a cold.

Reading

TESTED

Structural Features of Literature
3.1 Articulate the expressed purposes and characteristics of different forms of prose (e.g., short story, novel, novella, essay).

Explanation

Prose includes both fiction and nonfiction works. Fiction includes short stories, novellas, and novels. Though the subject matter may be serious, the purpose of fiction is to entertain the reader and offer insight into life. Nonfiction includes essays. Essays have various purposes, depending on the author's goal.

a. A short story is a brief work that tells a story about fictional, or imaginary, characters. A short story has the following elements:
   • plot (sequence of events),
   • setting (time and place of action),
   • characters (people, animals, or imaginary beings),
   • theme (main idea).

b. A novella is a short fiction book that includes all the elements of a short story, such as plot, setting, characters, and theme. The characters in a novella and other works of fiction may change and grow as the story progresses, but they have consistent personality traits throughout.

c. A novel is a long fiction book. It also includes elements such as plot, setting, characters, and theme. These elements are usually more developed in novels, given their longer length.

d. An essay is a nonfiction work that deals with real-life issues. Essays may be personal and informal, describing an event in the author's life in an entertaining manner. Other essays have a formal tone and deal with serious subjects. Their purpose may be to instruct or persuade readers.

Example

The following example is a description of a short story's characteristics.

   • *I am reading a work about two imaginary characters who live in England during World War II. It has a plot, a setting, and a theme. The work is short and fictional, so I know it is a short story.*

Understand the Skill

Write a short essay in which you compare the characteristics of short stories and novels.

Choose the letter of the best answer to each question.

1. Which of the following deals with real-life events?

   A. essay

   B novel

   C. short story

   D. novella

2. What is the time and place of action in a story called?

   A. plot

   B. character

   C. setting

   D. climax

3. What is a short story?

   A. a long work of fiction

   B. a brief work that tells a story about imaginary characters

   C. literature written in verse form

   D. literature about real-life events

4. Which of the following sentences does *not* work with the others to develop consistent character?

   A. Jed rarely spoke, and when he did, he chose his words with care.

   B. Jed dressed for comfort not for looks.

   C. Some people were afraid of Jed, but his friends knew they could trust him.

   D. At parties, Jed liked to sing funny songs in a goofy, high voice.

5. Which of the following would likely take you the longest to read?

   A. essay

   B. short story

   C. novella

   D. novel

6. Which answer *best* describes the setting found in the following sentence?

   In the 1920s, Annie worked as a housekeeper and cook in a house on a Montana farm.

   A. a city dwelling in the 1920s

   B. a housekeeper and a cook

   C. a farm in the 1920s

   D. the mountains of Montana

Reading

> **Narrative Analysis of Grade-Level-Appropriate Text**
> **3.2** Identify events that advance the plot and determine how each event explains past or present action(s) or foreshadows future action(s).

Explanation

The plot is the sequence of events in works of prose. Events that move the plot along include conflict, rising action, climax, and resolution. These events help to explain the actions of characters. They may also foreshadow, or hint of, actions to come.

a. Conflict involves a struggle between two opposing forces. An external conflict occurs when a character is pitted against an outside force. This force can be another character, an event, or even nature. An internal conflict occurs when a character struggles with inner doubts or feelings.

b. Rising action occurs when conflicts develop within the plot, catching and maintaining the reader's interest. Rising action builds suspense within the plot. The reader is unsure what will happen next and eagerly reads on to find out.

c. The climax is the point of greatest suspense or intensity in the plot. It usually comes near the end of the story.

d. Resolution follows the climax. It describes the results of the climax.

Example

The following example is a description of events that advance the plot.

- Conflict: *A young boy and his mother move to a new town. They have trouble making friends.*
- Rising action: *While exploring the town, the boy enters an old, abandoned house. He falls through the floor and is trapped in the basement.*
- Climax: *The townspeople come together to search for the boy. He is rescued.*
- Resolution: *The boy and his mother settle into their new life with their new friends.*

Understand the Skill

Authors often draw from personal experiences when writing fiction. Give an example of conflicts, internal or external, that you have faced in your life that could be turned into prose.

Choose the letter of the best answer to each question.

1. While stranded on a mountain ledge, two boys have to overcome cold, discomfort, and biting insects. What do these challenges represent?

    A. external conflicts

    B internal conflicts

    C. predictions

    D. foreshadowing

2. Identify the climax in the following passage.

    A boy sees a snake lying still in the road. He bends close to look at it. Suddenly, the snake moves. The boy jumps back.

    A. A boy sees a snake lying still in the road.

    B. He bends close to look at it.

    C. Suddenly, the snake moves.

    D. The boy jumps back.

3. Which of the following *best* describes the events in a plot?

    A. Events increase the tension or lead up to the resolution.

    B. Events are unrelated to the story.

    C. Events affect only the internal conflict in the story.

    D. Events affect only the external conflict in the story.

4. Which of the following sentences expresses a conflict you might find in a short story?

    A. Don worked at the bank on Elm Street in the middle of town.

    B. Don and Fred were brothers.

    C. Both Don and Fred liked to eat hamburgers.

    D. Both Don and Fred wanted to marry Sue Ellen.

5. Which of the following events is *most* likely foreshadowed by the description of "the pelting rain drowned out the sound of any footsteps"?

    A. A character will lose her umbrella.

    B. A noisy group of people will run through the streets.

    C. A character does not know he is being followed.

    D. The sun is about to come out.

6. What is suspense?

    A. an animated story

    B. a feeling of joy or happiness at the way events turn out in a story

    C. any event that takes place at night

    D. a feeling readers get when they are unsure what will happen next but are eager to find out

Reading

> **Narrative Analysis of Grade-Level-Appropriate Text**
> **3.3** Analyze characterization as delineated through a character's thoughts, words, speech patterns, and actions; the narrator's description; and the thoughts, words, and actions of other characters.

Explanation

Characters are the people, animals, or imaginary beings in literature. Main characters are pivotal to the story. The plot revolves around them. Minor characters are less fully developed than main characters; they are used to help move the plot along.

An author uses characterization to create and develop the characters.

a. Direct characterization occurs when the author makes direct statements about a character. These statements might describe the character's appearance and background.

b. Indirect characterization occurs when a character reveals personal thoughts, words, and actions. This can be accomplished through dialogue, or the spoken words of a character. Indirect characterization also occurs when other characters interact with and think about a particular character.

Examples

The following are examples of characterization.

- Direct characterization: *Antonio Cruz and Felix Vargas were both seventeen years old. They were so together in friendship that they felt themselves to be brothers.*

- Indirect characterization: *"You know Lisa," Abbie said. "She gets angry at the smallest thing!"*

Understand the Skill

Write a brief dialogue between two characters that reveals something special about a third character.

Choose the letter of the best answer to each question.

1. Which word *best* describes a character who advises another character to be careful and to travel safely?

   A. cautionary

   B powerful

   C. carefree

   D. indecisive

2. What is characterization in literature?

   A. the cast of characters

   B. the lesson or moral of the story

   C. how a writer creates and develops characters

   D. the writer's point of view

3. In prose, what are the spoken words and conversations of characters called?

   A. dialogue

   B. speeches

   C. instructions

   D. arguments

4. Which of these lines of dialogue characterizes an impatient person?

   A. If you don't mind, I'd prefer to walk home.

   B. Stop looking at your watch. Let's just leave now!

   C. Take those cookies out of the oven. They must be done by now.

   D. The dance will be over in an hour. Then, we can go to my house.

5. Which of the following *best* describes a character who scowls and stamps his or her feet?

   A. happy

   B. cooperative

   C. dreamy and relaxed

   D. demanding and angry

Reading

> **Narrative Analysis of Grade-Level-Appropriate Text**
> **3.4** Identify and analyze recurring themes across works (e.g., the value of bravery, loyalty, and friendship; the effects of loneliness).

Explanation

Theme is the central message or insight into life found in a work of prose. Common themes in literature include:

- the value of qualities such as bravery and loyalty,
- the healing effects of love and friendship,
- the timeless beauty of nature,
- the everlasting bond between families,
- the devastating effects of loneliness, heartache, or war.

a. A stated theme is directly stated within a story. Often, it is found at the beginning or end of a story.

b. An implied theme is revealed gradually over the course of a story through events and the actions, words, and thoughts of characters. Implied themes are more common in literature than are stated themes.

Examples

The following are examples of a stated theme and an implied theme:

- Stated theme: *Loyalty is the most important thing in the world.* (Theme: value of loyalty)
- Implied theme: *When everyone turned against me, she stood by my side. I owe her my sanity. I owe her my life.* (Theme: value of loyalty)

Understand the Skill

Choose a theme for a short story. Explain why you selected that particular theme.

Choose the letter of the best answer to each question.

1. What is meant by the word *theme* in a story?

   A. Theme is the music written by a character in a story.
   B Theme is the central message or insight into life.
   C. Theme is the setting of a story.
   D. Theme is the way a story ends.

2. Which of the following would *not* make a good theme in writings about nature?

   A. The beauty of nature is timeless.
   B. Nature is to be preserved for all time.
   C. Time is not to be wasted.
   D. Inspiration can come from nature.

3. Which of the following sentences would *most* likely express the theme of a story?

   A. A stitch in time saves nine.
   B Dublin, Ireland, makes an interesting setting for a story.
   C. Honesty between two people is valuable when making important decisions in life.
   D. Spring 1998 was the beginning of Winnie's education.

4. Which of the following would *not* make a good theme for a short story?

   A. the strong bond between family members
   B. the history of the Civil War
   C. the healing beauty of nature
   D. the value of friendship

5. How is an implied theme expressed in a story?

   A. in the first sentence of the story
   B. within the introduction
   C. by the first character who speaks in the story
   D. through the characters, actions, and events in the story

6. What is true of a stated theme?

   A. It is expressed directly.
   B. It is revealed gradually.
   C. It is never revealed.
   D. It is only found in novels about states.

Reading

TESTED

> **Narrative Analysis of Grade-Level-Appropriate Text**
> **3.5** Contrast points of view (e.g., first and third person, limited and omniscient, subjective and objective) in narrative text and explain how they affect the overall theme of the work.

Explanation

Point of view refers to the narrator's voice in a text and the angle from which a story is told.

  a. In first-person point of view, the narrator is a character in the text. He or she is called *I* throughout the story. This point of view is particularly suited to stories that describe personal experiences.

  b. In third-person limited point of view, the narrator describes the emotions and actions of one character in the text. In this case, the narrator is called *he* or *she*. This point of view helps the reader to more fully understand the main character in a story.

  c. In third-person omniscient point of view, the narrator is not a character in the story. Instead, the narrator stands apart, and comments on the emotions and actions of all characters in the text. This point of view is helpful is showing how multiple characters react to an event.

Examples

The following are examples of points of view.

  • First person: *I know how it will go. Annie will ask for help with her homework. And as always, I'll agree.*

  • Third-person limited: *Sally wasn't sure how her father would react to the news. But she knew she had to tell him regardless.*

  • Third-person omniscient: *Chris was worrying about how they would find their way out of the forest. Rodrigo, however, was thinking about how he would describe their adventure when they got home.*

Understand the Skill

Write a few sentences from the point of view of your choice. Exchange sentences with a classmate. Identify the point of view of your classmate's prose.

Choose the letter of the best answer to each question.

1. Which detail in this passage could be known only by a first-person narrator?

   In my garden, I planted rows of beans, corn, lettuce, cucumbers, and tomatoes. I planted everything from seeds. It takes patience to wait for the seeds to sprout. I look forward to the day this summer when I can make a fresh salad with my own crops.

   A. I planted beans.
   B. I planted seeds.
   C. I look forward to making a fresh salad with my own crops.
   D. It takes patience to wait for seeds to sprout.

2. If an author tells a story from a third-person limited point of view, what will the reader know about the characters?

   A. the thoughts and feelings of all the characters
   B. the thoughts and feelings of only one character
   C. the thoughts and feelings of the narrator
   D. nothing about the thoughts or feelings of the characters

3. From which point of view is the following passage written?

   I saw Ashley an hour ago. She looked at me and smiled but didn't say anything. I wonder if she's keeping a secret from me.

   A. first-person
   B   third-person limited
   C. third-person omniscient
   D. second-person

4. Which of the following terms *best* describes the angle from which a story is told?

   A. the main idea
   B. the point of view
   C. the description
   D. the resolution

5. Which sentence is written from the third-person limited point of view?

   A. The contest was my idea, even though there were other suggestions.
   B. At the sound of the bell, he began to tug.
   C. Don't pull yet!
   D. Sandra tugged before the bell rang, but Carey waited for the signal.

6. In which situation would it be *most* appropriate to use third-person omniscient point of view?

   A. in writing a set of directions
   B. in describing a personal experience
   C. in describing an event that happens to a single character
   D. in describing the reactions of different characters to a dramatic event

Reading

TESTED

> **Literary Criticism**
> **3.6** Analyze a range of responses to a literary work and determine the extent to which the literary elements in the work shaped those responses.

Explanation

Writers may use literary elements in prose to evoke a certain response in a reader. These elements include juxtaposition, alliteration, comic relief, and allusion.

a. Juxtaposition involves placing different things next to each other in a story to stress similarities or differences among the things. Juxtaposition is used to influence the reader's emotions.

b. Alliteration is the repetition of certain sounds, usually at the beginning of words. Alliteration can create a pleasing, musical quality. Poets often use alliteration to emphasize words they want readers to notice.

c. Comic relief occurs when a humorous statement or event breaks the tension in a serious situation. The author can more easily change the direction of the plot and give the reader an emotional break in a dramatic story.

d. Allusion occurs when a writer refers to a famous person or event, imaginary or real. A reader who understands the allusion gains a deeper understanding of the writer's prose.

Examples

The following are examples of the literary elements juxtaposition, alliteration, comic relief, and allusion.

- Juxtaposition: *I went to the party because everyone else was going. I went to show them that I was different.*
- Alliteration: *What a world of merriment their melody foretells!*
- Comic relief: *John threw his plate across the room. We sat there, shocked. Then we heard a small sigh from grandpa. The mashed potatoes had landed on his bald head.*
- Allusion: *I felt like Joan of Arc as I started the game. I could take on anyone.*

Understand the Skill

Create a sentence using alliteration. Share your sentence with the class.

Choose the letter of the best answer to each question.

1. Why would a writer use comic relief in a story?

   A. to evoke an emotional response
   B. to break the tension
   C. to sound pleasing
   D. to refer to a famous artist

2. An author compares her father to Abraham Lincoln. What literary element is she using?

   A. comic relief
   B. alliteration
   C. juxtaposition
   D. allusion

3. The following passage was written by a literary critic. Read the passage, and then decide to which literary element the critic was responding.

   When a reader first encounters the Edgar Allan Poe poem "The Bells," he or she cannot escape noticing the musical quality of the lines. The regular beat and sounds of the poem create the unmistakable impression that the reader is actually hearing bells.

   A. comic relief
   B. alliteration
   C. juxtaposition
   D. allusion

4. Which literary element places things side by side for comparison's sake?

   A. comic relief
   B. alliteration
   C. juxtaposition
   D. allusion

5. Which of the following is an example of alliteration?

   A. laughter and smiles
   B. as strong as Hercules
   C. love and hate
   D. the wild, wild West

6. In which type of prose would you *most* likely find comic relief?

   A. a poem
   B. a drama
   C. a comedy
   D. an essay

Writing

> **Organization and Focus**
> **1.1** Create an organizational structure that balances all aspects of the composition and uses effective transitions between sentences to unify important ideas.

Explanation

Compositions can present information in the order of how things happened (time order) or explain where something is in relation to other things (spatial order). All writing should have a main purpose, or focus. Transitional words or phrases, such as *first, after that, however,* or *finally* indicate movement from one idea to another.

Examples

The following are ways to organize information, identify the main purpose or focus of writing, and use transitions.

- Time order presents the order in which events occurred, such as a story of what happened at school first in the morning, then in the afternoon, and finally after school. A historical narrative identifies a specific point in history, such as the declaration of war, and gives information about what happened before and after the event.
- Spatial order gives the reader a sense of where things are. For example, a writer may describe a room. The description might include the items in the room along with how they are positioned. Spatial order also can be used to describe things of great distance, such as the solar system. In this case, the position of the planets in relation to the sun could be described. Spatial order gives the reader a visual idea of where things are.
- The main purpose is the reason, or focus, of the writing. This includes writing to entertain or inform the reader, summarize information, compare or contrast people or events, or persuade the reader to think in a particular way.
- Transition words or phrases hold thoughts together. Use words and phrases such as *moreover, therefore, after that, furthermore,* or *in this way* to transition from one idea to another.

Understand the Skill

Choose a paragraph from a literature or history book. Identify the main purpose of the passage, the organization of it, and the use of transitions.

On a separate sheet of paper, complete each item as directed.

1. Combine the following two sentences with a transition that indicates time.

   The sun rose over the lake.
   I jogged along the path in time to my own heartbeat.

2. Rewrite the following three sentences to organize the ideas in time order.

   Sand crunched under my footsteps.
   A cool breeze alerted me that I was approaching the beach.
   I welcomed the lapping of tiny cool waves over my hot feet.

3. Rewrite the following sentences to organize the ideas in spatial order.

   Beyond the trail was the grassy verge and huge barrier boulders.
   At my feet was the gravel trail.
   Way out, as far as I could see, were the white puffs of sails on the blue water.

4. Write a brief paragraph comparing and contrasting a pen and a pencil.

5. Write three unified sentences about events in a story you have read. Clearly organize the sentences, using these transitions: *first, then, finally.*

6. Revise the following paragraph. Use transitions such as *however, since, because, therefore,* or *yet* to show connections between sentences.

   The Grand Canal in China is a constructed waterway. It is the oldest in the world. The canal is still used today. The canal is used to carry goods and people. It connects the regions of China.

7. Write the main purpose of the paragraph in item 6.

Writing

Organization and Focus
1.2 Support all statements and claims with anecdotes, descriptions, facts and statistics, and specific examples.

Explanation

Different types of supportive information are used in writing to engage the audience and provide overall clarity and meaning.

    a. An anecdote is a short, and often amusing, story that improves understanding.

    b. Description gives readers a better visual image of a character or setting.

    c. Facts provide factual support, while statistics provide mathematical data.

    d. Specific examples support a point the author is making.

Examples

The following are examples of the different types of supportive information.

- Anecdote: *I always had fun with grandpa. We would go fishing and he would tell me stories of when he was just a lad. I remember one time when he sat up against an old oak tree holding his fishing pole. With great seriousness in his voice, he told me how he once caught a shark right where he had his line now. When he saw my surprised face, he laughed so hard he had to put his fishing pole down on the grass.*

- Description: *Have you ever seen a sunrise on a cold winter morning? As the sun peaks over the horizon, a burst of red and orange fills the sky. Across the white ground, streaks of light sparkle and dance on the hard-packed snow.*

- Facts and Statistics: *The Civil War was fought from 1861 to 1865. Many battles resulted in over 600,000 deaths from mortal wounds and disease.*

- Specific Examples: *Hurricanes affect the southern part of the United States. For example, on August 28, 2005, Hurricane Katrina hit the southern coast.*

Understand the Skill

With a small group, write a paragraph with an anecdote, description, facts and statistics, or specific examples. Share and discuss your paragraphs.

Choose the letter of the best answer to each question.

1. Which statement is based on a fact?
   A. Sports ticket prices are increasing from $8 to $10.
   B. I think football is the most popular sport in the United States.
   C. Race car drivers are always good mechanics.
   D. Tennis is a very difficult game to play.

2. Which fact *best* supports the statement that Mt. Everest, located on the border of Nepal and Tibet, is the tallest mountain in the world?
   A. Mt. Everest is incredibly difficult to climb.
   B. According to the *2000 World Almanac*, the height of Mt. Everest is calculated to be 29,028 feet—778 feet higher than the next highest mountain.
   C. Tourism contributes to the economy of Nepal.
   D. K2 is the second-tallest mountain in the world.

On a separate sheet of paper, complete each item as directed.

3. Support one of the following statements with specific examples.
   A. Winter is the best season.
   B. Winter is the worst season.

4. Agree or disagree with the following statement using a specific example of your own.
   It is important for people to take on a challenge once in a while.

5. Support the following idea with an anecdote from your own experience.
   Handing in homework on time is a good study habit.

6. Write a description of your classroom.

Writing

TESTED

> **Organization and Focus**
>
> **1.3** Use strategies of note taking, outlining, and summarizing to impose structure
> on composition drafts.

Explanation

The ability to organize notes and develop an outline is important for creating a
composition's organizational structure, for writing a first draft, and for supporting
main ideas with facts, examples, or other essential information. A summary presents an
author's main ideas.

Examples

The following are examples of how to summarize ideas and information using organized
notes and outlines.

- Note taking: Take notes as you read. Use individual note cards. Each card should
  have a heading, such as *Inner Planets*. Add subheadings on your card as you take
  notes, such as *Mercury, Venus, Earth, Mars*. Write down the most important details.
  Do not pack too many details on one card. Your notes should be in your own
  words. Use quotation marks if you copy an author's exact words. Have a special
  card set aside for listing where you found your information. Organize your note
  cards into time or spatial order before you start writing.

- Outlining: Use your note cards or the passage to create an outline. Outlines are
  divided into main ideas and supporting details. Phrases or sentences are used to
  create an outline. They can be formal, like the following example, or structured in
  a way you prefer.

  I. *Problems leading to the Great Depression*

      A. *consumer spending*

          1. *overuse of credit*

          2. *advertising*

      B. *stock market crash*

          1. *stocks purchased on credit*

          2. *lack of attention to market signs*

Understand the Skill

As a class, outline a paragraph from a history book. Work in small groups to outline two
other paragraphs. Use the main ideas of the outline to write a summary.

Choose the letter of the best answer to the question.

1. Read the following information from which you could make several note cards. Which of the choices that follow shows the appropriate amount of information to put on one of your several note cards?

   Your brain, which is the control center of your body, has more than 100 billion cells. The nerve cells send impulses to every part of your body through the central nervous system. The central nervous system includes the spinal cord, which is protected by a series of bones called vertebrae.

   A. 100 billion cells in brain. Nerve cells send messages via central nervous system.
   B. 100 billion cells in brain. Nerve cells send messages via central nervous system. Bones protecting spinal cord are vertebrae.
   C. 100 billion cells in brain.
   D. 100 billion cells in brain. Nerve cells send messages via central nervous system. CNS includes spinal cord. Bones protecting spinal cord are vertebrae.

On a separate sheet of paper, complete each item as directed.

2. List the following steps in the order you might use them in composing an essay.
   Summarize the main ideas
   Take notes
   Outline ideas

3. Write a modified outline of the passage below.

   It has been talked about for several years, but now is the time to make sure we implement a recycling program in our school. Recycling reduces waste and thereby reduces pollution in our environment. It also prevents dumps from expanding, and that means we have more space in which to live. In addition, it is important for schools to teach students how taking small steps, such as recycling, can lead to large rewards. Students will more likely become socially active in other areas. By having a recycling program, we send an important message and we make our world a cleaner, safer place in which to live.

4. List three or four important points or events in a book you have recently read.

5. Write a brief summary of the passage from item 3.

Writing

TESTED

> **Research and Technology**
> **1.4** Identify topics; ask and evaluate questions; and develop ideas leading to inquiry, investigation, and research.

Explanation

The steps for conducting research include identifying a topic to research, writing questions about the topic, identifying where answers to the questions most likely will be found, and, finally researching the topic.

Examples

The following are examples of the steps needed to research a topic.

- Area of study: *extinct species*
- Topic identified: *the dodo bird*
- Questions to research:
  What was the dodo bird?
  Where did it live?
  When did it live?
  Why did it become an endangered species?
  When was it considered extinct?
  Where can dodo birds be seen today?
- Possible sources used to investigate the topic:
  Internet, encyclopedia, library book about extinct animals
- How research will be conducted:
  Use note cards
  Make an outline
  Keep a record of my sources
  Include facts and a quote, if possible
  Use time order for the report
- Summarize what was learned

Understand the Skill

In a small group, research a general topic, such as *Folktales*. Determine a specific topic to research, create a series of questions, a list of sources to investigate, and a plan for researching the topic. Share your research process and a summary of what was learned.

On a separate sheet of paper, complete each item as directed.

1. Write three questions that you would like to have answered if you were going to write a report about world hunger.

2. Write three questions about the subject of eagles that would help you focus your research for a research report.

3. Write three sources you could use to research your questions about eagles.

4. Write a specific question that would help you limit a research topic on video games.

5. Identify three sources you could use to research your question about video games.

6. Describe how you would organize what you learned while researching your question on video games.

Writing

> **Research and Technology**
> **1.5** Give credit for both quoted and paraphrased information in a bibliography by using a consistent and sanctioned format and methodology for citations.

Explanation

A citation is a source used for research, such as an encyclopedia, Web site, or book. A bibliography is a formal list of citations. There are accepted, or sanctioned, ways to write citations. A citation must be listed for every source paraphrased for research and for every quotation used in a research paper.

Examples

The following examples show the correct way to write citations. Citations are listed in alphabetical order. Punctuation is a very important part of every citation. Make a notation of the source for an in-text citation by listing the author and number of the citation in sequential order, for example, (Johnson 15).

- *Book:* Kelso, William M. *Jamestown: The Buried Truth.* Charlottesville: University of Virginia Press, 2006.
- *Encyclopedia Article:* "California," *World Book Encyclopedia of People and Places.* 2003 ed.
- *Magazine Article:* Hadingham, Evan. "Unlocking Mysteries of the Parthenon," *Smithsonian.* February 2008: 36–43.
- *Internet Source:* Include the author's name in the citation whenever the Internet source identifies the author of the Internet article. Note the date you accessed the Web site.
  White, Jack E. "Martin Luther King." *The Time 100: The Most Important People of the Century.* [Online. Internet.]12 Jan. 2008 < http://www.time.com/time/time100/leaders/profile/king.html>.

Understand the Skill

With a partner, write citations for four different sources. Write one of your citations on the chalkboard. Discuss the differences in how sources are cited.

Choose the letter of the best answer to each item.

1. Read the following passage. Then, choose the letter of the sentence that would require a citation in a research paper.

   World War II was the bloodiest conflict in the history of humankind. The war officially began when Germany invaded Poland on September 1, 1939. In a quick, devastating attack, known as a *blitzkrieg*, German forces used swiftly moving armored columns with close air support to overwhelm the inadequately prepared Polish Army. According to Walter Cronkite, the Poles were completely powerless in the face of the *blitzkrieg*.

   A. World War II officially began on September 1, 1939.
   B. Germany attacked Poland in the first official battle of World War II.
   C. According to Walter Cronkite, the Poles were completely powerless in the face of the *blitzkrieg*.
   D. German forces used swiftly moving armored columns with close air support.

2. Which of the following do you *not* need to credit as a source?
   A. a paraphrase of another person's opinion
   B. a summary of research findings
   C. a restatement of a generally known fact
   D. a quotation from an obscure poet

3. Which of the following shows the correct revision for the following book citation?
   Cooke, Alistair, *Memories of the Great & the Good*. New York: Arcade Publishing, 1999.

   A. Remove the period at the end of the citation.
   B. Change the colon to a comma after *New York*.
   C. Add quotation marks around *Cooke*.
   D. Replace the comma with a period after *Alistair*.

On a separate sheet of paper, complete the item as directed.

4. Read the passage below. Then, write the information from the passage that needs to be cited.

   New York City is a wealth of cultures and customs with a population of more than eight million. Each borough of the city has unique qualities, and people visit each for different reasons.

Writing

TESTED

Research and Technology
1.6 Create documents by using word-processing skills and publishing programs; develop simple databases and spreadsheets to manage information and prepare reports.

Explanation

Computer word-processing programs efficiently create a page of text that is well designed and clean, with the ability to add images, such as photos or drawings, to text. Computer spreadsheet programs quickly process mathematical data and allow the data to be presented as a bar, line, or pie graph. Computer database programs group a lot of information in several different and helpful ways.

Examples

Word-processing, spreadsheet programs, and databases offer a wide variety of features, including the examples discussed below. Computers also can be used to create multimedia reports that include videos, slides, computer-based models, and music.

- Word-processing Programs: Using a word-processing program allows text to be formatted in several ways including **bold,** *italic,* and <u>underline</u> with the click of a mouse or a keystroke. Columns, changes in margins, and bulleted lists are easily created. Computer spell-checker programs alert the user to misspelled words that can easily be corrected with a mouse click. However, students still need to know the correct spelling of certain words, such as homophones (hear, here) or words not part of the computer's spell-checker database.
- Spreadsheets: These programs allow for the user to easily add, subtract, and manage other types of mathematical processes for a large amount of data.
- Databases: Information in databases is entered into a variety of fields. The computer processes the various fields in different ways to track such things as the number of items in a store. When you use a computer search engine, you are tapping into a huge computer database.

Understand the Skill

With a partner, create a text document that includes a photo or other image, spreadsheet, or basic database. Share what you have created with the class.

Choose the letter of the best answer to each question.

1. Which computer-based program would you use to quickly and efficiently add the scores and penalty minutes of several teams competing in a basketball tournament?
   A. spreadsheet
   B. word-processing program
   C. database
   D. search engine

2. Which of the following do stores use to track a large amount of customer information?
   A. spreadsheet
   B. database
   C. search engine
   D. word-processing program

3. Which would be the *least* helpful in writing a report on the Vietnam War?
   A. search engine
   B. word-processing program
   C. spreadsheet
   D. spell-checker program

4. What is the *best* reason for using a word-processing program?
   A. It automatically organizes information that otherwise would be confusing.
   B. It allows text to be changed quickly and efficiently for a clean presentation.
   C. It checks the spelling of every word so there are a limited number of misspellings.
   D. It transmits information to a printer so reports can be revised at a later time.

On a separate sheet of paper, complete each item as directed.

5. Explain why you should not just rely on electronic programs that check spelling when you use a computer to write a report.

6. List three ways to present information for multimedia reports.

Writing

Evaluation and Revision
1.7 Revise writing to improve organization and word choice after checking the logic of the ideas and the precision of the vocabulary.

Explanation

Students should be able to evaluate and revise, or make changes, to improve the quality of their compositions. Revisions include choosing words that convey the author's purpose, improving the organization of the composition, and making sure ideas are presented in a clear and meaningful way.

Examples

Read and evaluate the following paragraph. Then read the suggested revisions.

Rudy look forward to the day! His cousins were coming to visit. He had spent the last week planning for this day. Rudy hasn't seen them for almost a year. They would look through the family scrap book. He thought looking at picures of when everyone was a baby would be fun. He thought they might watch a movie. He planned for them to listen to the band that was scheduled to play that night in the park

Suggested revisions:

- Change *look* to *looked* in the first sentence.
- Change the position of the third sentence.
- Change *hasn't* to *hadn't* in the fourth sentence.
- Use transition words: *first, second, finally.*
- Replace *fun* with a more descriptive phrase.
- Use an adjective to describe the type of movie.
- Fix the spelling of *picures.*
- Make *scrap book* one word.
- Change *he* to *Rudy* in at least one sentence.
- Add a period after *park.*
- Add *It would be a great day!* at the end of the story.

Understand the Skill

As a class, discuss the revisions. Suggest other possible revisions to improve the paragraph. Revise the paragraph, then read your revised paragraph aloud.

Choose the letter of the best answer to the question.

1. Choose the sentence that expresses the following meaning using precise language.

   An angry man rushed to the store.

   A. He closed the door and went to the store.
   B. He secured the door and ran to the store.
   C. He banged the door shut and strolled to the store.
   D. He slammed the door and charged to the store.

On a separate sheet of paper, complete each item as directed.

2. Write a brief paragraph describing a person you know. Review your work and replace any dull or vague words with vivid, precise ones.

3. Read the following introductory paragraph for an essay. Then, write which sentence does not belong in the paragraph and should be removed.

   Plays are not new. People have put on plays in a theater for thousands of years. I enjoy performing in plays. The first plays were staged in Greece in the sixth century B.C.

4. Revise the following sentence to include precise sensory details of touch and sight.

   Amanda sat on the beach.

5. Revise the word choice in the following sentence to suggest a fun-filled experience.

   The wind, temperature, and sounds of seagulls were in Hank's memory.

6. Revise the sentence in item 5 to give an impression of an unpleasant experience.

Writing

2.1 Write fictional or autobiographical narratives:

a. Develop a standard plot line (having a beginning, conflict, rising action, climax, and denouement) and point of view.

b. Develop complex major and minor characters and a definite setting.

c. Use a range of appropriate strategies (e.g., dialogue; suspense; naming of specific narrative action, including movement, gestures, and expressions).

Explanation

A narrative is a story. A fictional narrative is a created story. An autobiographical narrative is a story based on the author's real life.

a. Each narrative should have a plot line, or the order in which events happen. An author should choose a point of view (who is telling the story).

b. Each narrative should have main characters and less important characters as needed, as well as a well-defined setting.

c. Narratives can include dialogue, conflict, and suspense in order to move the plot along. Characters' actions are described by movement, gestures, and expressions.

Example/Understand the Skill

Read the following narrative of Trina's summer experience. This is autobiographical because the person who actually had the experience wrote the narrative. Use the rubric to evaluate the quality and effectiveness of the narrative. Complete the chart to show how you would improve the narrative.

Last summer was the best summer I ever had. My cousin, Trina, from New York came to visit. I had never met her before, but we became friends almost immediately. It took a little while for us to get to know each other. We talked a lot at first, mostly about school and things we like to do. I found out that she also likes astronomy. So, we tried to study the night sky as much as possible. We would just sit and look at the stars, trying to make pictures out of their patterns. Once in a while we would see a shooting star. That made watching the stars really special.

Trina and I also helped out at the park. In the summer, the park has a special program for little kids. We watched them while they played on the playground equipment and played games with them. I think Trina enjoyed that even more than I did. She said she would like to start a program like that when she returns to New York.

It was sad the day Trina had to leave. We promised to email each other as much as possible. I hope I can visit her in New York next summer.

Evaluate the narrative using the scoring criteria—with 4 being the highest score and 1 being the lowest score.

Rating Scale	Writing Criteria
1 2 3 4	**Plot:** How well does the narrative tell a story? (plot line)
1 2 3 4	**Characters:** How well are the characters in the narrative developed?
1 2 3 4	**Organization:** How well does the narrative transition from one time or place to another?
1 2 3 4	**Setting:** Are there enough details to develop a good setting for the narrative?
1 2 3 4	**Style:** Is the narrative interesting?
1 2 3 4	**Conventions:** Are the words spelled correctly?
1 2 3 4	**Word Choice:** Is the language in the narrative strong enough to create a good visual image?

Use the chart below to show how you would improve the narrative. First, write information about the characters, setting, or plot line that is lacking. Then, write how to improve the narrative.

Information that is lacking:	Information that could be added to improve the narrative:
1.	
2.	
3.	
4.	
5.	

Writing

2.2 Write responses to literature:
  a. Develop interpretations exhibiting careful reading, understanding, and insight.
  b. Organize interpretations around several clear ideas, premises, or images from the literary work.
  c. Justify interpretations through sustained use of examples and textual evidence.

Explanation

Literature includes stories and poems. Some literature is very short, like a short poem. Other literature is long, like a book. A literary work has well developed characters and setting. A response is a reaction to an idea posed by the author or poet. A response also is the answer to a question.

  a. The plot line can be complicated, so careful reading is important in order to make the story meaningful to you.
  b. You need to use what you know, and clues from the literary work, to have a clear understanding of the author's purpose in writing the story or poem. Organize each of your responses around a central idea in the literature. Analyze the mood, or feelings shown by the characters.
  c. Support each response with at least one example from the literature.

Example/Understand the Skill

Read the following short story. Answer questions about the story on the next page. Use the rubric to evaluate your responses.

The Summer Rain

It started out just about like every other day for the past week—hot, humid, and the promise of rain. *Not rain again*, I thought. Uncle Henry said we needed the rain. The fields had stopped growing, and the cattle were chewing dry, brown stubbles instead of long, succulent grass. Uncle Henry was about the smartest person I knew. He had grown up on a farm and seemed to know everything about animals. Tall, like my grandfather, Uncle Henry's long beard and shaggy hair tucked under a hat he had worn forever hid the fact that he had been a professor at a nearby college. His eyes seemed to dance when he talked, so that you wanted to listen to every word. "Why must it rain again?" I whined. He looked at me, smiled, and pointed to a newborn calf. This time Uncle Henry didn't need to say a word. I grew up just a little at that moment, and looked to the sky, hoping to see a rain cloud.

Answer the following questions. Support each answer with an example from the literary work.

1. What is the plot line of the story?

   _____

   _____

2. What is the author's purpose?

   _____

   _____

3. Why does the narrator say, "I grew up just a little at that moment"?

   _____

   _____

4. What did the narrator realize?

   _____

   _____

Evaluate your responses to the short story using the scoring criteria—with 4 being the highest score and 1 being the lowest score.

Rating Scale	Writing Criteria
1 2 3 4	**Evaluation:** How well did you answer the questions?
1 2 3 4	**Focus:** How well did you explain the author's purpose?
1 2 3 4	**Organization:** Did you give complete answers to each question?
1 2 3 4	**Support/Elaboration:** Did you support your answers with examples or quotes from the story?
1 2 3 4	**Style:** How clear are the points you made?
1 2 3 4	**Conventions:** Were all of your answers written in complete sentences?
1 2 3 4	**Word Choice:** How well do the words describe the characters?

Writing

2.3 Write research reports:
  a. Pose relevant and tightly drawn questions about the topic.
  b. Convey clear and accurate perspectives on the subject.
  c. Include evidence compiled through the formal research process (e.g., use of a card catalog, *Reader's Guide to Periodical Literature*, a computer catalog, magazines, newspapers, dictionaries).
  d. Document reference sources by means of footnotes and a bibliography.

Explanation

Writing a research report starts with the identification of a topic to study, followed by posing good questions to answer. Next, sources have to be identified where answers to the questions can be found. Finally, the information learned has to be presented in a clear way. You must document where information was found and give credit to authors who are quoted or whose ideas are paraphrased.

Example/Understand the Skill

As a class, discuss the steps shown below for conducting a research project on the Civil War. Then, evaluate the following framework below and on the next page using the rubric and chart on the next page.

Writing a Research Report: Steps for Getting Started

1. Narrow the topic to a specific area of research.
2. Write five specific questions to answer.
3. Cite three credible sources to use.
4. Write a framework.

RESEARCH REPORT FRAMEWORK

General Topic: The Civil War   **My topic:** The Battle of Gettysburg

1. Who were the most important commanders of the Union Army?
2. Who were the most important commanders of the Confederate Army?
3. What battles took place at Gettysburg?
4. What happened after the Battle of Gettysburg?
5. What difference did the Battle of Gettysburg make?

Sources to use: 1. A book on the Civil War from the library
                   2. A reliable Internet site on Civil War battles
                   3. My history book

The Battle of Gettysburg

I. The Union Army
- A. Ulysses S. Grant
- B. George Meade

II. Confederate Army
- A. James Longstreet
- B. Robert E. Lee

III. Battle of Gettysburg
- A. July 1, 1863
- B. July 2, 1863
- C. July 3, 1863

IV. After the Battle of Gettysburg
- A. Union Army
- B. Confederate Army

V. Importance of the Battle of Gettysburg
- A. to the Union Army
- B. to the Confederate Army

Evaluate the framework for the research project using the scoring criteria—with 4 being the highest score and 1 being the lowest score.

Rating Scale	Writing Criteria
1 2 3 4	**Focus:** How well was the topic narrowed?
1 2 3 4	**Focus:** How relevant are the questions?
1 2 3 4	**Organization:** How well is the report structured?
1 2 3 4	**Support/Elaboration:** How credible are the sources chosen?
1 2 3 4	**Style:** How well does the framework of the report conform to a formal style?
1 2 3 4	**Conventions:** How helpful is the outline in writing the report?
1 2 3 4	**Word Choice:** How well do the words used in your questions lead to finding factual information?

Use the chart below to show how you would improve the framework. Write where the framework needs improving. Then write your suggested improvement.

Places the research report framework can be improved:	My revision suggestions:
1.	
2.	
3.	

Writing

> **2.4 Write persuasive compositions:**
> a. State a clear position or perspective in support of a proposition or proposal.
> b. Describe the points in support of the proposition, employing well-articulated evidence.
> c. Anticipate and address reader concerns and counterarguments.

Explanation

A persuasive composition is a short nonfiction work that tries to convince a reader to think or act in a particular way. Persuasive writing is used in advertising, political speeches, editorial pages in newspapers, Internet blogs, and many other places. An effective persuasive composition:

- clearly states the author's position,
- includes evidence to support the opinion, and
- addresses other opinions on the topic.

Example/Understand the Skill

Read the following persuasive composition, or essay. Review the elements of a good persuasive essay. Then, use the rubric on the next page to evaluate the essay.

> It is important to understand how urban expansion affects farmland and forest. As cities expand, farmland is replaced with housing developments. This changes the lives of farmers who want to continue to farm but can't because the city is too close. It also affects the price of food because farm products have to be trucked from farther away. My grandfather once owned a farm but he had to sell it because the city was so close. He really wanted his family to take over the farm because he had lived on it all his life. It was really a sad day for him when all his farm equipment was auctioned off to farmers living much farther away.
>
> Urban expansion also affects forests. As we cut down forest for cities to expand, birds, deer, fox, rabbits, and other wildlife lose their homes. This reduces the population of wildlife. I read in my science book that when there is a disruption in a food chain, other parts of the food chain also are affected. So, we can't continue to disrupt the forest food chain. We need our forests!
>
> One solution is to build up in the cities instead of expanding urban areas into farmland and forests. We need more skyscrapers! This also will save on the cost of building roads.
>
> City planners should work to find ways to improve the cities and put more living areas into the existing cities. Then, farmers like my grandfather won't be forced to sell their homes, and forest animals won't die.

Evaluate the persuasive essay using the following scoring criteria—with 4 being the highest score and 1 being the lowest score.

Rating Scale	Writing Criteria
1 2 3 4	**Persuasive Quality:** How convincing is this essay?
1 2 3 4	**Focus:** How well does the essay present a strong, interesting argument?
1 2 3 4	**Organization:** How logical and consistent is the organization?
1 2 3 4	**Support/Elaboration:** How convincing is the supporting evidence?
1 2 3 4	**Style:** How clearly is the argument expressed?
1 2 3 4	**Conventions:** How correct is the grammar?
1 2 3 4	**Word Choice:** Was the language in the essay descriptive enough to create a strong impression?

Use the chart below to show how you would improve the persuasive essay. Add a suggestion to any key element of the essay that you think should be improved.

Element	My suggestions for improvement:
1. Persuasive Quality	
2. Focus	
3. Organization	
4. Support/Elaboration	
5. Style	
6. Conventions	
7. Word Choice	

Writing

2.5 Write summaries of reading materials:
  a. Include the main ideas and most significant details.
  b. Use the student's own words, except for quotations.
  c. Reflect underlying meaning, not just the superficial details.

Explanation

A summary retells the main ideas of something heard or read in a concise and organized way. It includes important details and tells how the material is meaningful.

Example/Understand the Skill

Read the following short article about the Emperor penguin. Then, read the summary of the article on the next page and use the rubric to evaluate the summary. As a class, discuss the summary. Explain your ratings and share your completion of the statements that follow the rubric.

The Emperor Penguin

The Emperor penguin is a fascinating bird. It is the largest of all penguins, growing up to 40 inches in height. Male and female Emperor penguins look alike. Their heads are blackish blue with yellow ear pads. And though their backs and sides are a blue-gray color, it is their white underparts that are most prominent. Their small flipper-like wings are used for swimming. There are about 200,000 pairs of Emperor penguins found only in Antarctica. They live on fish, squid, and crustaceans caught on dives up to 700 feet deep into the frigid waters of the region. An Emperor penguin can stay under water for up to 18 minutes.

In May, the female lays a single egg that needs 63 days of warmth to survive. The female balances the egg on her feet and carefully moves it onto the feet of the male penguin. He covers the egg with a special flap of skin and feathers. While the females leaves to feed at sea, the males protect the egg. In the worst of weather, the males shuffle into a tight circle while balancing the egg on their feet, constantly changing places so that the same penguins are not exposed to the blasting snow and wind hitting the animals on the edge of the circle. By the time the females return to reclaim the newly hatched penguin, the male will have lost up to a third of his weight and must hasten on his 60-mile walk to the sea to find food. He then returns to his mate to help raise the young penguin.

Read the following summary. Then, use the rubric to evaluate how well the summary addresses each element.

The Emperor penguin is a very special bird. It lives in Antarctica. It can dive 700 feet into the frigid water of the region to feed on fish, shrimp, and crustaceans. The female lays one egg that is carefully placed on the feet of the male until it hatches. The male Emperor penguin protects the egg with a flap of skin and feathers while the female leaves to feed. The male protects the egg through the worst weather. During that time the male loses about one-third of its body weight. After the egg hatches, the female penguin returns. The male then travels 60 miles to the sea to feed. It then returns to help parent the young penguin.

Evaluate the summary using the scoring criteria—with 4 being the highest score and 1 being the lowest score.

Rating Scale	Writing Criteria
1 2 3 4	**Purpose:** How well does the summary retell the information from the passage?
1 2 3 4	**Focus:** Does the summary restate the theme in the topic sentence?
1 2 3 4	**Organization:** Are transition words used to help the ideas flow?
1 2 3 4	**Support/Elaboration:** Does the summary include a quote or examples to support the topic sentence?
1 2 3 4	**Style:** Does the author of the summary avoid imposing his or her own opinion on the reader?
1 2 3 4	**Conventions:** Is the summary correctly punctuated?
1 2 3 4	**Word Choice:** How well does the summary paraphrase the article?

Complete the following sentences.

1. One detail I would have included in the summary is

_____

_____

2. One way to improve this summary would be to

_____

_____

3. Two important things to remember when writing a summary are

_____

_____

2

Written and Oral English Language Conventions

TESTED

> **Sentence Structure**
> **1.1** Place modifiers properly and use the active voice.

Explanation

Sentence modifiers include adjectives, adverbs, phrases, and clauses.

a. A modifier clarifies or expands meaning. A modifier should be placed close to the word it modifies for the meaning to be clear and effective.
b. The subject performs the action in active voice.
c. In passive voice, the action affects the subject.

Examples

The following are examples of modifiers, active voice, and passive voice.

- Adjective: *They sold the yellow house.* (*yellow*)
- Adverb: *He quickly ran up the stairs.* (*quickly*)
- Phrases: *After the game, we had chocolate ice cream cones.* (*After the game*)
- Clause: *The song, which I sang, is about a small village in Ireland.* (*which I sang*)
- Active Voice: *The student read the report.*
- Passive Voice: *The report was read by the student.*

Understand the Skill

Reread the examples of modifiers, active voice, and passive voice. Generate other sentences that give similar examples. Identify the modifiers and be ready to explain if the sentence is written in active or passive voice.

Choose the letter of the best answer to each question.

1. Which of the following sentences contains three adverbs?

   A. Tye warmly greeted the new visitors.
   B. Tye greeted the visitors warmly and enthusiastically.
   C. The very happy visitors warmly and enthusiastically greeted Tye.
   D. The new visitors accepted Tye's warm and enthusiastic greeting.

2. Which word is modified by the adjective *unusual* in the following sentence?
   The day was most unusual with its cloudless blue sky and moderate temperature.

   A. cloudless
   B. day
   C. sky
   D. temperature

3. In which one of the following sentences does the adverb modify an adjective?

   A. He painted gracefully.
   B. The colors were astonishingly vibrant.
   C. The colors blended well.
   D. The museum visitors looked for the painting eagerly.

4. In which of the following sentences does the adverb *only* refer to baby-sit?

   A. He will baby-sit only with his brother when the baseball game is on TV.
   B. He will baby-sit with his brother only when the baseball game is on TV.
   C. He will baby-sit with his brother when the baseball game is only on TV.
   D. He will only baby-sit with his brother when the baseball game is on TV.

On a separate sheet of paper, rewrite the following sentences in the active voice.

5. A herd of enormous African elephants was spotted by the scientists.

6. After a short speech was given by the principal, the awards were announced by the mayor.

Written and Oral English Language Conventions

TESTED

Grammar

1.2 Identify and use infinitives and participles and make clear references between pronouns and antecedents.

Explanation

Infinitives and participles are types of verbs. Pronouns and antecedents are types of nouns.

a. An infinitive is a verb form using *to* that can take the place of a noun, adjective, or adverb.

b. A participle is a verb used as an adjective.

c. A pronoun is a word used in place of a noun or more than one noun.
Personal Pronouns: *I, me, he, him, she, her, you, it, we, us, they, them*
Possessive Pronouns: *my, mine, her, hers, their, theirs, his, its, your, yours, our, ours*

d. A pronoun refers to an antecedent. The antecedent is the word or phrase replaced by the pronoun.

Examples

The following are examples of infinitives, participles, pronouns, and antecedents.

- Infinitive: *To study is the way to get good grades.* (as the subject of the sentence)
  She likes to study after dinner. (as an adverb modifying *likes*)
  He is the candidate to study before voting. (as an adjective modifying *candidate*)

- Present Participle: *I like to watch squirrels running in the trees.* (*running*)

- Past Participle: *The car sputtered, then came to a stop.* (*sputtered*)

- Antecedents: *Students went to class. They went to class.* (The pronoun *They* replaces the antecedent *Students.*) *The book belongs to her. It is her book.* (The pronoun *It* replaces the antecedent *The book.*)

Understand the Skill

Make sure that the antecedent of the pronoun is clear.

Unclear: The team liked playing basketball in the new school gym. It was beneficial for the team.

Clear: The team liked playing basketball in the new gym. It was a good place for them to practice.

Choose the letter of the best answer to each question.

1. Which of the following is an infinitive phrase?

    A. to watch a movie
    B. on the television
    C. banged her fist
    D. an interesting film

2. Which pair of words correctly completes this sentence?

    Rosa's family always brings _____ dog with _____ on picnics.

    A. its, her
    B. her, them
    C. their, them
    D. their, her

3. Which sentence contains incorrect pronoun-antecedent agreement?

    A. The girls left their equipment in the locker room.
    B. The first person in line may choose his or her favorite dessert.
    C. All the members of the committee are to turn in their reports.
    D. Each person must clean out their desk at the end of the year.

4. Which of the following sentences contains an infinitive?

    A. Alex wants to work for a magazine.
    B. It is hard working six days a week.
    C. It always rains on Sundays.
    D. I received a letter in the mail.

On a separate sheet of paper, complete each item as directed.

5. Correct the pronoun-antecedent agreement in the following sentence.

    Each boy brought their own snacks.

6. Write a question that contains a pronoun with *Emily* as the antecedent.

7. Write a sentence using the following infinitive phrase.

    to give advice

8. Write a sentence using the participle *leaping*.

Written and Oral English Language Conventions

TESTED

> **Grammar**
> **1.3** Identify all parts of speech and types and structure of sentences.

Explanation

A sentence is a complete thought and is divided into a subject and a predicate. Each sentence is made of different parts of speech.

a. A noun is a person, place, thing, or idea.

b. A pronoun takes the place of a noun.

c. A verb expresses an action or explains time, place, or state of being.

d. An adjective modifies a noun or pronoun.

e. An adverb modifies a verb, an adjective, or another adverb.

f. An article is used to give definiteness.

g. A coordinating conjunction joins other words or groups of words.

h. A preposition is used to show placement. A prepositional phrase begins with the preposition and ends with the object of the preposition.

i. An interjection is a word or phrase that expresses emotion.

j. A subject tells whom or what the sentence is about. A simple subject is the main word or group of words in the subject.

k. A predicate tells something about the subject. A simple predicate is the verb or verb phrase in the predicate.

Examples

The following are examples of parts of speech and sentence structure.

- Nouns: *Thomas Paine, Trenton*
- Pronouns: *he, she, it, they, our, we*
- Verbs: *jump, run, is, was, smell*
- Adjectives: *pretty, blue*
- Adverb: *quickly*
- Articles: *a, an, the*
- Coord. Conjunctions: *and, but, or*

- Prepositions: *at, on, by, through*
- Prep. Phrase: *at the new planetarium*
- Interjection: *Wow!*
- Subject: *The black terrier*
- Simple subject: *terrier*
- Predicate: *ran faster than the poodle*
- Simple predicate: *ran*

Understand the Skill

Write one sentence using different parts of speech. Following the teacher's instruction, write your sentence on a separate sheet of paper. Identify the different parts of speech.

Choose the letter of the best answer to each question.

1. Which sentence has a linking verb?

    A. The siren blared.
    B. We heard the wailing siren.
    C. The siren was loud and steady.
    D. Every Tuesday, the fire chief activates the siren.

2. What is the preposition in the following sentence?
   Charles carefully examined his test paper under the bright light.

    A. Charles
    B. carefully
    C. under
    D. examined

3. Which of the following sentences ends with a prepositional phrase?

    A. We usually help around the house.
    B. My sister always fills the dishwasher.
    C. The dog stands by the door wagging his tail.
    D. We finished the laundry.

4. Which part of a sentence describes whom or what the sentence is about?

    A. adjective
    B. phrase
    C. subject
    D. predicate

5. What is the simple predicate in the following sentence?
   The people cheered in support of their political candidate.

    A. people
    B. cheered
    C. in support
    D. political candidate

6. Which of the following sentences contains a coordinating conjunction?

    A. The road was bumpy yet passable.
    B. The road was bumpy.
    C. We drove along the bumpy, passable road.
    D. Bumping along, we drove slowly down the road.

Written and Oral English Language Conventions

TESTED

Grammar

1.4 Demonstrate the mechanics of writing (e.g., quotation marks, commas at end of dependent clauses) and appropriate English usage (e.g., pronoun reference).

Explanation

The correct use of punctuation is part of the mechanics of writing. Punctuation shows complete thoughts or breaks in thought.

a. Use a period at the end of each complete statement.

b. Use commas in the following ways: to separate two or more adjectives in a row; to separate independent clauses; to set off a nonessential phrase; to set off a dependent clause; and to set off *yes*, *well*, and *no*.

c. Use quotation marks when stating a person's exact words.

d. Always place commas and periods inside the quotation marks. Place question marks and exclamation points inside the quotation marks if the statement is a question or an exclamation. Otherwise, place them outside of the quotation marks.

Examples

The following are examples of different types of punctuation.

- Period: *The squirrel ran up the tree.*
- Comma: *tall, stately tree* (separates adjectives)
  vanilla, chocolate, and strawberry (separates nouns in a series)
  I like roses, yet daisies are nice. (separates independent clauses)
  Like me, Sara enjoys science. (sets off nonessential phrase)
  Washington, our first president, is a well respected historical figure. (sets off dependent clause)
  Well, red is my favorite color. (sets off *well*)
- Quotation Marks: *The mayor stated, "We are building a new community center this May."*

Understand the Skill

Write the following sentences on a separate sheet of paper. Make any necessary changes to punctuate the sentences correctly.

The mayor asked, "Will we build the new community center on Vine, Plum, or Locust Street."

Last night, it was so exciting to hear the mayor announce, "We will build a new community center"!

Choose the letter of the best answer to each question.

1. In which sentence do the subject and predicate *not* agree?

    A. The crowd rushes through the gates.
    B. The band plays a haunting melody.
    C. The class discuss the story they just read.
    D. The herd gathers at the watering hole.

2. Which punctuation sets off exact words, dialogue, or conversations of characters?

    A. parentheses
    B. colons
    C. question marks
    D. quotation marks

3. What is the adjective clause in the following sentence?

    Jennifer and Carlos were happy about their project, which they had worked on for more than a week.

    A. Jennifer and Carlos were happy about their project
    B. about their project
    C. which they had worked on for more than a week
    D. for more than a week

On a separate sheet of paper, complete each item as directed.

4. Change the word *Smiths* to *family* in the sentence below. Change the verb if necessary for correct subject-verb agreement.

    The Smiths have lived on our street for ten years.

5. Combine the following sentences into a single sentence with an introductory phrase.

    Thomas Jefferson wrote the Declaration of Independence. He wrote it in 1776.

6. Rewrite the following sentence using quotations marks and commas correctly.

    Be nice to your sister said Tom's mother.

Written and Oral English Language Conventions

TESTED

Punctuation
1.5 Identify hyphens, dashes, brackets, and semicolons and use them correctly.

Explanation

Hyphens, dashes, brackets, and semicolons are other important punctuation marks used in writing. Each has a specific purpose.

a. Use a hyphen to divide a word at the end of a line; for compound numbers and fractions; with prefixes such as *ex*, *self*, and *all*; and to connect compound adjectives.

b. Use a dash to show a change in thought.

c. Brackets help explain parts of a quotation or when a word is changed for clarity.

d. Use a semicolon to connect independent clauses not joined by *for, but, yet, or, so,* and *nor*; to connect independent clauses joined by *for example, therefore, however, instead,* and *furthermore*; and when a series of items contains commas.

Examples

The following examples show the use of four important punctuation marks.

- Hyphen (-): *three-fourths, all-star, rain-soaked*
- Dash (—): *I suggested we celebrate my birthday by opening presents first—a good idea, if you ask me—but my parents didn't agree.*
- Brackets ([ ]): *"Fourscore and seven years ago [87 years ago] our fathers . . . ."*
- Semicolon (;): *We decided to go to the movie tonight; however, Jenny won't be able to join us.*

Understand the Skill

Read the following sentences to understand the proper use of hyphens, dashes, brackets, and semicolons.

It was the coldest night of the year; the astronomy club spent three-fourths of an hour stargazing.

The best plan—to build on the west field—will begin in mid-May.

The hockey tournament included the Polars, tournament champions; the Ice Hawks, second place; the Lightning, third place; and the Firebolts, fourth place.

Choose the letter of the best answer to each question.

1. Where is the hyphen needed in the following sentence?

   He bought 200 pounds of gravel to spread on the 40 foot driveway.

   A. 200-pounds
   B. gravel-to spread
   C. 40-foot
   D. drive-way

2. Which sentence uses the semicolon correctly?

   A. The roller coaster turns you up-side-down; hold onto your hat.
   B. Who brought the plates, napkins; and cups?
   C. Look; here's the merry-go-around.
   D. We are having fun; when will Ryan return?

3. Which sentence uses the hyphen correctly?

   A. I like to play out-side in the snow.
   B. When-ever I hear my favorite song, I feel happy.
   C. I like to spend time with my friends-who doesn't?
   D. He is a self-taught violinist.

4. Which sentence uses the semicolon correctly?

   A. The ice show performers are here; please welcome them.
   B. Shall we sit in the upper row; or more toward the middle?
   C. Oh; there's been an accident.
   D. The entertainment was great; and everyone cheered the performers.

5. In which of the following sentences is the dash used correctly?

   A. That is my sixth—grade notebook.
   B. I'm flabbergasted—just completely surprised.
   C. The bill passed by a two—thirds vote.
   D. I prefer black—and—white photographs.

6. In which of the following sentences are brackets used correctly?

   A. "When, in the [time] of human events . . ."
   B. "[When in the course] of human events . . ."
   C. "[When in the course of human events . . .]"
   D. ["When in the course of human events . . ."]

Written and Oral English Language Conventions

TESTED

Capitalization
1.6 Use correct capitalization.

Explanation

Capital letters signal the beginning of a new thought or note a word of special importance.

Examples

The following examples illustrate how to correctly use capital letters.

- Capitalize the first word in every sentence and the word *I*.
- Capitalize the first word of a quotation.
- Capitalize proper nouns. Proper nouns include the names of particular persons (*Thomas Paine*), places (*Yellowstone National Park*), or things (*Hubble Space Telescope*).
- Capitalize proper adjectives. Proper adjectives are formed from proper nouns; for example, *Spain* becomes *Spanish*.
- Capitalize the names of historical events and historical periods.

Understand the Skill

Read the following sentences to understand the correct use of capital letters.

Incorrect: *the zoo announced the birth of a baby polar bear.*
Correct: *The zoo announced the birth of a baby polar bear.*

Incorrect: *The director announced, "this will be the best play of the season."*
Correct: *The director announced, "This will be the best play of the season."*

Incorrect: *The movie, starring john wayne, will be shown on monday, tuesday, and Saturday.*
Correct: *The movie, starring John Wayne, will be shown on Monday, Tuesday, and Saturday.*

Incorrect: *The spanish name for "brother" is* hermano.
Correct: *The Spanish name for "brother" is* hermano.

Incorrect: *My favorite historical period is the american revolution.*
Correct: *My favorite historical period is the American Revolution.*

Choose the letter of the best answer to each question.

1. Which of the following sentences uses capitalization correctly?

   A. Thanksgiving is celebrated every november.
   B. George washington was the first president of the United states.
   C. Napoleon was a french emperor.
   D. Rome, Venice, and Florence are all Italian cities.

2. Which of the following is a proper noun that should begin with a capital letter?

   A. automobile
   B. pasta
   C. lincoln
   D. island

3. What signals the beginning of a sentence?

   A. a question mark
   B. a capital letter
   C. quotation marks
   D. parenthesis

4. Which of the following is a proper noun that should begin with a capital letter?

   A. city
   B. liberty
   C. sacramento
   D. mayor

5. Which sentence shows the correct rewrite of the following sentence?

   we decided to go to grandma jones's house for thanksgiving.

   A. we decided to go to grandma Jones's house for Thanksgiving.
   B. We decided to go to Grandma Jones's house for Thanksgiving.
   C. We decided to go to grandma Jones's house for thanksgiving.
   D. we decided to go to Grandma jones's house for thanksgiving.

On a separate sheet of paper, rewrite the following sentences using correct capitalization.

6. the spanish word for "hello" is *hola*.

7. the movie *star wars* was popular for a long time.

8. what i really like to do is visit jamestown at least once a year.

Written and Oral English Language Conventions

TESTED

Spelling
1.7 Spell derivatives correctly by applying the spellings of bases and affixes.

Explanation

The spelling of some base words changes when certain endings are added to the word.

a. A base word has no prefixes or suffixes added to it.

b. An affix can be either a prefix or a suffix.

c. A prefix is one or more letters added before the base word. A prefix changes the meaning of the base word. Common prefixes include *un-, mis-, il-, re-, pre-,* and *im-.*

d. A suffix is one or more letters added after the base word. A suffix changes the meaning of a word. Common suffixes are *-ly, -ness, -less, -able, -er, -est, -ful,* and *-ing.*

Examples

Several spelling rules apply when affixes are added to a base word.

- When a prefix is added to a base word, the spelling of the base word remains the same: *pre + view = preview*

- When the suffixes *-ness* and *-ly* are added to a base word, the spelling of the base word remains the same: *like + ness = likeness, final + ly = finally*

- When a suffix is added to a base word ending in *y*, the *y* changes to *i* before the suffix is added: *fly + er = flier; merry + ly + merrily*

- Drop the final *e* before adding a suffix that begins with a vowel: *place + ing = placing; write + ing = writing*

- Leave the final *e* before adding a suffix that begins with a consonant: *peace + ful = peaceful; safe + ly = safely* (Exceptions: *true + ly = truly; argue + ment = argument*)

- Change the *y* to *i* before adding a suffix if there is a consonant before the *y: hurry + ed = hurried; try + ed = tried*

- Double the final consonant before adding the suffix in one-syllable words, if the consonant is preceded by a vowel: *set + ing = setting*

Understand the Skill

On a separate sheet of paper, apply common affixes to the following words: *real, happy, race, grace,* and *employ.*

Choose the letter of the best answer to each question.

1. Which of the following words is *not* spelled correctly?

   A. immensity
   B. density
   C. scarceity
   D. humidity

2. Which of the following words correctly spells the word meaning "the most untidy"?

   A. messiest
   B. messyist
   C. messyest
   D. mesiest

3. Which of the following words is the correct spelling for "petty" + "ness"?

   A. pettyness
   B. pettyeness
   C. pettiness
   D. petteyness

4. Which of the following words is spelled correctly?

   A. sillyness
   B. silliness
   C. sillness
   D. silleness

5. Which of the following words is *not* spelled correctly?

   A. intensity
   B. rareity
   C. hostility
   D. gravity

On a separate sheet of paper, add the suffix *-ity* to each root word given. Make any spelling changes necessary.

6. severe + ity

7. sane + ity

8. grave + ity

Listening and Speaking

Comprehension
1.1 Ask probing questions to elicit information, including evidence to support the speaker's claims and conclusions.

Explanation

When listening to a report or speech, it is important to concentrate on what a speaker says, looking for facts. Listen for main ideas. After the speech, ask clear questions that require the speaker to support any claims with evidence.

Example/Understand the Skill

Listen while a classmate delivers the following speech. After you've listened, ask challenging questions to deepen your understanding of the topic. Consider the evidence given to support the speaker's position, and evaluate your understanding of the rubric on the next page.

> I think making students wear uniforms in school is a bad idea. Many middle schools in the United States require students to wear ugly uniforms, including schools in large cities, such as New York City, Long Beach in California, and Kansas City in Missouri. Some schools report that violence in the schools decreased and attendance increased after students were forced to wear school uniforms. But, that's not true for most schools. Not every family can afford to buy uniforms. And, what about a student whose religion requires a certain type of dress? It's not fair. I hope we never are required to wear uniforms at our school.

Circle the score that best represents your listening comprehension for each of the scoring criteria—with 4 being the highest score and 1 being the lowest score.

Rating Scale	Listening Comprehension Criteria
1 2 3 4	**Focus:** How well did I identify facts presented by the speaker?
1 2 3 4	**Evaluation:** Did I listen to the speech with an open mind?
1 2 3 4	**Drawing Conclusions:** How well did I understand the main idea presented by the speaker?
1 2 3 4	**Attention:** How well did I sustain interest in the presentation?
1 2 3 4	**Word Choice:** How well did I identify persuasive words?
1 2 3 4	**Thinking Critically:** Did I think of questions I could pose while the speaker was speaking?
1 2 3 4	**Analyzing:** How well do my questions sort fact from fiction?

Complete the following chart of questions you could ask the speaker. First, write the statement made by the speaker that prompted your questions. Then, write a question you would like to ask the speaker.

Speaker's statement that prompted my question:	My question:
1.	
2.	
3.	
4.	
5.	

Listening and Speaking

Comprehension
1.2 Determine the speaker's attitude toward the subject.

Explanation

When listening to a report or speech, it is important to evaluate the difference between fact and personal opinion. Listen carefully for loaded words that indicate the speaker is presenting a personal belief instead of a fact.

a. Listen for words of personal belief, such as "I think" or "In my opinion."
b. Listen for balance in how the ideas are presented.
c. Listen for personal bias toward the subject.

Example/Understand the Skill

Divide into groups of four. Ask one member of the group to read the following speech about logging. Use the rubric on the next page to evaluate the speaker's viewpoint on the subject.

> We should stop cutting trees in our national forests. Trees are important to the environment. We need trees to make oxygen for all of us to breathe. There are eighteen national forests in California, including the Sequoia National Forest and the Tahoe National Forest. Our state will soon run out of trees if we do not stop cutting them, and people will not have any more oxygen to breathe. People can rent cabins, camp, and fish at our national parks. They have a lot of fun doing that. I think people enjoy camping in national forests more than at state parks because there are so many trees. Some people think that we need to cut trees in a national forest to keep the forest healthy, but it seems to me that we should rely on natural ways, like forest fires, to maintain our national forests.

Circle the score that best represents your listening comprehension for each of the scoring criteria—with 4 being the highest score and 1 being the lowest score.

Rating Scale	Listening Comprehension Criteria
1 2 3 4	**Focus:** How well did I separate fact from opinion?
1 2 3 4	**Evaluation:** How well did I determine the attitude of the speaker?
1 2 3 4	**Drawing Conclusions:** How well did I determine if the information was backed up by examples or details?
1 2 3 4	**Attention:** How well did I listen for bias in the presentation?
1 2 3 4	**Word Choice:** How well did I identify loaded words?
1 2 3 4	**Thinking Critically:** How well did I identify exaggerated information included to convince me to agree with the speaker?
1 2 3 4	**Analyzing:** How well did I listen for a balance of ideas presented in the speech?

Complete the following chart of comments about the content of the speech or questions you could ask the speaker to clarify fact from opinion. First, write the statement made by the speaker that prompted your comment or question. Then, write the comment you have or question you would like to ask the speaker.

Speaker's statement prompting me to wonder about fact and opinion:	My comments or questions to ask:
1.	
2.	
3.	
4.	
5.	

Listening and Speaking

> **Comprehension**
> **1.3** Respond to persuasive messages with questions, challenges, or affirmations.

Explanation

When listening to a report or speech, be willing to challenge an idea if you think it sounds unbelievable or carries a strong bias. Likewise, if you are persuaded by an opinion that seems reasonable and workable, make statements (affirmations) to show how and why you agree.

a. Ask questions that request facts to support statements of opinion.

b. Ask questions that require the speaker to clarify his or her reasoning.

c. Respond with facts or reasons that support the speaker's opinion.

Example/Understand the Skill

In groups of three, designate a classmate to deliver the following speech about school vending machines. Listen to the speech. One member of the group will write and ask questions that will require the speaker to clarify what was said. The other member of the group will support the speaker's position. Use the rubric on the following page to evaluate the discussion.

> Why does our school continue to sell soda in our school vending machines? It is very unhealthy. Not only does soda contain a lot of sugar, which is very bad for teeth, but many sodas contain a lot of caffeine. Everyone knows too much caffeine can be harmful. Students come to school and grab a soda from the vending machine. They have a soda during study hour and again at lunch. After school, it's back to the vending machine for another soda. That's a lot of caffeine! No wonder students can't concentrate! Let's ask the school to replace soda with water or sports drinks. That way the school will not be losing money made from the machines, and students will have a healthier diet. Who knows? Maybe the entire school grade point average will improve!

Circle the score that best represents your listening comprehension for each of the scoring criteria—with 4 being the highest score and 1 being the lowest score.

Rating Scale	Listening Comprehension Criteria
1 2 3 4	**Focus:** Did I listen without bias?
1 2 3 4	**Evaluation:** How well did I focus on the facts presented in the speech?
1 2 3 4	**Drawing Conclusions:** How well did I determine the facts used to support the speaker's position?
1 2 3 4	**Attention:** Did I take a strong position for or against the speaker's position?
1 2 3 4	**Word Choice:** How quickly did I identify loaded words?
1 2 3 4	**Thinking Critically:** Are my questions worded so they ask the speaker for additional facts or reasons?
1 2 3 4	**Analyzing:** Are my affirmations supported by facts or good reasoning?

Do you support the speaker's point of view or strongly disagree with it? If you support the speaker's point of view, write affirmations you could express to the speaker. But, if you disagree with the speaker's point of view, write questions that would require the speaker to back up statements with facts or reasoning.

Affirmations I could express:	Questions I could ask:
1.	
2.	
3.	
4.	
5.	

Listening and Speaking

Organization and Delivery of Oral Communication

1.4 Organize information to achieve particular purposes and to appeal to the background and interests of the audience.

Explanation

When asked to present a report or essay on a topic, your job is to find ways to make the topic interesting for those who are listening to your presentation.

    a. Have a thesis, or a central idea, that you want your listeners to understand.

    b. Choose details that your audience will understand and respond to.

    c. Have a clear beginning, middle, and end to your report.

    d. Vary your sentence lengths.

    e. Include examples or a visual aid, such as a poster, to add interest.

Example/Understand the Skill

Read the following description of an oral report. Use the rubric on the next page to determine if the purpose of the report is clear. Evaluate if the presenter found ways to make the report interesting to himself and to his audience.

Kyle is asked to present an oral report on the solar system. Kyle enjoys art and likes science, but science has never been his first interest. He decided to look through some astronomy books to get some ideas on a good way to present what he knew about the planets, the asteroid belt, and the sun. He opened a book of photos on the planets taken by the Hubble Space Telescope and had a great idea.

The day before his report, Kyle stayed after school building a solar system out of Styrofoam balls. He has spent quite a bit of time learning why the planets are different colors. For two weeks, he read up on each planet, painting differently sized Styrofoam balls the colors of the planets, just like he saw them in the astronomy book. When it came time for his report, he used the solar system he had built to explain all about the position of the planets, their rings, and why they are different colors. He was very proud of his work and enjoyed showing his solar system to the class. After the report, he answered many questions.

Evaluate the organization and delivery of the report using the scoring criteria—with 4 being the highest score and 1 being the lowest score.

Rating Scale	Organization and Delivery of Oral Communication Criteria
1 2 3 4	**Focus:** Did the student show interest in the subject?
1 2 3 4	**Evaluation:** Was the student able to create interest for his listeners?
1 2 3 4	**Drawing Conclusions:** Did the student's report have a thesis, or central idea?
1 2 3 4	**Attention:** How effective were the visuals or other aids used by the student to help explain the topic?
1 2 3 4	**Preparation:** How well prepared was the student?
1 2 3 4	**Thinking Critically:** Overall, how would I rate this presentation?

Rethink each of your ratings. Explain your reasoning for each rating. Then, write any suggestions that might improve the science report.

My explanation for each rating:
1. Focus:
2. Evaluation:
3. Drawing Conclusions:
4. Attention:
5. Preparation:
6. Thinking Critically:
7. Suggestions for improvement:

Listening and Speaking

> **Organization and Delivery of Oral Communication**
> **1.5** Arrange supporting details, reasons, descriptions, and examples effectively and persuasively in relation to the audience.

Explanation

Every oral communication should have a theme, or main focus. In order to persuade the audience, all details, descriptions, and examples should support and explain the theme.

a. Make sure your reasons and examples are clear and do not leave your audience wondering what you were trying to explain.

b. Make sure your reasons can be supported by factual data.

c. Vary the type of examples and descriptions to keep interest high.

d. Present your information in a logical order so your audience has no trouble following your flow of ideas.

Example/Understand the Skill

Listen while a classmate delivers the following speech. With a partner, use the rubric on the next page to evaluate the speech. Then, rewrite the speech for a more organized delivery.

Hello,

My talk is on ways to save the rain forests. I like rain forests. Many beautiful, fascinating, and endangered animals live in the world's rain forests. They provide important medical benefits for humans. One way to save the rain forest is to recycle as much paper as possible. For example, cut up and staple paper only printed on one side to make small notepads instead of buying new ones. Rain forest trees convert carbon dioxide into oxygen. These trees are important to maintain our ecology and air quality. Another way to save the rain forests is to buy rain forest products, such as nuts, bananas, and avocados to support the economy of rain forests without having to cut down the trees. Some conservation groups even suggest ways to help buy acres of rain forests so they won't be cut down. Did you know that thousands of acres of rain forests are destroyed every year? This is a world problem that needs a worldwide effort to solve. We need to save our rain forests.

Evaluate the organization and delivery of the speech using the scoring criteria—with 4 being the highest score and 1 being the lowest score.

Rating Scale	Organization and Delivery of Speech Criteria
1 2 3 4	**Focus:** Does the oral communication arrange supporting information effectively?
1 2 3 4	**Evaluation:** Will the audience be able to clearly follow the flow of ideas?
1 2 3 4	**Drawing Conclusions:** Will the details, examples, and other information presented be factual?
1 2 3 4	**Attention:** Will the examples and other information presented keep the audience interested?
1 2 3 4	**Preparation:** How well planned does the presentation look?
1 2 3 4	**Thinking Critically:** Is there enough variety of examples and descriptions to serve the purpose of the oral communication?

Reorganize the speech in a way that you think will create a more organized delivery. Then, explain your reasoning for your reorganization.

My rewrite to improve the rain forest speech:
1)
2)
3)
4)
5)
6)
7)
8)
My reasons for arranging the speech this way:

Listening and Speaking

> **Organization and Delivery of Oral Communication**
> **1.6** Use speaking techniques, including voice modulation, inflection, tempo, enunciation, and eye contact for effective presentations.

Explanation

Interest can be created though effective use of voice, such as the rising and falling of the voice, how fast the speaker speaks, and the emphasis given to certain words or phrases. The flow of words should be well timed and clear.

a. Vary your modulation, or the rise and fall of your voice.

b. Vary your inflection, or the stress you place on certain words, in order to add emphasis and importance to words and phrases.

c. Vary the tempo, or speed, of your words, and make sure you do not rush through your presentation.

d. Make sure you enunciate, or state your words so they are clearly understood.

e. Make eye contact with your audience.

Example/Understand the Skill

Give an oral report on poems written by Dr. Seuss. Choose a classmate to be your audience. First, present a short biography about Dr. Seuss. Make sure to make eye contact with your audience. Vary your voice modulation, inflection, and tempo. Be sure you speak clearly. Ask your classmate to use the rubric on the next page to help you evaluate your oral report. Then, ask your classmate to write a list of suggestions to improve your presentation.

Today I practiced my oral report on poems written by Dr. Seuss. My friend Amy was my audience. First, I gave a short biography about Dr. Seuss. I held my cards up, but Amy said it was hard to see my face because the cards were so high. Even though I practiced reading my cards so I wouldn't have to use them, I found that lots of times I was looking down. Amy said that when I looked down my voice became softer and she couldn't hear what I was saying very clearly. Then, I read *Green Eggs and Ham*. When I read the poem softly to myself, my voice would go up and down, but when I read it to Amy my voice sounded flat. Amy also said that sometimes I read parts of the poem too fast. I didn't realize I was doing that, so I'm glad she told me. I'm going to practice at home tonight. I want to do a great job tomorrow.

Evaluate the organization and delivery of the practice session using the scoring criteria—with 4 being the highest score and 1 being the lowest score.

Rating Scale	Organization and Delivery of Oral Communication Criteria
1 2 3 4	**Focus:** How well did I make eye contact with my audience so that I looked confident?
1 2 3 4	**Evaluation:** How well did I vary the modulation of my voice?
1 2 3 4	**Drawing Conclusions:** How well did I add stress to the right words so that the listener understood the humor in the poems?
1 2 3 4	**Attention:** How good was the tempo of my voice?
1 2 3 4	**Preparation:** How well did I enunciate the words so that it looked like I was well prepared?
1 2 3 4	**Thinking Critically:** Overall, how good was my oral communication?

Finish the student's journal by writing five suggestions to improve her report. Then write how each suggestion will improve her report.

Suggestions to improve the report:	How the suggestion will help the report:
1.	
2.	
3.	
4.	
5.	

Listening and Speaking

Analysis and Evaluation of Oral and Media Communications
1.7 Provide constructive feedback to speakers concerning the coherence and logic of a speech's content and delivery and its overall impact upon the listener.

Explanation

Constructive feedback includes ideas and examples for improving oral and media communications. Constructive feedback is not criticism, but rather a set of helpful suggestions for making oral and media communications more coherent, or understandable.

Constructive feedback can include the following suggestions:

- Make the content of the message clear.
- Quickly capture the attention of the audience.
- Know your audience.
- Use persuasive words.

Example/Understand the Skill

Divide into groups of four. Ask one member of the group to read the following speech about sea creatures. Use the rubric on the next page to evaluate the logic of the speech's content, its delivery, and its overall impact. Among your group, discuss your constructive feedback.

Equipment used: computer, screen, projector, memory stick, CD player, whale sounds CD

Welcome to my report on creatures of the sea. [*click on first image of North America*] Oceans cover much of the world. In fact, scientists tell us that oceans cover about 70 percent of Earth. That's a lot of water! Under the surface of the world's oceans lies a fascinating world. [*click on image of bioluminescent fish*] I mean, just look at this fish! This strange looking fish lives deep in the ocean. It's called the anglerfish. Wow! Did you ever see such an odd-looking animal? Part of it actually glows in the dark to attract and catch prey. [*click on image of squid*] Above the deep sea where anglerfish live are giant squid that can reach lengths of 26 feet and more. Just imagine! The long tentacle of one of these giants can reach 18 feet long. Let's see, that's about half the width of our classroom. But things get bigger yet. Did you know that giant squid have been found in the stomachs of whales? [*click on image of a sperm whale*] Whales also are fascinating animals. They make the most interesting sounds. Just listen! [*play first track of whale sounds CD*] The picture shows a sperm whale. It can grow to be 50 feet long. It has a large brain that can weigh up to 20 pounds. It also produces a special waxy substance that protects it from bites from sharp squid beaks. These are just some of the many creatures found in the sea. Thank you for listening to my report. Are there any questions?

Evaluate the speech using the scoring criteria—with 4 being the highest score and 1 being the lowest score.

Rating Scale	Analysis and Evaluation of Oral and Media Communication
1 2 3 4	**Coherence:** How coherent was the communication?
1 2 3 4	**Logic:** How well did the individual present ideas that seemed logical?
1 2 3 4	**Word Choice:** How effective was the word choice?
1 2 3 4	**Media Presentation:** How well did the individual use the media to convey information?
1 2 3 4	**Delivery:** How effective was the delivery?
1 2 3 4	**Impact:** How effective was the overall impact on the listener?

Provide constructive feedback to improve the effectiveness of the speech.

Constructive Feedback:
1. Coherence:
2. Logic:
3. Word Choice:
4. Media Presentation:
5. Delivery:
6. Impact:

Listening and Speaking

Analysis and Evaluation of Oral and Media Communications

1.8 Analyze the effect on the viewer of images, text, and sound in electronic journalism; identify the techniques used to achieve the effects in each instance studied.

Explanation

Today information comes to individuals in many electronic ways. Television, the Internet, cell phones, and other electronic media convey information in an instant. Electronic journalism has the advantage of using both video and audio to capture interest and broadcast news and other information in a very effective way. You should be able to identify these techniques as electronic journalism:

- Computer-generated presentations
- Internet Web sites that are constantly updated
- Video presentations with sound
- A video and audio "webcast" posted on an Internet site

Example/Understand the Skill

Read the following description of a group plan for a computer-generated report on global warming. Use the rubric to evaluate the plan. With a partner, conduct research on the benefits of recycling. Describe how you would use electronic journalism to create an oral report on the topic.

> Tara's group decided they would use the computer to present their oral report on global warming. They spent a week researching the subject and then pooled together what they had learned. They decided on the following plan for their oral report:
>
> - Use the computer to put together a slide show on global warming.
> - Create visually interesting slides that are animated.
> - Have individual slides of graphs and maps that support our belief that global warming is occurring.
> - Have a couple slides that show a photo collage of animals affected by global warming.
> - Have a couple slides on parts of the world affected by global warming.
> - If possible, include a short video of an iceberg collapsing.
> - Add a sound track to the presentation.
> - Have Tara act as narrator, or add voice-over to the presentation.
> - Use the large screen in the classroom for the presentation.
> - Limit the slide show to 10 minutes.

Evaluate the organization and delivery of the report plan using the scoring criteria—with 4 being the highest score and 1 being the lowest score.

Rating Scale	Analysis and Evaluation of Oral and Media Communication
1 2 3 4	**Effectiveness:** How well does the plan combine visual and audio aspects of electronic journalism?
1 2 3 4	**Audience:** How well will the presentation capture the interest of the audience?
1 2 3 4	**Word Choice:** How effective will the use of voice-over or a narrator be?
1 2 3 4	**Presentation:** How well will the choice of information serve the purpose of the presentation?
1 2 3 4	**Thinking Critically:** Overall, what rating should this electronic journalism presentation receive?

Think of how you would create an electronic journalism report on recycling. Then, list the ideas you would use to structure your report.

How I would use electronic journalism techniques for an oral report on recycling:
What I would use: _____   _____   _____   How I would structure my report: •   •   •   •   •   •   •   •   •

Listening and Speaking

> **2.1 Deliver narrative presentations:**
>   a. Establish a context, standard plot line (having a beginning, conflict, rising action, climax, and denouement), and point of view.
>   b. Describe complex major and minor characters and a definite setting.
>   c. Use a range of appropriate strategies, including dialogue, suspense, and naming of specific narrative action (e.g., movement, gestures, expressions).

Explanation

A narrative is a story that includes a plot line, major and minor characters, setting, and point of view. The plot line should include such elements as dialogue, conflict, suspense, specific action, gestures, and expressions. The theme of a narrative is the author's main idea or message.

When giving a narrative presentation, remember to use your speaking skills to make the story as interesting as possible.

   a. Create an interesting plot line by adding dramatic touches to your voice.
   b. Clearly explain the setting of the story, making descriptive words come alive for the listener.
   c. Use gestures, expressions, and movement to add suspense, mystery, or drama to the narrative.

Example/Understand the Skill

Work with a partner to develop a short play. Create a rough outline of your story, including general context, basic plot, and point of view. Once you have both completed your outline, exchange outlines with your partner. You will now write a play based on your partner's outline. Be sure to include a thorough plot line (including a beginning, conflict, rising action, climax, and denouement) and point of view. Add interesting twists to the plot and details about the characters. Include dialogue, suspense, and stage directions. Once you have both completed the plays, read them aloud to each other. Use the rubric on the next page to evaluate your partner's play.

Evaluate each play using the scoring criteria—with 4 being the highest score and 1 being the lowest score.

Rating Scale	Skill
1 2 3 4	**Development:** How interesting was the plot?
1 2 3 4	**Description:** How interesting were the characters?
1 2 3 4	**Description:** How well could you visualize the setting?
1 2 3 4	**Response:** How interested were you in how the play ended?
1 2 3 4	**Development:** How much suspense did the play have?
1 2 3 4	**Evaluation:** Overall, how would you rate this play?

On a separate sheet of paper, answer the following questions.

1. Which play did you prefer? Why?

2. What made the play you preferred more interesting?

3. What suggestions would you give to improve this play? List and explain three suggestions.

4. What three things are the most important for you when reading a narrative aloud?

Listening and Speaking

2.2 Deliver oral summaries of articles and books:
  a. Include the main ideas of the event or article and the most significant details.
  b. Use the student's own words, except for material quoted from sources.
  c. Convey a comprehensive understanding of sources, not just superficial details.

Explanation

A summary retells the main ideas of something heard or read in a concise and organized way. It includes supporting details. An oral summary clearly conveys the meaning and purpose of an article or book. When giving an oral summary, remember to use the following skills.

  a. Vary the stress you place on certain words to add emphasis and importance to words and phrases.
  b. Vary your modulation, or the rise and fall of your voice.
  c. Vary the tempo of your voice, but do not rush your presentation.
  d. Make sure you enunciate, or state your words so they are clearly understood.
  e. Make eye contact with your audience.

Example/Understand the Skill

Your teacher will read the oral summary of the Emperor penguin aloud without modulation or changes in tempo. Generate ideas to improve the oral summary. Your teacher will reread the summary employing your suggestions. Discuss the difference in the quality of the two oral summaries. In pairs, orally read the summary of the Emperor penguin to each other. Then, evaluate your oral summaries using the rubric on the next page.

The Emperor penguin is a very special bird. It lives in Antarctica. It can dive 700 feet into the frigid water of the region to feed on fish, shrimp, and crustaceans. The female lays one egg that is carefully placed on the feet of the male until it hatches. The male Emperor penguin protects the egg with a flap of skin and feathers while the female leaves to feed. The male protects the egg through the worst weather. During that time the male loses about one-third of its body weight. After the egg hatches, the female penguin returns. The male then travels 60 miles to the sea to feed. It then returns to help parent the young penguin.

Evaluate your oral summary by using the scoring criteria—with 4 being the highest score and 1 being the lowest score.

Rating Scale	Speaking Criteria
1 2 3 4	**Presentation:** How well did I place stress on certain words to add emphasis and importance to the words?
1 2 3 4	**Voice Control:** How well did I modulate my voice (making it rise and fall)?
1 2 3 4	**Voice Control:** How well did I manage the tempo of my voice by not speaking too quickly or slowly?
1 2 3 4	**Speech:** How was my enunciation?
1 2 3 4	**Connection:** How well did I make eye contact with the audience?
1 2 3 4	**Preparation:** How confident did I feel while delivering the oral summary?
1 2 3 4	**Evaluation:** Overall, how should my oral summary be rated?

On a separate sheet of paper, answer the following questions.

1. Identify five words or phrases that should be stressed when reading the summary orally.

2. Write an example of a sentence that needs to have the words rise and fall as they are spoken.

3. What effect does reading an oral summary too quickly have on the audience?

4. Do you find making eye contact with the audience difficult? Explain your answer.

5. Explain how practicing an oral summary before having to deliver it in front of an audience can build the confidence of the speaker.

6. Write one sentence to explain how you rated your oral summary overall.

Listening and Speaking

2.3 Deliver research presentations:
  a. Pose relevant and concise questions about the topic.
  b. Convey clear and accurate perspectives on the subject.
  c. Include evidence generated through the formal research process (e.g., use of a card catalog, *Reader's Guide to Periodical Literature*, computer databases, magazines, newspapers, dictionaries).
  d. Cite reference sources appropriately.

Explanation

The oral delivery of a research presentation involves identifying the topic, organizing information in a way the audience can understand it, citing credible sources, and conveying information in a clear and interesting way.

Example/Understand the Skill

Read the following description of a research presentation on the growth of railroads in the United States during the 1800s. Use the rubric on the next page and complete the chart that follows to evaluate the presentation. Discuss the strengths of the report as well as the areas needing improvement with your class.

Scott had created a colorful display of different types of trains that included a time line of when each train first ran. He also had two maps on his display that showed railway lines in 1840 and 1880. Scott added some old time locomotives from his collection of toy trains.

Scott's report lasted 20 minutes. He looked confident and spoke clearly. Scott began his report with the impact of the Civil War on the growth of trains. He then talked about how the building of the Erie Canal in the 1820s had helped encourage the growth of railroads. Scott highlighted the invention of the Morse Code in 1844. He explained how by 1860, about 50,000 miles of telegraph wire had been strung along the country's railway lines. Finally, Scott talked about the building of the Transcontinental Railroad. He explained how this railroad encouraged westward movement and impacted the growth of westward towns.

Throughout his report, Scott mentioned where he had found his information, such as on the Internet, in his history book, and in the encyclopedia. He also said that he had learned a lot by reading fictional stories about people who lived in the 1800s. The class enjoyed his report. Some took notes while he talked. Three students asked questions.

Evaluate Scott's research presentation by using the scoring criteria—with 4 being the highest score and 1 being the lowest score.

Rating Scale	Presentation Criteria
1 2 3 4	**Author's Purpose:** How well did Scott convey the purpose of his report?
1 2 3 4	**Organization:** How well did Scott present factual data?
1 2 3 4	**Research:** How credible were Scott's sources of information?
1 2 3 4	**Support:** How valuable were Scott's examples to the purpose of his report?
1 2 3 4	**Organization:** How good was the logical order of information Scott presented?
1 2 3 4	**Technology:** How well did he make use of media?
1 2 3 4	**Connection:** How interested did the audience seem in Scott's report?
1 2 3 4	**Evelution:** Overall, how would you rate Scott's report?

Use the chart to note the strengths of Scott's report. Then note suggestions for how the report could be improved.

Skills needed in a research presentation:	Presentation strengths:	Suggestions for improvement:
Presentation of facts		
Use of credible sources		
Information presented in a logical order		
Use of examples or presentation of details		
Use of media		
Confidence		
Clear voice		
Engage the audience in the topic		

Listening and Speaking

2.4 Deliver persuasive presentations:
   a. State a clear position or perspective in support of an argument or proposal.
   b. Describe the points in support of the argument and employ well-articulated evidence.

Explanation

When you deliver a persuasive composition, you try to convince the listener to think or act in a particular way. You may be challenging an idea or bias carried by others. Your ideas must appear reasonable and possible. The delivery of persuasive compositions emphasizes the loaded words found in the composition.

Example/Understand the Skill

Listen as two volunteers read the parts of Ed Mason and Mayor Smith in the speeches below. Use the chart on the next page to evaluate the persuasive qualities of each speaker. Explain which individual was more persuasive and why.

Ed Mason, head of the local efforts to build a community zoo:

Fellow citizens. We need this zoo. Our youth must understand the importance of wild animals in the world's ecology and value the animals that still grace the world's dwindling animal reserves. Today, wildlife habitat is quickly shrinking. We are losing species every day. Even in our own community, we see evidence of the effect humans have on wildlife. Where are the songbirds that once returned to our area? What happened to the geese that graced the wetlands that no longer exist? We need to address the importance of animals. Having a small zoo in our community will do this.

Mayor Smith responded:

With all due respect, we simply cannot afford a zoo. We need new roads. We need to expand our middle school. Our parks need new play equipment. Yes, wildlife is important, but building a zoo means a huge increase in taxes. And, I'm not convinced that it can be built in such a way that our community will be safe. Wild animals are not safe. The proponents of this zoo are not talking about songbirds and geese. They want to have bears and leopards in this zoo. It just doesn't make any sense.

Evaluate the persuasive qualities of both speeches by using the scoring criteria—with 4 being the highest score and 1 being the lowest score.

Rating of 1st Speech	Persuasive Qualities Criteria	Rating of 2nd Speech
1 2 3 4	**Evaluation:** How convincing was the speech?	1 2 3 4
1 2 3 4	**Persuasion:** How well did the speaker make use of persuasive words?	1 2 3 4
1 2 3 4	**Logic:** How well did the speaker appeal to reason?	1 2 3 4
1 2 3 4	**Connection:** How important were the ideas to the community?	1 2 3 4
1 2 3 4	**Support:** How strong were the points made?	1 2 3 4
1 2 3 4	**Audience:** How well did the speaker know his audience?	1 2 3 4
1 2 3 4	**Technique:** How well did the speaker appeal to emotion?	1 2 3 4
1 2 3 4	**Logic:** How well did the speaker pose a solution to the problem?	1 2 3 4

On a separate sheet of paper, answer the following questions.

1. Which speech do you find more convincing? Why?

2. Which speech makes a better appeal to reason? How?

3. Which speech appeals more to emotion? In what way?

4. Do the speeches solve or complicate a problem? Explain your answer.

Writing Support for Narrative Essays

STANDARD

1.1 Sentence Structure: place modifiers properly, and use the active voice

Sentence Structure

- A modifier clarifies or expands meaning.
- Sentence modifiers include adjectives, adverbs, phrases, and clauses.
- A modifier should be placed close to the word it modifies for the meaning to be clear and effective.
- The active voice expresses a subject doing something: *He broke the dish.* Another way to state this is to express what is done to something: *The dish was broken by him.* (This is the passive voice.)

Timed Writing for Tested Prompt

Format and Details:

The prompt gives specific directions about what to write and targets a specific standard.

Writing Prompt: Write a narrative essay about a favorite summer experience. Your narrative should have a beginning, middle, and an end. Use at least ten modifiers in your narrative. Use the active voice when writing your narrative.

Academic Vocabulary:

A **narrative** is a story. The setting is the time and place it takes place. Every narrative has characters and a plot. When you write in **active voice,** the subject performs the action.

🕐 Minute-by-Minute Writing Guide

Complete these steps.

1. Prewriting (5 minutes)
Read the prompt carefully and completely. Look for keywords such as those in the sentence underlined above, which will help you understand the assignment.

2. Organizing (5–10 minutes)
Create a graphic organizer, such as a story structure chart, that will help you plan out the beginning, middle, and end of your story. Use an idea web to think about details.

3. Drafting (15–20 minutes)
Use your story structure chart and idea web to write your narrative. Develop the plot line of your story. Establish your setting. Make your characters interesting by adding details about them from your idea web.

4. Revising and Proofreading (5 minutes)
Quickly reread your draft, correcting as you go.

Reflect on Your Writing

Circle the score that best represents your draft for each of the scoring criteria—with 4 being the highest score and 1 being the lowest score. Then, use your observations to revise your draft and create a final draft.

Rating Scale	Writing Criteria
1 2 3 4	**Analysis:** Does your narrative tell a story?
1 2 3 4	**Focus:** Does your story have a main character?
1 2 3 4	**Organization:** Does your essay have a beginning, middle, and an end?
1 2 3 4	**Support/Elaboration:** Are there enough details to develop the characters and setting of your story?
1 2 3 4	**Style:** Is your story interesting?
1 2 3 4	**Conventions:** Did you use at least ten modifiers?
1 2 3 4	**Word Choice:** Did you use active voice?

Revise Your Writing

When completing a timed writing activity, you only get time to do what is necessary. Now, review your draft and identify 3 or 4 elements that you would revise if you had more time. Use the chart below to revise your writing.

Draft Sentence	My Revision
1.	
2.	
3.	
4.	

Writing Support for Narrative Essays

Grammar

- An infinitive is a verb form using *to* that can take the place of a noun, an adjective, or an adverb.
- A participle is a verb used as an adjective.
- A pronoun is a word used in place of a noun or more than one noun.
- An antecedent is a noun or noun phrase to which a pronoun refers.

Timed Writing for Tested Prompt

Format and Details:

The prompt gives specific directions about what to write and targets a specific standard.

Writing Prompt: Write a summary about a recent shopping trip or sporting event. Include descriptions of the most interesting things that happened. Use an example of an infinitive, a participle, and a pronoun. Make a clear reference between every pronoun and its antecedent.

Academic Vocabulary:

A **summary** describes the most important details or events. An **antecedent** is the word or phrase replaced by the pronoun.

⏱ Minute-by-Minute Writing Guide

Complete these steps.

1. Prewriting (5 minutes)

Read the prompt carefully and completely. Look for keywords like the ones underlined above, which will help you understand the assignment.

2. Organizing (5–10 minutes)

Create a graphic organizer, such as an idea web, that will help you determine the most important things that happened while on your shopping trip or at the sporting event. Use a sequence chart to think about what happened first, second, and last.

3. Drafting (15–20 minutes)

Use your idea web and sequence chart to write your summary. Start your summary with a topic sentence. Add details to your summary. Remember to use transition words.

4. Revising and Proofreading (5 minutes)

Quickly reread your draft, correcting as you go.

Reflect on Your Writing

Circle the score that best represents your draft for each of the scoring criteria—with 4 being the highest score and 1 being the lowest score. Then, use your observations to revise your draft and create a final draft.

Rating Scale	Writing Criteria
1 2 3 4	**Evaluation:** Does your summary describe the most important things that happened?
1 2 3 4	**Focus:** Does your summary begin with a topic sentence?
1 2 3 4	**Organization:** Does your summary explain what happened first, next, and last?
1 2 3 4	**Support/Elaboration:** Are there enough details for your reader to visualize the shopping trip or sporting event?
1 2 3 4	**Style:** Is your summary interesting?
1 2 3 4	**Conventions:** Did you use at least one infinitive, participle, and pronoun?
1 2 3 4	**Word Choice:** Do the pronouns correctly replace their antecedents?

Revise Your Writing

When completing a timed writing activity, you only get time to do what is necessary. Now, review your draft and identify 3 or 4 elements that you would revise if you had more time. Use the chart below to revise your writing.

Draft Sentence	My Revision
1.	
2.	
3.	
4.	

Writing Support for Narrative Essays

TESTED

STANDARD

1.3 Grammar: identify all parts of speech and types and structure of sentences

Grammar

- A sentence is a complete thought and is divided into a subject and a predicate.
- Each sentence is made of different parts of speech including nouns, verbs, and adjectives.
- A subject tells whom or what the sentence is about.
- A predicate tells something about the subject.

Timed Writing for Tested Prompt

Format and Details:

The prompt gives specific directions about what to write and targets a specific standard.

Writing Prompt: Write a narrative essay that describes your favorite place to visit. Include several details about your favorite place. Use as many parts of speech as possible. Remember to place each modifier close to the word it modifies.

Academic Vocabulary:

A **conjunction** is a word that joins other words or groups of words (*but, and, or*). An **interjection** is a word or phrase that expresses emotion (*Terrific!*).

⏱ Minute-by-Minute Writing Guide

Complete these steps.

1. Prewriting (5 minutes)

Read the prompt carefully and completely. Look for keywords such as the ones underlined above, which will help you understand the assignment.

2. Organizing (5–10 minutes)

Create a graphic organizer, such as a story structure chart, that will help you plan out the beginning, middle, and end of your story. Use an idea web to think about details you want to add to your story.

3. Drafting (15–20 minutes)

Use your story structure chart and idea web to write your narrative. Develop the plot line of your story. Establish your setting. Make your characters interesting by adding details about them from your idea web.

4. Revising and Proofreading (5 minutes)

Quickly reread your draft, correcting as you go.

Reflect on Your Writing

Circle the score that best represents your draft for each of the scoring criteria—with 4 being the highest score and 1 being the lowest score. Then, use your observations to revise your draft and create a final draft.

Rating Scale	Writing Criteria
1 2 3 4	**Purpose:** Does your narrative tell a story?
1 2 3 4	**Focus:** Does your story have a well-developed setting?
1 2 3 4	**Organization:** Does your story have a beginning, middle, and an end?
1 2 3 4	**Support/Elaboration:** Are there enough details to help your reader visualize your favorite place to visit?
1 2 3 4	**Style:** Is your story interesting?
1 2 3 4	**Conventions:** Can you identify five different parts of speech used in your narrative?
1 2 3 4	**Word Choice:** Does your narrative use a variety of interesting words to describe your favorite place to visit?

Revise Your Writing

When completing a timed writing activity, you only get time to do what is necessary. Now, review your draft and identify 3 or 4 elements that you would revise if you had more time. Use the chart below to revise your writing.

Draft Sentence	My Revision
1.	
2.	
3.	
4.	

Writing Support for Narrative Essays

Grammar

- Use a comma to separate two or more adjectives in a row; separate nouns in a series; separate independent clauses; set off a nonessential phrase; set off a dependent clause; and set off *yes, well,* and *no* when they begin a sentence.
- Use quotation marks when stating a person's exact words.

STANDARD

1.4 Grammar: demonstrate the mechanics of writing (e.g., quotation marks, commas at end of dependent clauses) and appropriate English usage (e.g., pronoun reference)

Timed Writing for Tested Prompt

Format and Details:

The prompt gives specific directions about what to write and targets a specific standard.

Writing Prompt: Write a summary of the past week at school. Your summary should include interesting details about the main events that happened. Use at least one example of each comma skill. Use quotations to enclose at least one quotation.

Academic Vocabulary:

A **summary** is a word that joins other words or groups of words (*but, and, or*). An **interjection** is a word or phrase that expresses emotion (*Terrific!*).

⏱ Minute-by-Minute Writing Guide

Complete these steps before you begin writing.

1. **Prewriting** (5 minutes)

   Read the prompt carefully and completely. Look for keywords like the ones underlined above, which will help you understand the assignment.

2. **Organizing** (5–10 minutes)

   Create a graphic organizer, such as an idea web, that will help you determine the most important things that happened during the past week at school. Use a sequence chart to think about what happened on each day.

3. **Drafting** (15–20 minutes)

   Use your idea web and sequence chart to write your summary. Start your summary with a topic sentence. Add details to your summary. Remember to use transition words.

4. **Revising and Proofreading** (5 minutes)

   Quickly reread your draft, correcting as you go.

Reflect on Your Writing

Circle the score that best represents your draft for each of the scoring criteria—with 4 being the highest score and 1 being the lowest score. Then, use your observations to revise your draft and create a final draft.

Rating Scale	Writing Criteria
1 2 3 4	**Purpose:** Does your summary describe the most important things that happened?
1 2 3 4	**Focus:** Does your summary begin with a topic sentence?
1 2 3 4	**Organization:** Does your summary explain what happened first, next, and last?
1 2 3 4	**Support/Elaboration:** Are there enough details for your reader to visualize the past week at school?
1 2 3 4	**Style:** Is your summary interesting?
1 2 3 4	**Conventions:** Did you use at least one example of each comma skill and at least one set of quotation marks?
1 2 3 4	**Word Choice:** Does your quotation show the exact words someone said?

Revise Your Writing

When completing a timed writing activity, you only get time to do what is necessary. Now, review your draft and identify 3 or 4 elements that you would revise if you had more time. Use the chart below to revise your writing.

Draft Sentence	My Revision
1.	
2.	
3.	
4.	

Writing Support for Persuasive Essays

Punctuation

Use a hyphen for dividing a word at the end of a line; for compound numbers and fractions (*three-fourths*); with prefixes such as *ex, self,* and *all* (*all-star*); and for connecting compound adjectives (*rain-soaked*). Use a dash to show a change in thought. Use brackets to help explain part of a quotation or when a word is changed for clarity. Use a semicolon when connecting independent clauses not joined by *for, but, yet, or, so,* and *nor.* Use a semicolon when connecting independent clauses joined by *for example, therefore, however, instead,* and *furthermore.* Use a semicolon when a series of items contains commas.

STANDARD

1.5 Punctuation: identify hyphens, dashes, brackets, and semicolons and use them correctly

Timed Writing for Tested Prompt

Format and Details:

The prompt gives specific directions about what to write and targets a specific standard.

Writing Prompt: <u>Write a persuasive essay on the importance of breakfast.</u> Include loaded words. Use at least two examples of hyphens, one dash, and one semicolon.

Academic Vocabulary:

A **persuasive essay** is a short nonfiction work that tries to convince a reader to think or act in a particular way.

⏱ Minute-by-Minute Writing Guide

Complete these steps.

1. Prewriting (5 minutes)

Read the prompt carefully and completely. Look for keywords like the ones underlined above, which will help you understand the assignment.

2. Organizing (5–10 minutes)

Create a graphic organizer, such as a cause-and-effect chart, to plan how you will present your reasoning on the importance of breakfast. List the ideas in order of importance to decide which ideas are the strongest to present.

3. Drafting (15–20 minutes)

Use your cause-and-effect chart to write your persuasive essay. Start your persuasive essay with a strong statement. Appeal to the reasoning and emotions of your audience. Remember to use persuasive words.

4. Revising and Proofreading (5 minutes)

Quickly reread your draft, correcting as you go.

Reflect on Your Writing

Circle the score that best represents your draft for each of the scoring criteria—with 4 being the highest score and 1 being the lowest score. Then, use your observations to revise your draft and create a final draft.

Rating Scale	Writing Criteria
1 2 3 4	**Evaluation:** How convincing is your persuasive essay?
1 2 3 4	**Focus:** Does your persuasive essay begin with a strong statement?
1 2 3 4	**Organization:** Does your persuasive essay present several strong reasons on the importance of breakfast?
1 2 3 4	**Support/Elaboration:** Are your reasons supported by examples?
1 2 3 4	**Style:** Does your persuasive essay appeal to your audience?
1 2 3 4	**Conventions:** Did you use hyphens, dashes, and semicolons in your persuasive essay?
1 2 3 4	**Word Choice:** Does your persuasive essay use loaded words?

Revise Your Writing

When completing a timed writing activity, you only get time to do what is necessary. Now, review your draft and identify 3 or 4 elements that you would revise if you had more time. Use the chart below to revise your writing.

Draft Sentence	My Revision
1.	
2.	
3.	
4.	

Writing Support for Narrative Essays

TESTED

STANDARD

1.6 Capitalization: use correct capitalization

Capitalization

- Capitalize the first word in every sentence and the word *I*.
- Capitalize the first word of a quotation.
- Capitalize proper nouns.
- Capitalize proper adjectives.
- Capitalize the names of historical events and historical periods.

Timed Writing for Tested Prompt

Format and Details:

The prompt gives specific directions about what to write and targets a specific standard.

Writing Prompt: <u>Write a narrative essay about planting a tree</u>. Your narrative should include main and minor characters. Include an example of each capitalization rule in your narrative essay. Remember to have a plot line and describe the setting in detail.

Academic Vocabulary:

A **minor character** supports the actions of the main character and helps the plot line to flow.

Minute-by-Minute Writing Guide

Complete these steps.

1. Prewriting (5 minutes)

Read the prompt carefully and completely. Look for keywords like the ones underlined above, which will help you understand the assignment.

2. Organizing (5–10 minutes)

Create a graphic organizer, such as a story structure chart, that will help you plan out the beginning, middle, and end of your story. Use an idea web to think about details you want to add to your story.

3. Drafting (15–20 minutes)

Use your story structure chart and idea web to write your narrative. Develop the plot line of your story. Establish your setting. Make your characters interesting by adding details about them from your idea web.

4. Revising and Proofreading (5 minutes)

Quickly reread your draft, correcting as you go.

Reflect on Your Writing

Circle the score that best represents your draft for each of the scoring criteria—with 4 being the highest score and 1 being the lowest score. Then, use your observations to revise your draft and create a final draft.

Rating Scale	Writing Criteria
1 2 3 4	**Purpose:** Does your narrative tell a story?
1 2 3 4	**Focus:** Does your story have a well-developed setting?
1 2 3 4	**Organization:** Does your story have a beginning, middle, and an end?
1 2 3 4	**Support/Elaboration:** Are there enough details to help your reader visualize the characters?
1 2 3 4	**Style:** Is your story interesting?
1 2 3 4	**Conventions:** Did you include an example of each capitalization rule?
1 2 3 4	**Word Choice:** Does your narrative use a variety of interesting words to describe the setting?

Revise Your Writing

When completing a timed writing activity, you only get time to do what is necessary. Now, review your draft and identify 3 or 4 elements that you would revise if you had more time. Use the chart below to revise your writing.

Draft Sentence	My Revision
1.	
2.	
3.	
4.	

Writing Support for Persuasive Essays

Spelling

- When a prefix is added to a base word, the spelling of the base word remains the same.
- When the suffixes *-ness* and *-ly* are added to a base word, the spelling of the base word remains the same. When a suffix is added to a base word ending in *y*, the *y* changes to *i* before the suffix is added. Drop the final *e* before adding a suffix that begins with a vowel. Leave the final *e* before adding a suffix that begins with a consonant. Change the *y* to *i* before adding a suffix if there is a consonant before the *y*. Double the final consonant before adding the suffix in one-syllable words, if the consonant is preceded by a vowel.

Timed Writing for Tested Prompt

Format and Details:

The prompt gives specific directions about what to write and targets a specific standard.

Writing Prompt: <u>Write a persuasive essay on the importance of teamwork.</u> Your persuasive essay should include loaded words. Include three words that have prefixes. Include four words that have suffixes.

Academic Vocabulary:

A **base** word has no prefixes or suffixes. A **prefix** is letters added before the base word. A **suffix** is letters added after the base word.

⏱ Minute-by-Minute Writing Guide

Complete these steps.

1. Prewriting (5 minutes)

Read the prompt carefully and completely. Look for keywords like the ones underlined above, which will help you understand the assignment.

2. Organizing (5–10 minutes)

Create a graphic organizer, such as a cause-and-effect chart, to plan how you will present your reasoning on the importance of teamwork. List the ideas in order of importance.

3. Drafting (15–20 minutes)

Use your cause-and-effect chart to write your persuasive essay. Start with a strong statement. Appeal to the reasoning and emotions of your audience.

4. Revising and Proofreading (5 minutes)

Quickly reread your draft, correcting as you go.

Reflect on Your Writing

Circle the score that best represents your draft for each of the scoring criteria—with 4 being the highest score and 1 being the lowest score. Then, use your observations to revise your draft and create a final draft.

Rating Scale	Writing Criteria
1 2 3 4	**Evaluation:** How convincing is your persuasive essay?
1 2 3 4	**Focus:** Does your persuasive essay begin with a strong statement?
1 2 3 4	**Organization:** Does your persuasive essay present several strong reasons on the importance of teamwork?
1 2 3 4	**Support/Elaboration:** Are your reasons supported by examples?
1 2 3 4	**Style:** Does your persuasive essay appeal to your audience?
1 2 3 4	**Conventions:** Did you spell words with prefixes and suffixes correctly?
1 2 3 4	**Word Choice:** Does your persuasive essay use loaded words?

Revise Your Writing

When completing a timed writing activity, you only get time to do what is necessary. Now, review your draft and identify 3 or 4 elements that you would revise if you had more time. Use the chart below to revise your writing.

Draft Sentence	My Revision
1.	
2.	
3.	
4.	

Writing Support for Narrative Essays

TESTED

Organization and Focus

Keep the following organizational concepts in mind when writing a narrative essay.

- Time order presents the order in which events occurred.
- Spatial order gives a sense of where things are.
- Main purpose is the reason, or focus, of the writing.
- Transition words hold thoughts together (*moreover, furthermore, after, then, finally*).

> **STANDARD**
>
> 1.1 Organization and Focus: create an organizational structure that balances all aspects of the composition and uses effective transitions between sentences to unify important ideas

Timed Writing for Tested Prompt

Format and Details:

The prompt gives specific directions about what to write and targets a specific standard.

Writing Prompt: Write a narrative essay about your classroom, using spatial order. Include a beginning, middle, and an end. Make sure the main purpose of is clear. Use at least five transition words.

Academic Vocabulary:

A **strategy** is a planned approach. Using graphic organizers helps you establish the main purpose and strategy for an essay.

🕐 Minute-by-Minute Writing Guide

Complete these steps.

1. Prewriting (5 minutes)

Read the prompt carefully. Look for keywords such as those underlined above, which will help you understand the assignment.

2. Organizing (5–10 minutes)

Create a graphic organizer, such as an essay structure chart, that will help you plan out the beginning, middle, and end of your essay. Use an idea web to think about details you want to add to your essay.

3. Drafting (15–20 minutes)

Use your essay structure chart and idea web to write your narrative. Develop your main idea. Use spatial details from your idea web to help readers picture the classroom.

4. Revising and Proofreading (5 minutes)

Quickly reread your draft, correcting as you go.

Reflect on Your Writing

Circle the score that best represents your draft for each of the scoring criteria—with 4 being the highest score and 1 being the lowest score. Then, use your observations to revise your draft and create a final draft.

Rating Scale	Writing Criteria
1 2 3 4	**Purpose:** Does your narrative essay tell a story?
1 2 3 4	**Focus:** Does your essay have a main idea?
1 2 3 4	**Organization:** Does your essay have a beginning, middle, and an end?
1 2 3 4	**Support/Elaboration:** Are there enough details to develop the main idea of your essay?
1 2 3 4	**Style:** Is your essay interesting?
1 2 3 4	**Strategy:** Does your essay use spatial order?
1 2 3 4	**Word Choice:** Did you use at least five transition words?

Revise Your Writing

When completing a timed writing activity, you only get time to do what is necessary. Now, review your draft and identify 3 or 4 elements that you would revise if you had more time. Use the chart below to revise your writing.

Draft Sentence	My Revision
1.	
2.	
3.	
4.	

Writing Support for Persuasive Essays

STANDARD

1.2 Organization and Focus: support all statements and claims with anecdotes, descriptions, facts and statistics, and specific examples

Organization and Focus

Know how to add the following when writing a persuasive essay.

- Anecdotes: short stories that explain points authors want to make
- Descriptions: explanations that use modifiers to help the reader visualize settings or characters
- Facts and statistics: specific information that is truthful and can be supported with data
- Specific examples: detailed descriptions of particular objects or events

Timed Writing for Tested Prompt

Format and Details:

The prompt gives specific directions about what to write and targets a specific standard.

Writing Prompt: Write a persuasive essay on a way to improve a park in your community. Propose a solution to a problem. Include an anecdote, facts and statistics, and a specific example.

Academic Vocabulary:

When you **propose a solution,** you suggest a way to solve a problem. Use details that show why a solution is needed and why it might work.

⏱ Minute-by-Minute Writing Guide

Complete these steps.

1. Prewriting (5 minutes)

Read the prompt carefully and completely. Look for keywords such as those underlined above, which will help you understand the assignment.

2. Organizing (5–10 minutes)

Create a graphic organizer, such as a cause-and-effect chart, to plan how you will present your reasoning. List the ideas in order of importance.

3. Drafting (15–20 minutes)

Use your cause-and-effect chart to write your persuasive essay. Start with a strong statement. Appeal to the reasoning and emotions of your audience.

4. Revising and Proofreading (5 minutes)

Quickly reread your draft, correcting as you go.

Reflect on Your Writing

Circle the score that best represents your draft for each of the scoring criteria—with 4 being the highest score and 1 being the lowest score. Then, use your observations to revise your draft and create a final draft.

Rating Scale	Writing Criteria
1 2 3 4	**Evaluation:** How convincing is your persuasive essay?
1 2 3 4	**Focus:** Does your persuasive essay begin with a strong statement?
1 2 3 4	**Organization:** Does your persuasive essay propose a solution to a problem?
1 2 3 4	**Support/Elaboration:** Are your reasons supported by examples?
1 2 3 4	**Style:** Does your persuasive essay appeal to your audience?
1 2 3 4	**Strategies:** Did you use an anecdote, facts and statistics, and a specific example?
1 2 3 4	**Word Choice:** Does your persuasive essay use loaded words?

Revise Your Writing

When completing a timed writing activity, you only get time to do what is necessary. Now, review your draft and identify 3 or 4 elements that you would revise if you had more time. Use the chart below to revise your writing.

Draft Sentence	My Revision
1.	
2.	
3.	
4.	

and its there

Writing Support for Narrative Essays

TESTED

Organization and Focus

Know how to use the following skills to write a summary.

- Notetaking: Use note cards to help you write a summary in a logical and organized way. Use quotation marks if you copy an author's exact words.
- Outlining: You can also use an outline for writing a summary. Outlines are divided into main ideas and supporting details. The main ideas of your outline become the main ideas of your paragraphs.

Timed Writing for Tested Prompt

Format and Details:

The prompt gives specific directions about what to write and targets a specific standard.

Writing Prompt: <u>Write a summary of a historical event that is of particular interest to you.</u> First, create a set of notes or write an outline to organize your summary. Make sure each paragraph has a main idea and supporting details.

Academic Vocabulary:

Supporting details are specific examples, anecdotes, facts, and descriptions that help explain a main idea.

⏱ Minute-by-Minute Writing Guide

Complete these steps.

1. Prewriting (5 minutes)

Read the prompt carefully and completely. Look for keywords such as those underlined above, which will help you understand the assignment.

2. Organizing (5–10 minutes)

Create a graphic organizer, such as an idea web, that will help you organize the details that are part of the historical event. Use a sequence chart to think about what happened first, next, and last.

3. Drafting (15–20 minutes)

Use your idea web and sequence chart to write your summary. Start with a topic sentence. Add details to your summary. Remember to use transition words.

4. Revising and Proofreading (5 minutes)

Quickly reread your draft, correcting as you go.

Reflect on Your Writing

Circle the score that best represents your draft for each of the scoring criteria—with 4 being the highest score and 1 being the lowest score. Then, use your observations to revise your draft and create a final draft.

Rating Scale	Writing Criteria
1 2 3 4	**Evaluation:** Does your summary describe the most important things that happened?
1 2 3 4	**Focus:** Does your summary begin with a topic sentence?
1 2 3 4	**Organization:** Does your summary explain what happened first, next, and last?
1 2 3 4	**Support/Elaboration:** Are there enough supporting details for your reader to understand the importance of the historical event?
1 2 3 4	**Style:** Is your summary interesting?
1 2 3 4	**Strategies:** Did you first create a set of notes or write an outline?
1 2 3 4	**Word Choice:** Did you use transition words?

Revise Your Writing

When completing a timed writing activity, you only get time to do what is necessary. Now, review your draft and identify 3 or 4 elements that you would revise if you had more time. Use the chart below to revise your writing.

Draft Sentence	My Revision
1.	
2.	
3.	
4.	

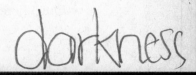

Writing Support for Expository Essays

TESTED

<table>
<tr><td>STANDARD
1.4 Research and Technology: identify topics; ask and evaluate questions; and develop ideas leading to inquiry, investigation, and research</td></tr>
</table>

Research and Technology

Know how to use these skills to plan a research report.

- Determine the area of study.
- Identify a topic.
- Ask questions that can be researched.
- Identify possible sources used to investigate the topic.
- Conduct research.
- Summarize what was learned.

Timed Writing for Tested Prompt

Format and Details:	Writing Prompt: Write a plan for a research report on volcanoes. Identify a specific topic to research. Write five questions to research. Explain how you will conduct your research.	Academic Vocabulary:
The prompt gives specific directions about what to write and targets a specific standard.		**Sources** used for research should be **credible.** A credible source is one that can be trusted to present factual information.

⏱ Minute-by-Minute Writing Guide

Complete these steps.

1. Identify a topic to research (5 minutes)

Narrow the area of study—volcanoes—to a specific topic that can be researched, such as where the majority of volcanoes occur in the world.

2. Write questions (5 minutes)

Think of five questions you could research that pertain to your topic of study.

3. Conducting research (10–15 minutes)

List five sources you could use to research your topic. Then, explain how you will conduct the research, including the use of note cards, outlining, or another system to gather information. What facts or examples will you research?

4. Drafting (10–15 Minutes)

Use your note cards or outline to write a plan for a research report. State your main idea. Explain which details you will use to support your main idea.

5. Revising and Proofreading (5 minutes)

Quickly reread your draft, correcting as you go.

Reflect on Your Writing

Circle the score that best represents your draft for each of the scoring criteria—with 4 being the highest score and 1 being the lowest score. Then, use your observations to revise your draft and create a final draft.

Rating Scale	Writing Criteria
1 2 3 4	**Evaluation:** How well will your research plan work?
1 2 3 4	**Focus:** Did you identify a topic that is possible to research?
1 2 3 4	**Organization:** Did you complete each step of the plan?
1 2 3 4	**Support/Elaboration:** How well will your questions guide your research?
1 2 3 4	**Style:** Did you identify facts or examples to support your research?
1 2 3 4	**Strategies:** How credible are the sources you have chosen?
1 2 3 4	**Word Choice:** How clearly written are your ideas?

Revise Your Writing

When completing a timed writing activity, you only get time to do what is necessary. Now, review your research plan and identify 3 or 4 elements that you would revise if you had more time. Use the chart below to revise your plan.

Research Plan	My Revision
1.	
2.	
3.	
4.	

Writing Support for Expository Essays

TESTED

Research and Technology

The following sources of information need to be cited properly in a bibliography: books, encyclopedia articles, magazine articles, Internet sources, and in-text citations.

STANDARD

1.5 Research and Technology: give credit for both quoted and paraphrased information in a bibliography by using a consistent and sanctioned format and methodology for citations

Timed Writing for Tested Prompt

Format and Details:

The prompt gives specific directions about what to write and targets a specific standard.

Writing Prompt: Write a summary of four different sources you could use to write a research report on Benjamin Franklin. Explain why the sources need to be credible. Explain which type of information needs a citation and which does not. Add a bibliography.

Academic Vocabulary:

A **citation** is a notation of a source. A citation gives credit to the author of something said or written. A **bibliography** is a formal list of citations.

⏱ Minute-by-Minute Writing Guide

Complete these steps.

1. Prewriting (5 minutes)

Read the prompt carefully and completely. Look for keywords such as those underlined above, which will help you understand the assignment.

2. Organizing (5–10 minutes)

Create a graphic organizer, such as an idea web, that will help you determine the different sources you might use for a report on Benjamin Franklin.

3. Drafting (15–20 minutes)

Use your idea web to write your summary. At the end, write the sources in the proper form. See the example citations at the top of the next page.

4. Revising and Proofreading (5 minutes)

Quickly reread your draft, correcting as you go.

Reflect on Your Writing

Circle the score that best represents your draft for each of the scoring criteria—with 4 being the highest score and 1 being the lowest score. Then, use your observations to revise your draft and create a final draft.

Rating Scale	Writing Criteria
1 2 3 4	**Evaluation:** Does your summary explain four different types of sources you could use for a report on Benjamin Franklin?
1 2 3 4	**Focus:** Does your summary explain why the sources need to be credible?
1 2 3 4	**Organization:** Is there one paragraph explaining types of sources and one explaining which information needs to be cited?
1 2 3 4	**Support/Elaboration:** Are your citations written correctly?
1 2 3 4	**Style:** Did you alphabetize your bibliography?
1 2 3 4	**Strategies:** Did you explain the importance of using reliable Internet sites?

Revise Your Writing

When completing a timed writing activity, you only get time to do what is necessary. Now, review your summary and bibliography and identify 2 elements that you would revise if you had more time. Use the chart below to revise your summary.

Summary/Bibliography Sentence	My Revision
1.	
2.	

Writing Support for Expository Essays

TESTED

Research and Technology

Know how to use the following computer-based programs to manage information and prepare reports:

- word-processing programs
- spreadsheets
- databases

<table>
<tr><td>STANDARD</td></tr>
<tr><td>1.6 Research and Technology: create documents by using word-processing skills and publishing programs; develop simple databases and spreadsheets to manage information and prepare reports</td></tr>
</table>

Timed Writing for Tested Prompt

Format and Details:

The prompt gives specific directions about what to write and targets a specific standard.

Writing Prompt: Write a plan for how you will use computer programs to manage information and prepare a report on a school survey of favorite meals served at school. Identify which computer programs you would use. Explain how you would use the programs to manage information and prepare a report.

Academic Vocabulary:

A **database** is an organized collection of information that can be accessed quickly. Information in databases is entered into a variety of **fields,** or categories.

Minute-by-Minute Writing Guide

Complete these steps.

1. Determine the type of information you will need (5 minutes)

Decide who will be part of your survey. Decide how you will conduct the survey.

2. Write questions (5–10 minutes)

Think of several questions you will ask in your survey. Your survey questions should provide you with specific data. For example, you could ask students to choose their favorite lunch item from a list of items.

3. Conduct research (15–20 minutes)

Explain how you will manage your survey data using a computer-based program or programs. Then, explain how you will use a computer-based program to prepare your report.

4. Write your plan (5 minutes)

Add an example of how your data might be presented. Then, make any last changes to your survey plan.

Reflect on Your Writing

Circle the score that best represents your draft for each of the scoring criteria—with 4 being the highest score and 1 being the lowest score. Then, use your observations to revise your draft and create a final draft.

Rating Scale	Writing Criteria
1 2 3 4	**Evaluation:** How possible will it be to conduct your survey, manage data, and prepare your report?
1 2 3 4	**Focus:** Did you write survey questions that will give you specific data?
1 2 3 4	**Organization:** Will you be able to create a database to manage your survey results?
1 2 3 4	**Support/Elaboration:** Will you be able to create a visual representation of the survey data using a computer-based program?
1 2 3 4	**Style:** How helpful are computer-based programs for you in managing survey information and preparing a report?
1 2 3 4	**Strategies:** How comfortable are you with using computer-based programs to manage data and prepare reports?
1 2 3 4	**Word Choice:** Did you use the terms *database* and *fields* correctly?

Revise Your Writing

When completing a timed writing activity, you only get time to do what is necessary. Now, review your survey plans and identify 3 or 4 elements that you would revise if you had more time. Use the chart below to revise your plan.

Survey Plan	My Revision
1.	
2.	
3.	
4.	

darkness

Writing Support for Expository Essays

TESTED

Evaluation and Revision

Know how to evaluate and revise to improve the quality of compositions, including:

- choosing words that convey the purpose of the composition
- improving the organization of the composition
- making sure ideas are presented in a clear and meaningful way

Timed Writing for Tested Prompt

Format and Details:

The prompt gives specific directions about what to write and targets a specific standard.

Writing Prompt: Write a summary of your plan when evaluating and revising your composition. Your summary should include time order. Explain what you do first, next, and last when revising a composition. Give two elements of a composition you always evaluate first. Explain how you would make sure that information or a story is presented in a clear and meaningful way.

Academic Vocabulary:

A **composition** is an essay. An **element** of a composition is something that is used to write it, such as correct spelling and punctuation.

🕐 Minute-by-Minute Writing Guide

Complete these steps before you begin writing.

1. Prewriting (5 minutes)

Read the prompt carefully and completely. Look for keywords such as those underlined above, which will help you understand the assignment.

2. Organizing (5–10 minutes)

Make a list of elements of a composition that you know need to be checked. Create a graphic organizer, such as a sequence chart, that will help you think about which elements you would check first, next, and last.

3. Drafting (15–20 minutes)

Use your elements list and sequence chart to write your summary. Start with a topic sentence. Explain important elements you would check. Explain your approach to making your composition clear and meaningful.

4. Revising and Proofreading (5 minutes)

Quickly reread your draft, correcting as you go.

Reflect on Your Writing

Circle the score that best represents your draft for each of the scoring criteria—with 4 being the highest score and 1 being the lowest score. Then, use your observations to revise your draft and create a final draft.

Rating Scale	Writing Criteria
1 2 3 4	How well does your revision plan make sure you evaluate the elements of your compositions?
1 2 3 4	**Focus:** Does your summary explain the main purpose of your revision plan?
1 2 3 4	**Organization:** Does your summary describe the order in which you use your revision plan?
1 2 3 4	**Support/Elaboration:** Did you give two examples of elements of a composition you evaluate first?
1 2 3 4	**Style:** How well does your revision plan work for you?
1 2 3 4	**Strategies:** How well organized is your revision plan?
1 2 3 4	**Word Choice:** Did you use the terms *composition* and *element* correctly?

Revise Your Writing

When completing a timed writing activity, you only get time to do what is necessary. Now, review your revision plan and identify 2 elements that you would revise if you had more time. Use the chart below to revise your plan.

Element	My Revision
1.	
2.	

darkness